Japan at the Millennium

Edited by David W. Edgington

Japan at the Millennium:
Joining Past and Future

UBCPress · Vancouver · Toronto

© UBC Press 2003

All rights reserved. No part of this publication may be reproduced, stored in a retrieval system, or transmitted, in any form or by any means, without prior written permission of the publisher, or, in Canada, in the case of photocopying or other reprographic copying, a licence from Access Copyright (Canadian Copyright Licensing Agency), www.accesscopyright.ca.

09 08 07 06 05 04 03   5 4 3 2 1

Printed in Canada on acid-free paper

National Library of Canada Cataloguing in Publication Data

Main entry under title:

Japan at the millennium : joining past and future / edited by David W. Edgington.

Includes bibliographical references and index.
ISBN 0-7748-0898-5 (bound) ; ISBN 0-7748-0899-3 (pbk.)

1. Japan – Social conditions – 1945- 2. Japan – Civilization – 1945- I. Edgington, David W. (David William)
DS822.5.J36 2003   952.05   C2003-910042-1

Canadä

UBC Press gratefully acknowledges the financial support for our publishing program of the Government of Canada through the Book Publishing Industry Development Program (BPIDP), and of the Canada Council for the Arts, and the British Columbia Arts Council.

This book has been published with the help of a grant from the Canadian Federation for the Humanities and Social Sciences, using funds provided by the Social Sciences and Humanities Research Council of Canada, and with the help of the K.D. Srivastava Fund. Funding was also provided by the Centre for Japanese Research, University of British Columbia.

UBC Press
The University of British Columbia
2029 West Mall
Vancouver, BC V6T 1Z2
604-822-5959 / Fax: 604-822-6083
www.ubcpress.ca

Contents

Figures and Tables / vii

Preface / ix

Acknowledgments / xi

Introduction

1 Joining the Past and Present in Japan / 3
David W. Edgington

Part 1: Economic and Political Systems / 19

2 Japanese Economics: An Interpretative Essay / 25
Keizo Nagatani

3 The Japanese Labour Movement's Road to the Millennium / 49
Lonny E. Carlile

4 Japan's High Seas Fisheries in the North Pacific Ocean: Food Security and Foreign Policy / 67
Roger Smith

Part 2: Japan's Identity and Youth / 91

5 Postwar Japan and Manchuria / 97
Bill Sewell

6 May the Saru River Flow: The Nibutani Dam and the Resurging Tide of the Ainu Identity Movement / 120
Millie Creighton

7 Pop Idols and Gender Contestation / 144
Hiroshi Aoyagi

8 A Century of Juvenile Law in Japan / 168
Stephan M. Salzberg

Part 3: Urban Living and Beauty / 189

9 Japan Ponders the Good Life: Improving the Quality of Japanese Cities / 193
David W. Edgington

10 Museum as Hometown: What Is "Japanese Beauty"? / 222
Joshua S. Mostow

Conclusion

11 Continuity and Change in Japan / 245
David W. Edgington

Contributors / 264

Index / 266

Figures and Tables

Figures

1.1 Rates of economic growth: 1960s, 1970s, 1980s, and 1990s / 7
1.2 Percentage of population aged 65 years and over by country, 1900-2030 / 10
4.1 Japanese fisheries production, 1908-50 / 69
4.2 Japanese prewar fishing areas and limits of authorized fishing areas during 1945-51 / 73
4.3 Production in four sectors of the Japanese fishing industry, 1959-69 / 78
4.4 Japan's fish catch and fish imports, 1965-96 / 82
4.5 Japan's percentage of self-sufficiency in selected foods, 1975-95 / 86
7.1 Idol Yumi Adachi assists in the 1999 Anti-Drug Campaign / 149
7.2 On the cover of the January 1998 issue of *Bomb!* Ryoko Hirose strikes a "cute" pose / 150
7.3 Examples of cute *shōjo* images from the Meiji period (circa 1890s) / 151
7.4 A cute idol undergoing a training session / 155
7.5 A scene from the Dance-Jet Agency's dancing exercise / 157
9.1 Diffusion of consumer goods and public infrastructure in Japan / 194
9.2 Japan's infrastructure priorities, 1870-1993 / 198
9.3 Regional core cities targeted as centres for local development under the Core Cities Law of 1992 / 213
10.1 Catalogue cover from *Nihon Bi Saihakken: Furi-Mukeba Japanesuku* (Japanesque – Rediscovery of Japanese Aesthetic Designs), Mitsukoshi Department Store, Nihonbashi, Tokyo (27 December 1994 to 15 January 1995) / 225
10.2 Catalogue cover from *Uīn no Japonizumu* (*Japonisme* in Vienna), Tōbu Museum of Art of Tōbu Department Store, Tokyo (20 December 1994 to 12 February 1995) / 232
10.3 Double-page spread from the catalogue for the exhibition *(Heisei 6-nendo Kokuritsu Hakubutsukan/Bijutsukan Chihō Junkai-ten) Nihon no Bi* (Annual Exhibition of National Museums and National Art Galleries Held in

Provincial Regions for the Year 1995: Japanese Beauty), Gunma Prefectural Museum of Modern Art (25 February to 26 March 1995) / 237
10.4 Catalogue cover from *Dentō to Kindai – Nihon no Bi* (Traditional Beauty in Japanese Art), National Museum of Modern Art, Kyoto (12 October to 13 November 1994) and National Museum of Modern Art, Tokyo (22 November to 18 December 1994) / 238
10.5 Handbill for an exhibition, *Keiga ni yosete* (Gathering Felicitations), the Museum of Imperial Collections, Sannomaru Shozokan Imperial Palace, Tokyo (4 January to 20 February 1995) / 241
11.1 The new Japanese central government structure, 2001 / 255

Tables
1.1 Japanese prime ministers, 1982-2001 / 8
9.1 Japan's infrastructure and housing standards compared with other countries / 195
9.2 Five-year (and seven-year) infrastructure plans of Japan's Ministry of Construction / 210

Preface

This volume is the product of interdisciplinary scholarship conducted under the auspices of the Centre for Japanese Research (CJR), part of the Institute of Asian Research at the University of British Columbia. Its purpose is to provide a critical multidisciplinary study of economic, political, social, and cultural changes occurring in Japan by situating these trends within the broad sweep of prewar and postwar history.

As Japan approached the new millennium, there was a sense of abrupt change, notably in national politics and economics. For instance, as this book was being prepared, much of the world was alarmed at Japan's inability to reform its economy. Yet not long ago, foreigners flocked to Japan to see how things were done. The Japanese economy was once the envy of the world, and its financial markets the source of stupendous wealth. In the late 1980s, many people were making matter-of-fact predictions that the age of Pax Americana would end in the 1990s, making way for the age of Pax Japonica. What a difference a decade makes! Apart from Japan's economic collapse, another recent and also worrying trend is the wave of political, bureaucratic, and business scandals that have hit the headlines over the past few years. These are testament perhaps not only to "system fatigue" in Japan but also to a widespread weakening of the special glue that has bound Japanese society into tightly knit groups since feudal times. Culture and other aspects of daily life are also changing in Japan. The country once known for its image of security was shocked by the 1995 Hanshin-Awaji earthquake that hit Kobe, and the Aum Shinrikyō gas attack on Tokyo's subway system.

How things change. Or do they? In light of these and other striking events, the major purpose of these essays is to reflect on processes of change and continuity in modern Japanese economic and social life. The book's central argument is that despite the apparent sense of uncertainty and even crisis in Japan today, it would be a mistake not to see strong continuities in Japan's social, political, and economic condition at the beginning of a new century and millennium. An ahistoric, shallow reading of sudden change and collapsing institutions must be deeply flawed. If Japanese society is changing – which it surely is – then that in itself is nothing new. In a very real sense, Japan is a country in which the past joins the future, or at the very least shapes the present.

This collection of essays is aimed at academics and students in the field of Japanese studies as well as those interested in comparative studies. Following an introductory essay on the essence of change and continuity in Japan, nine thematic chapters address how history has shaped both present circumstances and future challenges in aspects of economic, political, and social life. Of course, a handful of essays cannot deal fully with the myriad complex changes occurring in Japan at the dawn of the twenty-first century. Nonetheless, the contributing authors hope that they provide a better understanding of underlying trends in Japanese economic policy making and the labour movement and its links with political groups, resource management, attitudes towards China, the rights of minority groups, gender issues, youth and the criminal justice system, the quality of urban life, and aspects of the Japanese nostalgia boom. These substantive case studies document Japan in the final years of the last century. The closing chapter addresses the astonishing first six months of the administration of Prime Minister Koizumi Junichiro. Together, these essays show how the dawn of the twenty-first century is truly an intriguing bridge by which we can connect the past and future in Japan.

This book is the second volume of interdisciplinary research undertaken at the University of British Columbia's Centre for Japanese Research (CJR). The first, *Japan and the West: The Perception Gap*, was co-edited by Keizo Nagatani and David W. Edgington and published by Ashgate (1998). It deals with problems involved with Japan's internationalization *(kokusaika)* during the Tokugawa, Meiji, and postwar periods. Members of the CJR are currently engaged in the research of Japan on many fronts. Their investigations are wide-ranging and include basic issues in the humanities, language studies, culture and anthropology, history, economics, sociology, political science, geography, and other social sciences, as well as more applied areas in business management, technology issues, law, and environment and ecology. The CJR research project on "Reflections of Japan at the End of the Twentieth Century and the Start of the New Millennium" – from which this book draws – was funded by the Japan Foundation in Tokyo.

Note that Japanese words that appear in standard English-language dictionaries (such as Tokyo and Osaka) appear here without macrons. Japanese names are given in the Japanese order: family name first, except in citations of works published in Western languages, where they appear in the English order.

Acknowledgments

This book has been published with the help of a grant from the Humanities and Social Sciences Federation of Canada, using funds provided by the Social Sciences and Humanities Research Council of Canada. The editor and authors wish to acknowledge the financial support for this project given by the Japan Foundation and the Centre for Japanese Research, University of British Columbia. David W. Edgington also wishes to give due thanks to the Hampton Fund of the University of British Columbia for funding his research. Joe Clark typeset the original manuscript, and Eric Leinberger prepared the figures. The useful comments given by three anonymous reviewers are also gratefully acknowledged.

Japan at the Millennium

1
Joining the Past and Present in Japan
David W. Edgington

> Change in Japan never means the abrupt and fundamental giving up of the past.
>
> – A. Hernandi, *Japan's Socio-Economic Evolution*

A Century of Change

This volume brings together reflections and research on the link between history and the future of Japan in a time of growing volatility and change. The contributors all share a belief that the dawn of a new millennium offers an opportunity to consider contemporary Japan from a longer point of view. This book is integrated by a major theme – that complex changes currently unfolding in Japan can be understood in part by reference to past events and underlying consistencies in economic, political, and social life. The author of each chapter has approached his or her particular theme in this light, and recognizes that the year 2001 (when most of these essays were completed) represented an intriguing axis on which to assess various past trends as well as future trajectories. Waswo (1996, 163), writing about modern Japanese society since the Meiji period (1868-1912), notes that it is always tempting to see "the present as a historical turning point, and to assign to unfolding events or trends a significance that in the end they do not deserve." Still, as this chapter argues, the events of the last few years have been significant, and understanding Japan at the dawn of the millennium is made even more difficult by the concatenation of deep-rooted tradition and new circumstances.

The end of the twentieth century was celebrated in many countries, and no less in Japan. The *Japan Times* (the largest-circulation English-language newspaper) launched a series of review articles that reflected upon a number of important developments that had shaped the nation over the past 100 years. A wide range of subjects were canvassed, including political decentralization, the use of forestry resources, women's education, and the baby boom generation.[1] These and other reviews of Japan in the twentieth century provided engaging analyses of the country's emergence as a global power.[2] Spanning four periods (Meiji, Taishō, Shōwa, and Heisei), the twentieth century indeed brought historic change to Japan, from the building of a nation-state to the devastation of war, from the achievement of economic might on the international stage to the struggle to rebuild after the collapse of the "bubble economy." During a century of change, Japan's population has seen a dramatic transformation from rural life to urban society, from primarily agricultural work to primarily industrial and service sector occupations, and from moderate incomes to high incomes per capita. Nevertheless, at the century's end, the Japanese did not seem particularly appreciative of or buoyed by the country's startling successes. Instead they often showed apprehension or ambivalence about a wide range of reforms proposed or carried out by the Japanese government. These were being implemented with varying degrees of resolution to address the problems of a system no longer thought capable of meeting the challenges of contemporary Japan (Kingston 2001). The dawn of the new millennium provides, therefore, a platform for reflecting on the nature of a turbulent period in Japanese history. The opening year of the new millennium is also an appropriate time to take stock of Japan's likely future trajectory, in economic, social, and political terms.

The Turbulent 1990s
Why were the 1990s considered harbingers of turbulent change in Japan? Essentially, in this decade there emerged a new nexus of forces that threatened to undermine the stability and predictability of the postwar years. Disasters struck, the economy tumbled, and the social fabric unravelled. The government accumulated massive debts to maintain a semblance of prosperity; yet deep down few people felt that this prosperity was real. Specifically, the year 1990 opened with a stock market crash after the Japanese New Year holiday; in the next ten years, the country was beset by economic difficulties, resulting largely from the collapse of the bubble economy. In fact, the media dubbed the 1990s "Japan's Lost Decade" (Millett 2000). They noted that following rapid expansion in the late 1980s, the country faced a myriad of problems that sapped business and consumer confidence.

Stagnation in the economy revealed itself throughout the decade in asset (land and stocks) deflation, negative economic growth, corporate failures, and rising unemployment. A spate of national crises also hit Japan. In 1993 the ruling Liberal Democratic Party (LDP) fell from power for the first time in nearly forty years. That same year, a drought and rice crop failure occurred, necessitating the first-ever substantial imports of rice. In 1995 Japan suffered the Great Hanshin-Awaji (Kobe) Earthquake, which revealed that the country had inferior urban infrastructure and no crisis management plan for a major disaster. The sarin-gas attack in the Tokyo subway by the Aum Shinrikyō cult the very same year proved that the country was as vulnerable to oddball fanaticism as any other modern urban society. Various scandals involving government damaged the traditional respect for the bureaucracy and faith in political leadership. For example, during the decade, the Ministry of Finance failed to act decisively on the bad-loan problem of the major banks and housing-loan-related financial institutions. In 1996 the Ministry of Health and Welfare was implicated in the use of blood products tainted with the AIDS virus. Various corruption charges were levelled at politicians and government officials. During the late 1990s, a number of nuclear accidents occurred, notably at the Monju plutonium-based fast-breeder reactor and also at Tokaimura. Japan's image as a harmonious, crime-free society was also damaged following several bizarre murders for which there were no clear motives. In 1997 a male middle school student in Kobe was arrested as the suspect in a case involving serial killings and assaults on elementary school students. Vicious crimes also increased as criminals became younger and younger.[3]

A Nation Adrift
Besides these disturbing events, the country appeared to be in a state of flux and uncertainty. As the last century closed, it seemed that Japan had lost its traditional strong sense of direction. It was also clear that the postwar economic and political model had run out of steam and lost much of its credibility. More worrying at century's end was a sense of paralysis in the Japanese resolution to address its problems, giving rise to a general perception of a nation adrift (*The Economist* 2000). Throughout the 1990s, there was widespread dissatisfaction with the current system but little political vitality – within either the LDP or the opposition – with sufficient clout and popular confidence and vision to push through fundamental reforms. The goal of catching up with the West having been achieved, there appeared no other on the Japanese horizon to take its place. This is perhaps the biggest reason why the country appeared to be gripped by a vague sense of helplessness. People often feel tension and have a sense of purpose when going all out to achieve a critical objective. So it has been with Japan. Having reached Western consumption standards, Japan has failed to find a new national goal, and so has spent the last decade drifting aimlessly (Kingston 2001).

These challenges intensified in the opening years of the new millennium as the economic news worsened and people saw rising unemployment, negative economic growth, and a record number of bankruptcies (Katz 2001).[4] It was during this period of extreme despondency and rejection of the status quo that the LDP elected insurgent and maverick Koizumi Junichiro as party president, and therefore prime minister, in April 2001. Koizumi was Japan's tenth prime minister in just twelve years.

Unlike his predecessors, however, he appeared to take structural reform of the Japanese system seriously. He spoke openly about the likelihood of higher unemployment resulting from the changes to budgets and programs that he wished to introduce. He also broached the idea of reinterpreting Japan's constitution, which currently restricts the role the country's defence forces play in a regional or international crisis (*Oriental Economist* 2001). Nonetheless, despite Prime Minister Koizumi's overwhelming popularity among voters, there have been many critics of his reform movement, especially among the traditional "policy tribes" *(zoku)* who support rural electorates, farmers, small shopkeepers, and the construction industry. Whether the policy changes initiated by the Koizumi cabinet will succeed in turning the tide in Japan's decade-old malaise is unclear, but they certainly promise more volatility and uncertainty.

Making Sense of Change in Japan

Compared with earlier periods, these recent changes have been harder to analyze and understand, and it has become increasingly difficult to know how to interpret and characterize Japan, both as it reached century's end and as it shuffled into the new millennium. In part, I believe, this is because we are too close to certain events to have distance and perspective. In part also, the problem is that volatility is now everywhere and bound up in the concept of globalization and an increasing instability of economic, political, and social life (Friedman 2000). As noted by Eades et al. (2000), Japan is becoming transformed by globalization in a number of distinct ways, including intense economic competition and the infusion of Western ideas. Still, for the forty-five years or so following the end of the Second World War, it appeared that Japan's distinctive policy approaches alone had brought continuous growth in incomes and political stability. Hence the terms "economic miracle" and "Japan Inc.," which for a time were clearly embedded in accounts of Japan's success. So, at a more fundamental level, what has really changed?

First, the economic certainties of the early postwar years no longer hold and, as noted earlier, Japan's economy has stagnated for the last decade. Figure 1.1 shows that Japan's distinctive economic model brought high growth in the 1960s and moderate growth in the 1970s; since the early 1990s, however, the economy went into serious recession. By contrast, the United States – whose economic and social systems are often cited as being most dissimilar to Japan's – enjoyed prosperity for almost the whole of the last decade.

This comparison makes Japan's economic slump all the more conspicuous. Still, it was not so long ago that there was at least the perception of true prosperity, as by 1987 Japan became the world's richest nation in terms of GDP in comparative dollar terms, exceeding that of the US on a per capita basis. Hence, Japan attained its long-cherished goal of overtaking advanced Western nations. This new-found status turned out to be merely a chimera, however, one caused only by the startling realignment of currencies in global financial markets. Indeed, volatile currency realignments and a high-priced Japanese yen now threaten the very economic base of the country as manufacturing industries are driven offshore to cheaper locations, causing a "hollowing out" of production, downsizing of capacity, layoffs, and increased unemployment (Katz 1998). As economic growth plummeted in the mid-1990s, an array of Thatcher-Reagan conservative policies seemed congenial to many Japanese, in effect making market-oriented liberalization and deregulation of government controls seem more appealing than traditional dirigiste regimes. Japan's distinctive stockholder system and interpenetrating *keiretsu* (Japanese business group) structure also came under strain. Moreover, changes already under way in the financial sector since 1997's "Big Bang" reforms have prompted mega-bank mergers and companies crossing established *keiretsu* lines. In short, the comfortable accommodation of the traditional closed economy and long-term business networks were challenged at the same time that pressure for dramatic change and political realignment began to grow. Old-line manufacturing firms were more receptive to traditional forms of Japanese industrial policy in the 1970s. By contrast, however, many of the younger generation of cutting-edge companies today are more likely to support free-market arrangements (Porter et al. 2000; Lincoln 2001).

Second, the art of governance has fallen into a shambles. Political parties have come and gone, and political alliances formed and re-formed, the

Figure 1.1

Rates of economic growth: 1960s, 1970s, 1980s, and 1990s

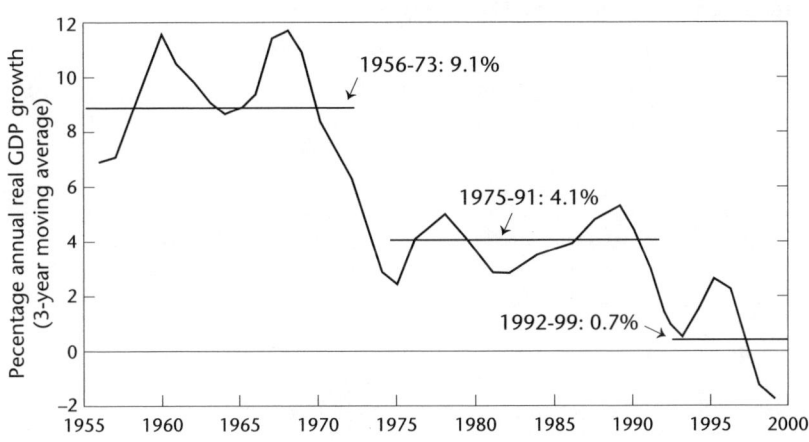

Source: Adapted from Katz 1998, updated with Economic Planning Agency data.

manifest aim being to remain in power. Table 1.1 shows the parade of prime ministers who have graced Japan's political leadership since 1982. In the sixteen or so years up to mid-2001, Japan had appointed twelve prime ministers. To be sure, Japanese politicians have never been held in high public esteem, but the public has always felt that a dedicated bureaucracy could rein in political excesses. As we have seen, however, during the 1990s even the bureaucracy saw its gleaming image tarnished by a torrent of scandals. Political reform and liberalization now threaten the traditional role of the bureaucracy as leaders and planners, a role that was established at the outset of the Meiji Restoration (1868). Economic slowdown itself has brought anxiety to the ruling consensus. Thus, small-scale farmers, shopkeepers, and construction companies have found less support for their taken-for-granted system of government protection. Conflicts between bureaucrats and increasingly independent-minded elements of the business and financial communities also became evident. Politicians in both local and central governments began to assert themselves with regard to the autonomy of their respective agency staffs (Carlile and Tilton 1998; Gibney 1998).

Third, there has been much realignment on the international scene. For instance, over the 1990s Japan's relationship with the United States, its traditional ally, changed. In particular, long-standing trade and investment disputes with the US appeared to gradually cool down. This period also saw stronger ties between Japan and the countries of the Asia-Pacific region, especially China. Indeed, the end of the Cold War in 1989 meant that Japan's security-based alliance with the US gave way to the discovery that these two countries were leaders of powerful global economic blocs

Table 1.1

Japanese prime ministers, 1982-2001

Years served	Name	Dates served
1982-87	Nakasone Yasuhiro	27 November 1982 - 6 November 1987
1987-89	Takeshita Noboru	6 November 1987 - 3 June 1989
1989	Uno Sosuke	3 June 1989 - 9 August 1989
1989-91	Kaifu Toshiki	9 August 1989 - 5 November 1991
1991-93	Miyazawa Kiichi	5 November 1991- 9 August 1993
1993-94	Hosokawa Morihiro	9 August 1993 - 28 April 1994
1994	Hata Tsutomu	28 April 1994 - 30 June 1994
1994-96	Murayama Tomiichi	30 June 1994 - 11 January 1996
1996-98	Hashimoto Ryutaro	11 January 1996 - 30 July 1998
1998-2000	Obuchi Keizo	30 July 1998 - 5 April 2000
2000-2001	Mori Yoshiro	5 April 2000 - 26 April 2001
2001-	Koizumi Junichiro	26 April 2001 -

Source: "Prime Minister of Japan and His Cabinet Web Site," <http://www.kantei.go.jp/foreign/index-e.html>, accessed July 2001.

(the North American Free Trade Agreement [NAFTA], and East Asia, respectively), and were therefore economic rivals as well. In the wake of the Gulf War, US-Japan differences on security also came to a head. During the first half of the 1990s, Japan appeared to be well placed to take advantage of Asia's own economic miracle. Following the "Asian flu" and currency meltdowns in 1997-98, however, the region's problems rebounded upon Japan. More recently, many have begun to worry about Japan's long-term ties to Asia and the possibility of it being bypassed by trading blocs negotiated between China and the Southeast Asian nations (*Japan Times* 2001).

Fourth, as Japan approached the end of the century, significant changes were afoot on the domestic front. For instance, it became harder to perpetuate the myth that Japan remained a society almost totally composed of people of the same class. As recently as the mid-1980s, the image of Japan as a homogeneous society was a common one in both Japanese and Western publications. By way of illustration, former prime minister Nakasone Yasuhiro could at that time legitimately contrast the presence of "blacks, Puerto Ricans and Hispanics" in the US with the absence of minorities in Japan (Eccleston 1989, 198). In this way, the Japanese majority could legitimately ignore the existence of its own special groups, such as the Ainu and Okinawans, and appear rightfully proud about its degree of social harmony. By the 1990s, however, the outside world began to force the Japanese to come to grips with their relative ethnic exclusiveness. In a rapidly globalizing epoch, even distinct cultures such as Japan often experienced feelings of loss of identity due to processes of international homogenization. While Japan has not become swamped by the West, the entry of foreigners and foreign investments into the country caused a cultural shock to the traditionally xenophobic Japanese society. In particular, the labour shortage of the late 1980s brought about an influx of foreign workers (mostly illegal) (Oka 1994). Other kinds of population shifts also began to cause tensions. Demographic change, combined with sustained policies against large-scale inward migration, led to fewer births and deaths and a rapid aging of the population. Indeed, the past decade or so has seen an enormous amount of attention paid to the implications of the speed at which Japanese society is aging (Ujimoto 2000). Figure 1.2 indicates that among Organization for Economic Co-operation and Development (OECD) countries, Japan will have the highest proportion of seniors in the early twenty-first century, with dramatic consequences for public pensions, health care, and corporate employment.

The Scope of This Book
The aims of this book are to place this period of turbulent change in historical context and to show that the break with the past is never complete. The essays are grouped around three major issues, each of which

has a contextual introduction. Although these essays contain different emphases and perspectives, two arguments appear throughout. The first is the need to connect the present with the past in order to understand Japan. As the quote at the beginning of this chapter suggests, it is not surprising that many aspects of contemporary Japan can readily find resonance with the past. Accordingly, each of these chapters reflects upon one aspect of Japan's situation at the end of the twentieth century, and then relates this to events and changes in the postwar years and, in certain cases, even back to Meiji Japan in the previous century.

A second theme, and one that is naturally more speculative, is that by confronting history, it is possible to achieve a more nuanced understanding of Japan's economic, political, and social trajectory in the years to come. Of course, not every important issue can be addressed here, and the major subjects covered in this book were shaped by the research interests of individual contributors. For instance, we do not deal expressly with the breakdown of the so-called 1955 political system and the hegemony of the LDP, which governed Japan for most of the period since the end of the Second World War (but see Pempel 1998; Curtis 1999). Readers will also have to turn elsewhere for a discussion of Japan's changing role in global security issues and its military presence (see, for example, Matthews and Matsuyama 1993; Mochizuki 1997). Furthermore, this book does not provide a general chronology of twentieth-century Japan. Rather, the objective here is more targeted: to look closely at a number of specific issues

Figure 1.2

Percentage of population aged 65 years and over by country, 1900-2030

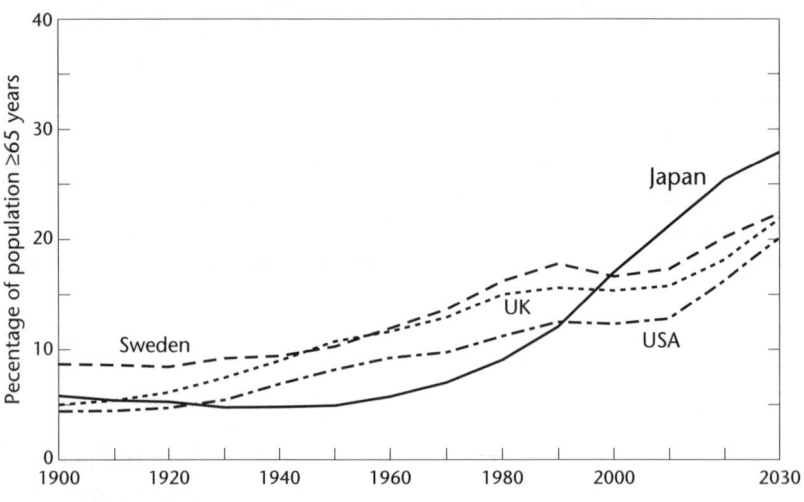

Source: Ministry of Health and Welfare data, contained in Foreign Press Center Japan 1999.

and then to trace how the past has influenced contemporary events and politics – whether it is the inability of the government to reform the economy to Western capitalist principles or its inability to effect significant improvements in the quality of urban life.

Part 1: Economic and Political Systems

This volume begins with three essays on economics and politics that lay out a broad context for addressing contemporary change. To date, Japan's economic and political system has been distinctive. Faced with the challenges of globalization and more intensive competition, however, the country's leaders have had to think how to reposition the country's economy. According to some, this means drastic restructuring of its industries and its financial systems along Western lines. The question also arises of whether the powerful forces of globalization will lead to Japan becoming more like the West. Many commentators think so and see Japan on the verge of conforming with Western norms (*The Economist* 1996). Campbell (1988) notes that in the West it is often assumed that underlying Japanese cultural and social traits are merely "feudal remnants," which can be easily pushed aside by the pressures of a modern economy in flux. In Chapter 2, Keizo Nagatani examines whether the Japanese economic system will converge along the lines of Anglo-American models of capitalism, or whether its earlier, distinctive Japanese approaches to economic development will continue. He concludes that full convergence towards the Anglo-American system is unlikely to occur. Commentators such as Dore (2000) also warn against assuming quick changes on the economic and business front.

Following on from this theme, it has often been argued that Japan's distinctive system has nowhere been more apparent than in the field of labour-management relations (Seike 1997). Yet, economic slowdown has meant that lifetime employment and other cornerstones of the labour market have become unviable. Indeed, many young people eschew the more traditional lifetime employment, and there has been a move to the so-called *freeter* generation (part-timers). All of these trends create problems for labour politics and unions. Faced with such dramatic shifts in the workforce and labour markets, what, in fact, is the future role of Japan's labour unions? This question is taken up in Chapter 3 by Lonny E. Carlile, who explores to what degree the established labour union system is changing. He argues that there has been a noticeable decline of the labour movement as a progressive political force in Japan, a decline that has been gradual and related to the changing organizational characteristics and strategies of various wings of the movement over the postwar period. Consequently, the labour movement will have to make some difficult choices if it is to survive as a meaningful social force in the twenty-first century.

A related dimension of shifting economic and political paradigms concerns Japan's external vulnerability to global changes, especially through its mammoth demand for natural resources. Truly, Japan at the new millennium continues to be a paradox. It is certainly a world power, despite its recent economic decline, but it also has many inherent weaknesses, including its dependence upon foreign sources of energy, food, and military security. Roger Smith addresses this issue in Chapter 4 and notes that Japan has long been obsessed with notions of economic security. In the past, this revolved around the important issue of how and where to obtain industrial resources. Now it is food security that is considered to be equally or even more important. Will the future be any different, even if Japan's economic structure continues to shift towards high-technology production and services and knowledge becomes more important than raw materials? Smith examines the history of fisheries management in the Pacific during the last century and reveals an overall trend of more stringent constraints placed on Japanese demands over time. He argues that there are important implications for future Japanese interests in the North Pacific Ocean. Besides territorial conflicts over fisheries with surrounding nations, such as Russia and South Korea, there is also the question of increasingly assertive nongovernmental organizations (NGOs) involved in environmental conservation, such as Greenpeace. These tensions bode ill for a country that continues to have to negotiate supplies of food and other resources from overseas sources.

Part 2: Japan's Identity and Youth

Japan's changing identity and youth are the subjects of the next four essays. It is often said that the Japanese spend more time and energy than perhaps any other people in trying to define what constitutes their particular national identity (Dale 1986). Japan has long been caught between Western-oriented modernizing visions on the one hand and traditional attitudes on the other. Today, as in the past, the perception of this nation is shaped very much by its context in the world. In the contemporary era, the forces of globalization and the steamroller of Western culture have tended to lead to an identity crisis. Certainly, Japan's task of managing its dependence on the world economy has raised new anxieties, and this is related not just to the issue of economic security. For example, Japan appears to be turning away from US hegemony and trying to create a role for itself in Asia. And as the contemporary world is now leaning towards the formation of regional blocs, then Japan's future lies at the centre of the Asia-Pacific bloc (Fukui 1994). But to what degree has its colonial past shaped its freedom to operate in Asia today? Japan and China comprise the most important relationship in the region, and it is conceivable that within a generation this relationship might become even more important and supplant even that between Japan and the US. Of course, for much of the past decade, cultivating closer and more diverse economic ties with China has been a major priority of the Japanese government. Certainly, Japanese business currently looks upon China as the most important location for its overseas factories. In developing new geopolitical and geo-economic strategies, however, problems left over from war, from history, continue to haunt Japan. But what can we learn from Japan's Asian colonial past? In Chapter 5, Bill Sewell examines how the historical memory of Manchuria impacts on contemporary identity in Japan. His study suggests that Japan's experience in Manchuria will greatly affect the country's ability to develop Sino-Japanese relations in the twenty-first century.

Domestically, Japan's identity crisis is also causing problems. For instance, Japan can no longer be said to be a homogeneous society and, as with many other countries, it will in the future likely become more and more a nation of new economic immigrants and minorities. Moreover, in a rapidly globalizing world, individuals and minority communities within nations seek some kind of shelter from internationalizing forces perceived as threatening. They often turn to narrow nationalisms and powerful separatist movements and demands for local independence. The Ainu of Japan are already doing this, and represent just one of a number of other diverse communities who continue to face discrimination (including the Koreans, Ryukyuans/Okinawans, Chinese, and foreign workers). In Chapter 6, Millie Creighton points out that the "Ainu problem" is not new. It has been a subject widely discussed among the authorities in Japan for a considerable time. She traces 100 years of the relationship between Japan's aboriginal people and mainstream Japanese society. Meanwhile, the bleak situation of the Ainu remains very much the same. This essay looks at contemporary Ainu resistance and how it creates a focus for the Ainu identity movement's efforts to gain international recognition of the Ainu as an indigenous people. Her study shows that Japan at the millennium is indeed at a crossroads in terms of the rights and recognition of indigenous and minority peoples.

"Youth culture" is driving a new identity for Japan, both in nearby Asia and in the rest of the world (Craig 2000). Paradoxically, Japanese pop culture is thriving at the same time that there is much angst over the aging of the Japanese population. The Japanese *shinjinrui* (younger generation) are quite different from the older generation as they do not have the same postwar experience of their parents, especially in terms of attitudes towards thrift and hard work. Indeed, many argue that the generation gap between the old and young in Japan may be most clearly seen in the attitude towards consumerism. In Chapter 7, Hiroshi Aoyagi examines important gender implications of one aspect of popular culture known as *aidoru poppusu* ("idol-pop"), represented by a series of female personalities who sing, dance, act, and are groomed by their managers for popular consumption. He concludes that the historical roots of this "industry" can be traced back to premodern images of femininity in Japan. Consequently, there are profound and disturbing ramifications for the role of women in Japan's growing entertainment economy. These reflect the many wider issues and setbacks of women's evolving position within Japanese society.

An even darker side of the new youth culture is the rising number of juvenile delinquents indulging in drugs and urban crime. They are represented in the image of the *Bosozoku* ("speed tribes"; see Greenfield 1994). Besides the economic and political changes noted earlier, Japan has witnessed a number of crimes associated with young people, indicative for many of perhaps an impending social crisis. There is the perception, at least, that failures in home and school education have damaged children's sensitivity and ability to deal with their problems, and that high schools and universities are not functioning as proper educational institutions (see, for instance, Hall 1998; Wray 1999). The rise of cults such as Aum Shinrikyō in the 1990s also revealed that the educational system had failed in the task of developing young people's abilities to understand and to make proper judgments on national and local issues as citizens (Metraux 2000). This increase in youth crime in Japan has led to heightened interest in the broader subject of the juvenile justice system. In Chapter 8, Stephan M. Salzberg traces the legal response to the problem of youth crime and the growth of Japan's juvenile justice system over the last 100 years. He looks at the evolution of the juvenile justice system, its historical roots, and the challenges that it now faces. While there has indeed been a rise in juvenile crime, he argues that the Japanese model of addressing this has been relatively successful and is unlikely to change in the foreseeable future.

Part 3: Urban Living and Beauty

A final set of essays concerns the link between the past and present in Japanese cities. As noted earlier, one of the most dramatic shifts in the past century was the transformation of Japan's population into a predominantly urban society. Indeed, because most Japanese live in cities, it is in the urban areas where many of the transitions reported above are being felt, such as economic restructuring and rapid social change. At the end of the century, the tension between urban and rural life in Japan came even more to the fore. Well-known commentator Kenichi Ohmae (1995), for example, berated the "civil minimum" policies of the Japanese government, whereby substantial subsidies are given to even the remotest islands and rural peripheries for postal services, water supply, electrical power, public works, and a host of other government-funded services. In part, this clearer split between the interests of urban dwellers and rural communities has been caused by the downturn in the economy and rising expectations about the quality of life. At the same time, however, increasing anomie among city residents has led to nostalgia for a simpler rural life.

David W. Edgington and Joshua S. Mostow consider these interrelated themes. In Chapter 9, Edgington examines why economic goals and rural development goals have always outweighed urban quality of life, and discusses the progress made in upgrading the amenities of Japan's cities over the last 100 or so years. He argues that despite the many plans aimed at making Japan a "quality of life superpower," there are very real constraints in upgrading Japanese cities in the years to come. In Chapter 10, Mostow analyzes the phenomenon of an increasing urban interest in Japan's rich and varied past, and finds that the fascination of urban consumers with art museum displays of traditional Japanese beauty is an evocative indicator of how the present is intertwined with the past.

Bridging the Past, Present, and Future
A general conclusion emerges from the various case studies, namely, that it would be a mistake not to see strong continuities in Japan's evolution. The final chapter of this book (Chapter 11) reviews the events of 2001. At the dawn of the new millennium, Japan reflected both sides of a national identity torn between tradition and modernity. Many features of Japanese economic, political, and social life remained intact, for better or worse, and so we should be cautious about any forecasts of rapid change. Japan's approach to structural reform has differed, and will differ, dramatically from that of North American and European countries, and so it will have to find its own way to adjust to the twenty-first century's pressures of global competition and global interdependence. This is likely to be based upon institutional adaptation, combining traditional attitudes towards managing change with strong government regulation and communal values.

By way of illustration, Nagatani and Carlile reflect on Japan's changing economy and labour politics. They conclude that an examination of economic uncertainty in Japan today has to recognize the underlying characteristics and strengths of a Japanese political economy, one that has survived more or less intact since the war years. Still, there are continuing and perhaps increasing weaknesses. Despite the country's shift to an industrial structure that is less dependent upon overseas materials, Smith finds that Japan has not been able to escape its need to negotiate supplies of food and other resources from outside. Sewell and Mostow detect aspects of the past, ranging from the feudal period to Japan's ill-fated invasion of China, continually reflected in Japan's changing image of itself in the years leading up to the end of the century. Edgington and Creighton find that although the country wishes to take its place as a prosperous member of the international community, there remain many dilemmas at home. These include the challenges involved in upgrading Japan's cities and the problems facing minority peoples, both of which have their roots in past actions and attitudes. Aoyagi and Salzberg find strong continuities in social and policy trends in the modern youth scene in Japan.

A second theme, considered by each contributor to this book, has been the connection between the present and the future. The book closes, therefore, with an essay written at the end of 2001 posing exactly how and to what degree change might occur. If some transformation in Japan is unavoidable due to the many structural shifts identified in this chapter, what are the necessary changes and how will they occur? How relevant is the reform government of Prime Minister Koizumi? The final chapter considers all of these issues.

Notes

1 See the "Century of Change" series of articles that appeared in the *Japan Times* throughout 1999, commencing with "Reshaping the Political Process: Plebiscites Giving Public an Outlet" (Murakami 1999).
2 For more general works dealing with Japan in the twentieth century, see Tsurumi 1987, Gordon 1993, Bailey 1996, Hane 1996, Thomas 1996, Waswo 1996, Allison 1997, Pempel 1998, Curtis 1999, and Kingston 2001.
3 For a review of these and other major economic, political, and social events of the 1990s, see Masuzoe 2000.
4 During the summer of 2001, many large electronic firms, such as Matsushita, Hitachi, and Toshiba, were forced to eliminate several thousand full-time jobs by offering redundancy payoffs to employees to quit. These and other corporate layoffs during the year were a stark reminder that Japan's job market was rapidly deteriorating, as company earnings slid and industrial output shrank. At the end of 2001, when this chapter was written, the unemployment rate stood at a record 5.5 percent. Economists and government leaders warned that bigger job losses might be ahead (see *Japan Today* 2001a, 2001b).

References

Allison, G.D. 1997. *Japan's Postwar History*. Ithaca, NY: Cornell University Press.
Bailey, P.J. 1996. *Postwar Japan: 1945 to the Present*. Oxford: Blackwell.
Campbell, J.C. 1988. *Politics and Culture in Japan*. Ann Arbor: Center for Political Studies, Institute for Social Research, University of Michigan.
Carlile, L.E., and M.C. Tilton, eds. 1998. *Is Japan Really Changing Its Ways? Regulatory Reform and the Japanese Economy*. Washington, DC: Brookings Institution Press.
Craig, T.J. 2000. *Japan Pop! Inside the World of Japanese Popular Culture*. Armonk, NY: M.E. Sharpe.
Curtis, G.L. 1999. *The Logic of Japanese Politics: Leaders, Institutions and the Limits of Change*. New York: Columbia University Press.
Dale, P.N. 1986. *The Myth of Japanese Uniqueness*. London: Croom Helm.
Dore, R. 2000. *Stock Market Capitalism: Welfare Capitalism: Japan and Germany versus the Anglo-Saxons*. Oxford: Oxford University Press.
Eades, J.S., T. Gill, and H. Befu, eds. 2000. *Globalization and Social Change in Contemporary Japan*. Melbourne: Trans Pacific Press.

Eccleston, B. 1989. *State and Society in Post-War Japan*. Cambridge: Polity Press.
The Economist. 1996. "A Survey of Tomorrow's Japan: The Compass Swings," 13 July (Special Supplement), 1-16.
—. 2000. "The Drift in Japan," 4 November, 20-21.
Foreign Press Center Japan. 1999. *Facts and Figures of Japan*. Tokyo: Foreign Press Center Japan.
Friedman, T.L. 2000. *The Lexus and the Olive Tree*. New York: Anchor Books.
Fukui, S. 1994. "Prospects for an Asian Trade Bloc: Japan, the Association of South-east Asian Nations and the Asian Newly Industrializing Economies." In T.D. Mason and A.M. Turay, eds., *Japan, NAFTA and Europe: Trilateral Cooperation or Confrontation*. Houndmills, Basingstoke, Hampshire, UK: St. Martin's Press, 164-88.
Gibney, F., ed. 1998. *Unlocking the Bureaucrat's Kingdom*. Washington, DC: Brookings Institution Press.
Gordon, A., ed. 1993. *Postwar Japan as History*. Berkeley: University of California Press.
Greenfield, K.T. 1994. *Speed Tribes: Days and Nights with Japan's Next Generation*. New York: HarperCollins.
Hall, I.P. 1998. *Cartels of the Mind: Japan's Intellectual Closed Shop*. New York: W.W. Norton.
Hane, M. 1996. *Eastern Phoenix: Japan since 1945*. Boulder, CO: Westview.
Hernandi, A. 1996. "Development versus Growth? Aspects of Quality Gaining Ground in Japan." In S. Metzger-Court and W. Pascha, eds., *Japan's Socio-Economic Evolution*. Folkestone, Kent, UK: Japan Library, 173-90.
Japan Times. 2001. "ASEAN, China OK Trade Zone," 7 November, 1.
Japan Today. 2001a. "Toshiba to Sack 17,000 Workers in Japan," 27 August. <http://www.japantoday.com>, accessed November 2001.
—. 2001b. "Jobless Rate Hits Record High 5.5% in Nov," 27 December. <http://www.japantoday.com>, accessed December 2001.
Katz, R. 1998. *Japan, the System that Soured: The Rise and Fall of the Japanese Economic Miracle*. Armonk, NY: M.E. Sharpe.
—. 2001. "Economy Heading Backwards." *Oriental Economist* 68(12): 3-4.
Kingston, J. 2001. *Japan in Transformation, 1952-2000*. Harlow, Essex, UK: Pearson Education.
Lincoln, E.J. 2001. *Arthritic Japan: The Slow Pace of Economic Reform*. Washington, DC: Brookings Institution Press.
Masuzoe, Y. 2000. *Years of Trial: Japan in the 1990s*. Tokyo: Japan Echo.
Matthews, R., and K. Matsuyama. 1993. *Japan's Military Renaissance?* New York: St. Martin's Press.
Metraux, D.A. 2000. *Aum Shinrikyō's Impact on Japanese Society*. Japanese Studies Vol. 11. Lewiston, NY: Edwin Mellen Press.
Millett, M. 2000. "Lost Decade Ends in Recession." *Sydney Morning Herald*, 14 March. <http://smh.com.au>, accessed March 2000.
Mochizuki, M.M., ed. 1997. *Towards a True Alliance: Restructuring US-Japan Security Relations*. Washington, DC: Brookings Institution Press.
Murakami, A. 1999. "Reshaping the Political Process: Plebiscites Giving Public an Outlet." *Japan Times*, 1 January, 1-2.
Ohmae, K. 1995. *The End of the Nation-State: The Rise of Regional Economies*. New York: Free Press.
Oka, T. 1994. *Prying Open the Door: Foreign Workers in Japan*. Contemporary Issues Paper No. 2. Washington, DC: Carnegie Endowment for International Peace.
Oriental Economist. 2001. "Koizumi Reforms Overshadowed by Events: Terror Abroad, Trauma at Home," 69(10): 1-3.
Pempel, T. 1998. *Regime Shift: Comparative Dynamics of the Japanese Political Economy*. Ithaca, NY: Cornell University Press.
Porter, M., H. Takeuchi, and M. Sakakibara. 2000. *Can Japan Compete?* Houndmills, Basingstoke, Hampshire, UK: Macmillan Press.
Seike, A. 1997. *New Trends in Japan's Labor Market: Changes in Employment Practices*. About Japan Series 22. Tokyo: Foreign Press Center Japan.
Thomas, J.E. 1996. *Modern Japan: A Social History since 1968*. London: Longman.

Tsurumi, S. 1987. *A Cultural History of Japan, 1945-1980*. 2nd ed. London: KPI.
Ujimoto, K.V. 2000. "The Aging of Japanese Society: Human Resource Management in Transition." In P. Bowles and L.T. Woods, eds., *Japan after the Economic Miracle: In Search of New Directions*. Dordrecht, Netherlands: Kluwer Academic, 169-84.
Waswo, A. 1996. *Modern Japanese Society: 1868-1994*. Oxford: Oxford University Press.
Wray, H. 1999. *Japanese and American Education: Attitudes and Practices*. Westport, CT: Bergin and Garvey.

Part 1
Economic and Political Systems

The essays in Part 1 all deal with aspects of Japan's economic and political systems and the link between history and current trends. The wider context throughout is the rhetoric of deregulation and reform that grew during the 1990s (Carlile and Tilton 1998; Gibney 1998). Many commentators now advocate a shift towards a more open or Western-style economy, even though this implies an end to distinctive Japanese approaches, including labour-management practices such as lifetime employment. Moreover, if Japan were to engage in freer trade with the rest of the world under a more liberalized regime, there would be many other implications, such as allowing its traditionally high self-sufficiency in food and other resources to wind down.

In Chapter 2, Keizo Nagatani shows how the Japanese economic system is organized along very different lines from that of the US. He reminds us that there is still a choice between capitalist regimes: the Anglo-American or "neoliberal" system of independent, profit-maximizing corporations versus the Asian-style system of state-administered corporatism. These alternatives are often referred to as the "shareholder" and "stakeholder" models of capitalism, respectively (Dore 2000). Nagatani is basically sympathetic to Japan's economic system, highlighting its creative balance between equity and efficiency, and a distinctive "coexistence principle," according to which the winners have to compensate the losers in society. He notes that this was laid down long ago, in the Meiji period, and based upon certain cultural values that today act as obstacles to the full adoption of Anglo-American economic reforms. He argues that Japan has historically found ways to adapt to external pressures and that the Japanese will continue to institute incremental reforms to good effect. An interesting counterpoint to this essay is the work of Professor Yoshio Noguchi of Tokyo University, who argues that many aspects of the Japanese economic system are not necessarily intrinsic to Japanese culture but rather were introduced as a wartime system during the years around 1940, and hence can be called the "1940 system" (Noguchi 1998).

There are certain pressures on the Japanese system, however, that must be addressed. One is the competition that has been brought to bear upon Japanese manufacturing from East Asian countries. Over the past fifteen or so years, the conditions under which the Japanese economy operates have changed substantially. Thus, South Korea and Taiwan emerged as locations of high technology and heavy industry during the 1980s and 1990s, and now hold positions of global leadership in these areas (Hobday 1995). By contrast, Michael Porter argues that there has been an almost total absence of new Japanese export industries during the 1990s (Porter et al. 2000). Japan must therefore reposition its economy and move even further into knowledge-based sectors and technologies. A second structural pressure is the need to address the dramatic transformation of information and communications technologies (often called the "third industrial revolution") that has unfolded in Europe and the United States over the last decade. The Japanese economy of the 1990s missed this important shift and largely failed to make the rapid transition from a catch-up economic system to one that facilitates creative innovation (Odaki 2000).

One image of the new economy in Japan is venture capitalist Masayoshi Son, the billionaire president of Softbank Corporation, who is responsible for half of all "e-business" initiatives in the country. Softbank was founded in 1981, and in the 1990s it became one of the first companies to dominate Japanese computer software and hardware distribution. It is now the single biggest investor in America's Yahoo!, owning about 28 percent of one of the leading Internet portals (*The Economist* 2000). Another is "Bit Valley" in Tokyo's trendy Shibuya district, which is Japan's own version of Silicon Valley. The name plays on Shibuya, which means "bitter valley." In just a few years since the mid-1990s, a lonely high-tech software and Internet field populated by a few Japanese entrepreneurs has blossomed into an industrial cluster of over 150 firms (Hamilton 2000). Another high-tech cluster is in Kyoto, where there are an estimated 300 high-tech start-ups. While these are not mature high-tech entrepreneurial clusters like Silicon Valley, they point to Japanese social and economic trends moving in the direction of entrepreneurship and information technology (Porter et al. 2000). In a postscript to his essay, Nagatani cautions against overenthusiasm for the information revolution and argues that this shift in the world economy may not necessarily place Japan at a disadvantage. Such a viewpoint is also supported by Eisuke Sakakibara (2000), former vice minister of Japan's Ministry of Finance. He has pointed out the strong continuities between the old economic regime and the new technology-driven economy.

Besides the transformation of the Japanese economy, management-employee relations are also evolving. In Chapter 3, Lonny E. Carlile notes an intriguing paradox, which is that while labour unions are moving closer to government policy, union membership rates are shrinking. To explain this, he carefully charts the history of Japan's labour movement over the past fifty years and notes that from its radical roots in the postwar years, it became more politically neutral over time. The wider context is that, unlike in other countries, the post-oil shock period in Japan saw a social contract emerge between labour and government. Essentially, the latter implicitly promised to maintain employment and institute welfare programs in return for the former keeping down wage demands (Garan and Mochizuki 1993). In the 1980s, Rengō (the National Federation of Private Sector Trade Unions) emerged, with the aim of unifying the newly tamed labour movement. Still, Rengō was subsequently able to advance labour policies in direct negotiation with the government bureaucracy and the Liberal Democratic Party (LDP), and Shinoda (1997) assesses that Rengō has made at least some contribution to improving workers' welfare in a difficult climate of economic recession, especially reduced work hours and improved child care facilities. By joining the moderate Rengō, therefore, Japanese labour has not sought to advance its aims through political confrontation, even at a time of recession and restructuring. Indeed, up to about 1997, restructuring in Japan was carried out with some sensitivity for workers' interests, especially compared with the US and Britain. Few employees were laid off abruptly, voluntary retirees received sizeable allowances, and retraining and alternative job placement within larger organizations were the norm rather than redundancies.

As the economy deteriorated, however, Rengō began to face criticism, especially from employees of small and medium enterprises as well as casual workers who had been driven into further difficulties and worsened economic conditions by continued low growth and globalization. After 1997 it became clear that even large companies were not averse to laying off core workers, normally protected by lifetime employment. For instance, the major companies NTT (Nippon Telegraph and Telephone Corporation) and Nissan Motor Company (owned mainly by France's Renault since 1999) caused quite a stir in 2000 when they laid off about 21,000 and 20,000 workers, respectively. Protest marches erupted in January 2000 when it was announced that Nissan was planning to lay off 14 percent of its workers. Significantly, it was another, more radical union, the National Confederation of Trade Unions (Zenrōen), not Rengō, that protested in Tokyo against these cuts. Most Nissan unions, which belonged to Rengō, did not oppose them (Goodspeed 2000).

What do all these changes amount to? Not all observers agree that an erosion of traditional corporate practices is taking place, and blame media hype for exaggerating the extent of the transformation (Dore 2000). They point out that American-style mass firing of workers is still not the norm in Japan, and possibly never will be. It is clear, however, that favourable employment conditions are shrinking and that the core workforce of many companies is declining. A shift towards more flexible pay and hiring practices is occurring and firms are steadily changing their compensation packages, notably by making greater use of merit pay. This is one reason why the traditional collective Shuntō wage-setting structure is quickly losing importance and giving way to the incremental growth of a more individualistic and market-oriented system. Finally, the use of part-time workers instead of full-time core workers is increasing, especially as restrictions on temporary workers *(sairyo rōdō)* are being lifted (Weathers 1999). The challenge for the labour movement is to manage these changes without allowing marginalization of less favoured workers or abandoning efforts to improve working conditions.

Yet another aspect of Japan's distinctive economic and political system has been its ability to keep at bay competition from the outside world. Such a system, however, has meant that Japan's consumers bear the high costs of such insulation. Recent calls for deregulation focus on opening Japan's markets even further to overseas suppliers, which in turn means a future reduction in Japan's resources and food self-sufficiency. This has exposed a deep-seated concern for the country's economic security, which is understandable given Japan's almost total lack of raw materials and its geographic isolation. At times, anxieties have run high about the nation's ability to secure long-term supplies of essential raw materials, particularly in the wake of the 1970s oil crisis. In the early 1980s, a policy of "comprehensive security" was launched by then Prime Minister Suzuki Zenko, who endorsed the notion of defining security broadly to include economic well-being and invulnerability to disruptions as well as traditional military security. The active use of diplomatic, economic, and cultural initiatives as well as a strong military defence to guarantee comprehensive security quickly arose in response to the first oil embargo (Akao 1983).

Roger Smith addresses these issues in Chapter 4 through a 100-year history of Japanese fisheries in the North Pacific Ocean. This study illustrates how Japan's postwar economy has had to operate within the confines of an international system. As he points out, the high seas fishing industry has seen a century-long struggle to secure sufficient resources for an expanding population and economy, and international forces have, over a period of time, imposed more and more restrictions on Japan's growing demands. Thus, Japan is currently embroiled in negotiations with Russia over northern Pacific salmon, and with South Korea over fishing in the waters around the Russian-held islands north of Hokkaido claimed by Japan (the disputed Northern Territories) (*Japan Times Online* 2001). Smith's essay also provides a link to many of Japan's contemporary environmental problems, particularly drift net fishing and whaling. Outside the North Pacific, Japan is also embroiled in high seas fisheries disputes over Southern Bluefin Tuna (Environmental News Service 1999). Besides these specific case studies, environmental groups such as Greenpeace and SeaWeb have been outspoken over Japan's huge appetite for fish in general (SeaWeb 2000a, 2000b). For example, Japan is often criticized for importing tuna for its lucrative sushi and sashimi markets from countries such as Taiwan, Indonesia, and South Korea, which are not signatories to any conservation agreement on this type of fish (SeaWeb 1997, 1998). For Japan there is much at stake in the coming years in the way it negotiates these disputes and criticisms, including its very food culture. Tottman (2000, 529) goes further and notes that "whether Japan should enter an era of industrial stasis and sustainability may for human-kind be the basic question that awaits an answer as the 21st century begins."

In short, these essays suggest that many historical forces are at work and there is no easy run for American-style reform or deregulation in Japan. Indeed, deregulation per se is unlikely to solve Japan's problems. Japan will have to find its own path, one that combines the need for efficiency with its own social values and sense of security. Certainly, Japan needs to improve productivity, and to do this it will have to allow more competition, labour market flexibility, and competition from imports. But nothing dictates that Japan has to accomplish these tasks in the same way that America or any other Western country does. Reform in Japan is not going to mean Americanization.

References

Akao, N. 1983. *Japan's Economic Security: Resources as a Factor in Foreign Policy.* Aldershot, Hampshire, UK: Gower.

Carlile, L.E., and M.C. Tilton, eds. 1998. *Is Japan Really Changing Its Ways? Regulatory Reform and the Japanese Economy.* Washington, DC: Brookings Institution Press.

Dore, R. 2000. *Stock Market Capitalism: Welfare Capitalism: Japan and Germany versus the Anglo-Saxons.* Oxford: Oxford University Press.

The Economist. 2000. "Japanese Banking: Soft Touch," 26 January, 87.

Environment News Service. 1999. "Japan Ordered to Halt Bluefin Tuna Take." <http://ens.lycos.com>, accessed August 2001.

Garan, S., and M. Mochizuki. 1993. "Negotiating Social Contracts." In A. Gordon, ed., *Postwar Japan as History.* Berkeley: University of California Press, 145-66.

Gibney, F., ed. 1998. *Unlocking the Bureaucrat's Kingdom.* Washington, DC: Brookings Institution Press.

Goodspeed, P. 2000. "Passive Japanese Unionists Protest Job Cuts at Nissan." *National Post* (Toronto), 26 January, 5.

Hamilton, T. 2000. "Japan's Dot-Com Double Vision." *Globe and Mail* (Toronto), 15 June, T1-2.

Hobday, M. 1995. *Innovation in East Asia: The Challenge to Japan.* Aldershot, Hampshire, UK: Edward Elgar.

Japan Times Online. 2001. "Protest Lodged by Tokyo over Fish Row," 3 August. <http://www.japantimes.co.jp>, accessed August 2001.

Noguchi, Y. 1998. "The 1940 System: Japan under the Wartime Economy." *American Economic Review* 88: 404-8.

Odaki, K. 2000. "Catching Up All Over Again." *Look Japan* 46(533): 22.

Porter, M.E., H. Takeuchi, and M. Sakakibara. 2000. *Can Japan Compete?* Houndmills, Basingstoke, Hampshire, UK: Macmillan Press Ltd.

Sakakibara, E. 2000. "Japan's Economy: A Global Context." Presentation given in Vancouver, 18 October. <http://www.jetrovancouver.org/Docs/SakakibaraBreakfast.html>, accessed December 2001.

SeaWeb. 1997. "Southern Bluefin Tuna Population at Lowest Levels Recorded: Report." <http://www.seaweb.org>, accessed August 2001.

–. 1998. "Bluefin Tuna Background." <http://www.seaweb.org>, accessed August 2001.

–. 2000a. "Japan Announces Intention to Expand 'Scientific' Whaling." <http://www.seaweb.org>, accessed August 2001.

–. 2000b. "Japan Goes Whaling in North Pacific: United States Announces Actions in Response." <http://www.seaweb.org>, accessed August 2001.

Shinoda, T. 1997. "Rengō and Policy Participation." In M. Sako and H. Sato, eds., *Japanese Labour and Management in Transition: Diversity, Flexibility and Participation*. London: Routledge, 187-214.

Tottman, C. 2000. *A History of Japan*. Oxford: Blackwell.

Weathers, C. 1999. "The Postwar Transformation of the Labor Force." In P. Heenan, ed., *The Japan Handbook*. New York: Glenlake Publishing, 182-201.

2
Japanese Economics: An Interpretative Essay
Keizo Nagatani

The Japanese economy has been in a deep recession for the past ten years. The average annual real growth rate from 1991 to 1999 was a meagre 1.7 percent (Economic Planning Agency 2000). The growth rates for fiscal years 1997 and 1998 were -0.7 and -1.9 percent, respectively, the first years of negative growth since 1974 (Nihon Keizai Shimbun 2000). The monetary and fiscal authorities have tried everything to pull the economy out of the recession. Thus, the bank rate was set at a historic low level of 0.5 percent in a bid to support the economic recovery. In February 1999, the Bank of Japan lowered this to 0.25 percent, resulting in interest rates of virtually zero. Fiscal authorities suspended the Fiscal Reconstruction Act and boosted public works spending to stimulate the economy. These strong policy efforts did not produce the desired results. In 1999 the government was determined to turn the economy around and declared an official forecast of positive 0.6 percent (Sakaiya 2000), but even this modest optimism was not shared widely among the populace.

The worst part of the Japanese system today, however, is not the economic recession itself but the mass psychological depression and the consequent loss of self-identity that permeates the system. In a sense, the current recession is a natural consequence of the big national gamble that the Japanese took during the "bubble economy" of the 1980s. The Japanese – governments, firms, and citizens alike – believing in eternal prosperity, went bullish on all fronts and lost. The household sector alone lost ¥200 trillion (roughly about US$1,000 billion) in net worth between 1990 and 1995; the banks and other financial firms were stuck with a huge amount of bad debts; and governments, both national and local, found themselves gazing at huge precommitted outlays and revenue deficits.

There is only one way out of the trouble: several years of perseverance and hard work, plain and simple. Up to the year 2001, no politicians or business leaders stepped forward to take the helm. Politicians appeared preoccupied with the same old power game, while Japan's business leaders appeared intent only on preying on the public purse. The once-powerful bureaucracy, smeared by an endless string of bribe taking and other scandals, lost the credibility and morale needed to steer a fatigued system. In short, the Japanese economy and politics have been in a state of flux without a clear sense of direction, giving observers both at home and abroad an impression that the Japan *maru*,[1] after decades of mostly smooth sailing, has run aground. Amid this chaos, the Japanese suddenly appeared to have lost all their self-confidence. It is often argued that the past success was just good luck that cannot be maintained in the new environment, and that the system needs to be overhauled to survive in the coming era of mega-competition, restructuring, and deregulation. The Japanese need to become cosmopolitans by ridding themselves of all their peculiar national traits, or so say the leading opinion makers in the nation. Certainly, the Japanese now face a major identity crisis.

The purpose of this chapter is to take stock of the Japanese economy at an important crossroads, namely after fifty years or so of postwar development that has raised the economy from the ashes to one of the most affluent in the world. How has Japan done so well for the past fifty years relative to virtually all other countries in the world? What has Japan done differently to achieve its great economic success? What was the essence of the "Japanese economics" underlying its economic policy formulation? How did it differ from Western economics? Can one expect the conditions, internal and external, that have supported the Japanese economy for the past fifty years to prevail in the future? If conditions were to change, or have already changed, where would the Japanese economic system go? Has it played out its historical role? Will Japan be increasingly Americanized in its social and economic management? Or will Japanese economics survive in the new era? What adjustments, if any, will it need in order to survive?

The next section discusses the importance of culture with regard to economic systems and provides a brief review of neoclassical economic theory, which is the dominant economic doctrine. Then follows a comparative analysis of American and Japanese economics within the neoclassical economic framework. The chapter concludes with a prediction about the future of these two economic systems (see also Nagatani 1998a).

Economic Culture and Neoclassical Economics

It is important to recognize certain basic connections between the economic culture of a nation (defined here as the value system or code of conduct its citizens hold in common) and the type of economics that forms the basis of the nation's economic policy making. This viewpoint accepts as fact that each nation has a more or less unique economics (so defined) of its own, the universality of the discipline promoted by academic economists notwithstanding.[2] That different peoples in different parts of the world have different lifestyles and outlooks on life seems indisputable. The natural environment – geography, climate, gifts of nature, and so on – determines to a large extent the manner in which the residents earn their living, develop religious beliefs, devise social rules and govern themselves, and form views about life and the world. The observed differences in the pattern of thought and behaviour among the different peoples of the world may be largely attributed to such people-specific cultural traits. It should be noted that these are the *collective* traits, or *ethos*, of a people, not those of the individual members. Human beings indeed seem far more similar at the individual level than at the collective level of races or nations.[3]

Some may argue that economics is an exception, and that different peoples are homogeneous when it comes to economic behaviour despite such cultural differences. Technical know-how in the spheres of production, distribution, and communication is shared across national borders, and business organizations move around the world fairly freely. Pressure for profits leaves little room for individual firms or nations to deviate from the prevailing mode. Consumption habits of different peoples have also become increasingly homogeneous as a result of the freer trade of goods. Even national economic policies appear to follow a similar trend towards rational homogenization, with neoclassical economics as a universal doctrine. Yet, beyond the veil of the universal economic doctrine and convergence thereto, one can recognize distinct "personalities" in the way various nations in the world practise economics. One can even say that neoclassical economics, which is currently the dominant doctrine, was itself the product of a particular economic culture representing a specific group of people sharing a common set of values and beliefs. A comparative analysis of American economics and Japanese economics below will illustrate these points.[4] To begin with, however, I will briefly survey the strengths and weaknesses of neoclassical economics.

That neoclassical economics was modelled after Newtonian physics is well known.[5] Newton's theory had two building blocks. One was the optimizing behaviour of natural objects; the other was the equilibrating behaviour of the system as a whole, tending towards a harmonious equilibrium once perturbed. Of these two building blocks, the former was developed in detail and passed numerous rigorous tests in the various fields of mechanics; the latter, in contrast, remained largely a teleology based not on scientific proof but on religious faith. Neoclassical economics borrowed everything, including its underlying faith, from the system of Newtonian physics. By replacing natural objects with individuals and equilibrium of the physical world with competitive (market) equilibrium, economists transformed this physical theory into an economic theory. The neoclassical theory paints an equally orderly picture of the economic system in which the forces of demand and supply bring prices to competitive general equilibrium. In this model, not only has every individual optimized activity, subject to his or her endowment of skills and resources, but also the equilibrium allocation of resources has achieved efficiency in the sense of Pareto for the system as a whole. (An allocation is said to be efficient in the sense of Pareto if it is impossible to improve one individual's welfare without reducing someone else's welfare by any further reallocation of the given societal resources.) Despite the many underlying strengths of this theory, a closer examination of a number of its loose ends is in order.

Static versus Dynamic Efficiency
According to Newtonian physicists, equilibrium is static in two senses. First, the process of equilibration is perceived as a passive response to isolated shocks from outside; it is essentially timeless. Second, equilibrium, once established, is assumed to stay put forever and has no sense of direction or evolution. The neoclassicist's notion of equilibrium therefore parallels that of the physicist. Just as physical equilibrium has no sense of direction and evolution, so neoclassical theory lacks a dynamic evolutionary content. It limits itself to the allocation of given societal resources under given tastes and technology and the system's capability to restore equilibrium when perturbed by exogenous shocks. As noted above, the centrepiece of neoclassical general equilibrium theory is the Pareto efficiency of competitive resource allocation. It corresponds to the state of maximized entropy in physics. Pareto efficiency is achieved through unfettered arbitrage operations by the market participants, even though monopoly and other barriers may get in the way of efficient resource allocation, just as a dam prevents two water levels from following the natural tendency to equalization.

Dynamic efficiency, however, deals with economic growth and so is a more inclusive concept than static efficiency. Indeed, it is of vital importance to discover how to achieve the long-term prosperity of an economic system. However, growth requires investment, in both human and non-human capital. But an important question is how much and in which uses? In other words, who is to determine how such an allocation of resources should occur? The neoclassical answer to these questions is pure and simple: the markets will do the job better than any conceivable alternatives, using price signals as a guide.[6] Yet one reason to be skeptical of the effectiveness of the market or decentralized solution for investment is that the decisions made by profit-seeking individuals tend to miss in aggregate the socially optimum level of investment systematically and exaggerate the magnitude of risk associated with the socially optimum level (Nagatani 1998b). This means that the benefit-cost analyses and investment decisions made by narrow-visioned individuals tend to miss the mark, and suggests that a more coordinated decision mechanism might do better than the markets. At any rate, those who lack the neoclassicists' faith in markets would be justified in searching for some alternative decision mechanisms for social investment.

Efficiency versus Equity
Despite the fact that the economists hold efficiency and equity as the two highest criteria of economic welfare, they have not been able to find a satisfactory compromise between them. Competition as a means of promoting excellence and efficiency does not serve equity well at all. Competition necessarily produces winners and losers. Economists tend to believe that the fiercer the competition, the better the quality of the winner's output and the social benefit derived from it, and that in order to increase the pressure of competition, the winner-take-all rule outperforms any others that allow for equity. This means that the loser's lot in a competitive system is a pretty sad one. Yet the only point that economists can agree on in terms of equity is the notion of *ex ante* equity in the sense of equal opportunities for all and of fair play. But such an *ex ante* notion of equity must be judged hollow in content. What counts most is *ex post* equity, in the sense of providing an equal share.[7] Thus, while efficiency and equity are regarded by many as the highest goals of economics, they are very different in character and require vastly different lines of attack. The neoclassical theory is silent on what these lines of approach are. It is therefore up to each nation to seek an ideal balance between the two goals. But what is ideal depends upon a nation's particular economic culture.

Microeconomics versus Macroeconomics
Strictly speaking, neoclassical general equilibrium theory emphasizes *microeconomic* behaviour and leaves no room for *macroeconomics*, which focuses on the social behaviour of individuals and the coordination of their plans into national aggregates. Thus, under the neoclassical model, once individuals make rational plans and once markets coordinate these plans perfectly, various aggregates would be the mere sums of individual activities. In other words, once one knew enough about individual behaviour, there would be nothing more to learn from studying aggregate behaviour.

By contrast, macroeconomics as we know it came from economist John Maynard Keynes, who was not a neoclassicist and who stressed the way in which informational imperfections and group psychology affected individual behaviour. In Keynes's view, the peculiar group psychology that affected markets was largely responsible for the fluctuations in aggregate production and employment and in the price level (Samuelson 1955). Moreover, he considered that these fluctuations were often something beyond the comprehension and control of maximizing individuals and yet responsible for a great deal of welfare losses (far greater in magnitude than the static welfare losses stressed by the neoclassicists) for individuals living in an economic system. Hence, a rationale is required for macroeconomics, or the science of studying ways to keep the aggregate economy on a stable and prosperous path through monetary and fiscal policies. But this is easier said than done. After fifty years of macroeconomic policy experiments, we are far from mastering the art!

Nationalism versus Globalism
Given the apparent universality of the neoclassical doctrine, economists are tempted to believe that they are scientists searching for universal truths and that the optimal solutions they find for their abstract models should apply to all. These beliefs, though justifiable within the given model frameworks, are conditioned by a set of premises many of which derive not from scientific proofs but from religious beliefs behind the doctrine. Yet if different peoples disagree on these premises, their faiths in and interpretations of the doctrine will necessarily vary. Hence the frequent spats and feuds among nations over the merits of free trade and other policy issues. True, the economists have won worldwide consensus on some fundamental propositions, such as that an economy with legislated *ex post* equity rules (such as a socialist regime) performs more poorly than one with legislated efficiency rules (such as a capitalist regime), and that open policies are better than closed policies for economic development. Beyond this basic consensus, however, nations will continue to hold different economic outlooks and make different policy choices.

In summary, therefore, the strengths of neoclassical economics are its solid structure, internal logical consistency, precision, and universality inherited from physics. Its highlight is the demonstration of efficiency of competitive general equilibrium, which, along with the optimizing behaviour of individuals, implies a perfect harmony between individual behaviour and that of the system. This magnificent proposition, hallowed as the Fundamental Welfare Theorem, hinges critically on the superb coordinating capacity of the markets. The weaknesses of the theory, on the other hand, are its static makeup and the consequent lack of dynamic sense of evolution, a lack of analysis of human beings as opposed to physical objects, and the lack of consideration of the role of culture as a regulator of human behaviour. It is these loose ends left by the theory that have spawned different versions of economics extant in the world.

In what follows, I shall elaborate on the use of neoclassical economics in the form of a comparative analysis of American economics and Japanese economics. To say that Japanese economics is different from American economics does not necessarily mean that Japanese economics is antineoclassical. Both economics can be thought of as variations within the neoclassical paradigm arising chiefly from its ambivalence or noncommittal attitude towards several key issues in economics: (1) how to organize capital markets for maximum dynamic efficiency of resource allocation, (2) how to strike an adequate balance between efficiency and equity, (3) how to construct information and incentive structures that bring together and coordinate micro and macro levels of the economy, and (4) the relative value placed upon globalism and nationalism. The apparent wide differences between the two types of economics are due, in my opinion, to the different manner in which the two nations have sought answers to these key issues.

American Economics

The United States is the land of neoclassical economics. No other country, not even Canada, comes close. American society operates on the principle of competitive individualism and grassroots democracy to a degree unmatched by others.[8] The US is a country made up of immigrants from all over the world and built on a vast expanse of land. Unlike in Canada and other new settlements where Old World rules and power came before people, Americans won independence from the Old World and built the rules for themselves. It was a land of the free. In America, with its small population and vast expanse of land richly endowed with resources, the purest form of competitive individualism proved to be an ideal social principle, for interpersonal conflicts were minimal. Each acre of land broken by a frontier was not only an addition to personal wealth but also a full addition to the nation's wealth.

It seems reasonable to say that America's unique history found a perfect match in neoclassical economics. The doctrine promoted free and atomistic competition, a faith in markets, and an emphasis on fairness based on equal opportunities for all and remuneration of factors by marginal productivity. This, together with an aversion to large establishments (including government) as potential sources of monopoly and infringement of individual rights and freedom, were all not only agreeable to Americans but also gave endorsement to what they had long been practising. Given their individualistic *Weltanschauung*, it is natural for Americans to believe that their economics should suit everyone in the world, and so they assume a missionary role in spreading the neoclassical gospel abroad.

Referring back to the loose ends of the neoclassical model mentioned earlier, the Americans naturally interpreted them to fit their tastes. First, on the question of static versus dynamic efficiency and the allocation of investment, the Americans took a stand that free and unregulated capital markets would do a better job than any other conceivable alternatives of allocating savings over competing investment projects. But this faith in capital markets is based on an unwarranted application of the Fundamental Welfare Theorem for static efficiency to dynamic efficiency. Competitive markets attain efficient resource allocation (under certain conditions) in a static setting through the power of arbitrage. As the participants engage in repetitive trade in a fixed environment, their knowledge of the prices and qualities of goods improves with the passage of time until everyone possesses perfect information about the price and quality of every good. If a good commands different prices at different trading posts, such differences would be arbitraged away instantly. Note that this "time" in statics is not the real time but a hypothetical computer time. In real-world capital markets, actual allocation needs to be completed in a finite real time subject to the uncertainty concerning the future profitability of various investment projects. Indeed, one of the most serious issues about the US economy in the last fifty years or so has been its weak investment record. Its investment ratio, namely, the ratio of gross fixed capital formation (both private and public) to GDP (gross domestic product), has been the lowest among the OECD nations for quite some time, ranging between 15 and 18 percent, in contrast to Japan's ratio of 30 percent. Moreover, while one-third of the total investment is carried out by the manufacturing sector in Japan, the American manufacturing sector accounts for only half that fraction. True, the US economy has grown strongly since 1992, and both its growth and productivity performance over the 1990s has been far superior to Japan's. Still, the American personal savings rate is a meagre 5 percent, and much of the nation's gross savings are being eaten away in the form of budgetary and trade deficits (Economic Planning Agency, various years; Executive Office of the President, various years). This certainly is not a very encouraging picture if the policy goal is the long-term prosperity of the US economy.

Second, the question of balance between efficiency and equity in America was settled in favour of efficiency. Equity has been interpreted as an *ex ante* equity or equality of opportunities, leaving the problem of *ex post* inequity among citizens as a matter of their personal responsibility. It is not surprising that the United States has by far the highest Gini coefficient (a measure of inequality) of all the OECD nations.[9] As the economy entered the prolonged period of recession in the 1970s, Americans' reaction was to strengthen competition both inside and outside of the economy. The buzzword for the policy makers was deregulation and creation of a level field so that individuals might pursue personal profits more fairly and freely. The freer competition gave enterprising individuals a chance to make a fortune (as junk bond promoter Michael Milken demonstrated) but also widened the gap between the successful and the unsuccessful. The income shares by quintiles show a steady rise for the rich and a steady decline for the poor during the past two decades. The financially drained federal government has not been able to maintain even existing social security programs. Unemployment insurance and other welfare programs have been cut back, and the number of citizens who cannot keep minimum health and automobile liability insurance has soared. Equity in the United States has thus proved to be a luxury good apparently to be enjoyed only in good times.

The fact of the matter, however, is that equity is really needed in bad times. To solve the problem of sharing a limited number of jobs and incomes among citizens in a civil manner in this age of slow growth requires something other than the principle of competitive individualism. As argued above, the substance of equity lies in *ex post* equity, that is, in the humane treatment of those who have lost the competition, after the fact. This notion is difficult to write into any social rule book because of the potentially devastating effects on motivation and efficiency. One might say it is a matter of ethics, or of heart, but I believe that the general morale of any nation's citizens depends critically on its presence. It is also clear that without the high morale of the citizens at large, a strong economy cannot be built. Neoclassical economics is silent about how to solve this problem of *ex post* equity. It has therefore been up to the Americans to invent their own solution.

The Americans believe that competitive individualism constitutes the best informational and incentive structures as it brings out the best in each individual. It is well known, however, that unregulated competition has certain elements of inefficiency,[10] so why should the Americans deny or fail to see the fairly obvious advantage of cooperation? I believe the reason goes deep into American culture. The Americans see the advantage of cooperation in theory but steadfastly deny that such a scheme ever works. They point to the wrong incentive structure built in the cooperative scheme, namely that an individual would put in an honest effort under the competitive scheme but would shirk under the cooperative scheme. He or she would join the cooperative team to claim the share of team profits but withhold the effort input. If everyone shirks, it is held, the team would collapse, which would mean the end of any cooperative scheme. So we must go back to a more competitive scheme, goes the argument, a competitive scheme that works because each individual earns the fruit of his or her own effort – nothing more, nothing less. In other words, the competitive model is believed to have the right incentive structure. Moreover, the Americans believe that the larger the gap in reward between the winner and the loser, the severer the competition and the better the outcome for society. Because of this, a "winner-take-all society" has come into being (Frank and Cook 1995). There are reasons to believe that there is such a thing as excessive competition, however. Thus, the well-known study of human behaviour in the prisoner's dilemma situation by political scientist Axelrod (1984) hints strongly at the possibility that individuals who are too competitive might drive society over the hill, by inducing their opponents to abandon any cooperative stance.[11] Indeed, it is difficult to make the case that competitive individualism is the best informational and incentive structure. I believe that if the Americans insist on this approach, it is not because of reason but because of their values or culture.

Third, American economics leads to a general inefficacy of macroeconomic policies. Thus, in the United States, where anti-government sentiments are particularly strong among the citizens, macroeconomic policy making has become a game between the policy maker and the citizens, each trying to outsmart the other. Typically, the policy maker estimates the behaviour of the private sector with the aid of economists and then tries to counteract it with a view to stabilizing the economy. The citizens, in the meantime, work hard to estimate what the government is up to and try their best to promote or protect their own interests, often to the frustration of the policy maker. The worst part of this game playing is that the information on which the policy maker acts is quite poor. The estimated consumption function, investment function, money demand function, and the like, which are used to forecast private sector behaviour and which policy makers often wish to counteract, are often too inaccurate to rely on, especially in times of change. Besides, the variety of lags inherent in policy actions has the danger of turning even a correct policy into an undesirable disturbance. Hence, the never-ending debate over rules versus discretion. But if discretionary policies are ineffective because of inadequate knowledge of private sector behaviour, and if fluctuations originate from the instability inherent in private sector behaviour, one cannot see a great benefit from fixing policy parameters such as the monetary growth rate and budgetary balance arbitrarily *ex ante*. Those who advocate rules must believe that the economy in the absence of government intervention is basically stable and efficient. Such a belief, though unwarranted either empirically or theoretically, is particularly strong in the United States.

Lastly, Americans' zeal to spread the neoclassical gospel to the rest of the world has, I am afraid, gone too far. They are oblivious (or ignorant) of the fact that theirs has been a unique case of perfect match between culture and doctrine and that their vast and rich soil assured a high labour productivity in agriculture from the start. This enabled them to escape the common pitfall of prolonged mass poverty in the developmental process. But others have not been so lucky. The countries in the Old World had centuries of experience of shared poverty before embarking on modern economic growth. Their long struggle towards prosperity has spawned a variety of communal rules and institutions that, in the main, restricted individual freedom for the sake of public good. Thus, in many societies, including Japan, personal profiteering was frowned upon traditionally as harmful to the peace and harmony of the community. Similarly, equity was put before efficiency and luxury was denounced as evil. Traditionally, the ruling class maintained wealth and power through established monopoly. When such traditional societies were thrown into the global race for modern economic growth and development, each had to find ways to reconcile its traditional values with those dictated by external competition and survival.

A fair number of countries chose to maintain their traditional values by closing themselves to the outside world. Most others took a cautiously open attitude of selectively importing foreign goods and technology with the ultimate aim of achieving a higher level of self-reliance. The few that took an unguarded open policy did so not on their own accord but under duress. No matter what course they chose, the process of development was a long struggle with themselves as much as with foreign rivals because modern economic growth required a massive socio-economic transformation of traditional societies. It is no wonder that success stories have been few.

At any rate, against the common experiences of the Old World countries, the US case must be deemed unique. First, Americans were spared the common problem of subsistence and shared poverty for survival, and so they did not need to worry too much about equity. Second, Americans did not have established ruling classes who lived off the populace and prevented the masses from enjoying the benefit of progress; consequently, competitive individualism in economics was as essential and natural for them as was equality in the theory of democracy. Americans are entitled to believe in what they do. But for them to believe that their way is also the best way for others is patently wrong.

Japanese Economics

In my opinion, the national traits of the Japanese people may be summarized by two characteristics. One is *ambiguity tolerance,* namely, the capacity to tolerate, if not accept, different views and opinions on any given issue, be it religious, political, economic, or even scientific in nature.[12] Instead of forcing a tournament among competing views in search of a single truth, as Americans would, the Japanese regard the very rivalry among different views as *the* truth. The other characteristic is *xenophobia,* that is, the fear of strangers (not necessarily foreigners). It incites an intense interest in strangers, in what they say or do. These two characteristics in combination, I believe, can account for virtually all the idiosyncrasies usually attributed to the Japanese people, including their economic behaviour.

Like most characteristics, these have both merits and demerits. The merits are that they enable the Japanese to take wide interest in and learn things abroad avidly without inhibition or loss of self-identity; to develop a keen sense of competition with others and a willingness to exert efforts to survive; to respect the virtues of competition but retain the warmth to salvage the losers in the race; and, most importantly, to develop a sense of balance among competing interests or goals. The demerits, on the other hand, are that they make the Japanese refrain from holding a firm conviction on any social issue, from using debates to get to the bottom of the issues, and from exercising the art of persuasion on others, especially in dealing with foreigners. In what follows, we shall see how these characteristics have manifested themselves in Japanese economic management. On the whole, however, the merits have overshadowed the demerits in the course of the social and economic management of the country. Let us validate this claim with an examination of Japan's policy choices, especially with respect to the neoclassical model's shortcomings.

First, on the issue of dynamic efficiency and investment allocations, Japan, like any other developing economy, initially faced the difficult yet urgent task of organizing the types of capital markets that would serve the national purpose adequately. To put it succinctly, the Japanese never had as great a faith as the Americans in open capital markets as a means of guiding a nation's intertemporal resource allocation. This pessimism about capital markets arose not so much out of actual testing as from a lack of opportunities to test. In the early stage of development, in the period 1868-1912, the government led the industrialization movement through its coercive power, using resources collected through taxation. Later, a handful of large capitalist families took over from the government as the main forces of industrialization. Their outfits were called corporations and their shares were traded in the two stock exchanges in Tokyo and Osaka, founded in 1874. However, without the wide participation of the public (who had no money to invest anyhow), the stock market was unable to function as a place for industrialists to raise capital or to maintain the liquidity of their IOUs. As a result, the market soon deteriorated into a playground for speculators.

Subsequently, corporate firms, then banks, security houses, and exchanges, were formed hastily. But lack of knowledge and experience needed to run these institutions properly forced Japan to take a shortcut. Instead of letting citizens at large accumulate knowledge and experience through trial and error, the government took the banks under its wing, made them the chief depository of citizens' savings, and directed them to allocate their funds for investment in accordance with the nation's developmental objectives. This system, though idiosyncratic in the eyes of Westerners, proved quite effective in minimizing the wastes inherent in more decentralized systems through the centralization of information and decision making. Since the Meiji period, each of the major *zaibatsu* (financial conglomerate) groups of enterprises had a bank at its centre as the financier for the family firms. Firms not belonging to these families also relied on banks of their choice as the main source of investible funds. In the postwar period, this practice of indirect finance became even more pronounced. At this time, the nation had to rely on the United States for technology and equipment but was short of hard currency to pay for them. Accordingly, about the only way for "nameless" Japanese corporations to obtain the requisite dollar loans was to have the somewhat better known banks do the negotiating and guaranteeing on their behalf. The now famous "main bank system" thus came into vogue. It was not so much a Japanese invention as an imposition by US financiers. The Japanese banks did a commendable job of financing investment throughout the critical stages of postwar reconstruction and development. Throughout the past thirty years, they financed corporate investment at interest rates consistently lower and more stable in real terms than those offered by American banks, in close cooperation with the government (Nagatani 1993).[13]

Second, the Japanese have shown a great deal of ingenuity and wisdom in securing a reasonable balance between equity and efficiency. Indeed, how to balance the two was a big problem faced by the leaders of Meiji Japan. Fukuzawa Yukichi (1834-1901), a prominent intellectual leader in that period, distinguished between private profits and public benefits and argued that the former were justified only insofar as they generated the latter. Shibusawa Eiichi (1840-1931), a leading business organizer, was adamant that the value of a business organization should be judged not by its profits but by its contribution to the public good. Moreover, they were reluctant to give individuals a similar privilege to pursue private gains. In short, Meiji Japan rejected competitive individualism in favour of peaceful coexistence. Consequently, in contrast to the American notion of *ex ante* equity, the Japanese favoured and developed the notion of *ex post* equity. In other words, the Japanese notion of equity is not just equality of opportunity but equality of actual share. I have called this the "principle of coexistence" elsewhere (Nagatani 1999). Whereas the Americans pursue competition without reservation (or remorse), the Japanese approve of competition only subject to the constraint of *ex post* equity. The Japanese recognize the virtue of competition as a means of raising efficiency but use it only if it is compatible with the principle of coexistence. Beneath it lies the Japanese philosophy that the economy is a common property of all citizens, that every citizen has the right to draw on it for his or her own subsistence, and that its use must therefore have this common good as the primary goal.

It seems fair to say that the coexistence principle is not for everyone. As an incentive structure, it runs the great risk of shirking by individual members, an expression of moral hazard. If it has succeeded in Japan, it was probably because Japan's traditional Confucian ethics kept the risk of shirking to a minimum. The overall result has been an efficient and equitable economy. Thus, during the 100-year period from 1870 to 1969, the US economy's average annual real growth was 3.7 percent, or 2.1 percent in per capita terms. In the same period, the Japanese economy grew at 4.2 percent or 3.0 percent per capita, respectively. This means that the US per capita real income increased eightfold, whereas Japan's increased by a factor of 19. If the period is extended to the present, the factor becomes approximately 10 for the US and 26 for Japan. As for the equity comparison, Tachibanaki (1999) cites some interesting statistics. Concerning wage income, the ratio of the ninth to the first deciles in 1995 was 2.8 for Japan and 4.5 for the US. With regard to asset holdings, the Gini coefficient for Japan (1984) was 0.52 and 0.79 for the US (1983). On the poverty question, the poverty ratio (the fraction of households having less than half of the average household income) stood at 7.5 percent for Japan (1989) and 18.4 percent for the US (1986). In the broader community of OECD members, the US is by far the most unequal society, whereas Japan has the lowest Gini coefficient for labour income and is ranked around the middle in terms of overall income and wealth distribution (Tachibanaki 1999).

It should be noted that most of these equitable customs were never formal rules of law. Yet Japanese society has managed to punish violators of customs quite effectively. The reasons for the successful practice of *ex post* equity are multiple. Probably the most important is the view of the world shared among the Japanese that certain things in life, including the outcomes of the competition in which they participate over the course of their lives, are, to a significant extent, beyond human control and a matter of luck. (Japanese gods, they believe, like to cast dice.) Winners therefore do not deserve full credit for their successes, and losers should not take all the blame for their failures either. Moreover, the Japanese are aware that a personal success usually carries with it a significant number of negative externalities in that behind every personal success are many who gave their wealth and lives for the cause. It follows from this perception that winners deserve something less, while losers deserve something more, than their respective "marginal products." Another way of describing the Japanese perception is that competition always has some elements of a zero-sum game.

Related to this is the Japanese notion and use of forgiveness. In Japanese society, when one individual fails in an attempt and causes damage to his organization in excess of his ability to repay, the organization reviews the individual's intent and manner of execution. If they are judged sincere, the organization forgives the individual's guilt in exchange for only a nominal penalty so that the individual can make a fresh start. More generally, long-standing feuds between individuals or organizations are routinely washed away with a ritual exchange of a glass of saké in the presence of a witness (usually a person commanding the respect and trust of both sides). Thanks to this constant cleansing of human relations through such forgiveness, the Japanese have been able to live and work peacefully together on their small and densely populated islands.[14]

Third, the above account also illuminates how the Japanese bring together and coordinate between micro- and macroeconomics. In the American version of neoclassical economics, the right of free choice of individuals comes first. What might happen in the aggregate as a result of individuals' free choice should not be their concern; the task of looking after the aggregate consequence should be left to some outside agency, presumably the government. Even if the government knew how individuals should behave for a desirable aggregate outcome, the feeling is that it should not preach or twist the arms of the individuals to follow its direction. Thus, if American consumers want to buy Japanese cars instead of American cars and cause mass layoffs in Detroit, it is not the consumers' fault but it is up to the government to take care of the problem. Confronted with this attitude at home, the US government has faced an even more onerous task of forcing its Japanese counterpart to commit to buying more American cars, which its own domestic consumers do not want. In short, American economics gives its citizens a free rein (microeconomics first) and leaves the government with the difficult task of aggregate adjustments (macroeconomics second). Micro and macro remain two disjoint subjects. The result is that the US government routinely must take a high-handed approach to shift the burden of adjustment onto foreign governments.

However, micro and macro levels are indispensable parts of sound economic policy making, and one without the other is just about meaningless. In the more holistic Japanese perception, micro and macro levels of economic activity must communicate with each other for coordination to further the goal of higher national economic welfare. Indeed, the two have been brought into one at the level of Japan's key industries. Thus, the Japanese *Keidanren*[15] has traditionally served as an intermediary between micro and macro. With its broad authority over industry, commerce, and finance, it has been instrumental in keeping lines of communication open between its individual member firms and the government. In this way, it has enabled the economy to reach a micro plan consistent with the macro target, or the macro target consistent with micro motives. The major advantage of the Japanese system in this regard is better information flow between the private sector and the government, which is in sharp contrast to the typically adversarial relations between the two sectors in the United States.

Fourth, on the issue of globalism versus nationalism, the Japanese, deep down, are on the side of nationalism, although they again often exercise their ambiguity tolerance and refrain from making a statement on it. The chief reason the Japanese are wary of a sweeping globalism, I presume, is its potentially devastating effect on equity. Equity is primarily a local or national concept, and one can give it any meaningful content only by reference to the given standard of living achieved in a local or national economy. At the level of the world, where one-quarter of the population enjoys forty to fifty times as high a standard of living as the remaining three-quarters, equity is an empty concept. The Japanese feel that the current fever over globalism is purely efficiency-driven, to the detriment of equity in both global and national contexts. The advanced industrial economies have been suffering from stagnation with increasing domestic inequity for the past two decades. What they are looking for in a freer global market is an expanded opportunity for their nationals to enrich themselves; it is certainly not aimed at sharing their affluence with the less fortunate abroad.

Globalization may also be interpreted as a cop-out from any forthcoming domestic inequity issue, as terms such as "winning the global competition" have often served as an effective argument against welfarism. For the Japanese, to follow this global trend is to risk destroying much of their economic culture, and the notably long-practised *ex post* equity principle. They are fully aware of the risk; and they are groping for ways to preserve the tradition with less friction abroad. Still, as noted earlier, for the Japanese the national economy is their common property, which has to provide a livelihood for its citizens for generations to come. Like any common property, however, it needs constant care to sustain productivity and to avoid "the tragedy of the commons." And the government and business have taken great care in order to nurture it. In other words, the Japanese see their economy as a renewable natural or national resource that requires measures of conservation; they would be loathe to let the rest of the world have a free ride on their property unless the outsiders are willing to conform to their rules.

The Future of Japanese Economics

The decade-long recession brought about by the collapse of the 1980s economic bubble has left a deep mark on the way the Japanese think of themselves and the world far beyond the recession itself. In the eyes of this expatriate, today's Japanese face an identity crisis. Popular opinion holds that Japan's past success was mere good luck, that Japan is not ready for the global era, and that the only way to survive in the new era is by shedding all its "Japaneseness" and transforming the system and the people after the American model. Deregulation, restructuring (that is, cost cutting by scrapping burdensome systems of insurance schemes and public subsidies), disclosure of information (centrally managed so far) to the public, and reorientation towards competitive individualism are key words that keep cropping up in news headlines and policy papers.[16]

Given that the Japanese economy is now at a crossroads and that it requires reorientation for the new millennium, a firm vision of the kind of economy the nation wants to have in the future is indispensable. Yet it is obvious that the inputs into such philosophizing must come first from reflections on the nation's own history and second from assessments of the global environment in which it operates. As it stands, the current Japanese restructuring campaign has none of the former and is being carried away with an exaggerated and glorified image of the latter. For instance, it totally ignores the important fact that Japan owed its past success not to victory in global price competition but to victory in the production of quality products.[17] In my opinion, the future prosperity of the Japanese economic system rests upon its ability to preserve a quality advantage and the superb communication network between consumers and producers that has supported it. This is the kind of vision that is needed to achieve successful restructuring. Once such a vision is established by national consensus, answers to other problems suggest themselves, as maintenance of the quality advantages requires certain organizational skills. Let me enumerate a number of key organizational elements vital to success in this sphere of quality competition.

The current campaign for indiscriminate "price busting" will do more harm than good. There are many administered prices in protected areas that deserve to be busted, to be sure, but Japan's high prices are also due to the high quality of the products. High margins on quality products are the source of high wages, and Japan should make every effort to keep them.

Although the government/big business partnership has claimed credit for the success in economic development, Japan's strength has always been in the incomparable breadth, vitality, and ingenuity of the small-business sector that comprises the capillary vessels of the communication network alluded to earlier. On the shop floors of the tens of thousands of "town factories," the owner-managers, designers, mechanics, and neighbourhood consumers hold conferences and experiments day in and day out on how to improve existing merchandise or design new ones. It is this coming together of information and technology in shop floor meetings that has helped Japan become a major world economic power. Japan's small businesses are better organizations than the now fashionable venture businesses of American origin in terms of information gathering, networking, and collective efficiency, in my opinion. Japan must make every effort to preserve this valuable national asset. Big businesses without capable small businesses will never amount to very much.

Rising unemployment is the overriding concern of the Japanese. The aggregate unemployment rate inched up from 2 percent during the 1980s to 4.9 percent in June 1999.[18] The first two quarters of 1999 registered positive real growth (7.9 percent in the first quarter and 0.9 percent in the second quarter at annual rates), yet the unemployment figures did not show any improvement. Job losses have spread over all age groups in the labour force and over firms of all sizes. Many large firms have announced plans to let go thousands of employees in the near future. If these layoffs were to be carried out as planned, the total number of unemployed, which stands at around 3 million, could easily rise to 4 million. Such a drastic loss of job security is capable of destroying the very heart of the Japanese system.

Attributing the recent economic woes to the Japanese system is wrong. The causes of the current recession lie in the national speculative mania and mismanagement during the 1980s. This was an instance of popular delusion, perhaps witnessed in history only once or twice in a century in various parts of the world. It had nothing to do with the "Japaneseness" of the Japanese system. To believe otherwise is bad economics, and bad economics can kill an otherwise robust economic system.

In many areas, the Japanese economy is basically sound. It certainly has enough vitality left in it, as evidenced by the 25 percent investment rate throughout the long recession of the 1990s, as opposed to the meagre 12 percent for the US economy (both figures are for 1997). Its international competitiveness has not weakened, as demonstrated by the strong performance of the export industries. If one assumes that the 25 percent investment rate will continue, that one-fifth, or 5 percent, of the 25 percent will be net new investment, and that the total factor productivity will keep increasing at half the average rate of the past forty years, then the Japanese economy's potential growth rate will be in the order of 2.7 percent even with a stationary or slightly declining population. This will certainly be enough to maintain the current level of affluence in the new century.

Conclusion

The past ten years have been largely wasted as far as the reorientation of the Japanese system goes. In the meantime, the Japanese system has been losing its "Japaneseness." Big businesses are increasingly turning to foreign firms for partnerships for survival, and they are dismantling the traditional long-term employment practices in the name of survival. Meanwhile, the government has so far been preoccupied with salvaging the banks by means of an ultra low-interest policy to stimulate the economy and the injection of public funds several times as large as the annual value-added of the banking sector. This has caused enormous pain and losses on the part of fund managers, such as life insurers and trust companies, of citizens at large in the form of lost interest income and much-reduced pension prospects (which means another heavy fiscal burden for the already debt-ridden treasury), and of small firms dependent on bank credits (as the banks burdened with bad debts have been in no mood to extend new loans at pitifully low interest rates). The general mood of society has been that of retrenchment, much of which would have been unnecessary had government and business leaders steered the ship more prudently and responsibly.

If this trend continues, I believe that the most valuable parts of the Japanese system will be lost. First, the time-honoured coexistence principle, which has provided a sense of security for all, will go. Tachibanaki (1999) points out that Japan's Gini coefficient has been on the rise, especially since the 1980s. The liquidation of employment contracts will no doubt accelerate the widening of income inequalities.

Second, the traditional practice of investment coordination (which itself was induced to a large extent by the coexistence principle) will give way to an allocation made through the open capital markets. As discussed earlier, the benefits of unregulated capital markets have been oversold. Rampant speculation and a smaller than expected contribution to long-term capital movements across borders have characterized such markets, at least so far. Most national savings – 80-90 percent in all the major economies – have been invested at home, and this strong home bias has remained even after the deregulation and globalization of capital markets. This means that the campaign has basically attracted only footloose speculative capital into the domestic arena, which in turn has dealt a heavy blow to national capital markets operating under different rules and produced a handful of big winners and countless losers, bearing out the theoretical concerns expressed above. The Japanese should regain autonomy and control over the allocation of national savings for domestic investment projects in accordance with a proper vision of the economy in the twenty-first century.

Third, Japan's traditional informational and incentive structures certainly need some modification but the basic idea behind them is worth preserving. It is hard to believe that the Japanese would be happy under the winner-take-all rule of the Americans. Their sense of sharing still seems strong. Nor would they tolerate the American way of leaving information as pure private goods and allowing individuals to make or lose fortunes on them. Ownership of knowledge and information is far more susceptible to monopoly and other rent-seeking activities than the ownership of ordinary physical goods. They should be recognized as public goods and should be regulated as such. Failure to do so would aggravate the growing inequities both within and across countries.

The most dangerous aspect of the sweeping globalist campaign of American origin is the elevation of their version of capitalism or free marketism to the height of a religion, despite its known shortcomings. The success of the campaign would seal the victory of neoclassicism. Any theory without rivals is no longer a scientific theory, however. Even within the broad framework of neoclassical economics, there is room for variations, as this chapter has laboured to point out. Diversity among national economies is natural and even rational, given the inseparability of economics and culture, and makes our life more interesting, to say the least.

Postscript
Since the time I first wrote this essay in 1997, the most notable change in the world economic scene has been the permeation of information technology, which has not only altered the way firms and individuals do business but also created new lines of business, such as e-commerce. Many words have already been spilt over this new technology and its great promise in the new millennium. From the long-term historical perspective, however, whether the "IT revolution" and the "new economy" organized around it will compare to the great technological inventions of the past, such as electricity and the internal combustion engine, is a moot question.

First, many of the computer-induced innovations have merely displaced traditional methods of doing business rather than adding new business. Business-to-business transactions through the Internet have merely replaced transactions through telephones and faxes. Business-to-consumer selling of books, cars, and other merchandise through the Internet has had the same effect. The mere novelty has attracted some new clients, but there are obvious limits to Internet purchases by consumers. Second, unlike electricity and the internal combustion engine, which created a huge and lasting new demand for transportation equipment, home appliances, and power tools, computers do not create such new demands for hardware. Third, unlike electricity and the internal combustion engine, which created a huge number of new jobs in the manufacturing sector, computers have no such promise. Fourth, the much-touted effect of computers to boost economy-wide productivity is based only on several years' observation; it is eminently premature to pass a scientific judgment (Gordon 2000).

Moreover, the increasing importance of information presents a new challenge to our economic thinking. Information as an economic good has a number of peculiar characteristics: free reproducibility (zero marginal costs of production), consumption and production externality (the value of information to the owner is dependent on how many others share it), and great quality uncertainty, to name but a few. In short, information not only has some of the features of a public good but also poses a new monitoring problem for the market. The sudden mushrooming of regional and bilateral free trade pacts of late is an indication that as the weight of world trade has shifted away from traditional commodities to services, informational difficulties regarding the quality of services have made the simple GATT-WTO (General Agreement on Tariffs and Trade-World Trade Organization) rules over commodities ineffective.

The more fundamental question is whether information should be left as a private good whose production, distribution, and consumption are left in the hands of individuals. We must bear in mind that a system based on the principle of competitive individualism is not an informationally efficient system (because of lack of communication and coordination among individuals). The Japanese system, by comparison, is a more efficient (and equitable) system when it comes to the management and use of information (centralization of information; better communication between government and business, between designer and shop-floor workers, and between producers and consumers). It remains to be seen how the competition between the two systems will evolve in the new century.

Acknowledgments
I have benefited from, among others, discussions with Toshiki Jinushi of Kobe University, who had independently arrived at a notion of *ex post* equity. His notion differs from mine, however. He stresses the fact that the long-term relationships typical among the Japanese allow credit and debt between two parties to cancel out each other over the long run. In this sense, his is a "long-term equity." My notion of *ex post* equity is based more firmly on Japanese aesthetics and regulates individual behaviour more directly and forcefully, although mine, too, presupposes long-term relationships. Discussions with James Mak of the University of Hawaii have also been very helpful.

Notes
1 Japan *maru* can be said to mean "ship of state."
2 For more details regarding these points, see Nagatani 1999.
3 Max Weber (1930) was the first to stress the connection between national culture and economic development. He identified the Protestant ethic as providing a uniquely fitting cultural background for modern capitalist development. He was perhaps right in this assertion, but he overstated his case when he denounced Confucianism in the same context as detrimental.
4 See also S. Kumon and H. Rosovsky 1990.
5 For a summary of its historical background, the reader is referred to Chapter 1 of Nagatani 1989.
6 For critiques of the neoclassical position, see Keynes 1936 and Stiglitz 1994.
7 Besides, we have reasons to believe that the US style of *ex ante* equity leads to unlimited competition that can be socially wasteful. See Frank and Cook 1995.
8 The Canadian reader should note that there is such a thing as Canadian economics that is distinct from American economics and, if I may say so, that Canadian economics is somewhere between American economics and Japanese economics. See Carlile 1998.
9 For an international comparison of inequalities, consult Tachibanaki 1999.
10 See Nagatani 1998a for a demonstration of this result.
11 In Axelrod's experiment (1984) with a set of strategies submitted by experts, a particular strategy called Tit-for-Tat was the runaway winner. This strategy is definitely not a winning strategy in individual matches; it is certain to lose to some shrewder strategies. Yet, by being nice (never be the first to defect), forgiving (retaliate without delay against any opponent who defects but get back into the cooperative mode as soon as possible), and simple (so that the opponent may easily understand its nice character), Tit-for-Tat came out the overall winner in the round robin tournament among all the entries by inducing

opponents to be nice and to be cooperative. The losing strategies were generally too anxious to fool the opponent, too harsh in punishing the opponent's defection, and too eager to win every game.

12 First and foremost, the Japanese have repeatedly demonstrated their capacity to tolerate ambiguities and reach compromise solutions in times of emergency for the sake of national interest. During the decade preceding the Meiji Restoration of 1868, the nation was on the verge of self-destruction. The country was split between the pro-Tokugawa wing and the anti-Tokugawa or Imperialist wing; the Western powers, notably Britain and France, were watching the situation like so many vultures trying to get a foothold on this small but strategically important island nation. Sensing the danger of colonization, the leaders of the two wings put aside their differences and achieved a smooth transition of power from the shogunate to the emperor. The new government, for its part, maintained the Tokugawa bureaucracy to preserve continuity. Modernization after the Western mode was the choice made by the Meiji government. Its vision, however, was again a compromise known as *wakon yōsai,* or "Japanese philosophy, combined with Western science and technology." The government then imported an assortment of Western laws and practices – Prussian constitution, French commercial code, American banking and education systems, for example. Beneath the Western facade, however, Japanese values and conventions remained alive and well. The Japanese demonstrated a similar capacity to tolerate ambiguities at the time of reconstruction after the Pacific War. They accepted the United States, the archenemy of yesteryear, as mentor overnight, and from the US learned the know-how necessary for survival. Trade disputes between them have arisen regularly over the past fifty years but Japan has managed to avoid serious confrontation and catastrophe with conciliatory tactics. Japanese governments have massaged American-made laws to suit the country's own values and conventions. Japan has often been criticized by the United States for its lack of "principles" and for engaging in opportunistic behaviour. In my opinion, however, it is precisely this lack of principles that has enabled Japan to avoid serious confrontation with the Western powers.

13 It goes without saying, however, that no capital market organization is perfect. A highly centralized organization such as Japan's has certain merits as well as demerits. The merits are an efficient use of economy-wide information, internalization of economic "externalities" inherent in decentralized investment decisions, and shielding of investment finance from speculative noises. The demerits, on the other hand, are loss of competitive minds on the part of the banks, relatively undeveloped open capital markets, severe discrimination against small business firms excluded by the banks, and inability of the system to adapt to large external shocks. When the economy is following the set course, the centralized system is more efficient than a decentralized system. But when the economy is hit by a large shock, the task of reorientation becomes harder the tighter and the more centralized the management of the economy is. These weaknesses are responsible at least in part for the spectacular bubble of the 1980s and the subsequent chaos the Japanese capital markets experienced. It would be rash, however, to conclude that the Japanese capital markets should therefore be overhauled and reorganized after the American model. The relative inability of a tightly controlled system to cope with shocks might very well be a fair price to pay for the high system performance in a stable environment.

14 Let me show some concrete examples of *ex post* equity devices from Japanese practice. The word *dangō* describes the old practice among firms in the same trade for the equitable allocation of contracts among themselves. The members gather together and decide that contract A goes to firm a, contract B to firm b, and so forth *before* the formal auction processes. General contractors (i.e., large construction firms) have recently been charged for this practice, which formally violates the Anti-Monopoly Law. True, such a practice contains elements of price fixing and other antisocial implications. On the other hand, each contractor has hundreds of subcontractors and, according to Japanese custom, it is responsible for feeding not only its own workers but also those of subcontractors. It is vital for the coexistence of all the members to have a system that distributes jobs equally. Although this is evidently an unacceptable practice in cultures of competitive individualism, the Japanese have, in the main, judged its benefits to outweigh the costs. The formerly government-owned National Railways was privatized in 1988 and broken up into

several regional JR (Japan Railways) companies. The three companies that share the most lucrative Tōkaidō Line (from Tokyo to Nagoya, Kyoto, Osaka, Hiroshima, and through to Hakata) have a definite advantage over the others, with the result that they enjoy profits while others suffer losses systematically. In order to keep all the JRs alive, the profitable three voluntarily began transferring part of their profits to the less fortunate ones, despite the fact that these companies are legally independent corporations. This is another example of Japan's *ex post* equity devices. A more recent and more important example is the initiative the Japanese government took to preserve employment at the time of sweeping restructuring by private firms. Fearing a massive loss of jobs due to restructuring that threatens to dismantle lifetime employment and seniority wages, the government intervened and pressured firms to *extend* the retirement age from the conventional fifty-five to sixty, using wage subsidies as bait. Nearly 80 percent of the firms have complied with the government's wishes and more are expected to follow. Without such a measure, Japan's unemployment rate, especially among the middle-aged and older would have risen sharply even more. This example brings out the Japanese notion of business firms as providers of jobs and incomes to the citizens in addition to serving the interest of the shareholders.

15 *Keidanren* (Federation of Economic Organizations) is the national umbrella organization for Japanese industry.
16 In February 1999, the newly organized Economic Rehabilitation Commission submitted a report to then-Prime Minister Obuchi Keizo. The report covers a wide range of social and economic issues (235 items in all) and offers advice on them. Comprehensive as it is, the report lacks a vision of an ideal organization of the economy towards which the restructuring should be targeted; it also lacks concrete solutions of the many issues enumerated. This I find quite disappointing. For example, the report had no analysis of what supported Japan's past success, where Japan's strengths and weaknesses lie especially in the new global era, what should be done about the coexistence principle, and how to restore the citizens' confidence in the system. On the sorry state of public finance, the report merely asserts that convincing the public of the soundness of treasury is of utmost importance, without spelling out the tax implications for the citizens. On scrapping of the multilayered insurance scheme and the consequent loss of a sense of security on the part of the public, the report merely stresses the need for improved safety nets, again with no mention of how they should be financed. In short, this report is little more than a long wish list without economics. See *Japan Times* 1999.
17 Japanese consumers have the most fastidious tastes for quality in the world (see Fields 1985, 1989). To them a movie camera that just makes movies is not good enough; they want it to be faster, lighter, smaller, and better-looking. Moreover, though very few farm products are sold abroad, anyone who has tried Japanese apples, pears, peaches, or grapes would agree that no foreign products match their quality. Being fussy about quality means that the Japanese are willing to pay more for a given quality improvement. Another traditional feature of the Japanese system is that the communication network between consumers and producers has been excellent and that the producers have been able to know what consumers want with little effort. Because consumers are willing to cover the additional cost of producing improved products, producers respond to the demand with ease. The result has been a system capable of supplying top-of-the-line products in the world market ranging from electronics to fruits and vegetables. In short, Japan's is a high-quality, high-price economy relative to other economies.
18 Data in this and the following paragraphs are taken from Barro 1997, Posen 1998, and Economic Planning Agency 1999.

References

Axelrod, R. 1984. *The Evolution of Cooperation.* New York: Basic Books.
Barro, R.J. 1997. *Determinants of Economic Growth: A Cross-Country Empirical Study.* Cambridge, MA: MIT Press.
Carlile, L.E. 1998. "Business and Government Relations in Canada and Japan: The 'Homestead' and the 'Public Vessel.'" In K. Nagatani and D.W. Edgington, eds., *Japan and the West: The Perception Gap.* Aldershot, Hampshire, UK: Ashgate, 109-32.

Economic Planning Agency. 1999. *The Current State of the Japanese Economy: Recovering from the Aftermath of the Bubble*. (In Japanese.) Tokyo: Economic Planning Agency.

–. 2000. *GNP Changes from the Previous Year at 1990 Prices*. <http://www.epa.go.jp/2000/g/qe001/nsa001-le.xls>, accessed December 2000.

–. Various years. *Kokumin Keizai Keisan Nenpō* (Annual reports on national accounts). Tokyo: Economic Planning Agency.

Executive Office of the President. Various years. *Economic Report of the President*. Washington, DC: United States Government Printing Office.

Fields, G. 1985. *From Bonsai to Levi's. When West Meets East: An Insider's Surprising Account of How the Japanese Live*. New York: New American Library.

–. 1989. *Gucci on the Ginza: Japan's New Consumer Generation*. Tokyo: Kodansha.

Frank, R.J., and P.J. Cook. 1995. *The Winner-Take-All Society: Why the Few at the Top Get So Much More Than the Rest of Us*. New York: Penguin Books.

Gordon, R.J. 2000. "Does the 'New Economy' Measure Up to the Great Inventions of the Past?" *Journal of Economic Perspectives* 14(4): 48-74.

Japan Times. 1999. "Plan Eyes Recovery in Next 10 Years," 27 February, 1, 12.

Keynes, J.M. 1936. *The General Theory of Employment, Interest and Money*. London: Macmillan.

Kumon, S., and H. Rosovsky, eds. 1990. *The Political Economy of Japan (Vol. 3): Cultural and Social Dynamics*. Stanford, CA: Stanford University Press.

Nagatani, K. 1989. *Political Macroeconomics*. Oxford: Oxford University Press.

–. 1993. "On the Recent Trends in the Japanese Financial Markets." In D.J. Dicks, ed., *Communicating with Japan: Images Past, Present and Future*. Montreal: Concordia University, 153-67.

–. 1998a. "Economics and Culture." *International Journal of Development Planning Literature* 13: 367-75.

–. 1998b. "Understanding Japanese Investment Behaviour: An Organizational Approach to Social Investment." In K. Nagatani and D.W. Edgington, eds., *Japan and the West: The Perception Gap*. Aldershot, Hampshire, UK: Ashgate, 133-52.

–. 1999. *Nihon Keizaigaku* (Japanese economics). Tokyo: Chuo Keizaisha.

Nihon Keizai Shimbun. 2000. "Economy: GDP Growth Expected in Fiscal 2000 but Solid Recovery Remains Elusive." In *Japan Economic Almanac*. Tokyo: Nihon Keizai Shimbun, 42-43.

Posen, A. 1998. *Restoring Japan's Economic Growth*. Washington, DC: Institute for International Economics.

Sakaiya, T. 2000. "The Past and Present of the Japanese Economy." Speech given at Yale University, New Haven, CT, May. <http://www.epa.go.jp/2000/b/0505b-daijinkouen-e.HTML>, accessed May 2000.

Samuelson, P.A. 1955. *Economics*. New York: McGraw-Hill.

Stiglitz, J.E. 1994. *Whither Socialism?* Cambridge, MA: MIT Press.

Tachibanaki, T. 1999. *Nihon no Keizai Kakusa* (Economic inequalities in Japan). Tokyo: Iwanami Shoten.

Weber, M. 1930. *The Protestant Ethic and the Spirit of Capitalism*. Translated by T. Parsons. London: Allen and Unwin.

3
The Japanese Labour Movement's Road to the Millennium
Lonny E. Carlile

The Japanese labour movement finds itself confronted by a paradox as it enters the new millennium. On the one hand, due to gains in the area in the last two decades, organized labour in Japan is in many ways more firmly ensconced in the nation's political and economic establishment than it has ever been in its history of over a century. On the other hand, despite this, it faces a situation in which its organizational and institutional foundation is eroding rapidly. The latter is perhaps most succinctly illustrated by the drop in union density to just 22 percent (Japan Institute of Labour 2001). More fundamentally, however, it can be seen in the alterations that are under way in the so-called Japanese employment system (lifetime employment, seniority wages, and enterprise unionism). Sociopsychologically, it is reflected in a widespread credibility gap that leaves many among the movement's rank and file with little sense of identification with their union and even less with the movement at large.

In the spirit of the various chapters of this volume, this essay looks back at the experience of organized labour during the last half-century and uses this retrospective to make sense of the Japanese labour movement's current situation. Unfortunately, space limitations permit only a summational discussion of broad trends, and the reader is encouraged to refer to cited references for more thorough discussion and empirical support of the points made.

The Post-Defeat Transformation, 1945-55
When Japan surrendered to the Allied Powers on 2 September 1945, there were, for all intents and purposes, no independent trade unions in the country, as unions had been effectively banned since 1941 and labour and management reorganized into "imperial rule assistance associations" *(sangyō hōkokukai)* modelled after the Nazi Labour Front. There was, however, a history of active unionism that dated back half a century. Furthermore, there was a cadre of surviving prewar union leaders who were anxious to

revive the movement in the context of a democratized and reformed Japan. Ideologically, the prewar labour movement was divided into three distinct wings: the communists, the noncommunist but Marxian left socialists, and the staunchly anti-communist moderate right. The organizational rivalry among these wings debilitated the relatively small prewar movement, which organized just under 8 percent of the employed population at its 1931 peak (Totten 1966; Large 1981; Scalapino 1983).[1]

A uniformly expressed sentiment among union leaders was that the postwar movement should not repeat its prewar mistake and should instead forge a unified movement that encompassed all three ideological wings in a consolidated national organizational structure.[2] In the early months of the Occupation, with the communists in jail and out of the picture, the moderate right and left socialists were able to forge a common organization that was given the name Sōdōmei. However, when the communists entered the picture following the Occupation Forces' release of political prisoners in early October, the unbridgeable hostility between the communists and the moderate right made unity impossible and the movement was soon divided into two national confederations: the noncommunist Sōdōmei and the communist-dominated Sanbetsu. Thus, ironically, a major legacy of the prewar labour movement for the postwar movement was ideological and political division. Thanks to this legacy, much of the energy of the postwar Japanese labour movement during its first half-decade was consumed by communist-anti-communist competition and a search for ways to overcome the resulting divisions.

A key legacy of the war and the immediate postwar years was a structural decentralization of the labour movement as a consequence of the predominance of the *kigyōbetsu kumiai,* or enterprise union form (Kawanishi 1992, 1-61; Weathers 1997). An enterprise union is a union in which the locus of organizational sovereignty – for instance, control over union finances and the right to call strikes – is found at the plant or company level. This predominance grew out of the fact that the devastation and dislocations wrought by the war made organizing difficult for prewar union leaders, and then an unusual confluence of factors caused unionization to spiral beyond their ability to consolidate.

On 5 October 1945, the Occupation Forces announced that trade unions were to be encouraged as part of a broader democratization program. Fuelled by this encouragement and by accelerating inflation, fears of job dismissals, and a variety of war-related resentments, unionization unfolded extremely rapidly. The number of unions grew from effectively zero to the point where by 1949 6.7 million workers, or about 56 percent of the employed workforce, were organized. In the absence of effective external guidance, Japanese workers utilized the social setting that they were most familiar with for their unionization efforts, and this happened to be the factory or plant. While labour leaders at the time saw these newly formed enterprise unions as a temporary phenomenon and sought to devise ways to amalgamate them into a proper framework of industrial unions and a unified national confederation, such efforts were hampered by the rivalry among the competing ideological currents. Later, management obstructed unionization along industrial lines by refusing to bargain on anything other than an enterprise or company basis.

The formation of Sōhyō in July 1950 was a further milestone in the evolution of the postwar Japanese labour movement.[3] Historically, it symbolized the movement's transcendence of its legacy of prewar communist-anti-communist rivalry. Organizationally, it made considerable strides in overcoming the previous politically based divisions of unions within industries by establishing a set of unified industrial federations – that is, federations of enterprise unions in a common industry – that substantially strengthened the movement's bargaining power in the labour market. It was hoped that Sōhyō, which was established as a joint project of non-communist unionists, would lay to rest once and for all the internal politically based rivalries of the labour movement. And, given the American backing that went into its creation, it was also assumed that the new organization would serve as a pro-American pillar supporting the emerging political economic paradigm of a bilateral US-Japan military alliance and economic recovery that was being constructed by the United States and Japan's conservative government (Schonberger 1979; Takemae 1982; Price 1991). However, rather than solidifying into a moderate, pro-American pillar and the centre of a unified labour movement affiliated with the International Confederation of Trade Unions (ICFTU), Sōhyō soon became an organizational vehicle for a militant, confrontational brand of politicized unionism that would remain a primary force in the Japanese labour movement over the next three decades.

Sōhyō's adoption of its distinctive brand of unionism was sparked by efforts in 1951 to conclude the San Francisco Peace Treaty, which would end the Occupation and formally restore Japan's national sovereignty (Dower 1979; Masumi 1985, 195-218, 268-70). Under the terms being put forward by the US, this was to be a partial peace treaty signed only by the noncommunist belligerents that fought against Japan. In addition, it was to be combined with the conclusion of a military alliance with the US that would include measures for Japanese rearmament and the continued stationing of US military personnel in Japan. Occurring as they did in a country whose population had suffered an ignominious defeat after fifteen years of incessant wartime mobilization, and while a hot war was in full swing in neighbouring Korea, these efforts led to the emergence of a fervently held streak of popular opinion that objected to the terms of the San Francisco settlement. There was also a fear that the treaty would serve as an entrée for the revival of prewar authoritarianism, as prewar politicians previously jailed by the Occupation for their collaboration with the wartime regime returned to politics.

Japanese workers were not immune to these currents, and in fact had various grievances of their own on top of the various concerns that were fuelling the "peace and democracy" movement. A change in US policy associated with the unfolding of the Cold War – from one emphasizing demilitarization and democratization to one focused on economic recovery and rearmament – began to impact Japanese labour relations. Labour militancy was seen as an obstacle to Occupation policy and efforts were made to reduce the power and influence of the movement. Among the steps taken, the one that had the most lasting impact was a decision during the summer of 1948 to rescind the right of public sector workers to strike. This move critically weakened the movement since the public sector unions were the largest and among the most militant unions at the time and had used the threat of massive strikes, occasionally implemented, to gain concessions from the government. These developments left a legacy of resentment and mistrust towards the government on the part of public sector unions. More generally, a set of harsh retrenchment policies in 1949 led to the dismissal of hundreds of thousands of unionists and to an employer rollback of labour movement advances made during the early years of the Occupation.

The unfolding situation galvanized anti-treaty unionists into action. The Japan Socialist Party (JSP), the party to which the noncommunist element of the labour movement was linked and which had been part of a centre-left coalition government, suffered a dramatic defeat in the January 1949 elections that saw their delegation in the Diet's House of Representatives reduced from 143 to 48. With a majority conservative government in power, labour lost the limited voice that it had in the centre-left coalition governments. With the JSP overshadowed in parliament by the ruling conservatives, the labour movement, led by Sōhyō, took on a highly political role. The Sōhyō convention of January 1951 and the conventions of the respective industrial federations were used as vehicles for mobilizing labour unions on behalf of a popular protest movement aimed at halting the San Francisco settlement and the perceived conservative rollback. Coming at a time when Sōhyō's organizational ethos was in the process of being defined, the exercise left a strong imprint. A close working relationship was cemented between Sōhyō and the JSP's staunchly anti-treaty left wing, to which Sōhyō unions provided funds, campaign manpower, and even candidates.

Although unable to stop the San Francisco Treaty, the politics of protest of the anti-treaty unionists succeeded in mobilizing an impressive level of mass support both inside and outside the labour movement. The experience was interpreted as a demonstration that appropriate political appeals at the top would provide the avenue for a closer identification with the lower levels of the labour movement, as well as that the labour movement could and should serve as the leading organizer of a political "countervailing force" *(gegenmacht)* that would check the conservatives' unbridled anti-democratic ambitions. As a result of the application of the "countervailing power" model, the history of the labour movement during the 1950s was punctuated by massive Sōhyō-led mobilizations against conservative initiatives. In the Diet, the JSP was seen as serving as a similar countervailing force in the arena of party politics. Sōhyō's militancy, in turn, precipitated a backlash from more moderate elements in the labour movement that led to the formation of competing organizations.

Confrontation and Accommodation, 1955-74

Between 1955 and 1973, the Japanese experienced an unprecedented period of prosperity that has come to be labelled the "era of high-speed growth." Double-digit GNP growth was accompanied by dramatic increases in labour productivity, wages, and employment levels. As a number of analysts have recognized, Japan's economic growth paralleled that of other advanced industrialized countries during roughly the same era in that it was sustained by a Fordist process. "Fordism" refers to a dynamic in a capitalist political economy wherein wage growth is effectively linked to productivity growth attained through capital investment. In such a system, high wages generate the demand needed to absorb the expanded supply that capital investment creates. Together they produce a "virtuous cycle" of stable employment and expanding consumption that was characteristic of the golden age of capitalism in the advanced industrialized countries during the 1950s and into the 1960s (Sabel 1982; Marglin and Schor 1990).

As students of the Fordist pattern have pointed out, the specific institutional arrangements that sustained Fordism varied considerably from country to country. In the United States, Fordism unfolded within the context of productivity-based "pattern bargaining" between leading employers in the manufacturing sector and leading industrial unions in a country. In Europe, "socialized consumption" in the form of redistribution of income through various welfare state institutions tended to play a much more prominent role. Japanese Fordism was distinguished, on the one hand, by the centrality of productivity bargains struck at the enterprise level (Price 1997; Kume 1998, 49-72). That is, in those industries where capital investment and productivity growth were most pronounced – notably, steel, autos, shipbuilding, consumer electrical goods (and later electronics) – union-management relations were grounded in an implicit promise by management to preserve the employment of regular full-time workers – who were also the members of the enterprise unions – in exchange for acceptance and cooperation in instituting productivity-enhancing capital investments.

Labour-management consultation forums were established nearly universally in Japan's largest firms and it became de rigueur for capital investment plans to be discussed in these forums and for new plants to be staffed first by transferees from existing plants, thereby preserving the employment of existing, unionized workers. Wage bargaining, in turn, was conducted by such unions on the principle that the increased returns from productivity gains made possible by these investments would be shared with workers in the form of increased wages at levels that would not jeopardize the competitiveness and future growth of the firm. Functionally, where this type of enterprise-level industrial relations prevailed, unions came to serve less as counterweights against management authority than as facilitators of corporate human relations strategies and as guarantors of the so-called Japanese employment system based on lifetime employment, seniority wages, and enterprise unions.

The other distinguishing feature of Japanese Fordism, in this case a macro phenomenon, was a distinctive system in which wages for both unionized and non-unionized workers were set during annual rounds of wage negotiations referred to as Shuntō, or "spring offensive" (Price 1997, 121-31; Sako 1997; Kume 1998, 73-106). Although atomized and conducted in circumstances where lifetime employment meant that a true *labour* market in the sense of the actual buying and selling of the labour was largely absent in the most critical sector of employees (i.e., permanent full-time workers in large corporations), the simultaneity of enterprise-level bargaining in the Shuntō system provided the basis for development of a "*wage* market" in which enterprise-level settlements were in fact quite sensitive both to settlements within their respective industries and to developments in the national labour market overall.

The facilitating institutions were the industry-level federations and various cross-industry labour councils. Union officials at both levels did their best to orchestrate enterprise-level negotiations in a way that would maximize the overall size of settlements attained. For instance, "pattern setters" in firms and industries that were highly profitable might be chosen to bargain and settle early in an annual Shuntō round in the hope that a high settlement there would spill over and ratchet up settlements in other firms and industries. From a Fordist standpoint, the Shuntō process served as a means of narrowing wage gaps between firms and industries and of sustaining consumption by distributing expanded purchasing power across the economy. As the rapid growth of the Japanese economy and the steady expansion of wages during the era of high-speed growth suggest, the enterprise-level productivity bargains were important in sustaining the virtuous cycle of production and consumption associated with Japanese Fordism in its heyday.

If the two sides of the Japanese Fordist coin were integrated functionally, the same was not true organizationally. On the contrary, this functional complementarity was the product of heated organizational rivalry and political contention between competing wings of the labour movement (Carlile 1994a). The Shuntō round, which was a Sōhyō invention, was seen, in line with the countervailing-power model, as a form of en masse mobilization that would help to overcome the inherent weaknesses of the predominant enterprise union format. The simultaneity of Shuntō bargaining, it was averred, would allow enterprise unions to drive harder bargains against management than they might otherwise, since it would free enterprise unions from the fear that other firms in the industry might take away market share if that union were to strike, and would make unions less likely to be convinced by management arguments that a generous wage hike would increase labour costs at the expense of competitiveness vis-à-vis rival firms, and thus employment and wages in the long run (Masumi 1995, 367).

The other pole around which the Japanese labour movement revolved during the high-growth era was a set of moderate national-level organizations that espoused a cooperative, accommodationist form of unionism. This consisted of national confederations that took shape as Dōmei in 1964 and also a gathering of metal industry federations formed in the mid-1960s that was named the IMF-JC (International Metalworkers Federation – Japan Chapter), after the international trade secretariat with which it was affiliated internationally. If one were to point to a key set of tenets in this line of unionism, they would be as follows: First, labour unions should be responsible, in the sense that their wage and other demands should be in line with what the economy could bear. Second, strikes and other applications of union organizational power for political purposes should be avoided. Both of these were fundamental criticisms of Sōhyō's style of unionism, and were interpreted as being in the spirit of the "free and independent" unionism enshrined in Sōhyō's original platform. In order to further its values in the arena of partisan politics, Dōmei aligned with the moderate Democratic Socialist Party (DSP) and competed with the Sōhyō-JSP bloc.

The demographics of the era of high-speed growth worked in favour of the Dōmei-IMF-JC camp. With the dramatic expansion of private sector employment in industries dominated by Dōmei-affiliated unions, the number of private sector workers affiliated with Dōmei surpassed those affiliated with Sōhyō during the mid-1960s. Sōhyō-affiliated private sector industrial federations, which established enterprise-level productivity bargains of their own, coordinated their activities with the Dōmei unions through the IMF-JC. If demographics favoured the Dōmei-IMF-JC brand of productionist unionism,[4] however, the socio-economic and political milieu of the high-growth era nevertheless left important niches that were hospitable to Sōhyō's confrontational style. The grievances and resentments of public sector workers continued to make the rank and file stalwart supporters of Sōhyō unionism. Rapid economic development created a variety of socio-economic grievances that exploded in such forms as the rebellion on Japan's college campuses, anti-pollution movements, and other social protest movements.

In the event, Sōhyō experienced great difficulty in harnessing these grievances, but their existence and the expansion of support for the left in local government elections over the course of the 1960s served to justify the Sōhyō-JSP bloc's political militancy. By the early 1970s, in fact, with the economy beginning to suffer from increasingly pronounced inflation, Sōhyō made an effort to link these newer popular grievances to its own political and labour market struggles. The culmination of this trend was the so-called People's Shuntō of 1974, which unfolded in the midst of a bout of double-digit inflation exacerbated by the oil crisis (Sōhyō Yonjūnen Shi Hensan Iinkai 1993, 574-604). In a manner reminiscent of the politicized struggles pursued by Sōhyō in the early 1950s, a variety of social demands were added to the roster of Shuntō demands, and the confederation made it a point to invite a variety of non-union anti-establishment organizations to the union rallies that it was sponsoring in conjunction with the Shuntō round. The record of the People's Shuntō in attaining its social demands was somewhat dubious, but the unions did achieve a whopping 33 percent average wage increase in that year's Shuntō bargaining. Unfortunately, galloping inflation quickly ate up any real gains in purchasing power, leaving the value of the wage hike that year at around zero in real terms.

In sum, then, during the era of high-speed growth, a certain systemic functionality emerged in the role of the Japanese labour movement vis-à-vis the Japanese political economy at large, but it was characterized by polarized competition between ideologically and organizationally conflicting tendencies. Sōhyō, on the one hand, pursued an externally oriented, anti-establishment mobilizational strategy that dominated the macro-level labour market and the public sector unions, as well as the arena of labour representation in party politics. On the other side, the Dōmei-IMF-JC line of unionism dominated the labour movement in the burgeoning private sector, largely at the micro level, and pursued its goal within parameters defined by management strategy. Overall, the existence of these two autonomous arenas of labour politics made it extremely difficult for the Japanese labour movement to develop the common strategy and unified organizational structure that would allow it to effectively and coherently pursue the general interests of Japan's working population.

The Labour Movement as a Force of Order, 1975-89

Punctuated as it was by two events that set in motion processes that ended the stalemate between Sōhyō militancy and Dōmei moderation, 1975 is widely recognized as a watershed in the history of the Japanese labour movement. One was the IMF-JC-affiliated unions' seizure of the initiative in the Shuntō. The other was the "Strike for the Right to Strike" by the public sector unions in late November.

Chastened by the debacle of the previous year's People's Shuntō, the government and employers, with Nikkeiren (Japan Federation of Employers Associations) at the helm, were determined to bring Japan's runaway inflation under control by holding the line on wages at 15 percent in the 1975 Shuntō round (Shimada 1982; Shinkawa 1984). The 15 percent figure was justified on the grounds that this was the anticipated level of inflation in the coming year. Miyata Yoshiji, president of the IMF-JC, and other enterprise-oriented unionists expressed their acceptance of this agenda. The official Shuntō coordinating committee, on the other hand, called for wage hikes that were double this figure. In the event, leading IMF-JC unions refused to follow the schedule prepared by the Shuntō committee and instead seized the initiative in the bargaining round by settling early with wage increases that were in line with the 15 percent target. These early settlements, covering as they did the nation's leading private sector industrial federations, took the wind out of the Shuntō committee's strategy. Overall, the average settlement for the round was just under the government-sanctioned 15 percent.

The timing of the second watershed event, the public sector unions' Strike for the Right to Strike, was the product of negotiations over the issue conducted in 1972, in which a final settlement of the issue was promised three years hence (Shinkawa 1999, 124-67; Sōhyō Yonjūnen Shi Hensan Iinkai 1993, 723-36). Sympathy for the public sector workers' demand for a restitution of strike rights had been increasing. The pro-strike elements, reflecting the confrontational logic that animated the militant public sector workers' movement, felt that a strong show of force at this point would provide the leverage needed to induce the government to pass the appropriate legislation. Buoyed by their Shuntō victory, however, the hawkish elements among the ruling conservatives were in no mood to compromise, and negotiations between the unions and the government went nowhere.

Matters came to a head on 26 November when the frustrated public sector workers union walked off the job, among other things shutting down the national railway system. The government insisted that it would not negotiate under the duress of an illegal strike. Dōmei openly sided with the government. Sōhyō's private sector unions did so tacitly. Public sympathy for the strikers withered once the strike began. In the face of this pressure and fearing defections, the public sector unions called the strike off on 3 December, 129 hours after the walkout began. The unions had gained nothing in the way of concessions. To add to their woes, the unions were subsequently held liable for damages stemming from the strike. All of this, moreover, occurred at a time when the mass media were being filled with stories of featherbedding, lax discipline, abuses, and inefficiencies among public corporation workers and management. Fulfilling the figurative role of the nail that sealed the coffin, the Supreme Court ruled that the strike ban was constitutional, thereby closing completely the possibility of an expanded interpretation of the law that had been at the heart of the public sector union strategy.

As for the lasting significance of these events, the 1975 Shuntō set the pattern for subsequent Shuntō rounds. On labour's side, de facto control over the bargaining process continued to be held by the IMF-JC unions, which worked with their respective managements to ensure that wage adjustments were in line with what were perceived to be the macroeconomic needs of the national economy. Functionally, whereas Shuntō had earlier been a process in which the pattern setters ratcheted up overall settlements, the settlements of the pattern setters now worked as a cap on the pattern takers. The tendency for wage hikes to exceed productivity growth that had become apparent in the late 1960s disappeared. Strikes, too, disappeared almost completely. Average annual wage increases soon settled into a pattern in which they were roughly in line with the rate of increase in labour productivity nationally. These, in turn, contributed to the maintenance of the low inflation rate, good export performance, and low unemployment in the Japanese economy that was lauded by the world as effective economic management. It is noteworthy as well that during this period, the Japanese economy began to rely more and more on exports as the engine of economic growth, while the relative importance of domestic private consumption declined (Rapp and Feldman 1979). There was, in other words, a shift away from the classic Fordist paradigm.

At the micro level, the altered productivity bargain, building on the foundation of the industrial relations systems brought into being earlier by cooperative unionists and their managements, encouraged a more pronounced dualism in the labour market.[5] On the one hand, a shrinking core workforce of unionized permanent employees came to take on quasi-managerial or technical roles. Less skilled, more labour-intensive, and less permanent work was increasingly farmed out to a lower-paid class of temporary, part-time, and, more often than not, female workers employed on a contract basis in a large company, or permanently or on contract in smaller, subcontractor enterprises. Although core workers were clearly better compensated and more secure in employment status, their working conditions did not necessarily improve. Among widely reported phenomena were increased labour intensity, an expanded role for performance-based compensation, and unpaid overtime.

The public sector unions' defeat in the Strike for the Right to Strike paved the way for a decline of confrontational unionism and for the enterprise-oriented unionists to gain hegemony (Tsujinaka 1993; Shinoda 1997). Initial moves towards unification of the national centres began in 1979. A long and protracted process led initially to a formal amalgamation of the private sector industrial federations in 1987. This was followed in 1989 by the inclusion of the public sector unions in a new national confederation, Rengō, that encompassed the bulk of Japan's unionized workers and subscribed to enterprise-oriented unionist principles.

Politically, the post-1975 emergence of enterprise-oriented unionism hegemony was accompanied by the forging of direct, unmediated relations between labour organizations and the governing conservatives and bureaucrats that reversed the estrangement of the 1950s. A key development was the formation of the Policy Promotion Labour Council in October 1976 (Inagami 1997). Formed by sixteen leading private sector industrial federations representing 3.6 million union members, the purpose of the council was to bring about "thoroughgoing reforms of policies and institutions," particularly in economic policy, employment policy, inflation restraint, and tax policy. These were to be attained by increasing the number of representatives on governmental advisory councils. Both the government bureaucrats and the ruling Liberal Democrats reacted positively, although the institutionalization of labour's participation in the policy process unfolded incrementally and gradually.

Several reasons were behind this new willingness to accommodate on the part of the previously hostile conservative establishment. Perhaps the most important was the growing perception among the governing elite that the Japanese employment system these union leaders personified was a critical supporting pillar of the social order. Another reason was the precariousness of the LDP's majority in the 1970s. With their ties to the DSP and the more moderate elements inside the JSP, the union leaders represented in the Policy Promotion Labour Council appeared to be an avenue through which to cultivate future parliamentary allies.

Subsequent councils, and eventually Rengō, continued to deepen their ties with the conservative establishment. This process by which the Japanese labour movement became embedded ever more deeply into the policy making and policy implementation of the Japanese state broadly paralleled similar developments in Western Europe and has been referred to as the rise of "neo-corporatism." Certain distinctive features characterized "Japanese-style neo-corporatism," however. Herbert Kitschelt (1994) noted that certain basic demands were pursued during the 1970s by Europe's labour movement-associated social democrats, who served as the vehicle for the rise of labour-inclusive neo-corporatism. Among these were two that are particularly useful in highlighting the distinctiveness of the path taken by the Japanese movement.

First, the European movements demanded state policies that would redistribute income and government-financed social welfare policies. Second, they pushed for legislative arrangements that would mandate co-determination or some other form of "control that would give nonowners of capital a say over investment and employment decisions in private enterprises" (Kitschelt 1994). In the postwar Japanese labour movement, welfare state politics was eclipsed by defence and security issues. This remained the case even as the salience of this constellation of issues began to decrease with popular acceptance of Japan's peace constitution-based status quo. In the meantime, the moderate unions chose to advance their interests through the vehicle of the firm. Under such a strategy, a big welfare state came to be seen as something that would undercut this strategy by becoming a drag on the international competitiveness of Japanese firms (Carlile 1994b). Instead of expanded welfare policies, during the latter half of the 1970s, unions tied to the Policy Promotion Labour Council pressed for policies designed to shore up the so-called Japanese employment system during a period of institutional stress caused by the post-oil crisis downturn. The unions also pressed for tax cuts that would raise the take-home wages of workers without putting pressure on corporate balance sheets. The same strategy also meant that Japanese neo-corporatism was generally devoid of efforts to externally erode the decision-making autonomy of company managements.

A zenith of sorts was reached when the Policy Promotion Labour Council, Dōmei, and other private sector unions backed in principle a neoconservative administrative reform movement being promoted by the high-profile Rinchō (the Second Extraordinary Commission on Administrative Reform). Included on the agenda, and eventually implemented, was the privatization of the national railways, NTT (Nippon Telegraph and Telephone Corporation), and other public corporations. This was significant because, by placing the industrial relations system of public corporations on a footing approaching that of the private sector unions, the privatization of public corporations ended up dramatically altering the dynamics and interests of the public sector labour movement in a way that brought them closer to the enterprise-oriented sensibilities that were animating the private sector unions (Mochizuki 1993; Weathers 1994).

Conclusion: Labour in Limbo, 1989-2000
As the Japanese labour movement contemplates its future course at the cusp of a new millennium, a second cycle in the evolution of the postwar labour movement seems to have run its course and circumstances demand that the movement reinvent itself yet again. A drastic alteration in the Japanese employment system around which the current movement is structured is now part of the agenda of management and the conservative government. The question is, should the movement dig in its heels and try to preserve the status quo, or should it concentrate its energy on a project whose aim is to realize labour's interests through a different set of institutions? This, in turn, begs the question of capacity. With a unionization rate of 22 percent and declining, does the labour movement have the capacity to resist alterations in the status quo of firm-level accommodation based on the so-called Japanese employment system? Can it mobilize the political, social, and economic resources to engineer changes in line with its preferences? Unfortunately, the more convincing answer to the last two questions at the moment is no. Neither the decentralized structure nor the ethos of Japan's enterprise union-based movement appears to incline it to move beyond the preparation of plans and position papers calling for dramatic change.

Proponents of enterprise-oriented unionism had understood their "responsible" approach to be something that would help advance the welfare of all Japanese workers. Competitive firms and a low-inflation economy would, it was felt, ensure that Japan would prosper, that Japanese workers would enjoy steady increases in real income, and that social stability and social equity would be maintained. The political and economic conditions of the latter half of the 1980s and 1990s, however, produced some rather ironic consequences.

The steady appreciation of the yen following the 1985 Plaza Accord put pressure on Japanese manufacturers in the export sector to cut costs and increase efficiency.[6] Japanese unions dutifully went along. The situation encouraged further dualization of employment. For unionized regular workers, this often translated into an intensification of work and the wrenching dislocation caused by transfers to far-flung parts of the country and, increasingly, overseas, as Japanese firms took advantage of the high yen to shift production overseas. As a consequence of the loose monetary policies associated with the so-called bubble economy of the late 1980s, leading firms found themselves flush with more cash than they could reasonably invest in labour-saving plants and equipment. The returns from *zaitech*, or the manipulation of financial assets, became a primary source of income for many large manufacturing firms. While this in and of itself did not necessarily hurt employees materially, huge amounts of money found their way into real estate speculation, and land prices skyrocketed. This put home ownership out of the reach of an ever-expanding portion of the labour force.

In the political arena, although the labour movement made considerable inroads into the conservative regime's policy-making process, it was unable to displace the farmers and small businessmen who were the mainstays of the conservatives' constituency. While the salaries of unionized employees showed the most modest of increases, the LDP protected the incomes of these client interest groups through various schemes that had the latent consequence of keeping the cost of living in Japan artificially high. This counteracted the positive material effects of the labour market in determining wages that the union movement had come to support. Workers, in effect, appeared to be bearing a disproportionate share of the burdens of adjustment to Japan's changed economic circumstances.

Shuntō wage hikes, in the meantime, continue to remain at historically low levels throughout the 1990s. Unemployment, currently hovering just below 5.0 percent, has been at historically high levels. New hiring has been reduced drastically where it has not been frozen, and in extreme cases, surplus regular employees have been dismissed. Indeed, in 1998 wage levels declined and the size of the workforce shrank in absolute terms, both of them for the first time since the government began tracking these in 1954 (*Rengō* 2000a, 3). In addition to establishing several pieces of new legislation that facilitate corporate restructuring, the government increased co-payments and cut back on benefits in pensions and medical care, as have private sector firms. Frustration with this state of affairs led the labour movement to realize that the approach in the 1990s mired the Japanese working population in a counterproductive, self-reinforcing cycle of employment insecurity and withering consumer confidence. Whereas the conflictual Fordism of the era of high-speed growth produced a virtuous cycle of expanding material prosperity, the cooperative unionist hegemony of the 1990s produced a vicious cycle of economic decline.

With the bursting of Japan's "economic bubble" in 1991 and the economic stagnation of the ensuing decade, even the Japanese employment system, the fundamental baseline of the labour movement, has come under attack. Firms that only a few years ago appeared to be invincible pillars of the Japanese employment system began to systematically reduce their workforces. In May 1995, Nikkeiren released a report in which it encouraged Japanese executives to radically transform their personnel policies in order to increase the "flexibility" of human resources. Under the plan, lifetime employment and seniority wages would be limited to a small number of management track employees (perhaps 10 percent of the workforce), with compensation to include a large merit component. The rest of the employees would be employed on a limited contract basis

(Shinkawa 1999). While it remains to be seen to what extent the Nikkeiren plan will be implemented by Japan's corporations, it is clear that Japanese firms are transforming their human resource policies in the direction of increased flexibility.

In the face of these dire circumstances, Rengō has begun to show signs that it is seriously re-examining its approach. Besides championing the obvious point that healthy wage hikes would help undo the effects of the consumer confidence trap that the economy is mired in, it has also begun arguing that the social safety net has to be expanded and fortified. It has begun championing the passage of an employment protection law to counterbalance the flexibility-fostering reforms that have been passed in recent years to facilitate management restructuring initiatives (*Rengō* 2000b). Attaining any of these, however, would require major changes in the structure and stance of the labour movement, and it is not at all apparent how the appropriate changes can be brought about.

On the party politics front, even as it strengthened its ties with high-level bureaucrats and the ruling Liberal Democrats, the labour movement struggled for years to effect new arrangements that would consolidate a political force capable of pushing forward a more worker-friendly policy agenda (Carlile 1994b, 1996). When the opposition parties began gaining ground as the ruling Liberal Democrats faced a public backlash over the imposition of the consumption tax and the Recruit Scandal in 1988-89, Rengō played a role in consolidating an opposition coalition.[7] This role was repeated when the LDP split in 1993. Rengō president Yamagishi Akira played a key role in cobbling together the eight-party, non-LDP coalition government of Hosokawa Morihiro. Rengō pressed for a merger of the DSP and JSP that would parallel the unification under way in the labour movement.

Despite a major loosening, however, the union-party relationship remained haunted by legacies of the past. Mistrust between the two ostensibly social democratic parties was a major factor in bringing about the resignation of the Hosokawa cabinet. The JSP bolted from the anti-LDP Hosokawa coalition and soon entered into a coalition with the former ruling party in 1994. Besides being fraught with historical irony, this brought back LDP rule, which the party has been able to sustain ever since through a shifting array of increasingly conservative coalitions. It was not until January 1999, when union-associated politicians and other elements merged with the newly formed, Rengō-backed Democratic Party that the two groups were again on the same side of the fence in national politics. The Democratic Party has remained in opposition so far, however.

Unfortunately, years of collaborative engagement with management within the context of the firm have created a union membership that is oriented towards management direction and the internal institutional arrangements of the firm. It is difficult indeed to picture a major strike occurring in a leading Japanese firm. With Shuntō itself now in decline as a growing number of unions distance their collective bargaining from the Shuntō schedule, the Shuntō "wage market" is becoming increasingly superfluous (Weathers 1997). One imaginable possibility is for the labour movement to use its new-found establishment credentials and electoral strategy to somehow induce the Japanese Diet to pass legislation that would use the regulatory power of the state to protect the status quo of the Japanese employment system. But here, too, it is hard to imagine that any kind of protection for labour can be attained without a major alteration of the status quo. Thanks to a quarter-century of systematic dualization of the workforce, the percentage of organized workers in the total workforce has decreased dramatically, and with it has come a decrease in the number of voters with a direct interest in preserving the status quo.

The current labour movement's situation resembles that of fifty years earlier, in that it will be necessary to develop an appeal that can gain the support of a substantial part of the non-union electorate. This, in turn, requires that the Japanese labour movement define its interest more broadly than it has in recent years, and in ways that would appeal not just to its rank and file but also to a broader spectrum of workers and citizens besides those formally affiliated with unions. Constituting, in effect, the exact opposite of a strategy of dualization, this would take the labour movement at the national level beyond its current role as a supplemental arm of enterprise-oriented unionism. This would be a dramatic change indeed. In any event, the new millennium finds the Japanese labour movement at a crossroads in a radically changed environment.

Notes

1 See also Gordon 1985, Gordon 1991, and Garon 1987.
2 For a detailed account of developments during this period, see Monogatari Sengo Rōdō Undō Shi Kankō Iinkai 1997-99.
3 Sōhyō (The General Council of Trade Unions of Japan) was Japan's largest federation of unions before 1987. It merged with the Japan Trade Union Confederation (JTUC-Rengō) in 1989. For a detailed account of Sōhyō's early years, see Sōhyō Yonjūnen Shi Hensan Iinkai 1993, 59-170.
4 Note that productionist unionism is an ideological orientation that emphasizes production, productivity, and collaboration with management in order to increase these measures. It can be contrasted with class unionism that emphasizes confrontation and struggle.
5 For an extremely thorough discussion of these issues, see Igarashi 2000. For accounts in specific industries and corporate settings, see Makino 1991 and Gordon 1998.
6 The Plaza Accord was an agreement reached by finance ministers of five major industrialized nations at New York's Plaza Hotel in September 1985. The signatories agreed to cooperate by market intervention to bring about a gradual decline in the exchange rate of the US dollar. As a result, the yen appreciated rapidly.
7 The Recuit Scandal involved the revelation in 1988 that a number of politicians and business leaders had profited from insider trading. Recruit is an information-publishing

conglomerate with property and telecommunications interests. The scandal led to the resignation of several cabinet ministers, including Prime Minister Takeshita.

References

Carlile, L.E. 1994a. "Sōhyō versus Dōmei: Competing Labour Movement Strategies in the Era of High Growth in Japan." *Japan Forum* 6: 145-57.
—. 1994b. "Party Politics and the Japanese Labour Movement: Rengō's New Political Force." *Asian Survey* 24: 301-16.
—. 1996. *The Left in Japanese Politics: Is There Movement toward a Third Pole?* JPRI Working Paper No. 17. Cardiff, CA: Japan Policy Research Institute.
Dower, J.W. 1979. *Empire and Aftermath: Yoshida Shigeru and the Japanese Experience, 1878-1954*. Harvard East Asian Monograph 84. Cambridge, MA: Harvard University Press.
Garon, S.M. 1987. *The State and Labor in Modern Japan*. Berkeley: University of California Press.
Gordon, A. 1985. *The Evolution of Labor Relations in Japan: Heavy Industry, 1853-1955*. Harvard East Asian Monograph 117. Cambridge, MA: Harvard University Press.
—. 1991. *Labor and Imperial Democracy*. Berkeley: University of California Press.
—. 1998. *Wages of Affluence: Labor and Management in Postwar Japan*. Cambridge, MA: Council on East Asian Studies, Harvard University.
Igarashi, J. 2000. "Rōdō Seisaku Katei no Hen'yō wa Naze Shōjita ka? Kume Ikuo *Rōdō seisaku katei no seijuku to hen'yō' o yonde*" (Why did the change in the labour policy process occur? Upon reading Kume Ikuo's *The Change and Maturation of the Labour Policy Process*). <http://oohara.mt.tama.hosei.ac.jp/iga/rousei.HTM>, accessed December 2000.
Inagami, T. 1997. "Seisaku Suishin Rōso Kaigi" (The Policy Promotion Labour Council). *Nihon Rōdō Kyōkai Zasshi* (Japan Institute of Labour Journal) 443: 70-71.
Japan Institute of Labour. 2001. "Main Labour Economic Indicators." <http://www.jil.go.jp/estatis/e0701.htm>, accessed August 2001.
Kawanishi, H. 1992. *Enterprise Unionism in Japan*. London: Kegan Paul International.
Kitschelt, H. 1994. *The Transformation of European Social Democracy*. Cambridge, UK: Cambridge University Press.
Kume, I. 1998. *Disparaged Success: Labor Politics in Postwar Japan*. Cornell Studies in Political Economy. Ithaca, NY: Cornell University Press.
Large, S.S. 1981. *Organized Workers and Socialist Politics in Interwar Japan*. Cambridge, UK: Cambridge University Press.
Makino, T. 1991. *Nihonteki Rōshi Kankei no Henbō* (The transformation of Japanese labour-management relations). Tokyo: Otsuki Shoten.
Marglin, S.A., and J.B. Schor, eds. 1990. *The Golden Age of Capitalism: Reinterpreting Postwar Experience*. Oxford: Clarendon Press.
Masumi, J. 1985. *Postwar Politics in Japan, 1945-1955*. Japan Research Monograph 6. Berkeley: Institute of East Asian Studies, University of California.
—. 1995. *Contemporary Politics in Japan*. Berkeley: University of California Press.
Mochizuki, M. 1993. "Public Sector Labor and Privatization Challenge: The Railway and Telecommunications Unions." In G.D. Allinson and S. Yasunori, eds., *Political Dynamics in Contemporary Japan*. Ithaca, NY: Cornell University Press, 181-99.
Monogatari Sengo Rōdō Undō Shi Kankō Iinkai. 1997-99. *Monogatari Sengo Rōdō Undō Shi* (The story of postwar labour movement history), vols. 1 and 2. Tokyo: Daiichi Shorin.
Price, J. 1991. "Valery Burati and the Formation of Sōhyō during the US Occupation of Japan." *Pacific Affairs* 64: 208-25.
—. 1997. *Japan Works: Power and Paradox in Postwar Industrial Relations*. Ithaca, NY: ILR Press.
Rapp, W.V., and R.A. Feldman. 1979. "Japan's Economic Strategy and Prospects." In W.J. Barnds, ed., *Japan and the United States: Challenges and Opportunities*. New York: New York University Press, 86-154.
Rengō. 2000a. "2000 Shunki Seikatsu Tōsō Book" (The 2000 spring livelihood struggle book), February, 2-11.

–. 2000b. "Rōdōsha Hogo hō no Susume" (Encouragement of a worker protection law), March, 8-12.
Sabel, C.F. 1982. *Work and Politics: The Division of Labour in Industry*. Cambridge, UK: Cambridge University Press.
Sako, M. 1997. "Shuntō: The Role of Employer and Union Coordination at the Industry and Inter-Sectoral Levels." In M. Sako and H. Sato, eds., *Japanese Labour and Management in Transition: Diversity, Flexibility, and Participation*. London: Routledge, 236-64.
Scalapino, R.A. 1983. *The Early Japanese Labor Movement: Labor and Politics in a Developing Society*. Japan Research Monograph 5. Berkeley: Institute of East Asian Studies, University of California.
Schonberger, H. 1979. "American Labor's Cold War in Occupied Japan." *Diplomatic History* 3: 249-72.
Shimada, H. 1982. "Wage Determination and Information Sharing: Alternative to Incomes Policy?" *Journal of Industrial Relations* 25: 177-200.
Shinkawa, T. 1984. "1975 Nen Shuntō to Keizai Kiki Kanri" (The 1975 spring offensive and the management of economic crisis). In H. Ōtake, ed., *Nihon Seiji no Sōten: Jirei Kenkyū ni Yoru Seiji Taisei no Bunseki* (The issues of Japanese politics: analyses of the political system through case studies). Tokyo: San'ichi Shobō, 189-232.
–. 1999. *Sengo Nihon Seiji to Shakai Minshu Shugi: Shakaitō Sōhyō Burokku no Kōbō* (Postwar Japanese politics and social democracy: the vicissitudes of the JSP-Sōhyō bloc). Kyoto: Hōristu Bunka Sha.
Shinoda, T. 1997. "Rengō and Policy Participation: Japanese-Style Neo-Corporatism?" In M. Sako and H. Sato, eds., *Japanese Labour and Management in Transition: Diversity, Flexibility, and Participation*. London: Routledge, 187-214.
Sōhyō Yonjūnen Shi Hensan Iinkai, ed. 1993. *Sōhyō Yonjūnen Shi* (Forty-year history of Sōhyō), vol. 1. Tokyo: Daiichi Shorin.
Takemae, E. 1982. *Sengo Rōdō Kaikaku: GHQ Rōdō Seisakushi* (Postwar labour reform: GHQ's labour policy). Tokyo: Tokyo Daigaku Shuppankai.
Totten, G.O. 1966. *The Social Democratic Movement in Prewar Japan*. New Haven, CT: Yale University Press.
Tsujinaka, Y. 1993. "Rengō and Its Osmotic Networks." In G.D. Allinson and S. Yasunori, eds., *Political Dynamics in Contemporary Japan*. Ithaca, NY: Cornell University Press, 200-13.
Weathers, C.E. 1994. "Reconstruction of Labour-Management Relations in Japan's National Railways." *Asian Survey* 24: 621-33.
–. 1997. *Japan's Fading Labor Movement*. JPRI Working Paper No. 35. Cardiff, CA: Japan Policy Research Institute.

4
Japan's High Seas Fisheries in the North Pacific Ocean: Food Security and Foreign Policy

Roger Smith

In this chapter, I examine the remarkably little understood topic of Japanese high seas fisheries in the North Pacific Ocean. This incorporates an account of the previous 100 years of change that aims to link past and present-day concerns. Also included are speculative comments on future directions, mainly regarding long-term access to food supplies. Overall, I argue that twentieth-century trends in Japanese fisheries, particularly the high seas fisheries, may serve as a useful example in trying to understand Japan's perennial quest for food self-sufficiency and resource security, while highlighting some of the challenges Japan's fisheries will face in the new millennium.

The focus here is on the North Pacific since this region has always been an important source of living resources for Japan's international fisheries. An examination of Japanese foreign policy with respect to fisheries illustrates a much larger theme relating to Japan's perennial quest for resource security, particularly food supply. Japan has long sought a way to secure access to food resources such as fish through trade, domestic production, and even colonial control. The Japanese view such an issue as a matter of survival, since whatever the level of industrial development the country may achieve, its economic and political security may be threatened if it remains highly dependent upon the external world for its food supply. This case study indicates that although Japan may continue to be an economic superpower, it is still vulnerable with respect to its basic food needs.

The Early Development of Japan's High Seas Fisheries

Japanese Fisheries

Japan has a long tradition of coastal, beach, and inland-water fishing that stretches back to well before 1900. It would be difficult to overstate the importance of fish in the diet of most Japanese and, consequently, their large role in the domestic economy. Fish products have constituted more than half of the animal protein consumed in Japan, compared with about 5 percent in the United States and Canada (Food and Agriculture Organization 1973). The natural productivity of the waters surrounding Japan, the lack of alternative food sources, and the concentration of population along the island's extensive coastlines led to the early intensive development of the local fishing industry.[1] Three distinct types of fisheries emerged in the early twentieth century, distinguished both by their areas of operation and by their techniques: coastal, offshore, and overseas.

Coastal fisheries were the oldest form of fishing in Japan. Such fisheries were largely conducted by village associations or diverse small-scale individual enterprises characterized by techniques requiring low capitalization such as nonmotorized boats, simple equipment, and small-scale production. Their methods of operation included beach seines, lift nets, set nets or traps, gill nets, and hook-and-line fishing within the customary three-mile zone, as well as shellfish and seaweed collection and inland freshwater catches. The principal species landed were herring, salmon, trout, yellowtail, tuna, horse mackerel, bream, sharks, cuttlefish, octopus, crab, shrimp, clams, and oysters (Espenshade 1946).

Offshore fishing, on the other hand, ranged from just outside the territorial sea to several hundreds of kilometres from the coast. Due to the higher costs for the equipment and mechanized boats capable of operating at such ranges, offshore fishing was largely conducted by companies and special associations utilizing large-scale purse seine fishing, two-boat power trawling, and line-and-pole tuna fishing techniques. The decentralized coastal fisheries with their low levels of capitalization were joined by new enterprise fisheries with much higher levels of capitalization as fleets extended into offshore areas. Such fisheries were largely based on tuna, skipjack, sardines, mackerel, cod, bream, sharks, flatfish, skipper, and mullet.

Because of the high cost and technical sophistication of refrigeration, diesel engines, and larger ships, overseas fisheries did not develop extensively before the mid-1920s. Even after the technology became available, only large companies, such as Taiyō Gyogyō and Nippon Suisan (Nissui), were able to provide the capital investment and organizational expertise necessary to turn international expeditions into profitable ventures. Such fisheries primarily operated motorized factory ships and trawlers off the coasts of Russia, the Kwantung Peninsula, Korea, Formosa, and the Japanese mandated islands in the mid-South Pacific, and "mother ship" operations in the Sea of Okhotsk, the Bering Sea, and the North Pacific high seas. The main species exploited were whales, sardines, tuna, skipjack, salmon, shrimp, and crab.

Coastal fisheries were the largest supplier of fish in the prewar period. However, while offshore and overseas sources of supply continued to amount to only a fraction of the coastal catch in absolute terms, their production increased 7.5 times from the mid-1920s to 1940 (see Figure 4.1) and continued to provide commercially valued species such as whales, crab, and salmon to the domestic market. Moreover, Figure 4.1 does not consider colonial fisheries, which supplied a yearly average of nearly 2.3 million tons of fish and whales – close to one-third of Japan's total production from 1935 to 1940 (Espenshade 1946, 132). Since Korean coastal waters provided most of this total, one must not underestimate the importance to the domestic market of fishing products supplied from outside Japanese coastal waters.

The increase in fisheries productivity was an important factor in the Meiji government's campaign of *fukoku kyōhei* (wealthy country, strong military) and in later governments' developmental strategies. Political leaders hoped that expanded fisheries would provide for the nutritional requirements of a rapidly growing population while simultaneously promoting enhanced economic activity in targeted industrial sectors. In 1905 the government enacted the Pelagic Fisheries Encouragement Act to facilitate the construction of large motorized fishing vessels. Subsidies were also provided from 1918 onward to aid in the construction and repair of mechanized ships. Moreover, the government offered subsidies in 1923 and again in 1932 to promote refrigeration technology and ice-making facilities, respectively (Niwa et al. 1957, 2). Such promotional policies greatly benefited those companies engaged in or expanding into overseas fisheries.

Japan's expanded fisheries productivity also had important environmental repercussions. Although general fishing effort in coastal and offshore

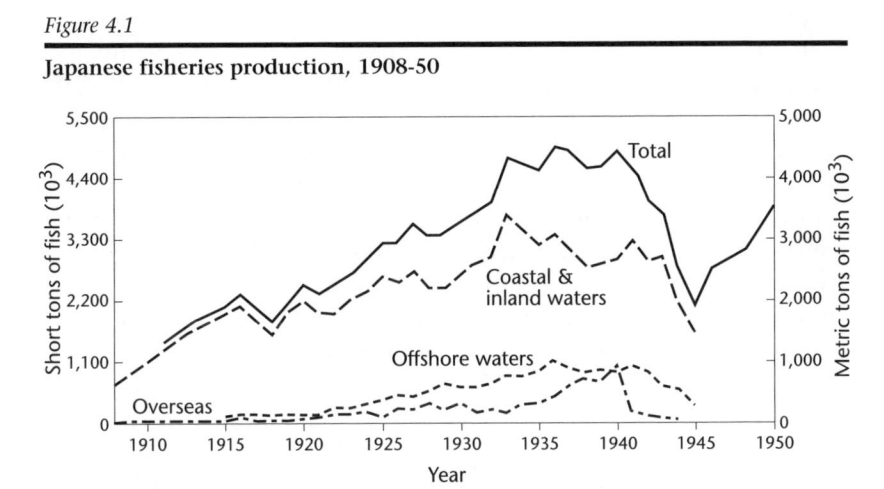

Figure 4.1

Japanese fisheries production, 1908-50

Source: Natural Resources Section GHQ, Supreme Command for the Allied Powers (SCAP), Tokyo; found in Ackerman 1953.

trawling grounds substantially increased after 1933, catch rates actually levelled off (Ackerman 1953, 444). This was an indication that the full utilization of marine resources had been achieved by the early 1930s and that further effort merely resulted in overfishing. Moreover, Japanese fishers earned a poor international reputation for their overexploitation of ocean resources. Japan's position as one of the world's major exploiters meant that its refusal to join the International Whaling Convention in 1936 doomed any global whale conservation efforts to only partial success at best (Johnson 1965, 396-411). The prewar failure of the convention's protective measures was largely attributed to Japan's absence from and non-compliance with the agreement. In addition, several exploratory salmon expeditions to Bristol Bay (located in Alaska) during 1936 also prompted the *Pacific Fisherman* (an influential North American industrial fisheries magazine) to warn of an impending "alien invasion" (*Pacific Fisherman*, late 1936 through 1937). Canadian and US fishers feared that intensive Japanese fishing would result in unsustainable yields and possibly deplete this valuable North American stock. Thus, the expansion of Japan's fishing activity led in some cases to excessive exploitation of fisheries resources, and engendered international resentment against its fishing practices.

The Early Oceans Regime
By the time Japan's fisheries extended operations into the high seas, a long-standing global oceans tradition was already firmly established. International maritime and fisheries law was predicated upon the principle of the "Freedom of the Seas" as originally outlined in Hugo Grotius's 1609 publication *Mare Liberum*. This principle maintained that no state or navy could own unenclosed seas or oceans. Unlike land, the seas were considered to be inexhaustible and inappropriable, and, consequently, did not share the qualities of property. Therefore, the high seas were open to everyone's use (Johnson 1965, 165).

Over the years, the *mare liberum* concept was modified with the widespread acceptance of "territorial seas." As a form of *mare clausiem*, the territorial sea allowed littoral states a three-mile zone of coastal water ownership – roughly the distance of a cannon-shot (Leonard 1944, 7). Outside this zone, however, freedom of the seas prevailed. While neither principle was codified in international law, they were nonetheless regularly used in practice. As Thomas Baty, an international jurist, once observed with regard to the three-mile limit: "The rule, while not infrequently attacked in theory, is supreme in practice. Diplomatists seldom or never question it; professors occasionally do. In the actual conduct of affairs, it is seldom challenged, and never successfully so" (Baty 1928, 503). No international organization, however, governed the application of these institutions. Consequently, no state or other actor could claim exclusive rights to any fish stocks in their natural habitat. Any actor was entitled to harvest fish anytime and anyplace, except within the narrow confines of territorial seas. In economic terms, fisheries resources were allocated upon the basis of an open-to-entry common property system (Sweeney et al. 1974, 179-92). This was coupled with a procedural device known as the Law of Capture, which provided that the capture of any fish from the ocean automatically transformed the common resource into the private property of the fisherman (Young 1982, 138).

The prevailing regime of freedom of the seas in international waters was therefore overwhelmingly favourable to the expansion of Japan's fishing activities. As steam and then diesel engine technology in conjunction with refrigeration facilities extended the range, catch capacity, and transportation ability of Japan's fishing fleets, no legal framework or property rights existed to restrict such development. The unlimited-entry nature of the common resource regime enabled any actors, including growing Japanese fishing companies, to expand their activities limitlessly into the international waters of the North Pacific and elsewhere to meet domestic consumption demands and export opportunities.

The International North Pacific Fisheries Convention

The Impact of the Second World War and Postwar Rehabilitation

The Second World War devastated Japan's domestic and international fisheries. By 1945 the tonnage of powered fishing boats declined to 40 percent of the 1940s total, while ice-making capacity fell to below half the prewar average (Niwa et al. 1957, 2). Many port facilities were rendered inoperable and required extensive repairs due to bomb damage. Moreover, the new Occupation authorities in the Supreme Commander for the Allied Powers (SCAP) headquarters declared Japan's traditional offshore and high seas fisheries areas off limits. As a consequence, fish catch dropped by half and fish consumption, a staple of the Japanese diet, fell by one-third from 1937 levels (the prewar peak), contributing to widespread undernourishment (Niwa et al. 1957, 2-3).

As the United States grew increasingly wary of communist encroachment in East Asia after 1947, however, Washington pushed for the revival of an economically strong Japan to serve as a bulwark in Asia. SCAP authorities soon identified the fishing industry as an area critical to Japan's economic revitalization. It was hoped that a strong fishery would both allow the Japanese to provide for their own food requirements while relieving the United States of burdensome aid expenses, and create the necessary impetus to rebuild essential economic sectors such as ironworks and shipbuilding.[2] Furthermore, exports of surplus fish products could provide much-needed hard currency and help build foreign exchange reserves. Thus, fisheries were promoted to alleviate the nation's postwar economic crisis, including serious food shortages, and to foster economic recovery.

Although SCAP initially suspended the movements of all vessels weighing over 100 tons in the interest of security following Japan's surrender, fishing vessels were exempted on 27 September 1945, within an authorized zone known as the MacArthur Line (shown in Figure 4.2). At the same time, the domestic government provided funds to reconstruct fishing boats, ice-making facilities, and coastal ports (Niwa et al. 1957, 3). By 1946, Antarctic whaling was also permitted to contribute to the nation's food supply. Japan's traditional fishing areas near Korea, China, and the Soviet Union remained closed due to considerable wartime resentment, security issues, and the fears of fish stock overexploitation. Nonetheless, SCAP authorities recognized that they would eventually be required to allow Japanese fishers to expand their activities eastward into the North Pacific and the Antarctic to meet domestic needs.

These promotional policies were so successful that by 1947 the restored fishing fleet tonnage exceeded prewar levels. In spite of considerable population growth, indigenous production of agricultural and fisheries food was sufficient to provide 66 percent of Japan's caloric requirements – close to prewar levels (Ackerman 1953, 153). Japan still suffered, however, from a food deficit of 11 percent even as late as 1950, according to SCAP studies.[3] Moreover, too many vessels led to additional problems of overfishing as catch intensity increased within the narrow confines of the MacArthur Line. To allow Japan to continue on its development path and to avoid ecological catastrophe, SCAP needed to extend or find new fishing areas for Japanese fishers. As a provisional measure to relieve some pressure on Japan's coastal fisheries, the MacArthur Line was extended in 1949 (see Figure 4.2).[4]

Tripartite Negotiations

Outside of Japan-US relations, the expansion of the high seas fisheries faced substantial opposition worldwide, stemming from Japan's previous lack of proper conservation practices. Accordingly, American fishing interests and Korean, Indonesian, Chinese, and Australian representatives pressured SCAP and the State Department to enshrine restrictions on Japanese fishing in the San Francisco Peace Treaty. Somewhat alarmed by the extent of these requests, Ambassador John Foster Dulles commented that the treaty was becoming an "international fisheries convention." He opposed such attempts largely to sidestep any singular opposition this might bring to the treaty as a whole and to avoid a punitive settlement with respect to Japan's international fisheries. In order to conclude the treaty as soon as possible, he felt that "this pressure had been resisted in every instance"

(Department of State 1951, 6: 1184). Consequently, Japan and the United States decided to negotiate the first fisheries treaty in an effort to establish a favourable precedent for subsequent peace treaty negotiations as well as to quickly open up an abundant fishing area for the Japanese. Washington also supported the conclusion of a Northeast Pacific treaty, with the inclusion of Canada, since an agreement for the Western Pacific and the Japan and China seas was still virtually impossible because of the political situation in Korea and China. Tripartite negotiations were held in Tokyo in November and December 1952. SCAP bestowed temporary sovereignty

Figure 4.2

Japanese prewar fishing areas and limits of authorized fishing areas during 1945-51

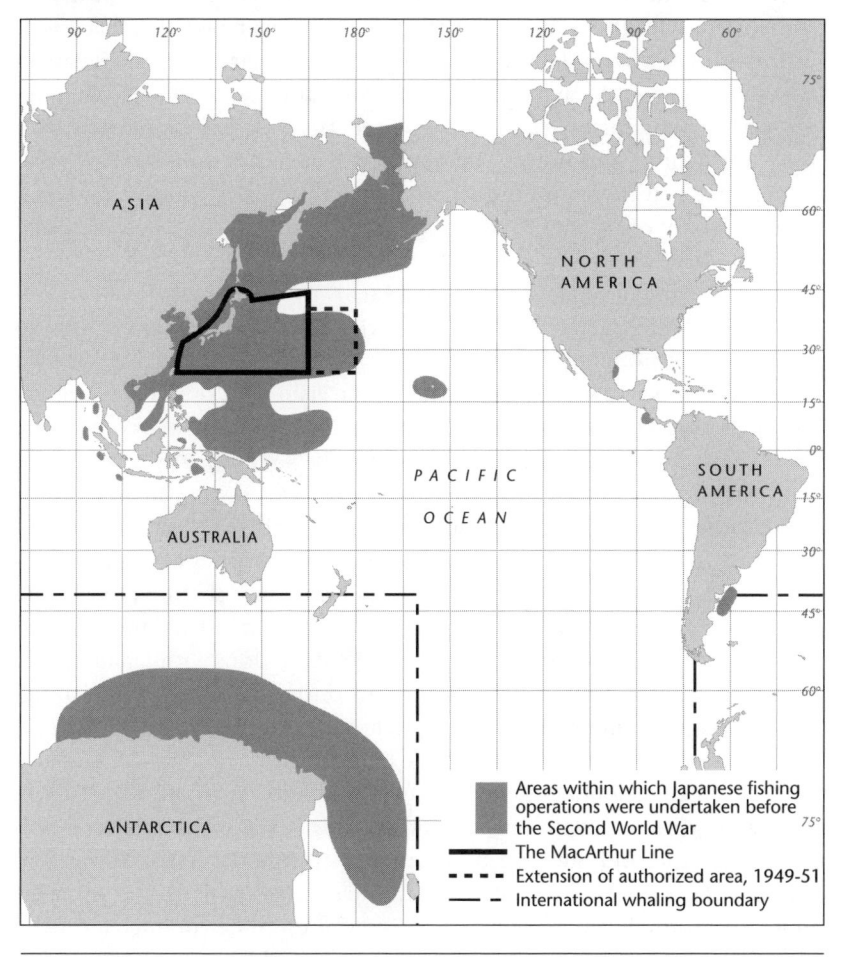

Legend:
- Areas within which Japanese fishing operations were undertaken before the Second World War
- The MacArthur Line
- Extension of authorized area, 1949-51
- International whaling boundary

Source: Natural Resources Section GHQ, Supreme Commander for the Allied Powers (SCAP), Tokyo; found in Ackerman 1953.

on Japanese authorities for the duration of the negotiations since the peace treaty had not yet been completed and full Japanese sovereignty had not yet been restored (Ministry of Foreign Affairs, n.d.).

The negotiation policy of the Japanese Ministry of Foreign Affairs was to defend the principle of freedom of the seas by avoiding any restrictions on fishing activities (Ministry of Foreign Affairs, n.d.). Moreover, the Japanese wanted to secure American and Canadian support for this principle through a mutual declaration that defended the freedom as a universal right. In the Japanese draft of the convention, Article 2 stated that "no country concerned under this convention is to be subject to discriminatory exclusion from the exploitation of any high seas fishing resource" (Ministry of Foreign Affairs 1951, 176). In other words, the Japanese argued that no restrictions should be applied to any single country in compliance with the standards of the earlier oceans regime, while conservation measures should be applied equally to all signatories. The Japanese negotiators hoped to avoid the adoption of any exclusionary principles for fear they might serve as adverse precedents in later negotiations with the USSR, China, and Korea. The ministry also emphasized the particular importance of fisheries to the economic revitalization of the postwar economy (Ministry of Foreign Affairs, n.d.), a persuasive tactic since Washington had already committed itself to the reconstruction of Japan through SCAP (Department of State 1953, 14: 1446-47).

Canadian and American fishing industries, on the other hand, sought to exclude Japan from any fishing at all in the Northeast Pacific. As resolved in the November 1950 meeting of the Pacific Fisheries Conference, a meeting held among American and Canadian industrial fishing companies, West Coast fishers encouraged their respective governments to negotiate with the objective of ensuring that "Japanese fishermen will stay out of the fisheries of the Northeast Pacific Ocean which have been developed and husbanded by the United States and other countries of North America" (*Pacific Fisherman,* January 1951, 15). Fishing industry advocates cited Japan's earlier "invasion" of the Bristol Bay salmon fishery in Alaska in 1936-37 as well as potential threats to peaceful relations with Japan as substantial reasons to impose an eastern limit on Japanese high seas fishing.

The US government, however, concurred with the Japanese Foreign Ministry's position with respect to the defence of freedom of the seas and the need for economic revival through fisheries expansion. Much more concerned with the communist victory in China, Soviet expansionary policy in East Asia, and the Korean War than with fisheries in the Bering Sea, the State Department was mostly attentive to security needs in Asia. As stated in a Central Intelligence Agency (CIA) special estimate conducted for the State Department in 1951, Japan would play a critical role in establishing an "East-West balance of power in the Far-East" and it would be important to secure markets and natural resources, such as fish, in noncommunist areas (Department of State 1951, 1: 204-5). Indeed, the fall of Nationalist China in 1949 raised urgent problems regarding the replacement of the very important and proximate mainland economy with one large enough to support the Japanese market while remaining friendly to American interests.

The tripartite negotiations were conducted with the understanding that the United States and Canada would allow Japan to fish in waters proximate to American coastal waters while making efforts to prevent Japan from entering selected, valuable North American fisheries, namely salmon, halibut, and herring. Thus, Japan would be able to develop an export market and provide for domestic consumption needs without having a directly adverse affect on valuable North American fisheries. While this oceans regime did not permit the total exclusion of Japan from such fisheries, the North American delegations pressured the Japanese to adopt some voluntary measures to reserve these stocks for Canadian and American exploitation. Perhaps owing to Japan's role in the negotiations as a vanquished nation, the Ministry of Foreign Affairs and the Ministry of Agriculture, Forestry and Fisheries agreed to a compromise whereby an abstention principle would be applied to Japanese fishers alone. Although the adoption of such a restriction may have seemed severe in terms of Japan's prewar experience (i.e., relatively unrestrained access to high seas fisheries), the agreement nonetheless opened up a vast fishing area beyond the diminutive zone authorized up to 1951 (see Figure 4.2).

The resulting agreement, known as the International Convention for the High Seas Fisheries of the North Pacific Ocean (hereafter the International North Pacific Fisheries Convention) was finally signed on 9 May 1952 and came into effect on 12 June 1953. The convention contained three important provisions. First, support for freedom of the high seas was included in the preamble in accordance with Japan's wishes (INPFC 1990). Second, the abstention principle was adopted in full but included in the appendix of the treaty. While not readily apparent, this section served as the operating basis for the new treaty. The Japanese in effect agreed not to fish herring, salmon, and halibut east of an Abstention Line demarcated at longitude 175°W (see Figure 4.2). Finally, the agreement established a supervisory organization, the International North Pacific Fisheries Commission (INPFC), to provide an annual trilateral forum, to coordinate dialogue, and to supervise biological studies on designated stocks.[5]

The International North Pacific Fisheries Convention, 1953-75
The International North Pacific Fisheries Convention (INPFC) established a regime that permitted the expansion of high seas fisheries activities in the North Pacific while protecting North American industry interests with respect to salmon, halibut, and herring. The immediate effect of the

convention was an end to the system of restrictions on Japanese fisheries, including the MacArthur Line, entitling Japanese fishers to operate in both the eastern and western portions of the North Pacific high seas. Japanese fishing companies vigorously expanded their fish catch after 1952 and the country soon regained its former status as the foremost fishing nation in the world. Total fish catch increased from 4.8 million metric tons in 1952 to 6.9 million metric tons in 1962 – nearly 15 percent of the world's total (Food and Agriculture Organization 1965, a-30, a-31). In the North Pacific,[6] pollack, salmon, squid, herring, sardines, whale, and crab fisheries, among others, became important food sources for the Japanese market.

Moreover, the adoption of new technologies and techniques enhanced the productivity of Japan's high seas fishing fleets. The introduction of sonar devices increased the efficiency with which they could locate and track schools of fish. While mother ship operations continued to be the dominant form of high seas fisheries until the 1960s, the new fishing technique of drift netting was increasingly adopted after 1952 and proved to be highly cost-effective. As a form of gill net that was allowed to drift in ocean tideways, drift nets were widely used because they did not require fuel to function and their vast size, at times as much as sixty kilometres long and fifteen metres deep, permitted a sizeable catch with little effort (Johnston 1990, 6). While drift nets were a particularly destructive and indiscriminate form of capture – frequently referred to as a "curtain of death" – they also enabled the Japanese high seas fisheries to rapidly expand their overall fish catch.

Despite adherence to limited abstention from certain species in the Northeast Pacific, Japanese fishing activities in this area, particularly of salmon, continued to expand. After a period of contentious fisheries relations, the Japanese managed to conclude bilateral fisheries agreements with both the USSR in 1956 and South Korea in 1965. While neither convention applied the abstention principle so feared by Japanese negotiators, Japanese fishing fleets were in no way guaranteed access to fisheries near either the Soviet or Korean coastlines. The two agreements provided an annual bilateral determination of quotas whereby the Soviet Union and South Korea sold access permits to Japanese fishers and vice versa, but reserved the right to unilaterally exclude foreign fishing from protected areas, such as Peter the Great Bay in 1957 and the entire Sea of Okhotsk during this period (Miles et al. 1982, 95). Nonetheless, the Japanese high seas fisheries were entitled to catch a vast amount of salmon and other species that were previously the exclusive preserve of coastal states.

In fact, notwithstanding various restrictions and limitations placed upon the high seas fleets in the Northeast and Northwest Pacific, Japan's total salmon catches between 1955 and 1961 were larger than those of the

United States, and in some years larger than the combined catch of the US and Canada (INPFC 1979, 20). A 1973 study conducted by Hiroshi Kasahara and William Burke concluded that in spite of the numerous international agreements governing the North Pacific fisheries, including the International North Pacific Fisheries Convention, more than 90 percent of fish stocks remained unregulated (Kasahara and Burke 1973, 43). Consequently, freedom of the high seas still prevailed in both principle and practice throughout most of the North Pacific.

The high seas fisheries, particularly those operating in the North Pacific, grew in importance relative to domestic fisheries as well as in terms of overall fish harvests. As indicated in Figure 4.3, distant-water fisheries surpassed inshore production in 1966 and, finally, offshore production in 1968. By 1975 Japan's North Pacific fisheries harvested 8,729,626 metric tons of fish, which amounted to 83 percent of overall Japanese production (Food and Agriculture Organization 1977, 4, 220, 222). Of this amount, 88 percent was harvested west of the Abstention Line in the Western Bering Sea, and near the Sea of Okhotsk and Kamchatka.

Thus, the North Pacific was a very important source of fish supply for domestic Japanese consumption. Moreover, while the convention may have protected valuable North American salmon fisheries from Japanese competition in the Northeast Pacific, it did not restrict catch levels and failed to regulate other commercial species within the rest of its North Pacific jurisdiction. Indeed, the convention regime had a fundamental weakness in that it was allocative and not conservationist in function. As coastal states around the North Pacific became increasingly alarmed at the declining state of fish populations in the two decades after its inception, the regime was unable to adapt to meet conservationist concerns or provide the regulations and quotas necessary for protection of fish stocks. The United States and Canada were unwilling to give additional regulatory power to the INPFC because of their reluctance to surrender aspects of national sovereignty to international institutions. Instead, both countries followed the growing global trend of expanding national jurisdiction at the expense of international authority.

The Extension of National Fisheries Jurisdictions

Japan's high seas fisheries prospered under the INPFC regime in the North Pacific during the 1960s and 1970s. Drift net fishing helped increase substantially, albeit indiscriminately, the catch of squid, salmon, and herring in the mid-ocean. As indicated earlier, the high seas fishing industry surpassed both coastal and offshore fisheries production by the end of the 1960s. The total production figure for Japan in 1975, 10.5 million tons of fish, represented a 150 percent increase from 1962 records; 83 percent of that total was caught in the North Pacific, including oceans surrounding Japan (Food and Agriculture Organization 1977, c-61, c-67). Consequently, Japan favoured the continuation of the freedom of the seas status quo as it entered into its third decade of the INPFC regime. In the last twenty-five years or so, however, a number of developments involving new approaches to oceans law and regulation conspired against Japan's increased access to living ocean resources.

The United Nations Conference on the Law of the Sea and the Enclosure Movement

After years of academic debate, the United Nations General Assembly finally decided to host a series of meetings – the United Nations Conference on the Law of the Sea (UNCLOS) – to codify the law of the seas and negotiate a new legal standard to reconcile the conservation concerns of coastal states with the right to open access to ocean resources. These UNCLOS sessions reflected a movement to protect coastal fisheries that was gaining momentum around the world. Within the North Pacific, as in other oceans worldwide, coastal states were becoming increasingly alarmed at the mounting evidence of overfishing and other forms of resource depletion, which brought to an end any belief in the age-old Grotian premise of the inexhaustibility of the oceans. Correspondingly, coastal states united in an enclosure movement to bring contiguous fishing

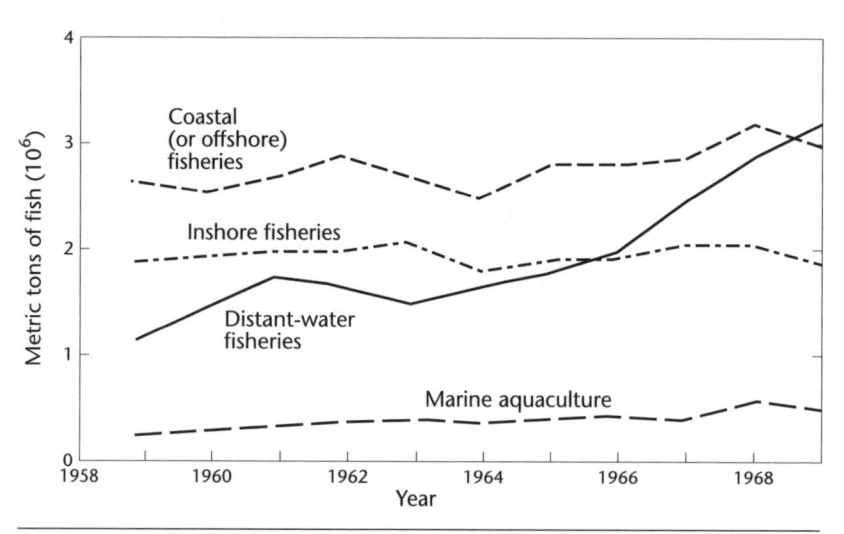

Figure 4.3

Production in four sectors of the Japanese fishing industry, 1959-69

Source: Based on data contained in Kasahara and Burke 1973.

areas under national sovereign control in the interest of more effective management and economic potential. By 1974 thirty-three nations declared extended fisheries jurisdiction beyond twelve nautical miles (about nineteen kilometres), but their declarations were not yet recognized in international law or custom (Eckert 1979, 129).

As UNCLOS launched into its third round of talks in 1973, the Japanese government recognized that it needed to address the increasingly influential enclosure movement. The simple advocacy of general freedom of the high seas would no longer suffice to counter coastal states' claims of extended jurisdiction. It became apparent at the first procedural session, held in New York in 1973, that special exclusive economic zones (EEZs) concerning coastal control of fisheries and other natural resources would dominate the forthcoming debate. In a talk to the Japan Press Club in May 1974, Director-General Shinichi Sugihara of the Japanese Foreign Ministry's Office for the Law of the Sea Conference declared that the government should abandon opposition to the 200-mile zones (about 320 kilometres). Instead, it should discuss the options for Japan to adopt its own economic zone (*Nihon Keizai Shinbun*, 29 May 1974). The ministry was particularly concerned that opposition to the adoption of EEZs by such states as China, Korea, or the Soviet Union might impinge upon Japan's control of its own coastal resources vis-à-vis foreign fleets.

The Japanese high seas fishing industry firmly opposed such an idea, however, and pressured the Fishery Agency of the Ministry of Agriculture, Forestry and Fisheries (MAFF) to resist the Foreign Ministry proposal. Consequently, the Japanese delegation to UNCLOS III, which consisted of officials from both ministries, remained split with regard to exclusive economic zones as it entered the Caracas negotiations in 1974. Although no convention text was entirely agreed upon at Caracas, the 200-mile EEZ concept was widely supported, most notably by the United States. Hereafter, the Japanese Fisheries Association and MAFF elected to reassess their policy in light of Japan's isolation regarding the fishery zone issue. The fishing industry abandoned its opposition to coastal states' extended jurisdiction in favour of advocacy of Japan's traditional fishing rights (Suisankai 1975, 93-94). In subsequent UNCLOS III negotiations, the Foreign Ministry and MAFF argued that living resources were the "common heritage of mankind," even if found within the 200-mile EEZs. Therefore, long-standing fishing countries such as Japan should enjoy access privileges based on traditional rights notwithstanding the new sovereign rights of coastal states (Ouchi 1978, 121). Moreover, the Japanese delegates argued that coastal states were no more capable of conservation or management of living resources than fishing states. Consequently, international organizations, such as the INPFC, should be strengthened and entrusted with such responsibilities.

Unilateral Enclosure in the North Pacific

Meanwhile, another significant development prompted the Japanese government to reconsider its ocean policy alternatives. As a result of the widespread acceptance of EEZs at the UNCLOS meetings, the United States passed the Fishery Conservation and Management Act in 1976 to establish its own 200-mile fishery conservation zone. This represented a reversal of US policy regarding freedom of the seas. Previously, Washington adhered to the principle of *mare liberum* to enable the free navigation of its vessels, largely for security concerns. This policy was finally relinquished in favour of protecting the 62 percent of fish species that were "fully utilized" or "overfished" within 200 miles of the American coastline, mostly in the Atlantic Ocean (Eckert 1979, 134). Washington was no longer willing to compromise domestic fishing interests in favour of Cold War policy, which included bolstering its key Asian ally, Japan.

The Soviet Union soon followed suit with the declaration of its own 200-mile fishing zone in December of the same year (Jackson and Royce 1986, 149). Finally, Canada announced its intention to establish a fishing conservation area of the same proportions effective 1 January 1977 (Johnson 1977, 88). Consequently, many of Japan's most valuable fishing areas in the North Pacific were unilaterally appropriated under national control by the beginning of 1977.

Japan was reluctant to declare its own fisheries zone for fear of implicitly sanctioning the unilateral declarations of EEZs that deprived it of many of its international fishing areas. The threat of an extended Soviet fishing area, however, prompted domestic fishing interests, particularly in Northern Japan, to defend their own coastal fisheries from the encroachment of Soviet fishers with the establishment of a counter fisheries jurisdiction (Yanai and Asomura 1977, 72-73). The Japanese Diet passed two laws, the Law of the Territorial Sea and the Law on Provisional Measures Relating to the Fishing Zone, that established a 12-mile territorial sea and 200-mile fishing area on Japan's eastern and northern coasts, effective 1 July 1977. It is worth noting that the fishing zone did not extend into waters contiguous to Korea or China since neither country claimed such zones at this time and the Japanese government wished to maintain the status quo in their fishery relations (Yanai and Asomura 1977, 74).

The US-led declaration of EEZs displaced the earlier INPFC multilateral arrangement in the North Pacific. Since most fisheries now fell under national jurisdictions, the 200-mile extensions deprived the INPFC of regulatory control over all fisheries with the exception of salmon. Under the renegotiated 1977 International North Pacific Fisheries Convention, a new Abstention Line was demarcated at longitude 175°E and applied only to salmon (INPFC 1990, 8-11). With regard to access to other species, Japan was required to engage in bilateral negotiations, which it concluded with

Canada, the Soviet Union, and the United States in 1977. Although Japan was entitled to stocks deemed surplus from coastal state catch quotas, its allocation diminished considerably over the next decade (Aoki 1976, 31-56). While the INPFC continued to conduct scientific surveys and monitor the Abstention Line until 1993, and continues to operate under the new name of the North Pacific Anadromous Fisheries Commission (NPAFC), it has never been vested with the powers necessary to enforce regional conservation measures.

The shift in resource regimes illustrates the catalytic role played by the United States in establishing customary international law in the postwar period. The US legitimized a global legal standard concerning resource use through sponsorship of the INPFC, and brought about the end of this system with the inauguration of the EEZ regime. In both cases, the US set an unchallenged precedent for other nations to follow, which may be a measure of its hegemonic leadership role.

As a result of this enclosure movement, Japan's high seas fisheries were deprived of a significant share of their traditional source of fish. According to catch statistics for 1975, close to 2.8 million tons of production fell within the United States's and USSR's exclusive economic zones – 27 percent of Japan's total catch (Yanai and Asomura 1977, 73). Moreover, almost half of Japan's total catch came from fisheries that fell within the 200-mile zones of other states, and 90 percent of this amount originated in the North Pacific (Johnson and Langdon 1976, 15). Thus, Japan lost much of the free access to living resources it was once guaranteed under the old regime of *mare liberum* and narrow territorial seas.

Domestic fisheries, on the other hand, gained substantially with the new exclusive economic zone. Japan's own fisheries jurisdiction expanded to nearly 376 square kilometres of ocean space, or fifty times as large an area as it controlled under the three-mile territorial sea rule (Food and Agriculture Organization 1984, 102). This resulted in a significant shift from high seas to coastal and offshore production. On balance, the new regime turned Japan into a net importer of fishery products at a real-term cost that has been increasing yearly since the mid-1970s. Thus, the dollar value of imports increased a drastic fifteen times up to the mid-1990s (see Figure 4.4), with a sharp rise in cost notable since 1986. This switch to importation is reflected in how Japan's two largest high seas fishing companies, Taiyō Gyogyō and Nippon Suisan, have diversified into other ventures and have essentially become import companies that have maintained some interests in domestic fish farming (marine aquaculture).

Drift Net Bans and the Whaling Issue
This section attempts to bring the account of Japan's North Pacific fisheries into the contemporary period with a brief consideration of two important

issues, drift net fishing and whaling on the high seas. After the inauguration of the EEZ regime, Japanese vessels continued to operate in the North Pacific outside the 200 nautical miles of both the Soviet and US zones in search of highly valued salmon and squid stocks. These vessels mostly utilized drift nets, which were a ruthless yet effective way to catch vast quantities of targeted fish, not to mention a high percentage of by-catch (e.g., seabirds and other creatures such as dolphins), at very little cost and effort. By the late 1980s, however, these fisheries also came under international scrutiny and pressure, so that by 1992 the Japanese government voluntarily banned drift net fisheries. This was another blow to an already dwindling high seas fishing industry (United Nations General Assembly 1998, 3).

As a result of the lobbying efforts of environmental nongovernmental organizations (NGOs), such as Earthwatch and Greenpeace, and Alaskan fishing interests, the US government passed its first piece of legislation concerning drift net fishing, the Driftnet Impact Monitoring, Assessment, and Control Act, in 1987. Lobbyists not only focused on the extensive

Figure 4.4

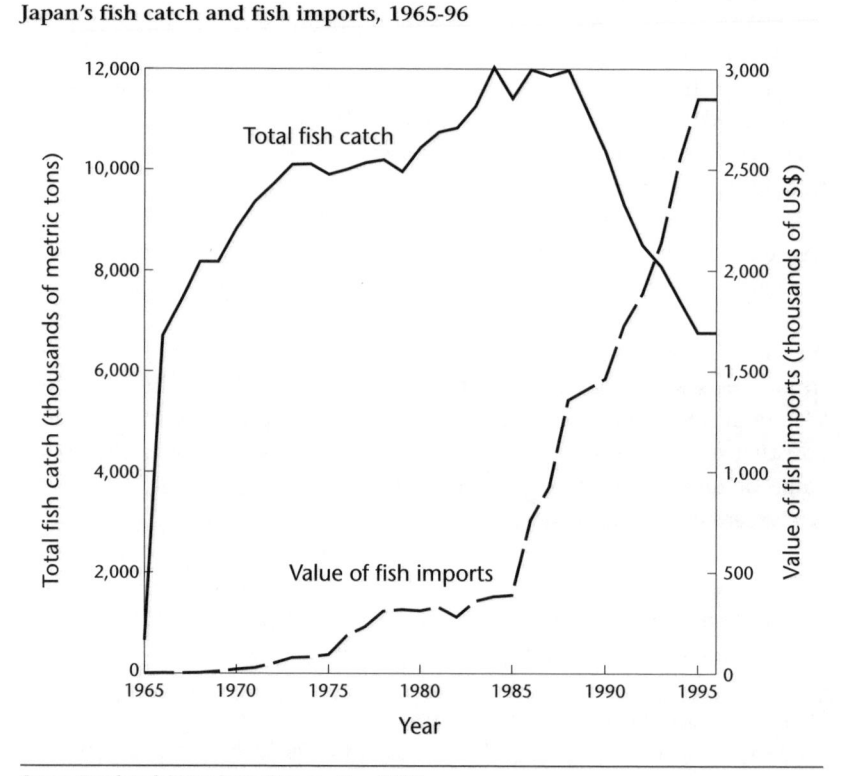

Japan's fish catch and fish imports, 1965-96

Source: Food and Agriculture Organization 1999.

environmental impact on mammals and seabirds but also claimed that alarming amounts of salmon were being captured in squid drift nets (Paul 1994, 5). The act was designed to allow the Secretary of State and the Department of Commerce to negotiate observer and enforcement programs for Bering Sea fisheries. It may be mentioned that this law was passed in spite of the INPFC's existing scientific mandate to permit observers on Japanese vessels, which suggests that the US placed little faith in the INPFC's monitoring or conservation capability.

The Commerce Department stepped up pressure to end the use of drift nets by issuing a regulation on 18 September 1991 stating that "fish taken with driftnets on the high seas will be banned from sale in the United States after July 1, 1992." This was done largely in response to the popular Dolphin Protection Consumer Information Act of 1990, but was also intended to protect valuable Bering Sea salmon stocks that were threatened by Japanese drift net fisheries (Gillnet Fishing Treaty 1997, 2). It provided a strong economic tool with which to enforce compliance with American wishes. The international community also stepped up pressure by supporting a ban on drift net fisheries. On 22 December 1989, the General Assembly passed UN resolution 44/225, later reaffirmed by UN resolution 46/215, that called for a 50 percent reduction of all drift net fleets by 30 June 1992 as well as penalties for countries that did not comply (United Nations General Assembly 1998, 1-3).

Japan responded to these foreign pressures by adopting a voluntary ban on drift net use. As of 31 December 1992, no more fishing licences were issued to drift net vessels. Although the government offered various compensation packages to adversely affected fishers, they were not given licences in other fisheries since most were already operating at full capacity. As a result, some fishers sold their equipment and boats overseas, mostly to companies in Taiwan and China. Others reportedly now operate under the flags of other nations although the owners remain Japanese. The ban on drift nets was a devastating blow to the remaining squid and salmon trawlers that Japan operated in the North Pacific. In their place, Chinese, Taiwanese, Korean, and other vessels continue to use drift nets illegally in an effort to catch valuable salmon and other species to fill the gap left in the Japanese market (Paul 1994, 5-6). In some ways, the problem has not changed, only the perpetrators.

Whaling is also an issue that has aroused considerable consternation in Japan and the ire of conservationists worldwide. This issue is important to the Japanese because it serves as a symbol of the kind of threat that unbridled conservationism may pose to all of Japan's future fisheries. It is feared that if other world fisheries achieve the notoriety and sympathy for protection that whales have, they too may be closed, never to reopen, much as the whaling fishery (Nagasaki 1994, 2).

Japan views its fight in the International Whaling Commission (IWC) to permit some harvesting as a fight for principle. What is at stake is not culture or the viability of small fishing villages, as Japanese representatives at the IWC frequently and unconvincingly assert, but the principle of "wise use," as the Fishery Agency calls it. Japan argues that the operating philosophy of the IWC is to manage an exploitable renewable resource through harvest allocations. Levels should be adjusted according to scientific evidence: to ban whaling when a species population is deemed endangered and to permit harvests when a stock has returned to healthy levels, which the Japanese argue is true for minke whales (Ministry of Foreign Affairs 1999). Japan feels, however, that the IWC has adopted only the philosophy of "non-use" and a system of irreversible moratoriums. It fears that this trend towards protection will not be reversed even if scientific evidence proves the return of healthy stocks.

In the case of both drift nets and whaling, the Japanese tend to see themselves as the victims of North American environmentalism. In neither case has there been the kind of popular support or sentiment in Japan that was present in North America and Europe, and that led to these bans. Much like the imposition of 200-mile fishery zones, it was external rather than internal pressure that brought about readjustments that dislocated fishing communities and tended to hurt Japan's international reputation. As a result, the Japanese tend to view foreign conservationists as a new enemy and as a serious threat to their traditional way of life (Nagasaki 1994).

Conclusions
The aim of this chapter has been to examine Japan's high seas fisheries in the twentieth century to illustrate a much larger theme of Japan's perennial struggle to secure access to natural resources. This struggle was sometimes facilitated, sometimes inhibited by the international system. In the beginning of the twentieth century, the international system provided an essential pretext for the uninhibited expansion of fishing on the high seas and colonial procurement on land. Although formalized colonialism was shattered with the defeat of Japan in the Second World War, *mare liberum* continued as part of a US-sponsored international system that was predicated on its Cold War strategy to rebuild Japan and coerce Japan's cooperation with the mutual defence agreement. Thus, the international system helped facilitate Japan's attempt to secure self-sufficiency in fish and other natural resources for most of this century.

This relatively unencumbered regime was severely restricted by the UNCLOS enclosures, and even further controls are likely in the future. Hence, in the twenty-first century, Japan must find a way to secure a stable supply of fisheries and agricultural products in the midst of a changing international framework, one that may be prone to disruption and realignment. Resource scarcity caused by environmental change and a growing world population will make this quest even more difficult.

While the twentieth century may serve as a useful example of Japan's efforts to provide for its food needs, the present century cannot be premised upon the same *mare liberum* regime that permitted unrestricted access for most of the past 100 years. Following the introduction of economic exclusion zones in 1976, Japan has been deprived of an important domestic source of food production. While Japan's coastal fisheries have expanded in size as a result of the new system, the overwhelming importance of high seas fishing to overall supply has meant that fish production has dropped and Japan has steadily become more reliant upon imports (Figure 4.4). This has had a negative impact on its self-sufficiency rate and serves as an example of the way the international system may inhibit Japan's domestic goals. Meanwhile, Japan's overall domestic production has been declining since it peaked in 1984, and at the end of the 1990s had fallen to early 1960s levels (Figure 4.4). The increase in the value of imports versus a declining value of domestic production has meant a steadily falling level of self-sufficiency in fisheries and a rising dependence upon foreign imports, most significantly from China, for an important protein supply. Japan's self-sufficiency rate for fish meat was a mere 56 percent in 1996, and for food in general (by calories) only 42 percent, the lowest among industrialized countries. The implications of this declining self-sufficiency rate for fish and other food products will be discussed in the concluding section, which deals with the challenges of the new century. The story of the high seas fisheries, therefore, typifies a disturbing trend in which Japan is losing self-sufficiency and potentially the ability to feed itself in a whole range of food sources (see Figure 4.5).

Challenges of the Twenty-First Century

Since the mid-1980s, Japan has arduously searched for alternative sources for its fisheries and access to other foodstuffs. As an island country poorly endowed with cultivatable land and burdened with a population that more than tripled in the last century, Japan has become highly dependent upon other countries to provide agricultural and fisheries products through trade. How to offset this dependence through greater domestic production or to minimize risk through stable trading regimes remains one of the great challenges for Japanese policy makers in the twenty-first century, one made more difficult in a world of dwindling natural resources and expanding populations. This concern is reflected in the 70 percent of Japanese who say they are worried about Japan's future food situation (Ministry of Agriculture, Forestry and Fisheries 1998, 7). Presumably, domestic production will continue to be an important goal in the effort to guarantee a reliable supply of essential foodstuffs and to offset anxieties over resource security. In this sense, Japan's experience in the twentieth century may provide guidance in the new millennium.

The Japanese demand for a stable food supply will intensify in this century as population, agricultural, environmental, and energy problems emerge to make securing a stable food supply even more difficult. In terms of fisheries, several factors may either diminish or enhance vulnerability of food supply regardless of which system of procurement is adopted. First, the basis of the security threat may be questioned. Although 50 percent of fish consumed is currently imported, this is due to the expensive tastes of Japanese consumers; tastes that can change in case of need. This may suggest that the self-sufficiency rate is underestimated. Moreover, Japan has a diverse supply of fish that, in an emergency, can meet most needs through domestic catches in coastal waters and a wide variety of trading partners from around the world. Lastly, the threat posed by diminishing world fish supply may be overstated in light of advances in fish farming. Cultivation

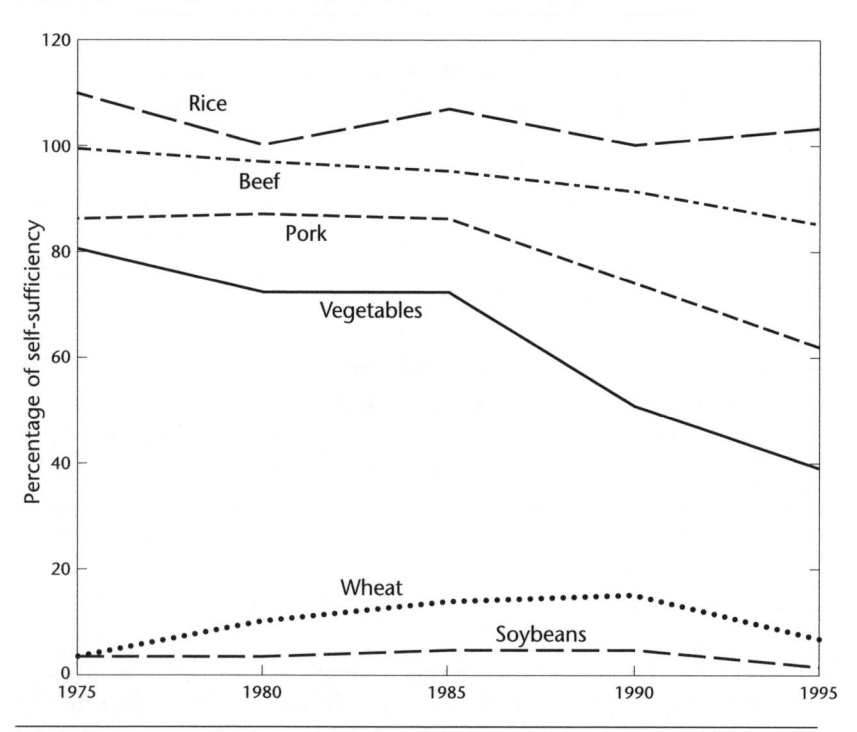

Figure 4.5

Japan's percentage of self-sufficiency in selected foods, 1975-95

Source: Based on data contained in Section 2-6, Ministry of Agriculture, Forestry and Fisheries 1999.

techniques for a variety of fish may produce an alternative supply for domestic production and remedy the problem of declining catches in the high seas.

Several other factors may increase Japan's vulnerability in this century, however. The first is related to the serious depletion of fisheries resources. Japan's most serious concern is that declining world fish stocks will eventually lead to a rise in prices that will seriously impact the country's food balance sheet and import costs. In addition, it is doubtful that Japan can truly meet its vast appetite with fish caught strictly within its 200-mile zone, since evidence suggests that many stocks are dangerously depleted and cannot sustain a sizeable, prolonged fishery. Parts of these waters are also fished by Korean and Chinese trawlers that compete directly for dwindling stocks with Japanese vessels. Moreover, Japan's domestic fishing industry is shrinking due to a small replacement rate for participants as fishers grow older and retire and the younger generation seeks work elsewhere.[7]

The worldwide spread of environmentalism and increasing concern for ocean resources, typified by the whaling controversy, may lead to the closure of even more fisheries.[8] Japan will have to fight for access to a resource that may be considered precious less in terms of money than in the interest of biological diversity. Meanwhile, rising environmental consciousness in Japan may also challenge the heretofore unquestioned practices of its fisheries, which may be a serious blow to an industry largely unscrutinized by its own consumers (Kawasaki 2000). Lastly, Japan must be prepared to face an uncertain political situation in East Asia, one that may even disrupt trade flows. This may be especially serious considering the magnitude of food imports that originate from China, a country traditionally antagonistic to Japan's interests. Difficulties may also arise if there is either a significant change in the international system, similar to the development of UNCLOS and the start of the 200 nautical mile economic exclusion zones. Problems may also result from a significant realignment of interstate relations, similar to Korea's switch from a colonial possession that once provided a significant supply of ocean resources into an independent country that is at times hostile to Japanese fishing activities.

Acknowledgments

I wish to thank several people for their assistance with this chapter. First of all, David W. Edgington provided sound editorial advice, support, and intellectual critique that served as a beacon to guide me through uncharted waters. Drs. Steve Lee, Bill Wray, and Diana Lary at the University of British Columbia and Kazutoshi Kase at Tokyo University offered valuable supervision and guidance in the course of this study. I also benefited a great deal from the conversations and commentary of a fellow Koerners (UBC graduate student pub) mariner, Colin Green, and the Koerners history crew.

Special thanks go to the Takase Foundation for their generous funding, which enabled me to travel to Japan for further research and made this study possible. Finally, Dr. Peter

Oblas at Tokyo University of Foreign Studies and Drs. Masao Nakamura, Keizo Nagatani, and Terry McGee at the Institute of Asian Research, UBC, were helpful with their inspiration and access to their research facilities.

Notes

1 The warm Kuroshio sea current surrounding Japan is largely responsible for providing the greatest source of diverse and plentiful fish species despite the country's relatively short fishing banks.
2 In 1949, SCAP spent 45 percent of its $515 million relief funds on food (Esterly 1980, 94).
3 This figure is based upon a consumption of approximately 1,900 calories per day out of an adult requirement of 2,250 calories per day.
4 In order to extend Japanese fisheries activities, the Japanese government first had to alleviate fears that Japan might once again ruthlessly overexploit common fisheries resources, and to demonstrate itself as an internationally responsible nation. In order to do this, the Japanese government sent the Yoshida Declaration to SCAP and various government missions announced Japan's willingness to abide by worldwide conservation standards and agreements regarding ocean resources. Accordingly, Japan joined the International Convention for the Regulation of Whaling in April 1951. Furthermore, the threat of overfishing in the authorized area also prompted Tokyo to make better use of available resources through more rigorous conservation measures beginning in 1950. Japan's first fisheries conservation law, the Law for the Prevention of the Exhaustion of Marine Resources, was enacted on 1 May 1950 to restrict catch rates within the MacArthur Line. This is not to say, however, that the Japanese hereafter adopted the "maximum sustainable yield" concept as a new operative management principle for all fisheries. The law was primarily designed as an ad hoc arrangement to mitigate an impending ecological crisis in the authorized zone. Japan sought to preserve the system of freedom of the seas by accepting voluntary constraints in the interest of conservation. The promotion of sound resource management principles also had important political implications for Japan. Most of the worldwide opposition to Japanese high seas fisheries – including American, Canadian, and Australian fishing industries – stemmed from Japan's previous lack of appropriate conservation practices. Tokyo's voluntary compliance with international standards, however, provided a reasonable justification for SCAP to permit an extended fisheries area for Japan. Hereafter, both Washington and Tokyo felt that an extension of Japan's fishing areas could best be accomplished through a multilateral agreement that set out rights and rules governing access and conservation in the North Pacific (Ministry of Foreign Affairs, Japan, n.d.)
5 Unlike several other extant fisheries organizations, such as the International Whaling Commission, the INPFC was relatively decentralized in its operations. It did not formulate quotas, could not enforce decisions upon its members, and did not have a formal dispute resolution process. While the INPFC supervised scientific studies of fish stocks and regularly employed conservationist language at annual meetings, it was not a resource conservation regime. Allocation of salmon, herring, and halibut was its effective function, not the management of environmental sustainability. Conservation considerations were the voluntary responsibility of each national government. The most important role of the INPFC was to reopen the North Pacific to Japanese fishing in the postwar era.
6 Both the Northeast and Northwest Pacific.
7 One may also question the basis of Japan's changing consumption habits and the credibility of fish farming as an alternative supply. While Japan has seen a rapid increase in the consumption of beef, pork, and chicken in the past twenty years, fish still remains the most important category of consumed meat, and will likely continue to be so in this century. Meat of all varieties excluding fish was consumed at a rate of 31.3 kilograms per person in 1996, while fish consumption was 38.2 kilograms per person. Fish consumption has increased 9 percent while the consumption of other meats has increased by 43 percent since 1975 (Ministry of Agriculture, Forestry and Fisheries 1999).
8 At present Japan remains relatively untouched by the environmental movement that has

so profoundly influenced other developed countries. Moreover, the Japanese tend to misinterpret this shift in values in other countries as a product of national policy rather than a grassroots concern for the future condition of global resources such as whales. They appear to have discounted the possibility that environmentalists might be motivated not only by nationality but also by a desire to protect the natural environment. Indeed, the natural-resource-based business community and environmentalists in North America and Europe have learned how to negotiate and accommodate each other's concerns with a remarkable degree of sophistication, a degree that is not reflected in the simplistic coverage by news sources or Japanese fisheries advocates. In this century, Japan too will need to accommodate rather than vilify environmental groups, especially as these will likely become more influential as resources become even scarcer.

References
Ackerman, E. 1953. *Japan's Natural Resources and Their Relation to Japan's Economic Future.* Chicago: University of Chicago Press.
Akaha, T. 1985. *Japan in Global Ocean Politics.* Honolulu: University of Hawaii Press.
Aoki, H. 1976. "200 Kairi to Nihon no Gyogyō: Beikoku Oyobi Soren no Tainichi Gyokaku Wariate o Chushin ni Shite" (200-Mile EEZs [Exclusive Economic Zones] and Japanese Fisheries: A Focus on Japanese Fishing Quotas by the United States and the Soviet Union). *Kokusai Mondai* 201: 15-25.
Baty, T. 1928. "The Three-Mile Limit." *American Journal of International Law* 22: 503-37.
Department of State, USA. 1945-55. *Foreign Relations of the United States.* Washington, DC: Department of State.
Eckert, R. 1979. *The Enclosure of Ocean Resources: Economics and the Law of the Sea.* Stanford, CA: Hoover Institution Press.
Espenshade, A. 1946. *Japanese Fisheries Production, 1908-46.* SCAP Natural Resources Section Report 95. Tokyo: Supreme Commander for the Allied Powers (cited in Ackerman 1953).
Esterly, H. 1980. "Overseas Fisheries and International Politics in the Occupation of Japan, 1945-1952." In L. Redford, ed., *The Occupation of Japan: Economic Policy and Reform.* Norfolk, VA: MacArthur Memorial, 92-123.
Food and Agriculture Organization (FAO). 1965-84. *Yearbook of Fishery Statistics.* Rome: Food and Agriculture Organization of the United Nations.
–. 1973. *Relative Importance of Trade in Fishery Products.* Rome: Food and Agriculture Organization of the United Nations.
–. 1999. FAOSTAT Fisheries Database. <http://apps.fao.org/egi-bin/nph-dp.pl?subset=fisheries>, accessed January 2000.
Gillnet Fishing Treaty. 1997. <http://www.american.edu/projects/mandala/TED/GILLNET.HTM>, accessed January 2000.
International North Pacific Fisheries Commission (INPFC). 1979. *Historical Catch Statistics for Salmon of the North Pacific Ocean.* Bulletin 39. Vancouver: INPFC.
–. 1990. *International North Pacific Fisheries Commission Handbook.* Vancouver: INPFC.
Jackson, R., and W. Royce. 1986. *Ocean Forum: An Interpretive History of the International North Pacific Fisheries Commission.* Farnham, VA: Fishing News Books.
Johnson, B. 1977. "Canadian Foreign Policy and Fisheries." In B. Johnson and M. Zacher, eds., *Canadian Foreign Policy and the Law of the Sea.* Vancouver: UBC Press, 52-99.
Johnson, B., and F. Langdon. 1976. "Two Hundred Mile Zones: The Politics of North Pacific Fisheries." *Pacific Affairs* 49: 5-27.
Johnson, D. 1965. *The International Law of Fisheries.* New Haven, CT: Yale University Press.
Johnston, D.M. 1990. "The Driftnetting Problem in the Pacific Ocean: Legal Considerations and Diplomatic Options." *Ocean Development and International Law* 21: 5-40.
Kasahara, H., and W. Burke. 1973. *North Pacific Fisheries Management.* Washington, DC: Resources for the Future.
Kawasaki, T. 2000. *Gyogyō Shigen: Naze Kanri Dekinai no Ka* (Why are fisheries resources surrounded by conflict?). Tokyo: Seizando.

Leonard, L. 1944. *International Regulation of Fisheries*. Washington, DC: Carnegie Endowment for International Peace.
Miles, E. 1982. *The Management of Marine Regions: The North Pacific*. Berkeley: University of California Press.
Ministry of Agriculture, Forestry and Fisheries, Japan. 1998. "Report Submitted to the Prime Minister's Office by the Investigative Council on Basic Problems Concerning Food, Agriculture, and Rural Areas." <http://www.maff.go.go.jp/ekihon/Report.html>, accessed January 2000.
–. 1999. "Abstract of Statistics on Agriculture, Forestry and Fisheries." <http://www.maff.go.jp/abst/form2/6ab/81A.html>, accessed January 2000.
Ministry of Foreign Affairs, Japan. n.d. "Kitataiheiyō no Kōkaigyogyō ni Kansuru Kokusai-jōyaku Kankei Ikken" (International treaties concerned with high seas fishing in the North Pacific). Microfilm Series B'0039.
–. 1951. *Tripartite Fisheries Conference, Tokyo, Japan, 1951*. Tokyo: Ministry of Foreign Affairs.
–. 1999. *Japan and the Management of Whales*. Tokyo: Ministry of Foreign Affairs. <http://www.mofa.go.jp/policy/economy/fishery/whales/index.html>, accessed January 2000.
Nagasaki, F. 1994. *Fisheries and Environmentalism*. Tokyo: Institute for Cetacean Research.
Niwa, A. 1957. *Japanese Fisheries: Their Development and Present Status*. Tokyo: Asia Kyokai.
Ouchi, K. 1978. "A Perspective on Japan's Struggle for Its Traditional Rights of the Ocean." *Ocean Development and International Law* 5: 107-34.
Pacific Fisherman. Various years. Seattle, WA: Miller Freeman Publications.
Paul, L. 1994. "The Impact of Driftnet Fishing on Sustainable Fisheries." In *High Seas Driftnetting: The Plunder of the Global Commons*. Kailua, HI: Earthtrust. <http://www.earthtrust.org/dnpaper/contents.html>, accessed January 2000.
Suisankai (Japanese Fisheries Association). 1975. "Chōki Shokuryō no Ikkan de Kakuritsu o: Kaiyōhō e Gyōkai Hōshin, Jisseki Kakuho no Sesshō nado Sanken" (Toward the settlement of Japanese long-term food requirements: the Japanese fishing industry will participate in negotiations and change its policy to accord with the Law of the Sea). 1084: 93-94 (cited in Akaha 1985).
Sweeney, R.J., R. Tollison, and T. Willet. 1974. "Market Failure, the Common-Pool Problem, and Ocean Resource Exploitation." *Journal of Law and Economics* 17: 179-92.
Yanai, S., and K. Asomura. 1977. "Japan and the Emerging Order of the Seas: Two Maritime Laws of Japan." *Japanese Annual of International Law* (21): 48-114.
Young, O. 1982. *Resource Regimes: Natural Resources and Social Institutions*. Berkeley: University of California Press.
United Nations General Assembly. 1998. *Report of the Secretary General on Large-Scale Pelagic Drift-Net Fishing, Unauthorized Fishing in Zones of National Jurisdiction and on the High Seas, Fisheries By-Catch and Discards, and Other Developments*. New York: United Nations.

Part 2
Japan's Identity and Youth

Part 2 consists of essays on selected issues related to Japanese identity and Japanese youth. These two themes are related as each author reflects upon how the memory of the past impacts upon contemporary society and culture in Japan. Following Morris-Suzuki (1998), identity is treated here at two different levels of scale.

To begin with, the identity of any nation, including Japan, is to a degree shaped by its contact with the outside world. In this light, many scholars have commented on the evolution of the China-Japan relationship (Howe 1996). Indeed, Japan's relationship with China is now an important component of its interactions with the Asia-Pacific region. For instance, China-Japan trade reached a record high in the opening year of the new millennium (2001), and as an export market for Japan, China now trails only the United States (*Japan Times Online* 2001). More and more Japanese firms are setting up factories in China, attracted by cheaper labour and other inputs (Cheung and Wong 2000). This trend reflects the working out of the so-called "flying geese model" of East Asian development, propounded by Japanese economist Akamatsu Kaname during the 1930s and 1940s (Akamatsu 1962). At the same time, however, it would be a mistake to portray Sino-Japanese relations as exclusively positive. The twenty-year period since 1978 saw rapid expansion of economic and political cooperation but it also gave rise to periodic conflicts (Zhao 1999). In the eyes of some analysts, this rapid expansion of cooperation belies a profound and underlying tension in the relationship, one that is rooted deeply in both culture and history. For example, animosity has occurred due to the reversal of roles between China and Japan as the natural "leader" of Asia in the past 100 years, and this was further exacerbated during the 1930s by the annexation of Manchukuo (Manchuria) as a colony of Japan (Young 1998). China at this time and in the years up to 1945 became part of Japan's notorious "Greater East Asia Co-Prosperity Sphere" *(Dai Tōa Kyoeiken)* (Korhonen 1996).

In Chapter 5, Bill Sewell examines this theme and how the image of Manchuria was displayed in postwar Japanese consciousness. Although Manchuria was once considered the "breadbasket of opportunity" and the single best hope for Japanese prosperity prior to 1945, the first three decades after the Second World War saw the image of Manchuria become a distant and blurred landscape for the Japanese. Sewell's study shows that published discussions of Manchuria initially fell into three simplistic categories: pained and apologetic memoirs, subdued but proud affirmations of Japanese contributions to Chinese development, and Marxist denunciations of Japanese colonialism – the last an aspect of a larger anti-capitalist perspective evident through Japanese academia. In the 1970s, however, curiosity and a gradual warming of Sino-Japanese relations led to surreptitious Japanese visits to the Manchurian communities that had once served as prewar homes, and to the general rebuilding of contacts and friendships long neglected. Change was also apparent in academic circles, as historians increasingly challenged the perspectives of the early postwar era. This led eventually to a veritable explosion of popular interest in Manchuria during the 1980s and 1990s. For Sewell, it suggests that perhaps now, finally, under the influence of the slow but continued dissemination of experience and understanding, Japanese society is confronting the record of its activities in China before 1945 more thoroughly, something unthinkable (and because of American complicity, unnecessary) during the Cold War.

At the level of the nation-state, contemporary Japan is often characterized as a homogenized and middle-class society. Certainly, this is an image that the Japanese authorities often portray to the rest of the world (Christopher 1984, 127). Nonetheless, the reality of past and present inequality belies such an assumption (Lie 2000). Indeed, the dominant paradigm of homogeneity has been challenged by a number of studies that have sought to locate the construction of this identity within appropriate historical contexts (e.g., Siddle 1996; Weiner 1997). Between 4 and 6 percent of the Japanese population are members of minority groups, many of whom suffer considerable discrimination. The principal minority populations are the Ainu, Burakumin, Chinese, Koreans, and Okinawans, and the most recent are the Nikkeijin – the returnees from Brazil. Of these, only the Burakumin are indigenous. Both Ainu and Ryukyuan/Okinawan populations were incorporated only during the late nineteenth century (Morris-Suzuki 1998). Present-day Korean and Chinese communities are largely a consequence of Japanese imperialism during the first half of the twentieth century (Weiner 1997). Other minorities, such as Vietnamese and illegal workers from Asia, came into Japan during the "bubble economy" of the late 1980s (Douglass and Roberts 2000).

At the end of the last century, despite the country's wish to further "internationalize" and engage the global community, many challenges still faced minority people at home in Japan. Millie Creighton traces 100 years of the relationship between Japan's aboriginal people, the Ainu, and contemporary mainstream Japanese, the *Wajin*. She shows that through social, economic, and legal treatment of the Ainu in the Meiji Era, the Japanese government sought to assimilate the Ainu into a homogeneous model of Japanese society. In the decades following the Second World War, discrimination against the Ainu was strong, and corresponding attempts at denial and passing for Japanese among members of the Ainu were common. About thirty years ago, the Ainu were considered a vanishing people by many. However, the 1980s and 1990s witnessed a strong resurgence of Ainu consciousness and a positive Ainu identity movement. One focus of this movement has been the political resistance to the Nibutani Dam over the Saru River, in the heart of the world's largest concentration of Ainu dwellers. In Chapter 6, Creighton looks at this resistance and how it created a focus for the Ainu identity movement and international recognition of the Ainu as an indigenous people. Her study shows that Japan at the millennium is indeed at a crossroads in terms of the rights and recognition of indigenous and minority peoples within its society.

Images of youth culture in Japan are treated in two different ways by the next two essays. In Chapter 7, Hiroshi Aoyagi examines the images of womanhood as portrayed in the conspicuous genre of popular cultural performances known as *aidoru poppusu* or "idol-pop." Since its emergence in the late 1960s, the pop idol has been represented by a series of personalities who sing, dance, act, and are groomed by their manufacturing industries for popular consumption. Numerous images of young pop idols appear on television programs, magazines, advertisement posters, and billboards, creating an enigmatic field in which gender stereotypes are shaped and reshaped to meet public demands, tastes, and interests. Using data gathered during ethnographic fieldwork, Aoyagi looks at the performances of female pop idols in the Tokyo-based entertainment industry. He argues that these manifest an ongoing gender contest in Japanese society between dominant and resistant images of Japanese womanhood. The historical roots of this contest can be traced back to the premodern ideological debate on the appropriate image of femininity in Japan.

Aoyagi's findings echo the opinion expressed by sociologist Joyce Lebra (1976, 297), who in the 1970s reported that "the majority of women in Japan, whether married or single, cling to the traditional definition of women as 'good wife and wise mother.' There has been no fundamental questioning of this traditional ideal." However, there can be no doubt that the position of women in Japan has improved over the last fifty years.

Their standard of living is among the highest in the world. Nonetheless, Japanese women lag behind their Western counterparts in most measures used for female advancement, such as gender equity in wages or political representation (Brinton 1993). Despite the ratification of the UN Convention for the Eradication of All Forms of Discrimination Against Women in 1985, the enactment of the Equal Employment Opportunity Law in 1986, the 1991 Childcare Leave Law, and the 1998 Elderly Care Law, women remain far behind men in the workplace in terms of job status and pay. In addition, partly as a consequence of inadequate government policies relevant to working women, birth rates are dropping and the family faces unprecedented strains because of the need to provide care for the aged (Bailey 1996).

Aoyagi's chapter on young pop idols leads to a discussion of youth and crime by Stephan Salzberg in Chapter 8. Among the many problems confronting Japanese society, youth problems receive extensive media coverage. These include stories about school violence *(kōnaibōryoku)*, bullying at school *(ijime)*, truancy, and the rise in youth crime (Watabe 2001). Indeed, the National Police Agency has pledged to step up its crackdown on juvenile crime in the wake of a perceived sharp increase in youth killings and other violent crimes (*Japan Today* 2001). While there may be a serious gap between the perception of increased criminal activity and reality, the increased attention paid to youth crime has led to greater interest in the broader subject of the juvenile justice system. More and more Japanese are coming to believe that the Juvenile Law, by exempting underage criminals from harsh punishment for their actions, is tempting people below twenty years of age to engage in violent behaviour. Under the present law, juveniles who have committed a serious crime are sent to juvenile halls for rehabilitation; upon parole, they are placed under the supervision of official and volunteer probation officers so as to return to normal society in accordance with the Offenders Rehabilitation Law. Some claim, however, that there has been a rise in recidivism among juveniles on probation. These factors have contributed to calls in the Diet for the Juvenile Law to be amended to provide for harsher punishments (Kondo 2000).

Salzberg traces the legal response to the problem of youth crime and the growth of Japan's juvenile system over the last 100 years. He argues that despite the many social changes in this period, Japanese courts have been surprisingly consistent in their approach to juvenile offenders. Three major pieces of legislation are examined. Japan's current core legislation is the 1948 Juvenile Law, enacted as part of the reforms of the US Occupation. This law reflects an American "social work" approach with highly paternalistic overtones, now abandoned in the US, where a tougher criminal law approach has in fact been adopted. Salzberg looks at the historical roots of the juvenile crime system and the challenges that it now faces. He argues that the Japanese model has to date been relatively successful and is unlikely to change in the foreseeable future. Nonetheless, the recent rise in heinous juvenile crimes led the Diet to revise the 1948 Juvenile Law in November 2000 to provide for tougher punishments. The revised law, which took effect on 1 April 2001, lowered the minimum age at which criminal offenders can be held liable for their crimes from sixteen to fourteen. Japanese law now defines a juvenile as a person aged fourteen to nineteen (Kondo 2000).

What do these accounts of tensions between past images and present-day realities amount to? First, it is apparent that the latest wave of globalization has been accompanied by a new upsurge in identity debates in Japan, consisting of both an anxious appraisal of its role in the world and reflections on how to respond to changes within the social fabric. While Japan certainly has to create a new relationship with neighbouring Asian countries, Chapter 5 illustrates how difficult this may be. A second point is that while Japan is certainly affected by international culture more than ever before, social attitudes about family roles and multiculturalism change very slowly. Neither is there likely to be a social revolution through the youth of the country. As evidenced in the essays by Creighton, Aoyagi, and Salzberg, conservative values in Japan show a certain tenacity not widely found in many other highly industrialized societies at the dawn of the millennium.

References

Akamatsu, K. 1962. "A Theory of Unbalanced Growth in the World Economy." *Weltwirtschafrliches Archiv* 86: 196-215.

Bailey, P.J. 1996. *Postwar Japan: 1945 to the Present*. Oxford: Blackwell.

Brinton, M. 1993. *Women and the Economic Miracle: Gender and Work in Postwar Japan*. Berkeley: University of California Press.

Cheung, C., and K. Wong. 2000. "Japanese Investment in China: A Glo-Cal Perspective." In S. Li and W. Tang, eds., *China's Regions, Polity, and Economy: A Study of Spatial Transformation in the Post-Reform Era*. Hong Kong: Chinese University Press, 97-132.

Christopher, R.E. 1984. *The Japanese Mind*. London: Pan Books.

Douglass, M., and G.S. Roberts. 2000. *Japan and Global Migration: Foreign Workers and the Advent of a Multicultural Society*. London: Routledge.

Howe, C., ed. 1996. *China and Japan: History, Trends, and Prospects*. Oxford: Clarendon Press.

Japan Times Online. 2001. "Japan-China Trade Hit Record-High in First Half," 10 August. <http://www.japantimes.co>, accessed August 2001.

Japan Today. 2001. "NPA Pledges Crackdown of Juvenile Crime," 21 September. <http://www.japantoday.com>, accessed September 2001.

Kondo, M. 2000. "Juvenile Crime." *Japan Echo* 27(5): 33-34.

Korhonen, P. 1996. "The Dimension of Dreams: Discussion of the Pacific Age in Japan 1890-1994." In S. Metzger-Court and W. Pascha, eds., *Japan's Socio-Economic Evolution: Continuity and Change*. Folkestone, Kent, UK: Japan Library, 123-41.

Lebra, J. 1976. "Conclusion." In J. Lebra, J. Paulson, and E. Powers, eds., *Women in Changing Japan*. Stanford, CA: Stanford University Press, 297-304.

Lie, J. 2000. "The Discourse of Japaneseness." In M. Douglass and G.S. Roberts, eds., *Japan*

and Global Migration: Foreign Workers and the Advent of a Multicultural Society. London: Routledge, 70-90.
Morris-Suzuki, T. 1998. *Re-inventing Japan: Time, Space, Nation.* Armonk, NY: M.E. Sharpe.
Siddle, R. 1996. *Race, Resistance and the Ainu of Japan.* London: Routledge.
Watabe, M. 2001. "Youth Problems and Japanese Society." *Japan Foundation Newsletter* XXVVIII (3-4): 1-5, 20.
Weiner, M. 1997. *Japan's Minorities: The Illusion of Homogeneity.* London: Routledge.
Young, L. 1998. *Japan's Total Empire: Manchuria and the Culture of Wartime Imperialism.* Berkeley: University of California Press.
Zhao, Q. 1999. "Japan and China." In P. Heenan, ed., *The Japan Handbook.* New York: Glenlake Publishing, 236-45.

5
Postwar Japan and Manchuria
Bill Sewell

> In the hearts of a generation who once lived there, all kinds of reminiscences remain, but Japanese rule of Manchuria has entered the realm of history.
>
> – Manshikai, *Manshū Kaihatsu Yonjūnen Shi*

These lines introduce the *Forty Year History of the Development of Manchuria*, probably the most influential postwar account of prewar Manchuria.[1] Intended to historicize Japanese activities into an ordered past, the study assumed that the recollections of the dwindling numbers of those who experienced Japanese rule in Manchuria would remain safely tucked away "in the hearts." Although the study was correct about the inevitability of historical change, its hope that the popular memories of Manchuria would gradually disappear proved premature. Curiosity regarding the three northeastern Chinese provinces did appear to disappear in the first two postwar decades, but a gradual turnabout in public interest occurred thereafter, peaking with the fiftieth anniversary of the end of the Second World War. Since then interest has again diminished, but only somewhat. Bookstores continue to devote significant shelf space to Manchuria, television documentaries occasionally discuss it, and announcements for reunions of Manchuria survivors still appear in major Japanese newspapers.

Given the apparent dearth of public interest earlier, this about-face suggests that Manchurian connections have an enduring significance in Japanese society. Indeed, evolving perceptions of Manchuria involve more than historical reassessment; they have been integral to the construction of a Japanese national identity throughout the postwar era. Even today, fifty years after the cessation of hostilities, perceptions of prewar and wartime Manchuria continue to help define post-postwar Japan. This perhaps becomes most evident when Manchurian isssues extend beyond the national sphere to intrude upon the international: Japanese and Chinese accounts of the occupation of Manchuria do not agree, and resolving this impasse has proceeded only gradually and partially.

It is important to note the significance of these issues. Manchuria was and is no sideshow (Dirlik 1991). The region received the bulk of the expanding Japanese presence in China. Chinese long contested Japanese activities, however, resulting in a painfully confused half-century of encroachment, resistance, subjugation, and collaboration. Although varied, the intense nature of this experience renders postwar discussions of it central to Chinese and Japanese perceptions of one another as well as of themselves.

After reviewing aspects of the Japanese experience in Manchuria, this chapter considers some of the published perceptions of Manchuria in the postwar era. As limitations of space prevent a thorough analysis of this growing literature, this chapter seeks instead to indicate some of the ways in which perceptions of Manchuria have intertwined with postwar constructions of national identity in Japan. Three distinct periods are apparent. While the first fifteen postwar years witnessed personal assessments that avoided discussing key aspects of the occupation, in the 1960s academics established a comprehensive theoretical framework for institutionalizing perceptions of Manchuria, but only while continuing to evade important, painful issues. Japanese academics began to address these lacunae only in the 1970s and 1980s. Although this paved the way for the explosion of public interest in the mid-1990s, it is worth noting that the hesitant nature of historical reassessment throughout the postwar era seems only to have encouraged popular interest.

The Japanese in Manchuria

To be sure, the subject of Manchuria could not simply disappear with submission and retreat – it only lay dormant, deep within the Japanese psyche. Many of the settlers, soldiers, merchants, and officials who went to Manchuria chose only initially not to speak publicly about their experiences. Why they came forward when they did, and not earlier, is illuminating. On the surface, many wanted to recount stories while still able to. A deeper reading suggests that the public presence of former Manchurian officials in postwar society, along with the inability of published accounts to satisfactorily explain the Japanese presence in Manchuria, influenced them more.[2]

The Japanese were not in Manchuria simply because corporations, government agencies, and the military dispatched them there. Thousands went willingly, settling in budding small towns or the commercial hubs of Dalian (in Japanese, Dairen; in Russian, Dalny) or Shenyang (earlier known as Mukden or Fengtian). The lure of economic gain was patent, and the resulting growth substantial. Only 16,612 in 1906, the Japanese civilian population in Manchuria rocketed past 233,000 in 1930 to top 1 million in 1940 (Manshikai 1964, 1: 84). As most did not stay permanently, the revolving Manchurian door touched numerous households in Japan one way or another, making it impossible for Manchuria to disappear completely from public consciousness after 1945.

Many Japanese prominent in postwar society manifested some connection with prewar Manchuria. A partial list of one-time residents includes men like Ueshiba Morihei (1883-1969), founder of the martial art of aikido, who served in Manchuria during the Russo-Japanese War. Drawn by the promise of a pristine frontier, he returned to Manchuria with Ōmotokyō proselytizer Deguchi Onisaburō in 1924 to create a heavenly kingdom on earth. Another was Abe Kōbō (1924-93), who lived in Mukden from the age of one to sixteen (until 1941) and likely experienced first among colonized others the sensations of alienation and urban isolation that he later wrote about so powerfully. It was disgust over Japanese rule that led him to use the Chinese rather than Japanese pronunciation of his personal name (Kimifusa). The renowned conductor Ozawa Seiji was born in Mukden in 1935. His personal name contains Chinese characters taken from the names of the two key plotters of the Manchurian Incident, Ishiwara Kanji and Itagaki Seishirō (McCormack 1991). Ozawa's father, a founding member of the Manchurian Youth League – a group formed in 1928 to encourage a more activist policy in Manchuria – was a proud supporter of the Incident (Fogel 1988, 134-39).[3]

Many Japanese intended to stay permanently, opening new lands for colonial settlement. Although the number of rural settlers never reached the official goal of half a million, the establishment of the puppet state of Manchukuo increased official support and spurred migration. The war's end found over 320,000 of Japan's rural poor scattered across Manchuria (Manshū Kaitakushi Kankōkai 1966, 827), especially in the north. Many returned to Japan only after experiencing work camps in China and the Soviet Union. Many never returned.[4]

This tragic experience conferred upon the more conspicuous figures in postwar Japanese society having some connection to prewar Manchuria a certain poignancy, perhaps especially those among Japan's leadership. It is well known that despite the disbanding of the Imperial Army and the dismembering of the financial conglomerates that worked closely with the military, most of the human capital of these organizations remained. This was particularly true in government administration. While the war crimes trials indicted some 6,000 – and hanged over 900 – many of whom were participants in Japan's administration of Manchuria, most of the empire's personnel were able to return to public life a decade later.

Perhaps the most well known of the rehabilitated was Kishi Nobusuke (1896-87). In the 1930s, Kishi was a "new bureaucrat" *(shinkanryō)* committed to state economic planning in close alliance with the military. Between 1936 and 1939, he worked in the Manchukuo government's economic control agency, organizing its five-year plans, an experience that served him well as Minister of Commerce and Industry in the wartime cabinet of Tōjō Hideki. Three years in prison as a suspected class A war criminal, however, did not prevent him from participating in postwar politics. Kishi helped orchestrate the formation of the Liberal Democratic

Party in 1955, and eventually served as prime minister between 1957 and 1960. Similarly, Yoshino Shinji (1888-1971), another "new bureaucrat," was a Manchuria Heavy Industries vice-president yet a postwar Minister of Transportation in Japan. In 1953 he was elected to the House of Councillors. Never did Yoshino have any qualms about using his Manchurian connections to get ahead in postwar Japan (Johnson 1982, 145).

Kishi and Yoshino were not alone. The consul-general at Mukden between 1925 and 1928 was Yoshida Shigeru (1878-1967), a strong proponent of expanding Japanese authority in prewar Manchuria and Japan's most powerful politician between 1946 and 1954 (Dower 1979). Prewar experiences were useful in rebuilding postwar Japan, and with the reverse course and the emphasis on practicality over ideology, thousands with suspect backgrounds returned to positions of influence. The postwar Japanese miracle was possible because a trained, if chastened, cohort helped manoeuvre it (Dower 1992). This was also true in academia. With regard to Manchuria, the most significant connection was the placement in universities of many of the South Manchuria Railway's Economic Research Bureau (Fogel 1988, xxvi-xxvii, 212-14).[5] Some reconstituted themselves as a private research organization, the Ajia Keizai Kenkyūjo (Institute of Developing Economies, or IDE).

Returnees from Manchuria had to adjust to new circumstances to restart careers, but a changed climate facilitated their rebirths. Changed Occupation policies coincided with a re-evaluation of perceptions among Japanese. Encouraged by the dissenting voice of the only Asian judge on the Tokyo tribunal, Radhabinod Pal, some contested the logic of the war crimes trials (Tanaka 1952). Others suggested that since Japan proved able to hold out for so long against more powerful enemies, imperial administrators must have done something right. Still others, bolstered by containment and the onset of the Cold War, noted that Japanese activities were in part directed against communism in Asia (Duus 1996). The IDE shared a similar point of view – the assumption that rational economic analysis and planning can improve society, enhance relations with neighbouring societies, and curb afflictions such as communism was widespread in Japan and never wavered (cf. Yamaguchi and Satō 1996).

This is as central to understanding Japanese activities in Manchuria before 1945 as it is to grasping Japanese perceptions of those activities after 1945. Rational development was the great hope of the Japanese empire. The first to enunciate this clearly did so initially in Taiwan but later more grandly in Manchuria. Rather than rely on military coercion alone, Gotō Shimpei (1857-1929), the first president of the South Manchuria Railway (Mantetsu), sought to induce Chinese acceptance of Japanese rule through the encouragement of economic development with a more judicious use of military force (Kitaoka 1988; Chin 1995). This basic orientation persisted, attracting many of Japan's promising bureaucrats to the railway. Mantetsu's leadership eventually included Matsuoka Yōsuke (1880-1946), the foreign minister who walked out of the League of Nations and brought Japan into the Tripartite Pact; Uchida Kōsai (1865-1936), a four-time foreign minister; and Sogō Shinji (1884-1981), the driving force behind the development of the *shinkansen*, Japan's "bullet train." Gotō Shimpei himself later served as mayor of Tokyo and foreign minister.

Although the Japanese occupation of Manchuria was authoritarian and at times brutal, Manchuria's significance to Japan did not involve only militarism and imperialism. Manchuria was also the site of Japan's most concerted overseas effort to effect a vision of the modern world. A late-developing country, Japan was state building at home while empire building overseas, and many Japanese saw in Manchuria not only a secure and complementary trading partner but also a place to articulate goals and ideals popular or useful at home. For Japanese, Manchuria thus became a tabula rasa upon which could be constructed new and expressly modern edifices. Manchukuo, too, was a laboratory geared to the creation of a new type of modern state, one in which state planning and racial harmony outlined a model society.

It is the mixed nature of this legacy that makes the assessment of Japanese involvement in Manchuria problematic. While Japanese tend to focus on the progressive aspects of this experience, Chinese, understandably, emphasize those more harsh. Each side – for their own reasons – selectively focuses on particular issues, resulting in the recurring disruptions in contemporary relations.

The focus here is on one side of that relationship: the evolution of postwar Japanese perceptions of Manchuria and what those perceptions signified about Japan.

Personal Perspectives

Japanese efforts to mould Manchuria failed, not simply because of military defeat but also because of the brutality of Japanese methods and the sterility of their visions.[6] One can only speculate how the Japanese would have come to perceive empire had Japan avoided war in 1937 or 1941 and maintained the empire, even if temporarily. With collapse and the occupation of the home islands, however, many Japanese addressed Manchuria first from the perspective of explaining expansion as a prelude to war and defeat. Others perceived activities in Manchuria against the backdrop of the war crimes trials that blamed a conspiratorial element within Japanese society. For them, the trials energized a popular and activist pacifism.

Ienaga Saburō (1913-), now famous for challenging government textbook policies, exemplifies the latter. Pointing to "anti-modern" forces at work as early as the Meiji Restoration (Ienaga 1953), Ienaga thought that Japanese imperialism and militarism were an indigenous force that required external subduing (Ienaga 1978). Because the Meiji legal system favoured the government and the military (Ienaga 1962), ordinary Japanese could not curb the indiscriminate use of state power by themselves (Ienaga 1965). Others agreed, igniting a brief debate on Meiji "absolutism" (Tōyama 1949).

Maruyama Masao (1914-97) similarly located the cause of Japanese expansionism within Japan, but blamed it instead upon an all-pervasive "emperor system" and the motivational power of "ultra-nationalism." For him the occupation of Manchuria was the logical outcome of an emperor-centred system of thought and organization that combined spiritual authority with state power. Permeating society, it prevented Japanese from recognizing the immorality of their actions (Maruyama 1963a). Japanese were easy prey for fascist radicals, and events in Manchuria helped tighten their grip: "the Manchurian Incident acted as a definite stimulus to Japanese fascism" (Maruyama 1963b). Intriguingly, Maruyama thought Japan's resulting nationalism reached its peculiar intensity because it was more like the powerful Asian nationalisms racking Korea, India, Southeast Asia, and China in the early postwar years than that of Europeans. These were "ethnic movements" *(minzoku undō)* seeking independence and revolution. Yet however unsettling Japan's ethnic movement was, it was temporary. In Maruyama's eyes, Japan's own nationalist excesses ended on 15 August 1945 and were now safely historicized in the past (Maruyama 1953, 6-7).

Maruyama and Ienaga were prominent academic critics of Japanese militarism in the early postwar era. They considered specific Japanese activities in Manchuria, however, only in passing. To his credit, Ienaga examined them to some extent later in his career, but his focus on the military as an autonomous and irrational element avoided examining Japanese society as a whole (Ienaga 1978). At the same time, Maruyama's analysis similarly diverted attention from society to particular militarist activists. Concentrating on pernicious but identifiable elements, Maruyama and Ienaga absolved society at large.

Former bureaucrats joined in the denunciation of militarism. Takasaki Tatsunosuke (1885-1964), a former vice-president of Manchuria Heavy Industries, the umbrella organization led by Nissan that implemented Manchukuo's five-year plans, echoed Ienaga by focusing blame on the ubiquitous and interfering role of the military. The military domination of Manchukuo obstructed business operations by entangling production and prohibiting international exchange. In the end, the military even contradicted the goal of Manchurian development and made a mockery of avowed slogans like "the kingly way" (Takasaki 1952, 74-76, 114-15).

In condemning the military, however, Takasaki did not question his own role. Accepting Manchurian development and Japanese expansion as necessary, Takasaki vented his frustrations, but offered only a limited critique. Presumably he was more content serving in the postwar Hatoyama and Kishi cabinets.

The indictment expressed by Komai Tokuzō (1885-1961), a Kantōgun (Kwantung Army) civil administrator and the first director of general affairs for the State Council of Manchukuo, was more searching. Noting the genuine Japanese commitment to improving Manchurian conditions, albeit for Japanese ends, Komai concluded that the seizure of Manchuria and the annexation of Korea were "foolish attempts" *(gukyō)*. To Komai, even though it enabled migration and encouraged economic growth, expansion only brought conflict. Komai, however, did not stop at condemning Japanese expansionism. Postwar American policies in Korea and China reminded him of prewar Japan's, and in publicly rebuking his prewar pronouncements, he wanted to terminate the new alliance between the US and Japan before it resulted in World War III (Komai 1933; Komai 1952, 319-31). Komai, a protégé of Nitobe Inazo, remained an idealist to the end.

Hoshino Naoki (1892-1978), an important Finance Ministry bureaucrat in the Manchukuo and wartime Japanese governments, also noted genuine Japanese desires to renovate Manchuria, but supposedly from the beginning, he himself questioned the morality of establishing Manchukuo. If so, he was an exception. Still, he admired his comrades' idealism, though he scorned their lack of realism. Komai, for example, had Manchurians' best interests in mind but had no practical experience. Kantōgun Chief of Staff Itagaki Seishirō came under a similar indictment – his amateurish organization of Manchukuo's taxes imperilled the state. Likewise, the Manchukuo government's celebrated strategy of "guidance from within" *(naimen shidō)* resulted in duplicate systems and administrative chaos.

Despite these misgivings, Hoshino accepted the Japanese presence in Manchuria and tried to justify it. Because Japan had no choice but to accept unequal treaties and a foreign presence itself when it first opened its doors to the world, Japan's occupation of Manchuria was a natural development to Hoshino – Japan became Manchuria's tutor, just as Japan had itself once been an apprentice. Hoshino thus boasted about Japanese accomplishments. Manchukuo's transportation network expanded, heavy industry developed, the population grew, and Manchukuoan exports shipped by way of the Trans-Siberian Railway helped keep Germany in the war (Hoshino 1963).

Manchukuo's successes reflected Hoshino's defence at the Tokyo War Crimes Trials. Pleading that he was merely an administrative official of a large and sovereign government, he claimed that he was personally responsible for nothing – a justification that led Maruyama to characterize Japanese fascism as "dwarfish," too timid to stand up to bureaucrats from above or radicalism from below (Maruyama 1963c). Seeing himself simply as a technocrat, Hoshino differed little from Himmler.

Itō Takeo (1895-1984) provided the perspective of a Mantetsu researcher. A self-described liberal, Itō joined the Economic Research Bureau upon graduating from Tokyo University in 1920, intending to study Chinese labour. Like many of his comrades, he was a product of the era of Taishō democracy, committed to a liberal world order and equal relations with the Chinese. He spent most of his time researching aspects of life in China that kindled a sincere warmth for the country and its people. His reaction to the Manchurian Incident, however, was ambivalent. Although he condemned the Kantōgun's usurpation of authority, he recognized that the army could not have acted without Mantetsu's organizational structure and preliminary research. Moreover, Itō disapproved of the new state chiefly because it did not embody its own ideals. To Itō, Manchukuo was an ad hoc and factionalized organization looking only to extend the Japanese empire. Ethnic harmony was a fantasy pursued by a few anticapitalist ideologues willing to collaborate with the military but of whom the military remained suspicious. Although Komai Tokuzō was genuinely pan-Asianist, he was also an opportunist willing to compromise and work with corporate capital. Still, Itō commended Komai for recognizing Manchukuo to be unfriendly to pan-Asianists and for resigning with Japan's recognition of Manchukuo. After that, "top-flight bureaucrats" from Tokyo, such as Hoshino and Kishi, took over, men more committed to the state than to progressive ideals (Itō 1975; Fogel 1988, 151). To Itō, men like Hoshino, Kishi, and Matsuoka Yōsuke were functionaries who perceived Manchuria simply as an economic "lifeline," a self-serving perception made popular in the war boom era of 1931-33 (Young 1998, 88-95).

The Manchurian Incident was an opportunity for men like these to extend the administrative reach of the Japanese state. Indeed, despite Itō's distaste for the military, he found he could also approve of the Manchurian Incident – it seemed to him that Mantetsu's revised Economic Research Association realized most completely Gotō Shimpei's original dream for Mantetsu's research staff. Founded in January 1932 to integrate Mantetsu research with the requirements of the military-dominated Manchukuo state hierarchy, and staffed by Mantetsu research personnel headed by Sogō Shinji, this was the agency that planned Manchukuo's economic development. Applied research reached its apogee under military rule.

The accomplishment was fleeting, however. The Manchurian Incident led inexorably to the mass arrests of Mantetsu researchers between September 1942 and June 1943, including Itō. Calling this a *"fascist assault and repression by the military of our scientific work,"* Itō's account attacked the ideologues and the military, leaving the reputations of the intellectuals largely untarnished (emphasis Itō's; Itō 1975; Fogel 1988, 203).

These six accounts illustrate the two general perceptions of Manchuria held by Japanese in the immediate postwar era. Ienaga, Maruyama, and Komai were more critical, but their work tended to focus on the effects of militarism on Japan only. Those most critical of Japanese militarism did not concern themselves with a close evaluation of Manchuria in the immediate postwar era. Manchuria was of distant and secondary importance. On the other hand, while Takasaki, Hoshino, and Itō were critical of the military, they accepted proudly Japanese economic endeavours in Manchuria. For them, Japanese activities in Manchuria were significant and undeserving of complete denunciation. To them, Japanese expansion entailed something progressive. Thus, while Ienaga, Maruyama, and Komai rejected militarism as a prelude to expansion and war, Takasaki, Hoshino, and Itō defined militarism more narrowly and rejected only the military's control of Japanese administration. Although they did not say so themselves, this latter view reflected most closely that of Japan's postwar administration, one that perceived reconstruction and growth to be Japan's primary needs. As such, economic management and scientific development became the rallying points for conquering the past. Only as the need for these goals flagged could other perspectives develop.

The Developmental Perspective

Global factors facilitated that initial outlook, as the widespread acceptance of the verdicts of the Tokyo Trials by American scholars enabled many Japanese to gloss over events in Manchuria. Stressing the differences between Japan and Nazi Germany, the diplomat-scholar Edwin Reischauer, for example, suggested, like Hoshino, that Japan had only acted as any other country would. In giving the Japanese occupation of Manchuria short shrift, Reischauer encouraged others not to examine it in great detail (Reischauer and Craig 1978).

The withdrawal of China from international exchange removed another external motivation to examine Manchuria critically. Until the end of the Cultural Revolution and the re-emergence of a China market, it was easy to disregard protests from the victims of Japanese activities in Manchuria. Of course, some Japanese did respond, perhaps most notably Itō Takeo. The isolation of the People's Republic of China, however, relaxed international pressure and allowed Japanese to cultivate pride in their Manchurian endeavours.

Three important contexts framed academic perspectives on Manchuria in the 1960s. One was the publication of important primary, especially Mantetsu, materials.[7] While facilitating study, however, these reports formed not only a backbone but also a boundary for scholastic analysis.

Seemingly exhaustive, they focused almost exclusively on economic development, primarily Japanese. The Chinese existed oddly disembodied – the population grew, acceded to treaties, established corporations, and sometimes existed in opposition, at which point they became "bandits." Friendly Chinese and other Asians either joined in the creation of a new society, at which point they acted like Japanese, or more ethnically, demonstrating traditional customs and attire. Japanese too could be guilty of orientalism (Tanaka 1993).

The re-publication of Mantetsu studies maintained the Economic Research Bureau's inherent bias – the abstract assessment of economic conditions and legal technicalities. Publications by the Manchukuo government were similar, despite attempts to be more stirring. This type of dispassionate analysis dovetailed with the second context-defining domestic development. Buoyed by a new, anti-militarist image and freed from police surveillance and the stigma of subversiveness, Marxism made great inroads among Japanese academics in the postwar era. Yet however insightful regarding economic and power relationships, Marxism has never satisfactorily addressed other issues arising from the imperialist experience, such as nationalism (Anderson 1991, 3-4). Thus, theoretical proclivities enabled postwar academics to neglect the darker aspects of Japanese activities and focus blandly on the occupation as an instance of global development.

Still, this new perspective was important. Japanese imperialism in a Marxist framework was no longer a purely Japanese issue – it became a problem of world history. Through this lens, Japanese activities in Manchuria were suddenly equivalent to American, British, or French imperialism elsewhere, especially if historians avoided Manchukuo and focused on Mantetsu as an element in an expanding capitalist system (Andō 1965). The most significant analysis of this kind was the *Forty Year History of the Development of Manchuria* (Manshikai 1964-65).

The Japanese were only one imperialist force, this study argued, and the Western powers were already dividing China before Japan ever procured a share. Moreover, since Manchuria was an "undeveloped wilderness" isolated from the modern global economy, the Japanese occupation of Manchuria was a natural occurrence. Japan was therefore only manifesting global trends. Yet portraying Japan's activities in Manchuria as part of a global process of imperialist capitalist development also allowed the authors to assert a measure of Japanese uniqueness. Despite what they saw as the common role of monopoly capitalism propelling all nations into imperialism, the authors suggested that – especially when contrasted with Russian imperialism – the Japanese developed Manchuria comparatively successfully and peacefully. Nor did the "pillaging style" *(ryakudatsuteki chūkai)* of European imperialism that occurred in America appear. Motivations behind imperialism also differed. While European and American imperialism occurred in part to obviate a working class revolution at home, Japanese imperialism occurred because it was a newly modern country. Becoming imperialist was like eliminating feudalism – both were necessary steps in the historical advancement of Japanese society. The authors thus concluded that the Japanese development of Manchuria was not purely for Japan's benefit: Manchurians gained too. Although not a study of modernization, the *Forty Year History* extolled the Japanese creation of a modern economy and infrastructure. In the end, Japan acted as a "midwife" *(josanpu)* for the region. Even Manchukuo was an experiment that ultimately aided the development of heavy industry (Manshikai 1964, 1: 31, 36).

The three large volumes of the *Forty Year History* detailed these assertions with an impressive array of statistics. Apparently comprehensive, though focusing mainly on Manchuria before the Manchurian Incident, it achieved a kind of intellectual pre-eminence in Japanese studies. Its scope was monumental and theory coherent. It also deflected attention from the darker aspects of the occupation and affirmed Japanese achievements. As such, it spoke to Japan's emerging self-confidence and delicately stated postwar nationalism, such as that which appeared around the era of the 1964 Tokyo Olympics.

Other sweeping studies followed that did not entail a Marxist approach but seemed to cover the remainder of Japanese activities in Manchuria. *The History of Colonizing Manchuria* recounted the various settlement programs encouraging Japanese emigration to Manchuria, including a large section on youth volunteers (Manshū Kaitakushi Kankōkai 1966). The no less weighty *Manchurian Migrants under Japanese Imperialism* followed (Manshū Iminshi Kenkyūkai 1976). The two hefty volumes of the *History of Manchukuo* recounted the goals and responsibilities of the various administrative departments of the puppet state (Manshū Kokushi Hensan Kankōkai 1970). Another large tome did the same for the Manchukuo military (Manshū Kokugun Kankō I'inkai 1970).

Together, these volumes presented the structures and goals of Mantetsu and Manchukuo as an overwhelming facade. Acknowledging Japanese imperialism in Manchuria, they left an impression that it proceeded in an organized manner with progressive goals. They ignored entirely, however, the more questionable aspects of the occupation. This perspective becomes more astonishing when the authors of these studies are considered. None of the 51 contributors listed in the *Forty Year History* appeared among the 20 researchers in the Mantetsu study group led by Andō Hikutarō (Andō 1965). Nor did any of the contributors to either of these take part in the *History of Colonizing Manchuria*, which listed 240 contributors, or the *History of Manchukuo*, which listed 105, and less than a dozen overlapped between the latter two. Historians of this generation agreed broadly that only development, planning, and rational administration constituted historical significance. Perhaps unsurprisingly, Hoshino Naoki and Kishi Nobusuke both took part in the latter two projects, as did former Nissan and Manchuria Heavy Industries chairman Ayukawa Yoshisuke (1880-1967).

The participation of Manchukuo officials in assessing Manchuria was the third contextual key apparent in the 1960s. Kishi Nobusuke himself chaired an enormous group memoir that included not only articles by Hoshino, Ayukawa, Sogō, and himself, but also an introduction (and calligraphy) by Kishi suggesting that Japanese endeavours in Manchuria were simply attempts to secure peace and prosperity for all of East Asia (Manshū Kaikoshū Kankōkai 1965). Politically significant participants in empire reinforced this perspective in *Dream and Reality of Founding Manchukuo* by attacking the limited acknowledgments of aggression made elsewhere (Kokusai Zenrin Kyōkai 1975). Iizawa Shigekazu made this clear in the introduction when he declared that the "movement to found a country" *(kenkoku undō)* was creative and inspiring, like drawing on a clean slate. Manchukuo was all about creating a new social system (Iizawa 1975). Hoshino Naoki, after commenting on some of the physical improvements such as dams and schools, agreed. Reconfirming the nature of the endeavour, he suggested that Manchukuo remained a fine example of the best ideals of the Japanese people (Hoshino 1975). Itō Musojirō, a former Manchukuo professor detained in the Soviet Union after the war, insisted that Manchukuo could be understood only in the broader context of an Asian revolt against the West, something he termed a "recovery movement" *(fukkō undō)* (Itō 1975). Ueno Takashi, former secretary to Manchukuo prime minister Zheng Lixu reminded readers of Zheng's and Komai Tokuzō's efforts to establish peace among the five largest ethnic groups of Manchukuo, something he insisted had never before been attempted in world history (Ueno 1975).

Analyses like these allowed historians to ignore the troubling aspects of the occupation and assert a version of events that portrayed Japanese activities as progressive. Contemporary discussions regarding the Japanese experience and developing economies elsewhere echoed this concern. Stressing the need for developed countries to help the undeveloped achieve political stability, Hara Kakuten recommended the Meiji and Mantetsu examples as useful models. His own studies of the Economic Research Bureau documented its utility through its gradually widening circle of interest to include China, Southeast Asia, and Siberia (Hara 1967, 1986).

Representing Japanese imperialism in these ways did not, however, go unchallenged. Suzuki Takashi, for example, grumbled loudly about studies like the ones listed above even as they appeared. For him, the involvement of former Mantetsu personnel in the compilation of the *Forty Year*

History and other works led not simply to a restricted perspective but also to an overly rosy account of Japanese activities that ignored many of the realities of the Manchurian experience (Suzuki 1971). A year later, perhaps the most important study of Manchuria of the 1970s, *Manchuria under Japanese Imperialism,* reinforced this criticism by confirming Japanese abilities regarding development but challenging the utility of that approach. Like Suzuki, these authors reacted strongly to the favourable views of Japanese activities in Manchuria as well as to the participation of former Manchukuo bureaucrats in works like the *History of Manchukuo.* They vowed to clarify the "characteristics of the economic management of Manchuria under Japanese imperialism" by bringing to the foreground the empire's "structural links" (Manshūshi Kenkyūkai 1972, i-iv). The four sections on economic control, finance, migration and labour, and land policy showed how the policies in the puppet state preceded similar policies at home and demonstrated that development required social regimentation. They also showed that Mantetsu's involvement was instrumental in the organization of Manchukuo, an issue the *Forty Year History* skirted. *Manchuria under Japanese Imperialism* did not go beyond the realm of policy, however, and failed to examine the entirety of the occupation.[8] An important revision examining bureaucratic control and the role of Nissan, it still avoided many of the darker issues of the occupation.

Towards a Comprehensive Account?

Japan's perspectives as to what happened in Manchuria began to change more radically in the 1980s, as its economic recovery allowed the overriding focus on growth to gradually dissipate. Indeed, before the bursting of the economic bubble, Japan's apparently complete recovery permitted society to consider a range of issues beyond development. Changes in the international arena also encouraged new perspectives, especially the reemergence of China and the spread of more searching questions by American academics in the wake of the war in Vietnam.

An important step towards a more comprehensive account was a series of articles in the communist daily *Akahata* (Red Flag) by Morimura Sei'ichi that found Japanese experiments on Chinese to be as gruesome as those of Nazi doctors in Eastern Europe. Eventually published as a book and translated into Chinese, Morimura's research helped open a public debate in Japan that questioned basic tenets of Japanese history (Morimura 1983; Takasugi 1982). In this, Ienaga Saburō re-emerged as a central figure. His lawsuits against government-mandated textbook revisions revolve essentially around the question of which version of empire to teach – that of the *Forty Year History* qualified by *Manchuria under Japanese Imperialism* or a view that considers also the harsher aspects of Japanese rule. Bureaucrats in the Ministry of Education prefer to consider the more heinous incidents of the occupation as anomalies so that the course of Japanese history remains generally progressive.

Academics studying Manchuria, however, continued to question such assumptions. Okabe Michio emphasized the experiences of pioneers to show that the popular image of modern, industrialized Dalian was not the Manchurian norm. He also questioned the goal of development itself by suggesting that development was simply to prepare for war against the Soviet Union. He also made a plea for the Japanese to examine rival sources in Chinese, Korean, Russian, and English (Okabe 1978). Nakamura Shigeo examined the repercussions of Japanese colonial development insofar as it contributed to the rise of a communist adversary (Nakamura 1984). Revisiting the materials on Nissan, Udagawa Masaru found that Nissan wanted to withdraw from Manchuria once Ayukawa Yoshisuke realized that the Kantōgun stymied growth by making it impossible to import foreign capital (Udagawa 1984, 1990). These works called into question fundamental assumptions of the prevailing orthodoxy.

The 1980s also witnessed the Japanese and Chinese hesitantly renewing acquaintances, and because prewar connections insured that Manchuria would be key to the Japanese rediscovery of China, fundamental questions about Manchuria also appeared in popular discussions. Taking the city of Changchun as an example, Japanese reports focused on a variety of topics. Some reacquainted the Japanese with Chinese life, especially under the changed, post-Mao circumstances (Ishige and Ruddle 1986; Yoshida 1988; Okawa 1989; Ebara 1996), and some featured the Japanese returning to the places of their youth, either literally (Kanai 1985) or photographically (Kokubun 1979; Kitakōji and Watanabe 1982). A number concerned themselves exclusively with the prewar era, some reminiscing about daily life (Fujise 1993), others novelizing it (Tani 1989). Some reported on idealistic Japanese who tried to improve society through personal endeavours such as establishing schools for the deaf and mute (Komatsu 1989).

Other studies examined rural life (*Nihon Shokuminchi Shi 2* 1978). Some investigated the macabre – Manchukuo's demise (Kishima 1986). The image of scattered villagers armed with farm tools heroically defending wooden stockades against Soviet armour especially captured the public's imagination. Although colonists amounted to only 17.4 percent of all Japanese in Manchuria, they accounted for 45 percent of Japanese casualties (Takasaki 1995, 10, 14).

The fiftieth anniversary of the end of empire found remarkable popular interest in Manchuria. Pictorial accounts and articles in popular magazines sketched the orthodox history of Japanese involvement in Manchuria repeatedly (*Manshū no Kiroku* 1995; Taiheiyō Sensō Kenkyūkai 1996; *Nichi Roku 20 Seiki* 1998). Personal stories remained popular – understandable because, given a different set of circumstances, some could imagine themselves going to Manchuria (Sugiyama 1996, 10).[9] Perhaps more indicative of the changed perceptions of Manchuria is its appearance as a setting in that ubiquitous barometer of the Japanese mood, *manga* (Japanese comics). The use of Manchukuo's former capital as a backdrop for cloak-and-dagger intrigue in Japanese comics illustrates graphically the return of Manchuria's acceptability to popular consciousness (Yoshikazu 1992).

Revived and expanded interest in Manchuria did not bypass Japanese academics. *The Administration of Manchuria under Japanese Imperialism* focused on the military and economic means of controlling Manchukuo (Asada and Kobayashi 1986). The wide-ranging *Studies on Manchukuo* not only examined the economic and administrative means of organizing the puppet state but also probed Manchukuo's culture (Yamamoto 1995). Komagome Takeshi explored this intriguing aspect further in *The Cultural Integration of Imperial Japan's Colonies* (Komagome 1996). The grand developmental perspective was slipping out of sight.

Other lenses were narrower. Imura Tetsuo's study of the Mantetsu Economic Research Bureau staff enlarged the account of Itō Takeo (Imura 1996). Yanagisawa Yū's studies of the Japanese merchant communities showed them to have been more activist than earlier assumed. (Yanagisawa 1992a, 1992b, 1993). Kaneko Fumio's analysis more pointedly called into question the nature and success of Manchurian development. Subordinate to Japan's needs, Manchurian industrialization could not help but be distorted, or "half-hearted" *(shōkyoku teki)*, in Kaneko's words. More significant, because development was confined only to certain regions, it was less spectacular than previously imagined (Kaneko 1993).

Despite these revisions, however, some research continued to portray Japanese activities as progressive. Koshizawa Akira, for example, found Manchuria's cities to be endowed with parks, modern amenities, and novel architecture. Compared with urban creations at home, Manchuria witnessed idealistic Japanese urban planning that postwar Japanese ignored entirely because of associations with war and imperialism (Koshizawa 1988, 1989).

The subtext of Koshizawa's argument is important – the ultimate focus of his research is Manchuria's significance for Japan (cf. Koshizawa 1991). By the late 1980s, however, this particular perspective was no longer readily acceptable. Nishizawa Yasuhiko, for example, chastised Koshizawa for his narrow range of sources – mostly Mantetsu and Manchukuo materials – and focus, noting especially Koshizawa's incomplete understanding of imperialism as a phenomenon. Indeed, Nishizawa found this to be a problem for colonial studies as a whole because it seemed to him that researchers often absolved civilians for imperialist activities (Nishizawa 1989). To him, imperialism was a system that encompassed almost every aspect of Japanese society in Manchuria, and architecture was no exception (Nishizawa 1996a). That this perspective is increasingly accepted is perhaps demonstrated most decisively in recent works like Yamamuro Shin'ichi's *Kimera* (Yamamuro 1993)[10] and the mammoth eight-volume series *Modern Japan and Its Colonies* (*Kindai Nihon to Shokuminchi* 1992-93). Japanese activities in Manchuria involved Japanese society as a whole and were implicit in the creation of Japan as a modern state. That was Manchuria's true significance for Japan.

Widening critiques of progressive activities in Manchuria coincided with examinations of more heinous events. These included primarily issues of chemical (Pin 1995; Obara et al. 1997; Osaki 1997) and bacteriological warfare (Watanabe 1993; Morimura 1997), as well as the painful stories of the "comfort women," many of whom were stationed in Manchuria (Suzuki 1993; Kurahashi 1994). The growing of opium as central to the Manchukuo economy is another emerging topic (Fujise 1992; Kurahashi 1996). Moreover, no longer do any of these topics emerge as anomalous. The partial acknowledgment of the comfort women, for example, led to the realization that the procurement of sexual services of Japanese women *(karayuki)* for military-organized prostitution was long-standing, and continued during the American Occupation for GIs (Kurahashi 1994; Yamada 1992). While such revelations are troubling to many Japanese, in calling attention to the means by which Japanese society achieved prosperity they encourage the Japanese to reconsider not only long-term official goals and policies but the values of contemporary society as well.

The potential inherent in this perceptual revolution may be none too late in arriving. Contemporary economic difficulties are the most severe since the era of the Manchurian Incident, and the failure to address current ills competently will likely refocus Japanese attention protectively. Recent elections already show an alarming return of nationalist rhetoric to political debate. It is against this backdrop that new studies of Manchuria appear. While contributors to journals like *Shōkun!* contest the veracity of the more nightmarish tales of the occupation, others continue to delve deeper.

Conclusion

Many non-Japanese are aware that Japanese activities in northeast China in the first half of the twentieth century were often horrific, yet it is important to understand that many Japanese have long perceived many of their activities there also to have been progressively idealistic. Japan secured Manchuria not only through military action but also through what could be extolled as enlightened management. However, while the postwar era witnessed the rebuking of prewar military actions, there was no similar process regarding the actions of the prewar bureaucracy, rendering their experiences problematic for later generations. Currently, the Japanese appear to be discovering that the attempt to dissociate themselves from the mishaps of the prewar era, much as Meiji Japanese attempted to dissociate themselves from the evils of the pre-Meiji Japan, cannot be done selectively. Calling into question one aspect of the prewar experience cannot help but call other aspects into question. Worse, there may be a kind of domino effect: questioning "progressive" aspects of the Manchurian experience cannot help but call into question the narrative of progress in Japan itself.[11] This is the unsettling dilemma that confronts the concerned public today, troubling fundamentally Japanese perceptions of national identity.

In another time and place, a revisionist historian seeking to alter perspectives in a different society suggested that in grappling with the nature of a country's impact on another, it is necessary to examine not only political and economic aspects of control but the progressive and humanitarian impulses as well (Williams 1962). In order to establish more stable relations in Asia, Japanese, too, would do well to acknowledge the detrimental consequences of what they consider to be the positive aspects of Japanese imperialism.

A wider awareness of the impact of the progressive must also include a readier acknowledgment of the negative. Recent revelations about leftover chemical weapons stockpiles suggest that other issues in Manchuria remain. As such, Manchuria continues to stalk Sino-Japanese relations. While the Chinese government has long demanded a public apology and appropriate reparations, the Japanese government has responded only by suggesting unofficial remuneration, something the Chinese refuse to accept.

It is important to note that both societies are to a large degree prisoners of their own postwar self-images. Japanese society, priding itself on development and progress, is reluctant to acknowledge publicly aspects of its occupation of Manchuria that suggest otherwise. In a similar vein, because postwar Chinese leaders manipulated an image of the Japanese other derived from the worst Japanese activities, the Communist Party cannot now readily accept a compromise either. The only way around this quandary appears to be for both societies to recognize the inadequacies of these images.

Yamamuro Shinichi has described Manchukuo as a "chimera": the Kantōgun provided the lion's head, the imperial system the sturdy goat's body, and Pu Yi – Manchukuo's "last emperor" – the dragon's tail. Japanese supporting one part did not necessarily condone the actions of the others but lived together as a single, if incongruous, organism. As such, more than being simply a puppet state, Manchukuo embodied conflicting points of view apparent in Japan itself (Yamamuro 1993). To some extent, contemporary Japanese – or any – society also resembles this chimera. However, while ominous black vans continue to blare patriotic slogans and anonymous threats continue to muzzle public debate, the growing awareness of society's interconnected nature suggests that some have learned the lesson of this particular chimera.

Puzzling out a national identity is a complex process of negotiation between the past and the present, by nature involving the public deliberation of competing perspectives. In the waning days of the twentieth century, views critical of Japanese activities in Manchuria appeared to be becoming orthodox. The challenge for the holders of this view has thus become to encourage society as a whole to acknowledge responsibility for Japanese involvement in Manchuria in a manner acceptable to the Japanese and their neighbours. This, however, is a task for the next half-century.

Notes

1 Although prewar Japanese came to perceive "Manchuria" as a separate or discrete entity, the term is of abstract utility only and is not a genuine geographic term. Of European origin, it designated only the homeland of the Manchus, but imperialist competition resulted in its reification. Chinese refer to the region historically as the "three eastern provinces" *(dongsansheng)* or, since 1945, as simply the "northeast" *(dongbei)*.
2 The torrent of memoirs from all walks of life is phenomenal. For the discussion of the traumatized views of migrant peasants, see Tamanoi 2001. For a good mix, see Uemura 1994 or Bungeishunjū 1984. The title of the latter work, published by a journal known for rightist tendencies, is indicative of another lingering if usually unspoken sentiment – that Manchuria was at one time "theirs." Another good example of nostalgic yearning in this vein is Manshū Kaikoshū Kankōkai 1965. This sentiment, of course, is not limited to Japanese. It was apparent among American perceptions of China after losing what was thought to be a noble cause. The success of the film *Titanic,* as popular in Japan as it was elsewhere, perhaps suggests a more current metaphor. Japanese in the 1990s were as fascinated with Japanese imperialism, especially as exemplified by the stately railway cars and hotels of the South Manchuria Railway (Mantetsu), as they were with that other fashionable and modern doomed enterprise. See Sekai Bunkasha 1988.
3 The Manchurian Incident involved the takeover of Manchuria by elements of the Japanese army stationed on the Liaodong Peninsula and along the South Manchuria Railway. It began with an explosion along the railway at Mukden – staged by provocateurs – on the night of 18 September 1931, and may be said to have ended with the establishment of the puppet state of Manchukuo on 1 March 1932, though mopping up of operations continued through December. The diplomatic rupture between China and Japan, however, continued until a truce was signed on 31 May 1933 at Tanggu. (Rather than accept an internationally brokered settlement, Japan withdrew from the League of Nations on 27 March 1933.) Initially named Regent, Pu Yi (the "last emperor") became Emperor of Manchukuo on 1 March 1934.
4 Of the 225,000 settlers recruited to Manchukuo, 34,000 were forced into work camps in Siberia, 46,000 died, and the whereabouts of 36,000 remained unknown after the war. Only 109,000 returned to Japan (Manshū Kaitakushi Kankōkai 1966, 827-29).
5 At war's end, the staff numbered 2,354. Many were noted for their liberal or leftist inclinations, and some remained in China after the war. On this fascinating institution, see also Young 1966, Egami 1980, Hara 1986, Imura 1996, and Kobayashi 1996. Because the exact name of this research organization changed often, it is referred to here simply as the Economic Research Bureau.
6 Japanese efforts to create something beyond imperialism are outside the scope of this essay. For an enlarged discussion of this issue, see Sewell 2000.

7 There were, for example, *Gaimusho* 1965-66, and *Gendaishi Shiryō* 1966, of which volumes 7 and 11 focused on the Manchurian Incident and volumes 31 to 33 on Mantetsu. Reprints of the *Manshū Hyōron* and the *Mantetsu Chōsa Geppō*, the journal and monthly compilations of the Economic Research Bureau, followed. Earlier studies were also republished, such as the Manchukuo government's *Ten-Year History of the Founding of Manchukuo* (Manshū Teikoku Seifu 1969) and Mantetsu's own history of the railway cities along its lines (*Mantetsu Fuzokuchi Keiei Enkaku Zenshi* 1977).
8 Despite its shortcomings, this work remains significant. While the opening piece by Hara Akira helps clarify the shifting policies of the 1930s, two of the other three authors, Kobayashi Hideo and Asada Kyōji, became leading authorities on the Japanese empire on the Asian mainland. See Kobayashi 1975 and Kobayashi 1993. Hara also wrote much about the economic impact of empire and edited several volumes of primary materials for publication.
9 One issue in particular brings this into focus in Japan, that of the returnees. Thousands of Japanese lost in the turmoil of war, mainly children, remained on the mainland in 1945 and Japanese newspapers today routinely carry pictures of adults seeking their biological families.
10 Likening Manchukuo's horrors to those that occurred at Auschwitz, Yamamuro reproves any who extol the puppet state's romanticized "good intentions." (A translation of this work is currently in preparation by Joshua Fogel.)
11 For one example of this dissident literature in English, see Hane 1982.

References

Anderson, B. 1991. *Imagined Communities: Reflections on the Origin and Spread of Nationalism*. Revised ed. London: Verso.

Andō, H., ed. 1965. *Mantetsu: Nihon Teikokushugi to Chūgok* (Mantetsu, Japanese imperialism and China). Tokyo: Ochanomizu Shobō.

Asada, K., and H. Kobayashi, eds., 1986. *Nihon Teikoku Shugi no Manshū Shihai* (The administration of Manchuria under Japanese imperialism). Tokyo: Jichōsha.

Bungeishunjū, ed. 1984. *Saredo, Waga "Manshū"* (Our "Manchuria"). Tokyo: Bungeishunjū.

Chin, E.I. 1995. "Gotō Shimpei, Japan's Colonial Administrator in Taiwan: A Critical Reexamination." *American Asian Review* 13(1): 29-59.

Dirlik, A. 1991. "Past Experience, if Not Forgotten, Is a Guide to the Future, or, What Is in a Text?" In M. Miyoshi and H.D. Harootunian, eds., *The Politics of History in Chinese-Japanese Relations*. Durham, NC: Duke University Press, 29-58.

Dower, J.W. 1979. *Empire and Aftermath: Yoshida Shigeru and the Japanese Experience, 1878-1954*. Cambridge, MA: Harvard University Press.

–. 1992. "The Useful War." In C. Gluck and S.R. Graubard, eds., *Showa: The Japan of Hirohito*. New York: Norton, 49-70.

Duus, P. 1996. "Japan's Wartime Empire: Problems and Issues." In P. Duus, R.H. Myers, and M. Peattie, eds., *The Japanese Wartime Empire, 1931-1945*. Princeton, NJ: Princeton University Press, xi-xlvii.

Ebara, T. 1996. "Dairen, Shin'yō, Chōshun, Harubin no ōki Naru Kanōsei" (The possibility of enlarging Dalian, Shenyang, Changchun and Harbin). *Chūgoku Keizai* (Chinese Economics) 370: 92-121.

Egami, T. 1980. *Mantetsu Ōkoku* (Mantetsu's kingdom). Tokyo: Sankei Shuppan.

Fogel, J.A. 1988. *Life along the South Manchurian Railway: The Memoirs of Itō Takeo*. Armonk, NY: M.E. Sharpe (originally published as *Itō Takeo, Mantetsu ni ikite*. Tokyo: Keisō Shobō, 1964).

Fujise, K. 1992. *Shōwa Rikugun "Ahen Bōryaku" no Daizai* (The crimes of the Shōwa military's "opium strategy"). Tokyo: Yamate Shobō Shinsha.

Fujise, T. 1993. *Chōshun-Shinkyō Hagoromomachi* (Changchun and Shinkyo's Hagoro District). Kagoshima: Fujise Takayuki.

Gaimusho. 1965-66. *Nihon Gaikō Nenpyō Narabi-ni Shuyō Bunsho* (Chronological tables of the main archives of the Japanese Foreign Ministry). 2 vols. Tokyo: Hara Shobō.

Gendaishi Shiryō (Materials on modern Japanese history). 1966. Tokyo: Misuzu Shobō.

Hane, M. 1982. *Peasants, Rebels, and Outcastes: The Underside of Japanese History.* New York: Pantheon.
Hara, K. 1967. *Gendai Ajia Keizai Ron* (Modern Asian economics). Tokyo: Keisō Shobō.
–. 1986. *Mantetsu Chōsabu to Ajia* (Mantetsu's Economic Research Bureau and Asia). Tokyo: Sekai Shobō.
Hoshino, N. 1963. *Mihatenu Yume: Manshūkoku Gaishi* (Unfinished dreams: an unofficial history of Manchukuo). Tokyo: Diamondo.
–. 1975. "Tairiku no Yume wa Ikite Iru" (Continental dreams still live). In Kokusai Zenrin Kyōkai, ed., *Manshū Kenkoku no Yume to Genjitsu* (Dream and reality of founding Manchukuo). Tokyo: Kenkōsha, 272-85.
Ienaga, S. 1953. "Han Kindai Shugi no Rekishiteki Seisatsu" (Historial reflections on anti-modernism). *Rekishigaku Kenkyū* (Historical Studies) 165: 31-41.
–. 1962. "Shihōken no Dokuritsu no Rekishiteki Kōsatsu" (A historical study of the independence of judicial power). *Shigaku Zasshi* (Historical Journal of Japan) 71(1): 1-44.
–. 1965. *Minobe Tatsukichi no Shisō Shiteki Kenkyū* (Historical studies on the thought of Minobe Tatsukichi). Tokyo: Iwanami Shoten.
–. 1978. *The Pacific War, 1941-1945: A Critical Perspective on Japan's Role in World War II.* New York: Pantheon Books (originally published in 1968 as *Taiheiyō Sensō*).
Iizawa, S. 1975. "Hakkan ni Tsuite" (Concerning [the] publication [of this work]). In Kokusai Zenrin Kyōkai, ed., *Manshū Kenkoku no Yume to Genjitsu* (Dream and reality of founding Manchukuo). Tokyo: Kenkōsha, 6-9.
Imura, T. 1996. *Mantetsu Chōsakabu: Kankeisha no Shōgen* (Mantetsu's investigators: the testimony of the participants). Tokyo: Ajia Keizai Kenkyūjo.
Ishige, N., and K. Ruddle. 1986. "Genkan no Chōshun Jiyō Ichiba" (The state of Changchun's free markets). *Kikan Minzoku Gaku* (Ethnic Studies Quarterly) 10(1): 28-37.
Itō, M. 1975. "Ajia no Fukkō Undō to Manshū Mondai" (Asia's recovery movement and the Manchurian problem). In Kokusai Zenrin Kyōkai, ed., *Manshū Kenkoku no Yume to Genjitsu* (Dream and reality of founding Manchukuo). Tokyo: Kenkōsha, 12-44.
Johnson, C. 1982. *MITI and the Japanese Miracle: The Growth of Industrial Policy, 1925-1975.* Stanford, CA: Stanford University Press.
Kanai, S. 1985. *Pekin, Harupin, Chōshun, Shin'yō no Tabi* (A trip to Beijing, Harbin, Changchun, and Shenyang). Nagano: Kanai Saburō.
Kaneko, F. 1993. "Shokuminchi Tōshi to Kōgyōka" (Colonial investment and industrialization). In *Kindai Nihon to Shokuminchi* (Modern Japan and its colonies), vol. 3. Tokyo: Iwanami Shoten, 27-50.
Kindai Nihon to Shokuminchi (Modern Japan and its colonies). 1992-93. 8 vols. Tokyo: Iwanami Shoten.
Kishima, M. 1986. *Manshū 1945 Nen* (Manchuria, 1945). Tokyo: Chikyūsetsu.
Kitakōji, K., and M. Watanabe. 1982. *Chōshun, Kitsurin* (Changchun, Jilin Province). Tokyo: Kokusho Kankōkai.
Kitaoka, S. 1988. *Gotō Shimpei: Gaiko to Bijyon* (Gotō Shimpei: diplomacy and vision). Tokyo: Chūō Koronsha.
Kobayashi, H. 1975. *Daitōa Kyōeiken no Keisei to Hōkai* (The formation and collapse of the Greater East Asia Co-Prosperity Sphere). Tokyo: Ochanomizu Shobō.
–. 1993. *Nihon Gunseika no Ajia* (Asia under Japanese military rule). Tokyo: Iwanami Shoten.
–. 1996. *Mantetsu: "Chino Shūdan" no Tanjō to Shi* (Mantetsu: the birth and death of an "intellectual pack"). Tokyo: Yoshikawa Kōbunkan.
Kokubun, H. 1979. *Saraba Shinkyō* (Shinkyō). Tokyo: Kokusho Kankōkai.
Kokusai Zenrin Kyōkai, ed. 1975. *Manshū Kenkoku no Yume to Genjitsu* (Dream and reality of founding Manchukuo). Tokyo: Kenkōsha.
Komagome, T. 1996. *Shokuminchi Teikoku Nihon no Bunka Tōgō* (The cultural integration of imperial Japan's colonies). Tokyo: Iwanami Shoten.
Komai, T. 1933. *Dai Manshūkoku Kensetsu Roku* (The founding of Manchukuo). Tokyo: Chūō Kōronsha.
–. 1952. *Tairiku e no Higan* (Eagerly to the continent). Tokyo: Dai Nihon Yūben Kōdankai.
Komatsu, N. 1989. "Kyū Manshūkoku Sekijūjisha Shinkyō Rōa Gakuin-shodai Gakuin

Tashiro Kiyō ni Tsuite" (Concerning Tashiro Kiyō, the first president of the Red Cross Deaf-Mute School in Shinkyō, Manchukuo). *Miyagi Kyōiku Daigaku Kiyō: Nibun Satsu Shizen Kagaku-kyōiku Kagaku* (Bulletin of Miyagi University of Education) 24: 127-40.

Koshizawa, A. 1988. *Manshūkoku no Shuto Keikaku: Tōkyō no Genzai to Mirai o Tou* (The planning of Manchukyo's capital: an inquiry into the present and future of Tokyo). Tokyo: Nihon Keizai Hyōronsha.

–. 1989. *Harupin no Toshi Keikaku* (City planning in Harbin). Tokyo: Sōwasha.

–. 1991. *Tōkyō no Toshi Keikaku* (City planning in Tokyo). Tokyo: Iwanami Shoten.

Kurahashi, M. 1994. *Jugun Ianfu Mondai no Rekishiteki Kenkyū* (Historical studies of the military "comfort women" problem). Tokyo: Kyōei Shobō.

–. 1996. *Nihon no Ahen Senryaku* (Japan's opium strategy). Tokyo: Kyōei Shobō.

McCormack, G. 1991. "Manchukuo: Constructing the Past." *East Asian History* 2: 105-24.

Manshikai, ed. 1964-65. *Manshū Kaihatsu Yonjūnen Shi* (Forty year history of the development of Manchuria). 3 vols. Tokyo: Manshū Kaihatsu Yonjūnen Shi Kankōkai.

Manshū Iminshi Kenkyūkai, ed. 1976. *Nihon Teikokushugika no Manshū Imin* (Manchurian migrants under Japanese imperialism). Tokyo: Ryūkei Shosha.

Manshū Kaikoshū Kankōkai, ed. 1965. *Aa Manshū: Kuni Tsukuri Sangyō Kaihatsusha no Shuki* (Ah, Manchuria: the private papers of national builders and industrial developers). Tokyo: Manshū Kaikoshū Kankōkai.

Manshū Kaitakushi Kankōkai. 1966. *Manshū Kaitakushi* (History of colonizing Manchuria). Tokyo: Manshū Kaitakushi Kankōkai.

Manshū Kokugun Kankō I'inkai, ed. 1970. *Manshū Kokugun* (Manchuria's National Army). Fukuoka: Ranshōkai.

Manshū Kokushi Hensan Kankōkai, ed. 1970. *Manshū Kokushi* (History of Manchukuo). Tokyo: ManMō dōō Engokai.

Manshū no Kiroku (Documents on Manchuria). 1995. Tokyo: Shueisha.

Manshū Teikoku Seifu, ed. 1969. *Manshū Kenkoku Jūnenshi* (Ten-year history of the founding of Manchukuo). Tokyo: Hara Shobō (originally published 1941).

Manshūshi Kenkyūkai, ed. 1972. *Nihon Teikokushugika no Manshū* (Manchuria under Japanese imperialism). Tokyo: Ochanomizu Shobō.

Mantetsu Fuzokuchi Keiei Enkaku Zenshi (The complete history of the management of Mantetsu's "attached lands"). 1977. 3 vols. Tokyo: Ryūkei Shosha (originally Dairen: Minami Manshū Tetsudō Kabushiki Kaisha, 1939).

Maruyama, M., ed. 1953. *Nihon no Nashonarizumu* (Japanese nationalism). Tokyo: Kawade Shobō.

Maruyama, M. 1963a. "Theory and Psychology of Ultra-Nationalism." Translated by I. Morris. In M. Maruyama and I. Morris, eds., *Thought and Behaviour in Modern Japanese Politics*. London: Oxford University Press, 1-24 (originally published May 1946).

–. 1963b. "The Ideology and Dynamics of Japanese Fascism." Translated by A. Fraser. In M. Maruyama and I. Morris, eds., *Thought and Behaviour in Modern Japanese Politics*. London: Oxford University Press, 25-83 (a lecture originally delivered in 1947).

–. 1963c. "Thought and Behaviour Patterns of Japan's Wartime Leaders." Translated by I. Morris. In M. Maruyama and I. Morris, eds., *Thought and Behaviour in Modern Japanese Politics*. London: Oxford University Press, 84-134 (originally published May 1949).

Morimura, S. 1983. *Akuma no Hoshoku* (The devil's gluttony). Revised ed. Tokyo: Kadokawa Shoten.

Morimura, T. 1997. *Ronsō: 731 Butai* (The Unit 731 controversy). Enlarged ed. Tokyo: Banshōsha.

Nakamura, S. 1984. *Chūgoku Kindai Tōhoku Chi'ikishi Kenkyū* (Revolutionaries against colonists: a history of northeast China, 1900-1949). Kyoto: Hōritsu Bunkasha.

Nichi Roku 20 Seiki (Twentieth-Century Daily Record). 1998. Vol. 2, no. 1, 6-13 January.

Nihon Shokuminchi Shi 2 (History of Japan's colonies 2). 1978. *Manshū: Nichi-Ro Sensō Kara Kenkoku-metsubō Made* (Manchuria: from the Russo-Japanese War to the founding and fall). Tokyo: Mainichi Shinbunsha.

Nishizawa, Y. 1989. "Manshūkoku no Shuto Keikaku" (The planning of Manchukuo's capital). *Ajia Keizai* (Asian Economics) 38: 109-13.

–. 1996a. *Umi o Watatta Nihonjin Kenchikuka* (Japanese architects who "crossed the sea" [to China]). Tokyo: Shōkokusha.
–. 1996b. *"Manshū" Toshi Monogatari* (Manchuria's cities). Tokyo: Kawade Shobō Shinsha.
Obara, H., A. Toshio, Y. Yukio, and O. Hisao. 1997. *Nihon Gun no Dokugasu Sen* (Japan's poison gas warfare). Tokyo: Nitchū Shuppan.
Okabe, M. 1978. *Manshūkoku*. Tokyo: Sanseido.
Okawa, Y. 1989. "Chōshun no Jidōsha Kōgyō" (Changchun's automobile factory). *Chiri* (Geography) 34(6): 92-99.
Osaki, K. 1997. *Akumu no Isan* (The devil's legacy). Tokyo: Gakuyo Shobō.
Pin, B., Y. Yuko, and M. Kyoshiro, trans. 1995. *Nihon no Chūgoku Shinryaku to Dokugasu Heiki* (Japan's invasion of China and poison gas weapons). Tokyo: Akashi Shoten.
Reischauer, E.O., and A.M. Craig. 1978. *Japan: Tradition and Transformation*. Boston: Houghton Mifflin, 247-77.
Sekai Bunkasha, ed. 1988. *Wasureenu Mantetsu* (Unforgettable Mantetsu). Tokyo: Sekai Bunkasha.
Sewell, W. 2000. "Japanese Imperialism and Civic Construction in Manchuria: Changchun, 1905-1945." Unpublished PhD dissertation, University of British Columbia.
Sugiyama, H. 1996. *Manshū Jojūku* (A Manchurian girls' school). Tokyo: Shinchōsha.
Suzuki, T. 1971. "Manshū Kenkyū no Genjō to Kadai" (The current state of "Manchuria" studies and its problems). *Ajia Keizai* (Asian Economics) 12: 49-60.
Suzuki, Y. 1993. *Jugun Ianfu Mondai to Seiboryaku* (The problem of military "comfort women" and sexual strategies). Tokyo: Miraisha.
Taiheiyō Sensō Kenkyūkai. 1996. *Manshū Teikoku* (The end of Manchuria). Tokyo: Kawade Shobō.
Takasaki, T. 1952. *Manshū no Shūen* (The end of Manchuria). Tokyo: Jitsugyō no Nihonsha.
Takasaki, Y. 1995. *Zetsubō no Iminshi: Manshū e Okurareta "Hisabetsu Buraku" no Kiroku* (The despair of immigrant history: the "undiscriminated villages" sent to Manchuria). Tokyo: Mainichi Shinbunsha.
Takasugi, S. 1982. *731 Butai Saikinsen no Ishi o Ou* (Pursuing the bacteriological warfare of Unit 731). Tokyo: Tokuma Shobō.
Tamanoi, M.A. 2001. "A Road to a 'Redeemed Mankind': The Politics of Memory among the Former Japanese Peasant Settlers in Manchuria." In T. Lahusen, ed., *Harbin and Manchuria: Place, Space and Identity*. Durham, NC: Duke University Press, 163-89.
Tanaka, M. 1952. *Nihon Muzai Ron* (On Japan's innocence). Tokyo: Taiheiyō Shuppansha.
Tanaka, S. 1993. *Japan's Orient: Rendering Pasts into History*. Berkeley: University of California Press.
Tani, M. 1989. *Chōshun Monogatari* (Tales of Changchun). Nagoya: Maruzen.
Tōyama, S. 1949. "Nihon Zettaishugi Seiritsuki no Mondai: Meiji Ishin no Shutaisei Ron o Chūshin Toshite" (The problem of eliminating Japanese absolutism: examining the autonomy of the Meiji Restoration). *Shigaku Zasshi* (Historical Journal of Japan) 58(3): 77-86.
Udagawa, M. 1984. *Shinkō Zaibatsu* (The new Zaibatsu). Kyoto: Nihon Keizai Shinbunsha.
–. 1990. "The Move into Manchuria of the Nissan Combine." *Japanese Yearbook of Business History* (7): 3-29.
Uemura, M. 1994. *Manshūkoku ni Umarete* (Born in Manchukuo). Tokyo: Keisō Shobō.
Ueno, T. 1975. "Jō Kōsho to Komai Tokuzō" (Zheng Lixu and Komai Tokuzo). In Kokusai Zenrin Kyōkai, ed., *Manshū Kenkoku no Yume to Genjitsu* (Dream and reality of founding Manchukuo). Tokyo: Kenkōsha, 337-46.
Watanabe, M. 1993. "731 Butai to Ienaga Tetsuzan" (Unit 731 and Ienaga Tetsuzan). In Chūō Daigaku Jinbun Kagaku Kenkyūjo, eds., *Nit-Chū Sensō* (The Sino-Japanese War). Tokyo: Chūō Daigaku Shuppansha, 275-302.
Williams, W.A. 1962. *The Tragedy of American Diplomacy*. Revised and enlarged ed. New York: Dell.
Yamada, M. 1992. *Senryō Jugun Ianfu: Kokusaku Baishun no Onnatachi no Higeki* (Military "comfort women" during the Occupation: the tragedy of female prostitution as national policy). Tokyo: Kōjinsha.

Yamaguchi, H., and H. Satō. 1996. *Understanding the Developing World: Thirty-Five Years of Area Studies at the IDE*. Tokyo: Institute of Developing Economies.
Yamamoto, Y., ed. 1995. *Manshūkoku no Kenkyū* (Studies on Manchukuo). Tokyo: Rokuin Shobō.
Yamamuro, S. 1993. *Kimera: Manshūkoku no Shōzō* (Chimera: a portrait of Manchukuo). Tokyo: Chūō Kōronsha.
Yanagisawa, Y. 1992a. "Kindai Nihon ni Okeru 'Kokusaika' no Kenshō: Nichi-Ro Sengo Nihonjin no 'Manshū' Shinshutsu" (Probing "internationalization" in modern Japan: Japanese in Manchuria after the Russo-Japanese War). In S. Ozeki, A. Takahashi, and Y. Chino, eds., *Kokusaika Jidai ni Ikiru Nihonjin* (Japanese living in the age of internationalization). Tokyo: Aoki Shobō.
–. 1992b. "Dairen Shōgyō Kaigijo Jōgiin no Kōsei to Katsudō: 1910-1920 Nendai Dairen Zaisei Hensen Shi" (The cosmopolitanism and activity of Dalian's commercial establishment: the transformation of finance in Dalian, 1910-20). In K. Iseki, ed., *Sentōki Nihon no Taigai Keizai Kankei* (Overseas economic matters of Japan at war). Tokyo: Nihon Keizai Hyōronsha, 301-58.
–. 1993. "Manshū Shōko Imin no Gutaizō" (A realistic picture of Manchuria's immigrant merchants). *Rekishi Hyōron* (Historical Review) 513: 42-53.
Yoshida, F. 1988. "Dairen, Shin'yō, Chōshun, Harupin no Tabi" (Travels in Dairen, Shenyang, Changchun, and Harbin). *Fainansu* (Finance) 24(5): 58-69.
Yoshikazu, Y. 1992. *Niji'iro no Turotsukii* (Rainbow coloured Trotsky). Tokyo: Chō Shuppansha.
Young, J. 1966. *The Research Activities of the South Manchurian Railway Company, 1907-1945: A History and Bibliography*. New York: Columbia University Press.
Young, L. 1998. *Japan's Total Empire: Manchuria and the Culture of Wartime Imperialism*. Berkeley: University of California Press.

6
May the Saru River Flow: The Nibutani Dam and the Resurging Tide of the Ainu Identity Movement
Millie Creighton

In Japan the New Year 2000 was officially the beginning of *Heisei 12*, marking the twelfth year in the reign of the presiding emperor, whose reign has been designated as the Heisei Era. Japan's late-twentieth-century international prominence and its concurrent use of the *seireki* or western[1] calendar means there is also awareness in Japan of the "new millennium" as frequently discussed in western countries. In western countries, there was a debate over whether the year 2000 was the first year of the new millennium, as popular millennium madness suggested, or, in keeping with existing conventions of counting centuries, the last year of the previous millennium. However, the year 2000 was for many "the millennium year," a phrase ambiguous enough to cover the situation either way, a humanly constructed liminal marker in time, a divider betwixt and between calling for a pause; a stop in the ongoing flow of life to reflect upon the past and think about the future (Turner 1967).

In pausing to consider Japan at the millennium, it is imperative to consider its Indigenous Peoples at this possible turning point in Japanese society. Whether the year 2000, as the millennium year, is the last year of the old millennium or the first year of the new one, the opening of the year on 1 January marked a sense of transition and the passing of the midway point in the Decade of Indigenous Peoples, designated by the United Nations as the decade from 1995 until the end of 2004. (Since this decade began on 1 January 1995 and continues until 31 December 2004, or until 1 January 2005, sometimes one will see this written as the decade 1995-2004, and alternatively as 1995-2005.) This decade designation followed the United Nations declaration of 1993 as the Year of Indigenous Peoples. Japan at the millennium is also at a possible critical turning point in terms of constructs of national identity. In the waning years of the old millennium, the work of minority groups, writings in the popular press, and academic scholarship all began to make serious inroads into the denial of diversity that underlies Japan's self-constructed identity as a "homogeneous nation," while, conversely, other elements within Japanese society sought to reaffirm the belief in a "one-people" nation united under the emperor.

In this chapter, which is in accord with Japanese scholar Baba's recognition of "the existence of several well-defined minorities"(Baba 1980, 61; see also Siddle 1997, 17) in Japan, I consider some of the concerns and activities of members of Ainu during the 1990s, in terms of their struggles for positive self-identity, a validation of their distinct cultural heritage within the national Japanese polity, and their growing international networking among the world's Indigenous Peoples in pursuit of these goals. It is based on research conducted in Japan's northern island of Hokkaido, in Nibutani, Akan, and Sapporo in 1993 and 1994 and Hakodate and Sapporo in 2000; in Vladivostok, Russia in 1994; and in other areas of Japan and Vancouver, Canada, during the decade of the 1990s. In this chapter, I will consider festivals and special activities conducted by Ainu to mark 1993 as the United Nations Year of Indigenous Peoples, along with other events and laws in the decade of the 1990s, in light of how these helped to focus attention on minority and Aboriginal issues in Japan.

I will also explore in greater detail a central issue that emerged in relation to Ainu identity concerns during this time, involving the protest against a dam project built on land in Nibutani considered sacred in Ainu tradition, and how this helped contribute to an Ainu renaissance movement, a further linking with other minority groups in Japan, and a fostering of international linkages with other Aboriginal groups worldwide. While focusing on Ainu, the article thus draws attention to the contemporary struggles within Japan of various minority groups to assert Indigenous or ethnic identities[2] against the monolithic construct of homogeneous Japan. It also discusses how Japan's nationally acclaimed goal of *kokusaika* (internationalization), originally directed at increasing interaction with nations and groups outside Japan, has helped induce greater reflexivity about social diversity and marginalized peoples within Japan.

Japan's Myth of Homogeneity and National Identity Symbols

Japanese society constructs self-identity around a strong assertion of homogeneity and the corresponding denial of diversity (Weiner 1997). This myth of homogeneity, continually reaffirmed by Japanese institutions and authorities, is echoed by many foreign writers. Christopher, for example, writes: "Racially and culturally, Japan is the most homogeneous of the world's major nations." He further links this to a Japanese ability to "preserve a keen sense of their own special identity" (Christopher 1983, 44). The pride taken in this asserted homogeneity is reflected in former Prime Minister Nakasone's 1986 speech in which he offended both American and Japanese minorities by claiming that Japan's IQ level was higher than that of the United States because Japan was a homogeneous society uncontaminated by minority groups. Some Japanese scholars like Baba suggest that the constant refrain of homogeneity leads to "unthinking acceptance," despite "the existence of several well-defined minorities" (Baba 1980). The denial of diversity is so strong that Japan responded to the United Nations charter calling for the elimination of discrimination against minorities with an official government statement in 1980 that there were no minorities in Japan. The government also noted that in countries where minorities did exist, Japan believed they should not be discriminated against (Creighton 1991; Sjoberg 1993; Siddle 1997, 40).

The denial of diversity in Japan has worked against minority struggles to counteract the negative effects of discrimination, to raise the standard of living of minority groups, which is usually lower than for mainstream Japanese, and to enhance a positive self-identity for minority group members, since by official definitions minority problems cannot exist, given Japan's dogma of a one-people nation. The United Nations international human rights covenant – the International Bill of Human Rights – maintains that "all peoples have the right of self-determination. By virtue of that right they freely determine their political status and freely pursue their economic, social, and cultural development" (United Nations 1978, 10-11).

The ability of groups such as Ainu to realize these rights, however, is made problematic by the nation-state's denial of their presence as distinct groups within the society. As Seymour (1993, 48) aptly points out, "the meaning of 'peoples,' is of course, not without ambiguity. It would seem to have some ethnic implications, but not apply when ethnic groups are intermingled among others. Thus, a 'people' must have some territorial integrity before they can claim independence."

In the case of minority groups in Japan, they are positioned within a national polity that has sought to deny the presence of distinct ethnic groups within the society. One way this is done is through the use of national symbols of identity that can theoretically be inclusive, but that somehow also serve to reinforce inclusion at the expense of conformity to the homogeneity model. Embedded within these symbols is the staging of Japan as a homogeneous society. The symbols reiterate the history of Japanese relations – with minorities both within Japan and in other Asian areas that Japan colonized – as a history of assimilation, or *dōka*, where assimilation meant "same-ization" or "Japanization" *(Nipponka)* (Robertson 1998, 92).[3]

Two prominent symbols utilized in the construct of a Japanese national identity based on the assertion of homogeneity are rice and the sun. In her treatise *Rice as Self*, Ohnuki-Tierney (1990) details how the contemporary Japanese sense of self is closely entwined with rice and rice cultivation. It is not just any rice that is associated with Japanese identity, but the short-grained polished rice, in contrast to the longer-grained varieties frequently found in other Asian countries (Creighton 1995a, 1998a). It is also specifically rice grown on Japanese land rather than the same variety grown outside Japan's national boundaries, including the seemingly similar short-grained variety grown in California, which many Japanese feel does not have the same taste value and which clearly does not have the same symbolic value. The strongly asserted symbolic association of rice with Japanese identity is tied to the suggestion that "one is what one eats." In this case, there is the suggestion that the Japanese eat not just rice but rice that is a product of the environment as linked to the national body. In this construct, the children of Japan are nourished by the sustenance produced by the national body, as infants are nourished by breast milk produced by their mothers' bodies, and hence are suggested to have return obligations to support and replenish the national body.

Although rice cultivation has an extremely important role throughout Japan, and archeological evidence indicates a long existence of rice cultivation, there are indications that it was not a central part of the diet of the earliest people for whom there are significant archeological records, the Jomon people, but a more central part of the diet of the later-arriving waves of immigration of the Yayoi people. Thus, assertions of Japanese identity bound to the universality of rice cultivation and consumption denies, or at least minimizes, the existence of groups within Japan whose subsistence was not rice-based, both in prehistory and in historic cases of culture contact. Notable among these was the Ainu, whose subsistence centred around fishing, hunting, and gathering until mainstream Japanese assimilationist policies channelled them into farming activities. A parallel situation applies to Okinawans at the southern reaches of the archipelago, for whom historically rice cultivation had a less prominent role in the diet. According to Takamiya (1997, 240), "while wet rice agriculture was accepted in many regions of Japan, in Okinawa it was not, because of environmental and climatic factors." Terasawa and Terasawa (1981) also conclude Okinawa's agricultural system centred around dry crops such as wheat, barley, and millet, which were better adapted to the Okinawan environment. In dominant cultural symbolism, crops such as millet are seen as a low-class food source, in contrast to highly valued rice.[4] Thus, the Japanese sense of self constructed around a unified agrarian heritage based on rice cultivation again serves to reinforce the denial of diversity in Japan, from the prehistoric past to the modern post-millennial present, and to denigrate the food cultures of groups in society that were based on other staples.

Another symbol of Japanese national identity is the sun. One common custom in Japan associated with the New Year, referred to as *hatsu hinode* (first sunrise), involves going to an ocean vantage point to view the first sunrise of the year. Since Japan is an insular country, there are many locations where the meeting of water and the horizon provide an excellent view of the apparent emergence of the sun at the breaking of day. This New Year's ritual of greeting the first sunrise of the year focuses attention on the place of human beings within the cycles of life and the natural universe, while reinforcing their social ties to each other. It should also be noted, however, that the sun as an important symbolic trope in Japan attempts to construct the social definition of human beings as specifically "Japanese" both in relation to the larger patterns of the natural universe and the orchestration of social ties within communities. Although the universe may send its sun to shine just as much upon the non-Japanese as the Japanese, national symbolism tends to treat the sun as a prominent marker of "Japaneseness."

The word for Japan, *Nihon*, means "the root of the sun." It is often more poetically translated to render Japan as "the land of the rising sun," hence again, *hatsu hinode*, or the first sunrise, like all sunrises, is subtly linked to national Japanese identity. The flag long used as Japan's national flag,[5] *Hinomaru*, which means the sun's circle, depicts a red ball symbolizing the sun, on a white background. This gave the name to the *Hinomaru Bentō*. *Bentō*, often translated as "lunch box," refers to a prepared meal people carry with them, which might be eaten at school, at work, while travelling, and so on. The *Hinomaru Bentō* provides a section of the meal as rice laid out in a rectangular shape, with an *umeboshi* (dried red plum) placed in the centre, creating a visual icon of the Japanese flag, the symbol of the national body, which people then physically consume and incorporate into their own bodies. It is noteworthy that the *Hinomaru Bentō* thus combines both symbols of national Japanese identity being discussed here, in the form of real rice with a representation of the sun.

Just as the sun becomes a symbol to highlight Japanese identity in contrast to non-Japanese, the sun does not seem to symbolically shine equally for all elements of the population within Japan. In the Japanese creation myth, the imperial line is thought to be descended from Amaterasu, the sun-goddess daughter of Izanagi. In the construction of homogeneous Japan, the Japanese populace is symbolically united under the emperor, to whom is granted mythic descent from the sun, "from time immemorial." Thus, sun symbolism as it is used to reaffirm the national polity and reinforce assertions of homogeneity works against minority groups in Japan such as resident Koreans, who after generations within Japanese society are still legally designated as "foreigners," and thus excluded from Japanese identity, and against groups like Ainu and Okinawans, who wish to establish claims to their own distinct cultural heritages, which in both cases involve claims to Indigenous status, given that their forebears pre-dated those of the mainstream *Wajin* ("Japanese") on the Japanese archipelago.

The following section considers problems created for Ainu by Japan's myth of homogeneity, and activities during the 1990s that highlighted

Ainu resistance. Despite the drawbacks created by over a century of assimilationist practices, and the national government's rhetoric of homogeneity, Siddle (1997, 17) points out that, "nevertheless, a striking 'ethnic revival' is underway among the Ainu" (see also Siddle 1996; Creighton 1995b; Sjoberg 1993; Hiwasaki 2000).

The Nibutani Dam and Ainu Resistance

Present-day Ainu reside predominantly in Hokkaido, the northernmost of Japan's four main islands, or the northern Tōhoku region of the main island, Honshū. Thus, in geographical space, as in the nationalized imagined community, they are peripheral to the Tokyo-based state core of power.[6] The national government's assertion of homogeneity is criticized by Ainu leaders. The abstract for a talk that was to have been given by Kayano Shigeru,[7] Japan's first Ainu member of the National Diet, at a 1994 conference in Vladivostok, Russia, said that his paper would "shed some light on the present-day Ainu initiatives to combat with the existing biases in public education system [sic] which is based on the conception of Japan as a homogeneous nation" (Kayano 1994a, 91).

Although Ainu festivals, exhibits, and even museums are maintained, these are treated as analogous to local cultural fairs or exhibits elsewhere in Japan, not as a recognition of Ainu as a minority group. According to Japan's official ideology of a one-people nation, Ainu have been assimilated and therefore, like *Wajin,* are simply *Nihonjin* (Japanese), although in both vernacular speech and scholarly writing, people routinely differentiate between the two. Japanese-born scholar Ohnuki-Tierney (1993, 5), for example, refers to her experiences with "both the Ainu and the Japanese," and makes statements such as, "I went back to Japan frequently, but I went directly to the Ainu people in Hokkaido and did not pay serious attention to the Japanese" (Ohnuki-Tierney 1994, 16). There are thus indications that the two categories are commonly distinguished despite official denial. Siddle describes this as the contradiction of race for the Ainu. On the one hand, Ainu are clearly differentiated from *Wajin* and thought of as a different racial category, either making it difficult for Ainu to "pass" as *Wajin* or creating psychological problems if they succeed. On the one hand, the rhetoric of homogeneity denies the distinct existence of Ainu, who are therefore left caught between these two contradictory stances (Siddle 1996; 1997, 26).

Japan's assimilationist policies contributed to the erosion of Ainu culture and the disadvantaged conditions of modern Ainu. Clear differences in general economic conditions exist. The majority of Ainu are in Japan's lowest income bracket (60.9 percent of Ainu compared with 21.9 percent of *Wajin*). The unemployment level of Ainu (15.1 percent) is nearly double that of *Wajin* (8 percent), reliance on social welfare is high, and educational levels are in sharp contrast to those of *Wajin* (Sjoberg 1993, 116).

Japan's assimilationist policies were consciously designed during the Meiji Era, the period beginning in 1868 during which Japan opened its formerly closed society to the outside world. Japan was then constructing a national identity of homogeneity that symbolically included a self-image as a rice-growing and rice-eating people (Ohnuki-Tierney 1993). Since Ainu subsistence was based on hunting and gathering, acculturation policies emphasized making them farmers. These policies conveniently denied their traditional land, hunting, and fishing rights. Of great bitterness to Ainu was the 1899 law called the *Hokkaido Kyūdojin Hogohō*. Although this law is frequently translated as "Hokkaido Aborigine Protection Act," this does not adequately convey the full meaning of the original. The *"kyū"* in the title means "former"; it is a prefix also used, for example, in referring to the "former" name of a married woman. A more appropriate translation is the "Hokkaido *Former* Aborigines Protection Act." The law's title asserts that once assimilated, the Ainu were no longer Aborigines. Kayano claims that the Japanese government, unlike other governments, made no attempt or even pretence to a treaty. He writes: "By contrast, there is not even a scrap of treaty between the Japanese and the Ainu. Instead, the 'Former Aboriginal Protection Act' was unilaterally imposed in 1899, in the name of protecting the 'unenlightened' Ainu" (Kayano 1999, 817).

This act, which remained in effect for nearly a century until 1997, made it illegal for Ainu to carry out their hunting and fishing practices – many were arrested for continuing their common cultural subsistence patterns – and allotted each family five hectares of land, forcing them to become farmers in conformity with symbolic constructs of national identity (Takakura 1960, 55, 56). Assimilationist policies also sought to discourage cultural practices and, of particular importance, to inhibit language use. According to Siddle (1997, 17), "government policies of relocation and assimilation aimed at the eventual extinction of the Ainu as a people, aided a system of 'native education' that actively discouraged Ainu language and culture" (see also Siddle 1996).

These assimilationist policies treated Ainu as an inferior culture whose members needed to be civilized. Such an attitude was not unique to the Japanese government, but has frequently characterized contact relationships with Indigenous Peoples elsewhere in the world. Boarding schools and mission schools were used as important agents of acculturation in the United States and Mexico (Berkhofer 1965; Szasz and Ryan 1988). According to Keller (1983, 152), the educational goals of schools for Natives in the US were "to demolish the Indians' communal life, to wreck tribal identity and values, and to implant a different individualist ideology." Residential schools in Canada sought to remove Native children from their community in order to transform them from "savages" to "the habits and modes of thought of white men."[8] Similar policies have been directed at Australian Aborigines (Anderson 1983) and the Maori of New Zealand (Binney 1987).

In the view of these assimilationist policies, erosion of Ainu culture and language were seen as advances towards acculturation and modernization, while Ainu themselves were often treated with condescension and contempt. One joke invoked the similarity between the word Ainu and the Japanese word for dog, *inu*. Using the expression "ah," and the Japanese copula *da* ("it is"), the pun was created, *"ah, inu da"* ("It's an Ainu" or "Oh, it's a dog!") (DeVos et al. 1983; Kayano 1994a, 51). Many Ainu felt ashamed of being Ainu and tried "passing." "Passing" refers to attempts to hide one's identity and pass as mainstream. If successful, it gained one greater acceptance in general society, but at the cost of psychological pain and fear of discovery. As for other minority groups in Japan, such as Burakumin ("hamlet people," descendants of an occupational outcaste group), passing could be most "excruciating when attempting marriage" (DeVos et al. 1983, 8).

The poignancy surrounding pressure to pass was revealed to me in 1994 by a woman working at the Sapporo headquarters of the Ainu association known as Hokkaido Utari Kyōkai.[9] This full Ainu woman, one of nine children, married a *Wajin* but is trying to raise her eleven-year-old son to be proud of his Ainu heritage. She knows that not all Ainu wish to reveal their identity. She said:

> When I was dating, I told my husband right out that I was Ainu. I didn't want to have to hide it. If we were going to get married I felt like I didn't want to pretend all my life that I was something else. Many people try to hide it, try to pass, always. Many people don't even want their spouses to know. Some want to make better marriages. Some are afraid of trouble. When there are fights for example, there is the fear the spouse will bring it up, and say "you're just Ainu" ... My son is eleven now. There are forty students in his class and he is the only Ainu, but he says openly "I am Ainu." One day they discussed Ainu in his class and he told everyone he was Ainu. He is not ashamed of this.[10]

This woman is one of many Ainu in Hokkaido today actively working towards a renewal of Ainu culture and a reaffirmation of positive Ainu identity. Ainu now engage in touristic presentations of their traditional culture not just for a livelihood but as a medium to educate the public about Ainu culture (Sjoberg 1993). Other activities include giving lectures or public presentations. In one such event, which I saw in Akan, an Ainu man presented the Ainu idea of "humanness" through a discussion of an Ainu concept:

In the Ainu language, the word Ainu means "human being" and the goal of life should be to live as a humanlike human being *(aynu neoan aynu)*. Now, what does this mean? Well, it includes things like consideration for other human beings. According to Ainu belief everyone was given two ears and one mouth, which shows that you should listen to other people twice as much as you talk.[11]

Another focus of the renaissance movement has been preserving the Ainu language. Language is an important marker of ethnicity and cultural identity. LePage and Tabouret-Keller (1985, 14) claim that language usage involves a "series of acts of identity" in which people make speech choices "to resemble those of the group or groups with which, from time to time, they wish to be identified" (118). Sagarin and Moneymaker (1979, 38) claim that even if language use has declined until it is "little more than a cultural fossil," it can "continue to be a symbolic rallying point for the ethnic group."

The Ainu language never had a writing system. Kayano spent years recording the speech of elderly Ainu speakers because he recognized that although archeological studies could give insights into past Ainu life and material culture studies could preserve artifacts, once gone the Ainu language could never be recovered: "When you dig in the earth, you find stone and earthen implements, but not words – not the words of our ancestors. Words aren't buried in the ground. They aren't hanging from the branches of trees. They're only transmitted from one mouth to the next" (Kayano 1999, 819).

In 1982 Kayano established Japan's first Ainu language school in Nibutani. By 1993 there were eleven Ainu language schools throughout Hokkaido. The Hokkaido Utari Kyōkai compiled and published a textbook for Ainu language instruction in 1994 (Hokkaido Utari Kyōkai 1994). By 1999 the number of Ainu language classes in Hokkaido had grown to fourteen. I visited the Ainu language classes held at the Hokkaido Utari Kyōkai headquarters in Sapporo. According to one woman involved at the centre, few people came at first, but the past five years had seen a sizeable and growing group of steadfast students: "The classes started about ten years ago. I think from about ten years ago there was a general beginning of an Ainu identity movement. People started saying we shouldn't be ashamed of being Ainu, we should be proud of it. As part of that the Ainu language classes started. Still, at that time not very many people came ... maybe only a couple of people each time. But from about five years ago, more people came, and more people were concerned about the Ainu language being lost."[12]

Language study also testifies to the long-standing presence of Ainu in Hokkaido, where an estimated forty thousand place names are of Ainu origin (Kayano 1999, 819).

Nibutani, located along the midpoint of the Saru River, an area important in Ainu belief, emerged as a central core of the Ainu revival. This is considered sacred land, since the god Okikurmikamuy is said to have been born here (Kayano 1994b, 7). In ancient Ainu beliefs, nature was sacred because humans received their sustenance from it. Other Ainu gods included Atuykorkamuy, god of the sea; Shirkorkamuy, god of the mountain forests; and Wakkauskamuy, god of river waters (Kayano 1999, 818). Nibutani symbolizes *Ainu moshiri* (Ainu land/community), a vital Ainu concept that connotes the harmonious coexistence of humans, gods, and nature (Ohtsuka 1994). Uemura discusses how the economic and subsistence life of the Ainu was harmoniously integrated in this concept of *Ainu moshir,* or *Ainu moshiri* (Uemura 1990, 205-89). According to Uemura, ideas of "development" and "progress" that did not harmonize with this ideal were not a part of Ainu life but were imposed on them by *Wajin,* based on their own goals and expectations – *Wajin no tame, no "keihatsu" to "shimpo"* ("Development" and "progress" for the sake of *Wajin*) (Uemura 1990, 222-35).

With close to 500 Ainu inhabitants, Nibutani has the largest remaining population of Ainu in Japan, and the world. It was a source of pride for many villagers when Kayano became the first Ainu in the National Diet. Rather than hide his Ainu identity or Nibutani village background, his book titles proclaim them through statements such as *"Nibutani ni Ainu to shite ikiru"* ("I [am determined to] live in Nibutani as an Ainu") (Kayano 1993). Nibutani was already home to the Museum of Ainu Cultural Resources, established by Kayano, who for decades personally collected Ainu artifacts. As part of the revival movement, the much larger Nibutani Ainu Culture Museum was erected in 1992, both as a museum and as a centre for Ainu studies. Museum pamphlets state that its purpose is to preserve the true history and culture of Hokkaido *(Hokkaido no rekishi to bunka no honto no gensen),* based on Ainu culture inherited up to the present generation *(gendai ni Ainu bunka o uketsugi),* pass this on to future generations *(mirai e tsutaete iku),* while aiming at the creation of new Ainu traditions *(arata na dentō no sōzō o mezashimasu).* The pamphlets claim that Nibutani is the *furusato,*[13] or "home place" of Ainu culture *(Ainu bunka no sato Nibutani).* Ohtsuka Kazuyoshi, Ainu specialist and curator for Japan's National Museum of Ethnology, pinpoints Nibutani as the heart of the Ainu identity movement.[14] Given Nibutani's pivotal role in the Ainu culture renaissance, a government decision to construct a dam in Nibutani had potentially profound effects on the modern construct of Ainu identity.

Japan is a small, highly mountainous island country with densely populated urban centres. Dams are frequently built in outlying rural areas to supply water to the cities. These projects most strongly affect rural dwellers because they are forced to sell their land and cannot easily relocate, given the closed nature of rural Japanese communities. In some cases, local rural dwellers welcome these projects because of the compensation sums, which can be large. In many cases, however, people are left with a sense of loss and powerlessness. These construction projects reflect the unequal relationship between urban centres and outlying areas in contemporary Japan, a hegemonic relationship that places not just Ainu but also rural *Wajin* at a disadvantage. Japanese journalist Honda Katsuichi (1993a, 181) claims: "The Japanese people who farm and fish have become the indigenous people," meaning that the government generally treats rural dwellers as it did Aborigines in the past. If the government wants land, it takes it, and there is usually little that rural communities can do about it (see also Honda 1991). A recent example supports this. In January 1999, an overwhelming 90 percent of area voters rejected a proposed government dam project in Tokushima prefecture. The government then announced that it would go ahead with the project despite the vote (Stoddard 2000).

When the Hokkaido government decided to build a dam in Nibutani, two hegemonic processes were involved: the relationship between urban government centres and village farmers, and the relationship between Ainu and *Wajin*. Plans for the dam, nearing completion by 1994, began in 1970. The dam was planned to provide a huge increase in water supply to the city of Tomakomai, located about 100 kilometres from Nibutani. In the high-growth decade of the 1960s, Tomakomai had been targeted for major development, including the decision to construct a huge industrial park there. During the slowdown of economic growth, the Tomakomai Industrial Park plan was cancelled. Although the main reason for the dam no longer existed, the Hokkaido government would not abandon the project, despite strong protests from Nibutani Ainu, Ainu scholars, and journalists.

When I mentioned the Nibutani Dam to a Tokyo engineer who specializes in dam construction, his response was, *"seijika damu!"* ("a politician's dam"). This expression reflects the idea that such projects benefit politicians and other special interests, given that large sums of money are often involved. Such large-scale construction projects are now being cited as an increasing cause of Japan's burgeoning national debt. Critics within Japan claim that such projects fill the pockets of the "iron triangle" of politicians, bureaucrats, and businesses, but do relatively little to help the local economy of the people (Stoddard 2000). Dam administrative offices in Japan provide written descriptions of their projects, including a rationale. The pamphlets distributed by the Hokkaido Development Bureau (HDB) stopped mentioning the aborted industrial park, and switched to a need to control occasional flooding of the Saru River, and the need for a general increase in industrial water supply to Tomakomai (Hokkaido Kaihatsukyoku 1990).

A feasibility study for the dam was done in 1971, but it did not include an assessment of the dam's impact on Ainu as an ethnic group or on Nibutani as a focal point of Ainu identity. Many Ainu protested the dam's construction but, given Japan's stance of homogeneity, their arguments that the dam violated their rights as an ethnic group held little weight. Some *Wajin* voices joined the protest. Dr. Ohtsuka, as curator at the National Museum of Ethnology, gave an ethnological perspective on the dam's potential impact in court. According to Ohtsuka:

> Nibutani is on the Saru River, a river that is very important in Ainu mythology and for the Ainu way of life. Nibutani is also the place where the greatest number of Ainu in Japan live. The Ainu take salmon from the river, they make food, and other traditional things there. They get medicines from the area, and know the trees. When the dam is finished this will all stop. The trees will be cut down, the water levels will change ... The Ainu struggle to maintain their identity is focused around Nibutani, and this will suffer.[15]

Compensation sums were large, but Ainu farmers were not given any choice about selling their land, something reminiscent of their earlier situation. Doubly demeaning was the fact that the land taken now was that "given" to Ainu under the Hokkaido Former Aborigines Protection Act when they were forced off their larger territories.

Some Ainu in the area went to court, but many did not. However, I did not meet any Ainu who actually said they supported the dam. Some Ainu households were heavily indebted for farm loans and saw little choice. An elected leader of a neighbourhood association expressed the pragmatic view, held by many households, that no matter what they did, the government would build the dam, so they should fight for the best compensation they could get rather than just refuse the dam.

Some Ainu households in Nibutani did begin a court case against the forced sale of their land. Claiming that they had not agreed to sell, they refused to accept the government payment. The money involved went to the *hōmukyoku*, a special government office where money is temporarily held for up to ten years while such cases are being decided. Japanese legal practices made it too difficult and too expensive for most Ainu to resist very long. After ten years, the money involved would revert to the payer – the government, leaving the households with nothing. An even bigger issue was that if people accepted the money within three years, it was considered compensation for a forced sale, but after three years it would be treated as income. Thus, those who resisted longer would be required to pay huge amounts of tax on the payment. One Ainu man said: "It's a kind of scare tactic, if you don't want to pay this huge tax on the land, then you feel you must sell."

By 1994, four years into the court case, only two Ainu farmers were still resisting the land sale. Kayano was one. In a television interview (*Portrait of Japan* 1991), he said:

They're building a dam without our consent. I never agreed to it. We Ainu have a right to live on our land and catch salmon. No one here is happy about it but others stopped complaining when they were offered large sums of money as compensation. Now there are only two of us left to protest, but I'm still fighting. It's a useless dam. I want the government to destroy that dam and grant us our traditional right to fish for salmon. *I want the world to hear this* [my emphasis].

The Ainu protest also raised concerns about environmental issues. By the year 2000, Japan had succeeded in damming all its rivers, finishing with a dam on the Nagara River on Honshu, which had previously held the distinction of being the last free-flowing river in Japan. Kayano (1999, 818) lamented the human destruction of nature, and the loss of humans' spiritual relationship with nature:

Today, I see dams on the rivers all over Hokkaido, many considered unnecessary, and many with no passage for fish ... It is as if we have felled a massive timber across the mouth of each river as a barrier to fish ... For their sake – for our sake – we should take out the "timbers." When human beings, myself included, continue destruction of nature, it reminds me of an old teaching. If we spit into the face of heaven, we can expect it back in our own faces.

The Ainu lost this round of the fight against the Nibutani Dam, but something was gained. The case brought national and international attention, resulting in appeals for better treatment of Ainu. It highlighted attempts to gain recognition of Ainu as a minority group, as an Indigenous People, and of their special relationship to the land. The Hokkaido court refused the Ainu claim to a special relationship to the land around the Saru River in its decision that issues of ethnicity and discrimination are not related to issues of development and the environment (*Hokkaido Shinbun* 1994a). In other ways, however, the government made concessions that acknowledge the distinct status of Ainu. Although the Ainu protest did not prevent the dam from being put into operation, it won a concession acknowledging that, at least on occasion, the Saru River should be allowed to flow more in accordance with its natural course. The government agreed to drain the river area surrounding the dam (symbolically "nullifying" the dam) for important Ainu festivals. Then, in a subsequent landmark decision in 1997 (to be discussed below), the Sapporo court reversed the earlier decision, recognizing the Ainu as a specific minority and as an Aboriginal group, and the dam as a violation of their rights to enjoy their ethnic heritage.

A frequently noted corollary effect of major development projects that adversely impact unempowered groups is that these often politically mobilize people or groups who were formerly inactive. According to Oliver-Smith (1991, 147), resistance to such dam projects has often forged a clearer sense of identity, helping a group develop better strategies to pursue its goals. The Nibutani Dam created such a focus for Ainu. During the dam protest, Kayano became the first Ainu member of the National Diet. Ainu individuals visited various foreign countries, giving talks to promote awareness of the dam and to protest it. They also promoted the Nibutani Forum, an international forum they hosted in Nibutani, Japan to commemorate the United Nations' designation of 1993 as the International Year of Indigenous Peoples. This forum was attended by people from many different countries throughout the world. An Ainu visit to Russia over the dam was reported in the Japanese press (*Hokkaido Shinbun* 1994b) and on Japanese television. Given Japan's keen awareness of outside countries, these international activities helped focus attention in Japan on the Ainu situation. The use of international covenants helped Ainu win recognition of their Aboriginal status in Japan, in the 1997 Nibutani Dam decision.

The Nibutani Forum and Ainu Identity
The decade of the 1990s was an extremely important one for reflection upon the status of Indigenous Peoples in Japan. Several events and activities were conducted by Ainu and by groups interested in their concerns and those of other minorities in Japan. Some of these events focused on gaining recognition of Japan's minority groups in contrast to the model of homogeneous Japan, while others more directly addressed the issue of Ainu Indigenous status.

Worldwide, 1992 was seen as a year commemorating 500 years since the beginning of Columbus's expeditions to the New World. To counterbalance activities planned to celebrate the idea of exploration, other events were held to mark recognition of the prior existence of Aboriginal Peoples. Tokyo's Meiji Gakuin University hosted a conference in 1992 to reflect on the 500 years since Columbus's arrival in the New World in relation to Aboriginal Peoples, particularly the Aboriginal Peoples of Japan. The conference provided a venue for stories from Ainu, Okinawan, and Uilta individuals. Okinawans comprise an Indigenous population on the Ryukyu Islands at the southernmost parts of the Japanese archipelago. Their ancestors are thought to predate those of *Wajin* on the Japanese islands. Just as Ainu were pushed northward by incoming waves of the predecessors of *Wajin*, it is believed that Okinawans were pushed southward. Uilta are an Indigenous group who inhabited northern areas of Japan; their numbers are now so small that many Japanese are entirely unaware of the group.

Partly as a realization of the need to focus on Aboriginal Peoples in the aftermath of celebrations to commemorate 1992 as the 500th anniversary of Columbus's "discovery" of the Americas – which, like other parts of the world, were already inhabited by Indigenous Peoples at the time of so-called discovery – the United Nations designated the following year, 1993, as the International Year of Indigenous Peoples. Ainu from Nibutani organized and hosted an international festival designated as the Nibutani Forum to commemorate the year. Before the Nibutani Forum, planned for August 1993, Meiji Gakuin University held a second symposium, in recognition of the International Year of Indigenous Peoples, in July. Held in Japan's political and economic core of Tokyo, this symposium helped publicize the upcoming Nibutani Forum to the general population, and encouraged city-dwelling *Wajin* to visit this village in Hokkaido for the forum. Kayano Shigeru, as an elder from Hokkaido, was one of the spotlighted Aboriginal speakers at the symposium, along with other special speakers such as renowned Japanese journalist Honda Katsuichi. Symposium press releases explained that its purpose was "to increase awareness of the significance of the up-coming events and the desire to create an era of harmonious coexistence with all ethnic groups, and to expand their circle of friends and supporters" (Meiji Gakuin University 1993).

One purpose clearly reflected in this press release for the event was that Ainu and other minority groups in Japan would work together to gain recognition of diversity within Japanese society in contrast to the model of homogeneous Japan, for the sake of all minorities in Japan.

In August the small village of Nibutani, home to the largest remaining Ainu concentration in the world, hosted the international Nibutani Forum. Representatives of Aboriginal Peoples throughout the world attended, spoke, and performed. The forum turned out to be a celebration for area Ainu of the culmination of their struggles to gain international recognition of their status as a distinct minority group and as an Aboriginal population. Notably, the international community, through the United Nations, granted them recognition of this status before Japan did. One formal announcement for the Nibutani Forum proclaimed: "Although after 1400 years of domination the Japanese government still declines to recognize the existence of the Ainu, the United Nations officially recognized the Ainu's indigenous status last December" (Nibutani Forum 1993).

That Ainu were able to gain this recognition by the UN shows how involved they were in such international organizations while networking with other Indigenous Peoples worldwide.

In the years following the Nibutani Forum, the struggles to gain recognition of minority and Indigenous rights within Japan continued. In 1994 the visit of an Ainu representative to Russia, speaking on contemporary Ainu issues and concerns (including but not limited to the Nibutani Dam), was telecast in Japan via satellite. In the same year, Kayano Shigeru, a man who had spent a lifetime of effort struggling to prevent the Ainu culture and language from fading away, became the first Ainu to be elected to

Japan's National Diet. Ainu international networking activities continued as well.

In 1995 members of minority groups in Japan participated in a minorities conference held in Vancouver, Canada. The conference was held at the activities centre of the Japanese Canadian Citizens' Association (JCCA), in conjunction with the National Association of Japanese Canadians (NAJC), to explore issues of minority groups within larger nations. One of the themes that emerged involved the differing experiences of minorities within a self-proclaimed multicultural society such as Canada, and within a society that asserts cultural homogeneity and denies diversity, such as Japan.

The 1997 Nibutani Dam Decision and the Ainu Cultural Promotion Act

As indicated earlier, despite a series of hearings and preliminary research, the Minister of Construction denied the petition to stop the dam project on 26 April 1993. The plaintiffs in the case, however, were able to begin a process of appeals (Levin 2001, 452-55). The case appeared to be shattered when the Sapporo court rendered its decision that there was no relationship between issues of ethnicity and issues of development, on 21 July 1994 (Creighton 1995b), but the Ainu struggle to free the Saru River, and for their own human rights, continued.

Then, after a long battle, the Sapporo court reversed this stance in 1997, in what has come to be known as the Nibutani Dam decision (Stevens 2001). The court declared the action of the government in pursuing the project illegal, only the second time in modern Japanese legal history that such a finding was made (Levin 2001, 422). The court took into consideration the history of injustices to the Ainu people. It also acknowledged the Ainu people as a specific group within Japanese society, and as an Indigenous People.

In order to win this decision, the Ainu plaintiffs and their lawyers again made skilful use of international institutions and codes. This included the use of the International Covenant on Cultural and Political Rights (ICCPR), particularly Article 27, which holds that minority groups have distinct rights, and the International Covenant on Economic, Social, and Cultural Rights (ICESCR), both of which Japan had ratified, along with the International Convention on the Elimination of All Forms of Racial Discrimination (ICERD), which went into effect in Japan in 1996.

These international covenants were effectively employed in conjunction with Article 13 of the Japanese constitution, which calls for the respectful treatment of individuals, recognizing their right to life, liberty, and the pursuit of happiness as long as it does not interfere with the public welfare. In its 1997 decision, the Sapporo court not only recognized the distinct and Indigenous status of Ainu, but proclaimed that their right to pursue and enjoy their cultural heritage had been abrogated by the construction of the Nibutani Dam, and that the government's actions in building it without due consideration of its effects on Ainu ethnicity were illegal (Levin 2001).

This would seem to be a major victory for the Ainu plaintiffs in the case. However, the court did not call for the removal of the Nibutani Dam, as they had wished. Instead, since the dam had already been built using public funds, the court deemed that its removal at that point would be against the public good. Thus, there remains debate over the extent this legal decision will truly influence social change in Japanese society, given the court's reluctance to order the removal of a development project once in place. Stevens, for example, notes that although the court found that the project would greatly impact Ainu culture, the decision might suggest that the concept of the public good could be used to override rights guaranteed by Article 27 of the ICCPR (Stevens 2001, 192). However, the court's recognition of Ainu Indigenous status, against the long-term background of homogeneity assertions, was itself considered by many to be a major victory for Ainu and other minorities.

Also in 1997, Ainu won another significant victory with the passage in the National Diet of the Ainu Cultural Promotion Act. This law, whose full title is "An Act for the Promotion of Ainu Culture, the Spread of Knowledge Relevant to Ainu Traditions, and an Education Campaign," was passed on 1 July 1997, and came into effect in September that year. The law focuses on the preservation of Ainu cultural traditions and the transmission of the Ainu language. Perhaps most importantly, the new law struck down and replaced the nearly century-old Hokkaido Former Aborigines Protection Act, which had sought to eliminate these very same markers of Ainu ethnicity in the name of assimilation. The new law, however, does not go so far as Ainu activists had wished, and did not include some of their proposed clauses, such as those relating to self-determination and access to natural resources. After seeing this progress in his long-term efforts to keep the Ainu language from disappearing completely, Kayano (1999) then turned his efforts to the struggle for recognition of the inviolability of Indigenous food cultures, and the right of Ainu to fish salmon.

The passage of the Ainu Cultural Promotion Act was a primary reason that Japan was chosen to host the eighth international Conference on Hunting and Gathering Societies (CHAGS) in 1998. CHAGS has consisted of a series of conferences, conceived in 1965, to deal with issues related to Indigenous foraging and post-foraging peoples in the modern world. In 1998 over 200 participants from around the world came to Osaka to participate in this conference, the last of the millennium. A major theme was the persistence and status of hunting and gathering societies at the millennium.

In his contribution to the conference, anthropologist Richard Lee recognized that Aboriginal hunting and gathering societies have indeed been affected by globalization, but spoke with renewed hope of the resilience of cultural survival despite threats of cultural homogenization coming from global processes. The abstract to Lee's paper (1999, 821) states: "It is remarkable that in spite of economic globalization, bureaucratic domination, and assaults on the cultural integrity of the world's 'small peoples' something of value has persisted. Against all odds, these societies have maintained some portion of their life-worlds outside of the capitalist world system, showing that even in this hard-bitten age of globalization other ways of being are possible."

The Nibutani Forum and other events hosted or attended by Ainu provided a venue through which Ainu could proclaim to the world that Japan's Indigenous Peoples are still here despite a century of government assimilationist policies directed at erasing their distinctive traditions and languages. As an Aboriginal People, they have adapted to the contemporary world but they have not vanished (Riddington 1987; Creighton 1995b).

Conclusions and Commencements

Ainu have a very real presence in modern Japan, and have been active in forging stronger ties with other minority groups in the country. They have also emerged as important actors on the international stage, networking with other Indigenous Peoples throughout the world. Kayano (1999, 817) points out that he has travelled to foreign countries twenty-four times, always making sure to meet with Indigenous People wherever he goes. An Ainu visit to Russia, and the Japan/Canada minorities conference held in Vancouver, shows that Japan's Indigenous Peoples are making their presence known to the world. The United Nations designation of 1993 as the International Year of Indigenous Peoples, and of the decade 1995 through 2004 as the Decade of Indigenous Peoples, have helped create a forum to do this.

For the last two decades of the twentieth century, Japan was wrapped up in a national promotional campaign for *kokusaika* (internationalization). The goal was consistent with Japan's increased affluence and prominence in the world arena, but contradictory to Japan's insular and exclusionary history and its desire to retain an ideology of cultural homogeneity. Internationalization implies an awareness of social and cultural diversity and a valuing of these. This is at odds with the value Japanese society has long placed on social and cultural homogeneity. The dominant symbols of Japanese identity are tied to this. Ohnuki-Tierney (1993) argues that rice, like the sun (Ohnuki-Tierney 1990, 206), was used as a dominant symbol of self-identity to help bolster the idea of homogeneity. This was a dual process of forming Japanese identity in contrast to foreigners, while making minorities in Japan conform to the homogeneity model.

Internationalization, as a Japanese goal, has fostered increased Japanese interactions with foreigners and has also had the unexpected consequence of prompting greater reflection on Japan's own minority groups. Concerned with world opinion, Japan has faced greater pressure to reconsider its stance on homogeneity since the United Nations recognized Ainu as an Indigenous People. The incorporation of international covenants and conventions helped lead to the 1997 Sapporo court decision on the Nibutani Dam, which recognized the Ainu as a distinct minority group within Japan and as an Indigenous People. This paved the way for recognition of other minority groups. The linking of Ainu with Indigenous Peoples throughout the world, and the participation of people from all over the world at events such as the Nibutani Forum and CHAGS, which address issues relevant to Japan's Indigenous Peoples, cannot go unnoticed in Japan. By internationalizing the problem and focusing attention on these groups in foreign countries, Ainu create news within Japan, bringing greater recognition of Japan's diversity.

In the summer of 1999, the Japanese government passed the *Kokkikokkahō* (National Flag and Song Act), officially designating *Hinomaru* (the circle of the sun), as the national flag and *Kimigayo*, a song of reverence to the emperor, as the national anthem, after five decades of debate over these contested symbols (Creighton 2000). Many observers, inside and outside Japan, felt that this act suggested renewed attempts to reinvigorate the dominant symbols of Japanese identity used to underscore the idea of Japan as a homogeneous nation. Minorities in general have been reluctant to accept these symbols, because the emphasis on the Japanese imperial system implicit in them detracts awareness from other backgrounds in the country. Like the decision to build the Nibutani Dam in an area that has the world's largest remaining concentration of Ainu and that is considered sacred in Ainu mythology, the passage of the flag and anthem act towards the end of the millennium revealed Japan's inability to value diversity or consider the ethnological implications of actions for specific minority groups. In contrast to the new awareness of diversity in Japan, the act's passage reiterated the long-standing ideology of the homogeneity of the Japanese populace under the emperor.

Japan at the millennium is at a crossroads in terms of the rights and recognition of Indigenous Peoples and other minorities. On the one hand, throughout the 1990s, Ainu and other groups prompted recognition of minority concerns within Japan, while international activities helped to increase this awareness. Inroads have been made into the myth of Japan as a homogeneous society. Longstanding assertions of identity do not die easily, however, and there appear to be renewed efforts by segments of Japanese society to keep in place the known ways of national identity formation.

Given Japan's new role in the international community, some scholars and minority representatives underscore why it is of value *to Japan* to reconsider its stance on its own social diversity. Kayano's plea to Japan as a member of the Ainu people is important not just to Ainu themselves but also to other minority groups in Japan: "Issues concerning ethnic minorities are being rethought in earnest the world over today, and great effort is being expended to reverse the eradication of minority cultures and languages. I want Japan to take meaningful steps and not be left behind in what is happening throughout the world" (Kayano 1994b, 153).

As one millennium concludes, a new one commences. At this critical reflective juncture, it is hoped that issues concerning ethnic minorities are earnestly being rethought the world over, with a view towards shaping a more enlightened future that enhances the survival of cultural diversity and the various forms of human knowledge that have developed through the ages. The designation of 1995-2004, a decade bridging old and new millennia, as the Decade of Indigenous Peoples, shows international awareness of Indigenous Peoples at the millennium. Inside and outside Japan, Ainu have sought recognition that despite historic loss of land and contemporary forced land sales, despite extensive cultural destruction and language loss, despite a century of degrading assimilationist practices, they have not vanished, but are very much present as living members of a distinctive Indigenous cultural tradition in Japan at the millennium.

Acknowledgments
The Social Sciences and Humanities Research Council of Canada provided a grant to study the effects of dam construction projects on rural communities in Japan, under which parts of the research conducted in Hokkaido and Tokyo were undertaken. The Japan Foundation provided additional support for research on contemporary Ainu activities, which funded some of the research in Japan and the visit to Vladivostok, Russia, for the Ainu presentation there. Additional funds received through the Centre for Japanese Research (CJR) at the University of British Columbia have also been helpful in providing insights. A related research article, "The Non-Vanishing Ainu: A Damming Development Project, Internationalization and Japan's Indigenous Other," which focuses on the contemporary Ainu identity movement and the Nibutani Dam case, appears in Creighton 1995b.

Notes
1 In this essay, I have followed the convention now used by some authors of writing words such as "western" and "westernization" without capital letters. This convention questions the previous rationale of capitalizing, and thus giving a sense of priority to, such words. Similarly, "second world war" is written entirely in lower case to avoid elevating the importance of wars, which some have suggested is inherent in the custom of capitalizing the first letters of these words. In keeping with the policy of the Native Law Centre (see Levin 1993, x) and growing international practice, the words "Aboriginal," "Native," and "Indigenous" are capitalized wherever they appear unless quoted from another source. Japanese words appear with macrons in this article, in keeping with customary romanization practice, except in such cases as Japanese names attached to English publications when these did not have macrons in the original publication form, and for words that

commonly appear in English writing without macrons, such as place names like Hokkaido, Ryukyu, Tokyo, and Honshu. In these cases, the words have a macron when they occur as part of a longer Japanese phrase, but not when they stand alone as part of the English text or in neologisms of combined Japanese and English formation.

2 The issues discussed in this paper involve those related to ethnicity and Aboriginality. Japan's proclamation of a homogeneous society has hindered the ability of minorities to gain recognition as distinct groups within the society. Ainu were officially recognized by the United Nations as an Aboriginal group before 1993. Although this article is related to issues of ethnicity in the more general sense of that word, which recognizes diversity within societies, it is noted that the words "ethnic" and "ethnicity" are sometimes considered problematic when used in relation to Aboriginal or Indigenous Peoples. This is largely because these words have frequently been associated with immigrant groups, whereas Indigenous Peoples claim a prior existence in an area or country (Levin 1993, x). However, I use the words "ethnic" and "ethnicity" as employed by Glazer and Moynihan (1975), to refer to any group, whether of minority or majority status or of Indigenous or immigrant origin.

3 In his contribution to the book *Ideology and Practice in Modern Japan,* Harumi Befu traces the ambivalence in contemporary Japan towards certain of the symbols discussed here. In particular he discusses the problematic associations with the emperor as well as symbols associated with him such as the song *Kimigayo* (since 1999 legally Japan's national anthem). These symbols retained their associations both with Japanese prewar militarism and with attempts at *dōka* ("same-ization," or the process of making the same) or assimilation of other Asian peoples in order to maintain a notion of Japan as a homogeneous nation despite the colonization of other Asian peoples into the Japanese polity. He sees the rise in popularity of *Nihonjinron* (theories on the Japanese) as part of a quest to find alternative symbols of Japanese identity. *Nihonjinron,* as a genre particularly popular in the 1970s and 1980s, also tends towards essentializations of Japaneseness, thus reiterating a suggestion of ultimate homogeneity.

4 An example of this can be found in the Kurosawa film *The Seven Samurai,* in which a group of peasants, attempting to hide their poverty and needy condition, prepare a dinner with rice for the samurai they are asking to help them. One of the samurai realizes what is going on and exposes the poverty of the peasants, who can afford to eat only millet themselves.

5 The *Hinomaru* flag came into wide use after the second world war, replacing the Rising Sun flag because of the association of the latter with Japanese militarism and imperialism that had helped give rise to the war. Although commonly used as the Japanese flag, *Hinomaru* also remained very controversial as a national symbol, and many thought it still retained a symbolic contamination of militaristic associations. As a result, many voices within Japan continued to protest the use of *Hinomaru,* arguing that it had never been officially adopted by the National Diet as Japan's national flag and hence should not be used. Similar debates focused on the use of *Kimigayo* as the national anthem. In 1999, after decades of such debates and resistance, Japan's National Diet, amid much controversy, passed the *Kokkikokkahō* (National Flag and Song Act) designating *Hinomaru* as the national flag and *Kimigayo* as the national anthem.

6 This sense of distance from the central geographical core of Japan, along with a distancing from the core of identity of rice agriculturalists, can often be inferred by readers of works on Ainu, whether or not this was relevant to the author's intent, as, for example, in Uemura's (1990) book title description of the Ainu as "Traders of the Northern Sea" *(Kita no Umi no Koekishatachi).*

7 Mr. Kayano was scheduled to give this talk in person. However, because he became a member of the National Diet in 1994, he was unable to attend the conference and the paper was presented in his absence.

8 The view that Natives were savages who needed to be civilized is clearly evident in statements made by Canadian Prime Minister John A. Macdonald in the House of Commons on 9 May 1883, when Canada was considering adopting an American model of "industrial" or residential schools for Native children (House of Commons 1883):

> When the school is on the reserve, the child lives with its parents, who are savages; he is surrounded by savages, and though he may learn to read and write, his habits,

and training and mode of thought are Indian. He is simply a savage who can read and write. It has been strongly pressed upon myself, as head of the Department [of Indian Affairs], that the Indian children should be withdrawn as much as possible from the parental influence, and the only way to do that would be to put them in central training industrial schools where they will acquire the habits and modes of thought of white men.

See also Haig-Brown 1988 and Dyck 1991.

9 *Utari*, an Ainu word meaning "friend" or "comrade," was combined with the Japanese word *kyōkai*, meaning association, to form the name of these Ainu organizations. Many of the Ainu I spoke with asserted that even this name reflects discrimination, since the word *Utari* is used because Ainu felt too embarrassed to openly use the word Ainu. When it began as a registered organization in 1946, it was actually named the Hokkaido Ainu Kyōkai (Hokkaido Ainu Association). During the organization's general annual meeting of 1960, however, it was decided to change the name to Hokkaido Utari Kyōkai because, according to the records of those discussions provided by Honda (1993b, 136), "some of our members still feel uncomfortable to have the name Ainu which used to be considered a derogatory word." In 1961 the constitution was modified, and the name change went into effect in May 1962. Some Ainu are now actively encouraging a shift in title back to "Hokkaido Ainu Kyōkai."

10 Discussion held in Sapporo, Japan, 1994.
11 This presentation took place in Akan, Japan, 1994.
12 Discussion held in Sapporo, Japan, 1994.
13 For discussions of *furusato* as a symbolic trope in Japan, see Robertson 1987, 1988, and 1991, and Creighton 1998b.
14 Discussion held in Osaka, Japan, 1994.
15 Discussion held in Osaka, Japan, 1994.

References

Anderson, C. 1983. "Aborigines and Tin Mining in Northern Queensland: A Case Study in the Anthropology of Contact History." *Mankind* 13: 473-98.

Baba, Y. 1980. "Study of Minority-Majority Relations: The Ainu and the Japanese in Hokkaido." *Japanese Interpreter* 1: 60-92.

Befu, H. 1992. "Symbols of Nationalism and *Nihonjinron*." In R. Goodman and K. Refsing, eds., *Ideology and Practice in Modern Japan*. London: Routledge, 24-46.

Berkhofer, R.F., Jr. 1965. *Salvation and the Savage: An Analysis of Protestant Missions and American Indian Responses, 1787-1862*. Lexington: University of Kentucky Press.

Binney, J. 1987. "Maori Oral Narratives, Pakeha Written Texts: Two Forms of Telling History." *New Zealand Journal of History* 21: 16-28.

Christopher, R.C. 1983. *The Japanese Mind*. New York: Fawcett Columbine.

Creighton, M. 1991. "Maintaining Cultural Boundaries in Retailing: How Japanese Department Stores Domesticate 'Things Foreign.'" *Modern Asian Studies* 25: 675-709.

–. 1995a. "Japanese Craft Tourism: Liberating the Crane Wife." *Annals of Tourism Research* 22: 463-78.

–. 1995b. "The Non-Vanishing Ainu: A Damming Development Project, Internationalization and Japan's Indigenous Other." *American Asian Review* 13(2): 69-96.

–. 1998a. "Weaving the Future from the Heart of Tradition: Learning in Leisure Activities." In J. Singleton, ed., *Learning in Likely Places: Varieties of Apprenticeship in Japan*. Cambridge, UK: Cambridge University Press, 190-227.

–. 1998b. "Pre-Industrial Dreaming in Post-Industrial Japan: Department Stores and the Commoditization of Community Traditions." *Japan Forum* 10(2): 127-49.

–. 2000. "The Legislation of *Kimigayo* and *Hinomaru* as State Symbols: Igniting Memories of War and Peace, Minority Issues in Japan, and Nikkei Identity Outside Japan." Unpublished manuscript, presented for Japan Forum Series, Reischauer Institute of Japanese Studies, Harvard University, Cambridge, MA, February.

DeVos, G., W.O. Wetherall, and K. Stearman. 1983. *Japan's Minorities: Burakumin, Koreans, Ainu and Okinawans. Report No. 3*. London: Minority Rights Group.

Dyck, N. 1991. *What Is the Indian "Problem": Tutelage and Resistance in Canadian Indian*

Administration. St. John's, NF: Institute of Social and Economic Research, Memorial University.
Glazer, N., and D.P. Moynihan, eds. 1975. *Ethnicity: Theory and Experience*. Cambridge, MA: Harvard University Press.
Haig-Brown, C. 1988. *Resistance and Renewal: Surviving the Indian Residential School*. Vancouver: Tillacum Library.
Hiwasaki, L. 2000. "Ethnic Tourism in Hokkaido and the Shaping of Ainu Identity." *Pacific Affairs* 73: 393-412.
Hokkaido Kaihatsukyoku. 1990. *Sarugawa Sogo Kaihatsu Jigyo: Nibutani Damu* (Saru River comprehensive development project: Nibutani Dam). Muroran: Sarugawa Damu Kensetsujigyosho.
Hokkaido Shinbun. 1994a. "Nibutani Damu Soshō Do to Kuni 'Ainu Minzoku' Kenkai Shimesazu: 'Jigyō to Chokusetsu Kankei Nai' Sapporo Chisai Saishū Kaitō o shomenteishutsu" (The Hokkaido government and central government not publicizing views of Ainu land court case regarding Nibutani Dam: Sapporo court decides "no relationship between ethnicity and development"), 21 July.
–. 1994b. "Nibutani Damu Soshō: Genkoku, Kaigai Hatsuhokoku e, Asukara Urajio de Kaishi" (Nibutani Dam court case: claimants to give first overseas presentation in Vladivostok), 28 August.
Hokkaido Utari Kyōkai. 1994. *Akoroitaku (Akor itak): Ainugo Tekisuto 1* (Ainu language textbook, vol. 1). Sapporo: Shadanhōjin Hokkaido Utari Kyōkai.
Honda, K. 1991. "Nibutani Damu to Nagaragawakako Damu no Nihongata Kozo. *Asahi Jānaru*." (The Japanese way is revealed through the Nibutani Dam and Nagaragawa Dam. *Asahi Journal*), 27 September.
–. 1993a. "Development as Invasion." In J. Lie, ed., *The Impoverished Spirit in Contemporary Japan: Selected Essays of Honda Katsuichi*. New York: Monthly Review Press, 180-82.
–. 1993b. *Senjūminzoku Ainu no Genzai* (The Indigenous Ainu today). Tokyo: Asahi Shinbunsha.
House of Commons (Canada). 1883. *Debates*, vol. 14, at 1107-8.
Kayano, S. 1993. *Kokkai de "Charanke": Nibutani ni Ainu to shite ikiru* (I'll tell it in the Diet: I live as an Ainu in Nibutani). Tokyo: Shakai Shinpō.
–. 1994a. "The Ainu Foundation Stone: The Present Situation of Ainu Language, Oral Literature and the Culture in Hokkaido." In *Bridges of the Science Between North America and the Russian Far East, 45th Arctic Science Conference: Abstracts, Book 2*. Vladivostok, Russia: Dalnauka, 91.
–. 1994b. *Our Land Was a Forest: An Ainu Memoir*. Boulder, CO: Westview Press.
–. 1999. "Ainu and the Salmon, 8th International Conference on Hunting and Gathering Societies: Foraging and Post-Foraging Societies." *Bulletin of the National Museum of Ethnology* (Osaka) 23(4): 815-20.
Keller, R.H., Jr. 1983. *American Protestantism and the United States Indian Policy, 1869-82*. Lincoln: University of Nebraska Press.
Lee, R. 1999. "Hunter-Gatherer Studies and the Millennium: A Look Forward (and Back), 8th International Conference on Hunting and Gathering Societies: Foraging and Post-Foraging Societies." *Bulletin of the National Museum of Ethnology* (Osaka) 23(4): 821-45.
LePage, R.B., and A. Tabouret-Keller. 1985. *Acts of Identity: Creole Based Approaches to Language and Ethnicity*. Cambridge, UK: Cambridge University Press.
Levin, M.A. 2001. "Essential Commodities and Racial Justice: Using Constitutional Protection of Japan's Indigenous Ainu People to Inform Understandings of the United States and Japan." *New York University Journal of International Law and Politics* 33: 419-526.
Levin, M.D., ed. 1993. *Ethnicity and Aboriginality: Case Studies in Ethnonationalism*. Toronto: University of Toronto Press.
Meiji Gakuin University. 1993. Symposium press release. Tokyo: International Year of Indigenous Peoples Symposium Preparatory Committee.
Nibutani Forum '93 Organizing Committee. 1993. Announcement and invitation for Nibutani Forum '93. Nibutani: Nibutani Forum Files.
Ohnuki-Tierney, E. 1990. "The Ambivalent Self of the Contemporary Japanese." *Cultural Anthropology* 5(2): 197-216.

–. 1993. *Rice as Self: Japanese Identities through Time*. Princeton, NJ: Princeton University Press.
–. 1994. *Illness and Culture in Contemporary Japan: An Anthropological View*. Cambridge, UK: Cambridge University Press.
Ohtsuka, K. 1994. "Senjūminzoku no Kankyōkan to Kyōsei no Shisō – Ainu Minzoku o Chushin ni" (The view of Indigenous People on the environment and their ideas of coexistence – from the focus of the Ainu). *Kankyō Jōhō Kagaku* 23: 17-22.
Oliver-Smith, A. 1991. "Involuntary Resettlement, Resistance and Political Empowerment." *Journal of Refugee Studies* 4: 132-49.
Portrait of Japan. 1991. Hosted by Richard Chamberlain, produced and written by Rick King, co-produced by Patricia Bischetti and Liza Levine, series produced by Takashi Shirai. New York: Turner Broadcasting System.
Riddington, R. 1987. "Omaha Survival: A Vanishing Indian Tribe That Would Not Vanish." *American Indian Quarterly* 11: 37-50.
Robertson, J. 1987. A Dialectic of Native and Newcomer: The Kodaira Citizens' Festival in Suburban Tokyo." *Anthropological Quarterly* 60(3): 124-36.
–. 1988. "The Culture and Politics of Nostalgia: *Furusato* Japan." *International Journal of Politics, Culture and Society* 1: 494-518.
–. 1991. *Native and Newcomer: Making and Remaking a Japanese City*. Berkeley: University of California Press.
–. 1998. *Takarazuka: Sex and Politics and Popular Culture in Modern Japan*. Berkeley: University of California Press.
Sagarin, E., and J. Moneymaker. 1979. "Language and Nationalist, Separatist and Seccessionist Movements." In R.L. Hall, ed., *Ethnic Autonomy – Comparative Dynamics: The Americas, Europe and the Developing World*. New York: Pergamon Press, 18-37.
Seymour, J.D. 1993. "The Rights of Ethnic Minorities in China: Lessons of the Soviet Demise." *American Asian Review* 11(2): 44-56.
Siddle, R. 1996. *Race, Resistance and the Ainu People of Japan*. London and New York: Routledge.
–. 1997. "Ainu, Japan's Indigenous People." In M. Wiener, ed., *Japan's Minorities: The Illusion of Homogeneity*. London: Routledge, 17-49.
Sjoberg, K. 1993. *The Return of the Ainu: Cultural Mobilization and the Practice of Ethnicity in Japan*. Chur, Switzerland: Harwood.
Stevens, G. 2001. "The Ainu and Human Rights: Domestic and International Legal Protections." *Japanese Studies* 21: 181-98.
Stoddard, S. 2000. "Japan's Debt 'a Time Bomb.'" *Vancouver Sun*, 5 February.
Szasz, M.C., and C. Ryan. 1988. "American Indian Education." In W.C. Sturtevant and W.E. Wasburn, eds., *Handbook of North American Indians, vol. 4, History of Indian-White Relations*. Washington, DC: Smithsonian Institution, 284-300.
Takakura, S. 1960. "The Ainu of Northern Japan: A Study in Conquest and Acculturation." *Transactions of the American Philosophical Society* 50(4).
Takamiya, H. 1997. "Subsistence Adaptation Processes in the Prehistory of Okinawa." Unpublished PhD dissertation, University of California at Los Angeles.
Terasawa, K., and T. Terasawa. 1981. "Yayoi Jidai Shokōbutsu-shitsu Shokuryō no Kisoteki Kenkyū" (A fundamental study of the plant foods of the Yayoi period). *Kashihara Kokogaku Kenkyu Kiyo* 5: 1-129.
Turner, V. 1967. *The Forest of Symbols*. Ithaca, NY: Cornell University Press.
Uemura, H. 1990. *Kita no Umi no Koekishatachi: Ainu Minzoku no Shakai Keizeishi* (Traders of the Northern Sea: The Ainu people and [Japanese] society's economic history). Tokyo: Dubunkan.
United Nations. 1978. *International Bill of Human Rights*. New York: United Nations Office of Public Information.
Weiner, M., ed. 1997. *Japan's Minorities: The Illusion of Homogeneity*. London: Routledge.

7
Pop Idols and Gender Contestation
Hiroshi Aoyagi

One area of Japanese culture that will certainly continue to attract attention in the new millennium is the role played by women in society. In a country where womanhood has been characterized in relation to a century-old ideology of *ryōsai kenbo* (good wife, wise mother), changes that strike at the core of the sexual hierarchy are difficult to attain. This ideological model, coined by the Ministry of Education during the period of state formation in the late nineteenth century, marginalized women from the public arena by defining the home as their primary place for activities. In this ideological matrix, the role of women was as agents of biological and social reproduction (Ochiai 1989, 1997a, 1997b; Boiling 1998). Its reinforcement by a variety of male-governed institutions has affected the lives of many women throughout the twentieth century. Still, a sentiment advocating the greater public participation of women has been present, and is today even more alive and visible.

In this chapter, I investigate how gender is socially constructed in a conspicuous genre of popular cultural performances known as *aidoru poppusu*, or "idol-pop." This consists of a series of adolescent personalities – *aidoru*, or "pop idols" – who are commodified as public role models in adolescent fashions and lifestyles. Since the late 1960s, many pop idols have appeared on television programs, singing melodramatic love songs, dancing to peppy electronic tunes, and acting in dramas. Numerous images of pop idols have also appeared in popular magazines and advertising posters, with coquettish smiles and shapely poses.[1]

Although their apparent crudeness has been ridiculed by adult critics from time to time, pop-idol performances continue to produce a vital domain of popular culture sponsored by media institutions and business corporations that specialize in trend creation. Hundreds of young people participate in contests each year, hoping to become idols. Many support groups and fan clubs develop as idol candidates strive to make a career that can be traced through numerous media events and publications. Many successful idols become popular abroad, especially in other Asian countries, where various homegrown personalities also emerge to represent local youth cultures.

Part of becoming adolescent role models in the burgeoning pop-idol industry involves the embodiment of gender ideals. Pop idols define classy images of the time through their role playing. With this premise, I focus on female pop-idol performances as a dramatization of public tastes involving women in Japan. What are the popular images of adolescent femaleness represented in pop-idol performances, and why are these images popular? How have these images changed over time, and what factors have contributed to this change? What speculations can one make for the new millennium? The subsequent discussion examines these problems.

Much has been written recently about popular cultural performances, such as films, pop music, and fashion, using theories and methods that are derived from sociology and communications, and contributing to the development of the hybrid discipline called "cultural studies" (e.g., Ewen 1976; Williamson 1980; Frith 1983, 1988; Fiske 1989a, 1989b; During 1993).[2] While some of these studies offer textual analyses, others try to explain the relationship between texts and contexts. This study will approach the idol-pop phenomenon ethnographically, as a field of cultural production where one can observe particular individuals, groups, and institutions organize themselves as they interact with each other. During field research in Tokyo, I followed particular pop-idol candidates to training sessions and observed how they embodied images of adolescent femaleness. Interview commentaries and conversational data that illuminate performers' and producers' thoughts on these distinct role models are included. The subsequent analysis will place these cases in a larger context: the position of women in Japanese society. Pseudonyms are used for all informants and company names that appear in the following discussion. Translations of quotations and excerpts from Japanese sources are mine.

The Fantastic World of Cute Idols

One way in which the entertainment industry establishes its place in a society is through the development of fictitious characters and relationships that can provide the public with an ongoing sense of the world. Many of these art forms are commodified each year, shackling human desire to a drive towards certain styles of conformity (Haug 1986; Barnouw and Kirkland 1992). From the perspective of the Japanese entertainment industry, a consumer society is composed of *taishū*, or aggregates of consumer groups to which commodities are sold. Some of my informants in the industry referred to their activities as "mass-control" *(taishū sōsa),* whose goal is to mould consumers' desires through stylish images and narratives. What trend institutions offer to the people is generally perceived by Japanese consumers as purported teachings through which one presumably acquires information on the needs, wants, and pleasures of the greatest number of people, and obtains greater harmony with one's social surroundings (Yano 1997, 337; see also Ivy 1993).

In this socio-cultural setting, adolescents emerged as a segment whose active involvement in the creation of lifestyles can contribute to the reproduction of consumer culture. Adolescents, characterized in Japan as current consumers and the future labour force, are the key constituent of the nation's socio-economic well-being. They are occasionally referred to as "infomaniacs" *(infomaniakku)*, implying that an intense focus is placed on their ability to socialize by negotiating an appropriate lifestyle through their mutual interaction and information exchange. Japanese adolescents get together "to share the latest on their favorite pop-music stars, news on where to buy that great shirt, or what CD rental shop has a special offer this week. The young teen is intensely focused on being appropriate, and she negotiates the path by testing on friends what's learned in the media – discovering who she is by what her friends like to wear, to hear, to buy" (White 1993, 14).

In friendship grounded in consumer culture, adolescents constitute the market-driven aspects of coming of age that continue to feed the trend industry. It is to this end that idols and their manufacturing industry employ cultural strategies that can create marketable adolescent personalities.

Pop-Idol Performances as the Embodiment of Youth Culture

Pop idols project themselves as what Ogawa (1988, 122, 123) calls "quasi-companions" *(gijiteki nakama)*, who provide their followers with a virtual sense of intimacy, a feeling that affirms a cultural emphasis on interconnectedness in Japan.[3] Although this companionship is understood as artificial and therefore realized only in fantasy, the intimacy it evokes can be as strong as that shared among friends. A former editor-in-chief of pop-idol magazines told me in an interview that two of the primary functions of idols are to empathize with the experiences and emotions of those who undergo youth, or *seishun no mon* (literally, "the gateway to youth"), and to develop a sense of growing up together with the audience: "Pop idols enact the role of compassionate partners who can comfort adolescents, sharing problems which are typical to that age-group such as emotional tensions and ambiguities, sexual curiosities, a sense of conflict with society, search for the meaning of life, and so on. Pop idols can share these problems with the audience by expressing their ideas and opinions, providing their teenage fans with a sense of communal ties, and growing up together with these fans." Thus, idols and their manufacturing industry create a social space in which adolescents can socialize with one another.

The following excerpt from an essay written by Matsuda Seiko (who debuted in 1980) provides evidence of the sense of empathy evoked by a pop idol: "Seiko is so happy to meet you!! As a singer and an 18-year old girl, I feel for the first time that I can become independent. Please watch over me warmly forever!!" (Matsuda 1980, cover page). Similarly, Satō Atsuhiro, a former member of a popular male idol group, *Hikaru Genji* (1987-94), writes in his published essay: "I want to establish a personal position as a singer, actor and all else put together! Yet, this may still be too vague to be called a dream ... Although I am still at a stage where I am working hard, please keep watch over me. Let's continue to spend time together" (Satō 1991, 215). Both Matsuda and Satō build on their companion statuses and call upon the readers to empathize with their "will to mature." Statements such as these are observed throughout many commentaries made by pop idols, contributing to the development of peer solidarity.

Pop idols evoke empathy through the lyrics of their songs as well. These dwell on the well-worn themes of being in love. For instance, in a song titled "One Summer Experience" *(Hito Natsu no Keiken)*, released in 1974, female idol Yamaguchi Momoe sings: "I will give you the most important thing a girl has to give, I will give you the most important thing she treasures in her little heart." In the song "Sorrow with Regards" *(Yoroshiku Aishu)*, released in the same year, male idol Hiromi Gō sings: "I want you to believe in my love more sincerely, I want to live with you." In her 1995 hit song "Try Me," popular female idol Amuro Namie sings: "I want to send you my heart faster than anyone else, so you must try me, my love is waiting to wrap you up!" These examples from smash hits are a small portion of a great many narratives epitomized by pop-idol songs to provide adolescent consumers with romantic fantasies. Each envisions an affectionate tie between the singer and any listener (indicated as the relationship between "you" and "me"), generating the shared sense of intimacy among all subjects.

Activities designed to build and maintain the social solidarity between pop idols and their fans are carried out to a degree and with a uniformity that have no apparent equivalent in the American pop-star scene. These include handshaking ceremonies *(akushu kai)*, get-togethers with fans *(fan no tsudoi)* where fans can talk and play games with their favourite idol, public photo shoots *(satsuei kai)* where idols strike poses for amateur photographers, known as "camera kids" *(kamera kozō)*, and periodic correspondence with fans by letter. When idols release CDs or publish photo albums, autograph ceremonies *(sign kai)* are held for buyers at retail outlets.[4] There are "idol hotlines" for fans wishing to hear recorded idol messages, and Web pages where they can browse through idol images and profiles. All of these practices are part of materializing the imagined companionship within a controlled environment.

Popular idol magazines, such as Gakken's *Bomb!* contain idol photos, feature interviews, and commentaries, followed by readers' columns consisting of letters and homemade idol cartoons. Together these sections constitute an interactive space wherein pop idols can "speak" to the readers with solidly predictable advice about being loyal in friendships, being hardworking at school, and holding on to one's dream in life (White 1995, 266). The evocative power of pop idols is sometimes borrowed by government institutions in their campaigns to attract public attention. For instance, selected pop idols perform as "one-day police officers" organized by the National Police Agency, calling on the public, particularly young people, to follow traffic rules. Others appear in events promoting national health, as in the case of Yumi Adachi, who appeared as "the citizens' representative" in the 1999 Anti-Drug Campaign organized by the Ministry of Health (Figure 7.1). The list of such rituals is endless.

The "Cute" Style
Until the early 1990s, the most common feature embodied by pop idols to enhance the sense of companionship was cuteness. *Kawaiko-chan,* or "cute girls and boys," became a synonym for pop idols in the 1970s and 1980s (Figure 7.2). According to Kuroyanagi Tetsuko, the former host of the prestigious Japanese music countdown program *The Best Ten* (1969-89), people adore cute idols for their sweetness, which evokes the sense that "they should be protected carefully" (quoted in Herd 1984, 77, 78).[5] Young female pop idols who carry the cute style too far are called *burikko,* or "childish girl," a mildly derogatory term, first used to describe Matsuda Seiko.

To express cuteness, pop idols generally smile with clear, sparkly eyes. They also strike coy poses. The cute image encompasses not only pretty looks but also a heartwarming style, such as singing, dancing, and speaking in a sweet, meek, and "adorable" way. Cuteness is also expressed by a form of handwriting that consists of rounded characters, written laterally in contrast to normal Japanese script. Many of these characters, often considered by adults as "deformed" due to a "lack of discipline," appear in pop-idol autographs and handwritten letters with childlike drawings of hearts, flowers, stars, and animated characters.

To be sure, the cute style is by no means a recent Japanese invention but has clear historical roots. The Japanese word for cute, *kawaii,* can be traced back to its classical form, *kawayushi,* which appears in poetry and stories from the premodern era. This term is also a derivation of *kawaiso,* or "pitiable," a term that implies the vulnerability of the subject (Yamane 1986; Kinsella 1995). The "cuteness" observed today in pop idols closely resembles "sweet little girls" *(otome)* or "cute Japanese women" *(yamato nadeshiko)* images from the late nineteenth and early twentieth centuries (Figure 7.3).[6] In fact, cuteness was considered to be the main feature of *shōjo,* the term coined at the time to signify the "not-quite-adult" femaleness of unmarried girls. As Robertson shows, this characterization contributed to the socializing policy of the modernizing state by effecting an increase in

Figure 7.1 Idol Yumi Adachi assists in the 1999 Anti-Drug Campaign. *Top:* In the opening ceremony of the campaign, Yumi smiles with former prime minister Obuchi Keizō (26 June). *Bottom:* A campaign poster featuring Yumi. (Courtesy of Sun Music Production and the Ministry of Health)

Figure 7.2 On the cover of the January 1998 issue of *Bomb!* Ryoko Hirose strikes a "cute" pose (© Gakken Co. Ltd.).

the number of years between puberty and marriage as a period of preparation for marriage (Robertson 1998, 63, 65; Murakami 1983; Ōtsuka 1989).

The contemporary manifestation of the cute style signals young Japanese women's rebellion against adult culture – a form of female-led youth culture that emerged in the mid-1960s and expanded over the next three decades, the time in which Japan reached the height of its economic growth. To be cute was to be "infantile and delicate at the same time as being pretty," and to participate in the formation of an adolescent utopia where people can be forever young, childlike, and liberated from the filthy world of adult politics (Kinsella 1995, 220; Ōtsuka 1989; Yamane 1990; Miyadai et al. 1993).

By the mid-1990s, however, the star of the cute idols was burning less brightly. One explanation for this decline is the appearance of a large number of pop idols and idol-like characters, which led to the term "pop idols" becoming one that could be applied to almost any genre as long as performers seemed cute. In the eyes of many people, this thorough penetration of the cute style has diminished its public appeal as well as the commercial value of cute idols.

Figure 7.3 Examples of cute *shōjo* images from the Meiji period (circa 1890s). These are part of a postcard series called "Contemporary Popular Figures" *(Tūsei Fūzoku Hyakushi)*, featuring popular geisha girls of the time.

An alternative explanation is the decline of the cute style itself. A central tenet of cuteness, childlike innocence, could go only so far as a form of rebellion. Young female performers who projected more powerful and sensual images (including young female rock-and-roll artists) came to the fore, leading to the creation of a new category: the "post-idol."[7] The following section will detail this transition.

Pop Idols and Gender-Role Competition

The assumption underlying the current investigation is that gender is a performative construct, a mode of enacting the received norms that surface as the styles of the flesh. Repeated practice of normative sexual behaviours produces a body that in gesture and appearance is recognizably "feminine" or "masculine" (Bartky 1990, 65; Butler 1990). Delving into the process in which female pop idols are physically shaped as a cultural institution provides a means of uncovering how these young Japanese women negotiate their images in a social field. By attempting to win public recognition, they enmesh themselves in the gender discourses and sexual stereotypes that are presented to them by the pop-idol agencies that train them.

The current shift in the public preference from cute idols to sensual post-idols reflects the era in which the traditionally male-dominated socio-economic system is considered to be on the verge of a breakdown and restructuring (a phenomenon known in Japanese as *risutora*, from the English "restoration"). This era has also been one in which women are said to be becoming more powerful and outspoken than ever before in the public sphere (*onna no jidai*, or "the age of women"). My interest here is to investigate how these changes and perceptions are influenced by and manifested in the way young female performers package themselves as commodities. With this in mind, I will compare two cases in which I followed particular idol candidates to training sessions and observed how they embodied images of adolescent femaleness.

Reproducing Cute Idols

The first group of female candidates I studied intensively in 1996 included three individuals in their mid-teens, Yuka, Mari, and Chieko, who had just been recruited by a pop-idol promotion agency, Cutie Smile, Ltd., through auditions. Cutie Smile has specialized in pop-idol manufacturing since the early 1990s. Nagabayashi Akihiko is a male producer and the decision-maker of this agency. A former pop-idol manager, now in his mid-forties, Nagabayashi has worked in the entertainment industry for nearly half of his life. One of his assistants, Komobuchi Takeshi (male), specializes in voice training, while another assistant, Wakasugi Yokō (female), directs choreography. Both of these assistants are in their late twenties. The agency holds concerts from time to time, attended by approximately 500 fans, mostly men between the ages of eighteen and thirty-five.

Two- to three-hour training sessions, including voice training and choreography lessons, took place three evenings per week in a studio located next to the agency's main office. While Komobuchi and Wakasugi instructed the trainees most of the time, Nagabayashi interrupted whenever he felt it was necessary. Nagabayashi called this interruption "quality control," the purpose of which was to "make sure that performers can perform properly in the end." Nagabayashi was specific about how performers should speak and act on stage, and he required them to repeatedly practise articulating with childlike innocence and enthusiasm. These appeared to be difficult for Yuka and Mari, who were not used to singing and speaking in such a manner in their everyday lives.

In a two-hour voice training session, Komobuchi played a tune with a guitar and made each trainee sing a lyrical line over and over again until he was satisfied, then asked the next trainee to do the same. Nagabayashi occasionally stepped in to push the trainees harder towards refining certain parts. The following excerpt is a typical example of this interaction, in this case between Yuka (Y), Komobuchi (K), and Nagabayashi (N). My observations are enclosed in brackets.

The setting: Y practises singing with a microphone in her hands, K coaches her, and N observes the two from his seat at the back of the studio.

Y: [sings a line] "It's so wonderful to fall in love, but it's difficult to be loved ..."
K: Stretch out this "loved" part ... Yes, that's good! Alright ... On to the next part ...
Y: "When one wants to capture happiness, it's so difficult not to rush ... "
K: Good! Okay, that's it. Good enough.
N: [looks frustrated] What do you mean "good enough," Komobuchi!? Can't you tell that the "happiness" part is not articulated right!? Do it once more!
Y: *Hai!* [a humble confirmation in Japanese] "happiness ... "
N: [looking frustrated] The whole line, idiot!
Y: *Hai!* "When one wants to capture happiness, it's so difficult not to rush ..."
N: Put more heart into "happiness," would you!? ... Like "happiness ..." [demonstrates a childlike articulation]
Y: *Hai!* "Happiness ..." [tries her best to sound childlike]
N: It's "happiness ...." [demonstrates again]
Y: "Happiness ..." [repeats with a childlike smile on her face]

N: Try the whole line again.
Y: *Hai!* "When one wants to capture happiness, it's so difficult not to rush ..."
N: "Difficult not to rush ..." [demonstrates]
Y: *Hai!* "It's so difficult not to rush ..."
N: Too strong! Why can't you get the cuteness!? It's "difficult not to rush ... " [demonstrates] Try to exaggerate it!
Y: *Hai!* [looking a bit tense, she pauses for two seconds to take a breath] "When one wants to capture happiness, it's so difficult not to rush ... " [tries her best to sound childlike]
N: Next.
Y: *Hai!* "Let's have the courage to say 'I love you' ..."
N: "I love you ... " [demonstrates]
Y: "I love you ..."
N: [three-second pause] Okay, go on to the next part ... [looks unsatisfied but leaves it as it is for now; signals Komobuchi to take over]

Tension filled the air during such an extensive drill, and the trainees could not prevent the weariness from showing on their faces towards the end.

Choreography lessons centred on making predominantly feminine gestures (Figure 7.4). Pensive poses and melancholy expressions were often made as the trainees waved their bodies "softly" from left to right. These, according to Nagabayashi, signify a youthful femininity that evokes empathy in the minds of the viewers. Over the course of the four-week training period, Yuka and Mari became increasingly frustrated by these gestures. One day, Mari came out of the studio with tears in her eyes as she was scolded by Nagabayashi for not mastering the style. Later, she recalled this event as one of the most unpleasant experiences of her life. As I pursued the reason, Mari said that the gestures required by Nagabayashi made her look excessively "coy" and "submissive," creating a "fake personality" that was no longer herself, and she felt "extremely uncomfortable" about it. Both Yuka and Mari felt that their sexualized bodies and images were out of their control, but they could not do much about it because it was their job *(shigoto dakara shikata ga nai)*.

Wakasugi, who had worked as a choreographer at Cutie Smile for some time, was sympathetic about the sense of discomfort felt by many of her trainees: "Sometimes I feel bad because they [the trainees] have to play the [feminine] character that they don't really want to play. All of them struggle at the outset [of their training period] as they try to become someone who they have never experienced being before. For those who are willing to overcome that struggle, however, there is a point at which they embrace the cute character as part of themselves, and that's when they really grow.

They become apparently more enthusiastic and confident, and their skills improve dramatically."

This statement indicates that the candidates' willingness to compromise with the image provided by their agency influences the rate at which they acquire performing skills. During the period of my observation, I failed to see Yuka and Mari grow in the way Wakasugi described that some willing performers would grow.

For Chieko, however, adopting the excessively cute and childlike character was simply one of many tasks she expected to fulfill in show business – something she attended to enthusiastically. When I asked her whether she ever felt uncomfortable about her performances, she replied: "Not really. It is my job and it is something I enjoy doing very much. I eventually want to become someone who is adored by everyone. Please provide me with your support, too, as I will do my best to keep it up!"

This showed the association Chieko had made between embodying the cute style and attaining prestige, which together constituted her identity as a performer. It also showed how motivated she was in adopting this adolescent gender role – she even tried to pull the researcher into buying her cute character!

In sum, I found that performers had different attitudes towards embracing the crafted image of adolescent femininity. To the extent that these performers were willing to adopt it as part of their expertise, they accepted the

Figure 7.4 A cute idol undergoing a training session (photo by the author).

image. To the extent that they could not identify themselves with the sexist stereotypes, the embodiment of the cute style was met with resistance.

Becoming Vibrantly Sexual

The Dance-Jet Agency became a powerhouse of the emerging pop-idol category of "idol dancers" *(dansukei aidoru)*. Performers who belong to this category are also referred to as "post-idols" *(posuto aidoru)*, who mark the era in which idols can no longer attract the public by simply being cute. Idol dancers gained nationwide recognition in 1995 with the debut of Namie Amuro, a leading figure of current adolescent fashion and lifestyle.

Many enthusiastic Amuro fans were called "Amurors," and the "Amuro style," signified by wavy long hair, darkly coloured and thinly trimmed eyebrows, tight shorts, an exposed belly button, and long high-heeled boots, created a sensation in the fashion and cosmetic industries. This appearance became a stereotype of all idol dancers as well as a symbol of the so-called *garu,* or "gals," a point to which I will return in the next section.

I followed 30 students as they underwent singing and dancing practice at the Dance-Jet Agency in the summer of 1996. Most of the approximately 200 students who attended this training school were young females between the ages of eight and twenty-two, who were recruited through a series of auditions. An instructor of this school, Keiko, was a former cute idol who debuted in the late 1980s but retired after a year or so. She coached the students with several other instructors, all in their midtwenties. For students who attended the school, Keiko was a "big sister" whom they could confide in, rather than an official instructor or a former pop star. The general atmosphere was informal and friendly, but all students were serious about their training. Once lessons began, their attention sharpened, their bodies were filled with energy, and they were transformed from shy teenage girls who giggled during breaks into confident dancers who concentrated on brushing up on their performing skills.

Iwaki Yoshihiro, the president and founder of the Dance-Jet Agency, spent most of his time in his office next to the studio, where he met with guests from big companies and local government bureaus to discuss business. He came into the studio occasionally to observe how things were proceeding, but he rarely interrupted. Small children who took dancing lessons were accompanied by their parents, who sat at the back of the studio to observe how their little ones performed.

In sharp contrast to the ideal image described by Nagabayashi, Iwaki's version of adolescent femaleness does not represent a form of delicate femininity. For Iwaki, or Iwaki-*sensei* (Master Iwaki), as students call him, "being oneself" is the single most important driving force in performances: "[It is important] to allow one's energy to flow from within, without any external constraint. This enables the actor to act from the bottom of her heart and soul. By being pure, she can open herself up to anything and everything, and give to the performance all that she can. It's the primary step in becoming a professional actor." Iwaki incorporates an active idea of "purity" to signify actors' subjectivity, or the sentiment of acting with one's total being, rather than using the term in a more orthodox way to represent an objectified self.

Students met twice a week: one day for voice training, another to practise dancing. In voice training, students lined up in the mirrored studio, put their strength into their bellies, and sang as loud as they could for about one hour. In dancing, students shook their bodies to the rhythm (Figure 7.5). Dancing was practised in a free style, where each student invented her own way of moving the body. Keiko and other instructors taught basic dancing skills, such as how to make steps or turn the body around, but there was no choreography in any strict sense. The heat generated by students' bodies raised the temperature of the studio, which was already hot and steamy. Soon they were dripping with perspiration, but everyone thought that they were "having a good sweat" *(ii ase o kaite iru)*. At day's end, students formed a circle to reflect upon their performances and discuss some of the problems they found during their lessons, as a way of mutual encouragement.

The kind of crafted femininity that I observed at Cutie Smile was absent from the Dance-Jet Agency. What I encountered instead was an expression of vibrant sexuality that incorporated "quick," "sharp," "powerful," and even

Figure 7.5 A scene from the Dance-Jet Agency's dancing exercise (photo by the author).

"aggressive" body movements – similar to the style represented by American hip-hop artists, or pop singers such as Janet Jackson and Madonna. All body parts waved dynamically with fast foot shuffles. Frequent fist making made little dancers appear even more "big and strong." Students occasionally made crotch-grabbing gestures and touched under their breasts when they danced, suggesting that they were preening for the audience in an overtly sexual way. Seeing young girls strike some of these poses was quite shocking, and I even wondered if some of them really understood what they were doing.

Some students I interviewed considered that this style was "cool and sexy," and it represented the so-called *tsuyoi onna no jidai*, or the "age of the powerful women." Others indicated that it gave them a sense of liberation and self-empowerment. When I asked Keiko to tell me how she compared this overtly sexual style with the cute style she represented back in the late 1980s, her reply indicated a significant emotional and attitudinal contrast:

> The cute character I played back then was a made-up image that oppressed my individuality, and I did not enjoy trying to live up to that image at all. The only thing that kept me going was my hunger for fame ... The kind of sexiness that I am expressing now through my dance comes from within myself. It's what I really am or what I can really be, and I don't have to present a fake self or lose my control over it ... I don't have to feel bad any more about trying to satisfy people with an invented character that is not really myself.

This confirmed the willingness of Keiko and her colleagues to break away from the old stereotype of adolescent femaleness through a new, self-affirmative style of sexualized performance.

However, the new sexual assertiveness in post-idols has not actually entirely eclipsed its "cute" antecedent. My interviews with male Amuro Namie fans revealed that the performances of Amuro Namie and all the rest of the idol dancers were offshoots of cute idols' male-attracting gestures. A female Amuro fan told me that Amuro was just another cute idol when she was not singing on stage: "She appears to be very feminine when she is not performing, and I love that gap between her acting and her real personality. She is cute when she doesn't perform, and powerfully sexy once she begins performing."

This indicates that in spite of the assertion that the so-called post-idols allow new sexual assertiveness for women, they essentially back up the existing gender-role expectations and sexual stereotypes for adolescents – whereby female subjects continue to be sexually objectified by many, especially male, viewers.

As far as Amuro herself was concerned, there was one clear goal in mind, as she commented in a television interview: "I would be happy to be widely adored by anyone and everyone ... not only by women of my age, or men, or something like that" (*Golden Disc Prize Special*, NHK, 3 May 1996).

What mattered for her was her popularity. The fact that she and her style were being discussed widely by many people was a sign that she was accomplishing the dream of self-establishment. In the winner-take-all system of capitalism, the cultural debate on gender is a good bait for the public, and also for profit-makers to feed on – as long as they can.

Producing Gender Roles through Idol Performances

The century-old gender ideology "good wife, wise mother" *(ryōsai kenbo)* was first championed by officials in the Ministry of Education in the late 1890s, differentiating women's role as homebound wives and mothers from that of men. The history of women in modern Japan can be understood as the struggle between state policies, which consistently discouraged women from entering the public arena, and female-led social movements, which opposed the state's ideological apparatus.

Good Wife, Wise Mother

The image of "good wife, wise mother" was developed by the ideologues, whose goal was to transform Japan from a feudal state to a modern nation that was strong enough to stand up to the Western imperialist superpowers. Under the government's plan to institute a strong "family-state" *(kazoku kokka)* headed by the patriarchal emperor, women were expected to contribute to the national welfare by serving the male family head at home and devoting themselves to the bearing and upbringing of children, the nation's future workforce (Ohinata 1995, 200). With this vision, the state marginalized women from almost all aspects of public life.

Prewar laws denied women the right to vote, to organize politically, and, before 1925, to attend or speak at political meetings (Sievers 1983, 52, 53; Uno 1993, 299). The 1898 Civil Code placed women under the authority of the patriarchal head, who could choose the family domicile, manage his wife's property, and make decisions on legal issues involving his family members (including marriage and divorce) (Kaneko 1995, 4, 5). While many women entered the job market from time to time, they were relegated to occupations considered to be supplemental to those of men, such as low-wage industrial workers, clerical attendants, teachers, nurses, domestic servants, and home-based workers (Kawashima 1995, 272-75). In education, the 1899 Girls' High School Law officially declared that the aim of secondary education for girls was to provide them with training to become "good wives and wise mothers" (Kaneko 1995, 5).

Although the 1947 democratic constitution forbade discrimination based on sex, cases show that throughout the postwar period, Japanese bureaucrats and politicians continued to inform their state policies with the vision of women as domestic agents. The provisions of the 1948 Eugenic Protection Law, for example, aimed at preserving the prewar role of women as mothers rather than their health as individuals. Reproductive policies served national interests rather than women's needs, suggesting that the postwar state still considered women as bearers of the nation's workforce, except that this time their wombs were borrowed to meet the labour needs of industry rather than those of households or the state (Uno 1993, 306).

Various restrictions were imposed on women's qualifications to work in companies, whereas men's pursuit of a career path was often taken for granted. In spite of the implementation of the 1986 Equal Employment Opportunity Law (EEOL), gender bias continued to exist in many Japanese companies, as reflected in salaries and occupational types.[8] In many, especially large, companies, female employees were often regarded as the "flowers of the workplace" *(shokuba no hana),* whose role was little more than decorative: to "brighten up" *(hanayaka ni suru)* the company atmosphere as assistants or extras.[9]

The typical career path of a permanent female employee, as envisioned by Japanese firms, was to be hired for a relatively low-skill, low-responsibility job out of high school, work until marriage, retreat to her motherly duties, and, if possible, return to work after her children were grown. This scenario was part of the state's labour policy, which in order to cope with a growing shortage of workers during the period of Japan's postwar economic growth, kept encouraging women to enter the labour force without reducing their responsibilities for household management and child care (Oūchi 1981; Uno 1993, 305).

The Ministry of Education continued to issue guidelines recommending that primary and secondary co-educational schools organize different curricula for men and women. This included making homemaking courses mandatory for high school girls (the practice followed by most high schools between 1969 and 1989), and placing female and male students on separate teams for sports-oriented activities (Hara 1995, 104). In many of these schools, female and male students continue to wear different uniforms, carry different school bags, and have separate classroom roll calls in which boys are consistently called first (Kameda 1995, 114).[10]

Japanese Womanhood: Transgression and Contestation

Against the forces that marginalized women in public spaces, there emerged a set of movements that aimed to redefine women's status. In the domain of politics, activists during the 1880s and 1890s stressed women's right to participate in public affairs. Labour strikes by women occurred as early as 1886, leading groups such as *Yūaikai* (Friendship Society) and

Sekirankai (Red Wave Society) to emerge and sponsor mass rallies against the textile industry and other corporate institutions to protect female workers from being exploited. Japan's first feminist organization, *Seitōsha* (Bluestocking Society), founded in 1911, published periodicals in which female intellectuals discussed various social and legal issues concerning women. *Shin Fujin Kyokai* (New Women's Association), founded in 1920, achieved the repeal of the law that barred women from political meetings. Women's right to vote was sought by another feminist organization, *Fusen Kakutoku Domei* (Women's Suffrage League), as well as similar groups that developed during the 1920s and 1930s (Sievers 1983; Kuninobu 1984; Bernstein 1991; Fujieda 1995).

In the popular culture of this era, the so-called modern girls *(moga)* epitomized the self-assertive attitudes of young middle-class women who rejected the submissive domesticity of *ryōsai kenbo*. These women modelled themselves after the so-called modern women or "flappers" of Europe and North America, who, by adopting the carefree, cosmopolitan fashion and lifestyle of urban women, rebelled against the establishment (Silverberg 1991).

In postwar Japan, the introduction of democracy led to the emergence of numerous movements and organizations. In the 1970s and 1980s, radical feminists such as Tanaka Mitsu, Atsumi Ikuko, and Ueno Chizuko criticized the idea of *ryōsai kenbo*. They questioned the inevitability of women's domestic destiny as they demonstrated the mechanism of societal domination as manifested in the state, family, and corporations (e.g., Tanaka 1972; Ueno 1994).

In the youth culture of the 1990s, a new image of adolescent femaleness, known as *gyaru* or "gals," began to replace the older *shōjo*. This image conjured up the figure of an assertive, self-centred young woman who is in no hurry to marry and who maintains a stable of boyfriends to serve her different needs (Robertson 1998, 65; Tanaka 1995). Contemporary "gals" reflect the antisocial attitude of the modern girls of the 1920s and 1930s. In fact, *gyaru* can be read as a Japanese revival and abbreviation of the French *garçon (gyarusonnu)*, one of the common terms used in the 1930s to denote a masculine female (Robertson 1998, 65).

A closer look at women's reactions to the state's sexual politics and gender management over time, however, reveals that the multiple positions taken by women cannot be reduced to a simple "pro/con" dichotomy. For example, under the great surge of nationalist sentiment during the wartime period (1930s and 1940s) that denounced feminism as being "anti-government," "unpatriotic," or "un-Japanese," leading female activists appealed to the idea of motherhood in order to proclaim their public identity (Kuninobu 1984; Mackie 1988; Uno 1993, 302).[11] Most women's associations that became active during the early postwar period (the 1950s and 1960s) sought to protect working wives and mothers outside the home with the assumption that women are primarily domestic agents (Uno 1993, 307). These cases show that from time to time, women's movements altered their goals in order to adapt themselves to the surrounding social environment.

Studies show that a considerably high proportion of Japanese adults are still trying to bring up their children in conformity with gender-appropriate behaviours.[12] Many mothers, especially those with small children, continue to believe that their motherly love and devotion are the keys to a child's development, and play the role of *kyōiku mama,* or "educational mothers." Parental attitudes towards child rearing show that parents constantly differentiate between boys and girls: boys are brought up with the expectation that they will become "active, brave, and strong," while girls are raised to be "obedient, polite, and non-argumentative" (Kashiwagi 1973, quoted in Kameda 1995, 110; Ohinata 1995, 207).

Many students actively reinforce their gender roles in classrooms, as in the case of a self-governed student council that is commonly found in primary and secondary schools. Here, a common understanding holds that girls run for vice chair, treasurer, or secretary, but never the chair; a girl who seeks the very top office is likely to be accused by her classmates of lacking common sense. In most sports-related club activities where both sexes are involved, women continue to participate as managers, if not cheerleaders, whose role is to assist the male players, for example, by putting away equipment, washing uniforms, and preparing meals.[13] Gender bias in schools can also influence students' academic career paths. More women enter postsecondary education than men, but most enter two-year colleges while men go to four-year universities in higher numbers (Kameda 1995, 110).

All these cases together imply that while the traditional image of *ryōsai kenbo* may be refuted by radical activists and movements representing women, many Japanese women do not contest this gender role but rather find comfort in conforming to it more or less. As much as *ryōsai kenbo* has failed to become hegemonic, it has also failed to become counter-hegemonic, and the ground for contesting the appropriate image of Japanese femaleness remains open.

Idol-Pop as Gender-Role Showcase

Situating pop-idol performances in this dynamic socio-historical setting reveals that the two observed images of femaleness in pop-idol performances, "cute" versus "sexy," are two different, optional images of female sexuality manufactured by idol-promotion agencies that try to establish their place in Japanese society. Cute idols advocate a traditional adolescent femininity that idealizes the image of the future *ryōsai kenbo* for young girls. A shift away from the cute style towards a more vibrantly sexual style in pop-idol performances appears to reflect the fact that Japanese women are breaking away from the traditional gender ideology and becoming more self-assertive. However, the current popularity of pop idols also proves the point that young girls continue to empower themselves in reference to the models that are provided by the industry. By constructing a contested terrain in which adolescent women can variably position and invent themselves as gender role models, the burgeoning industry continues to capitalize on the manipulation of female sexuality.

The competition between the two alternative images of femaleness in pop-idol performances becomes more explicit when one looks closely at the pop-idol manufacturing process. The compulsory practices of gender-role replication are welcomed and self-enforced by those who can identify themselves with what their agencies offer (as in the case of the Cutie Smile Agency), whereas they are resisted by those who see the gap between the assigned gender role and their subjectivity (as in the case of Dance-Jet). From the perspective of many, especially male consumers, however, these competing images continue to form part of their sexual fantasy.

Conclusion

This study has examined female pop-idol performances, focusing on the process by which young female performers evaluate and embody what they consider to be the appropriate image of adolescent femaleness. It has shown how Japan's entertainment industry bridges the gap between the state's gender ideology and the actual lives of young women.

Two distinct images of adolescent femaleness were identified in this discussion: the passive, submissive, and childlike femininity expressed by cute idols on the one hand, and the active, stylish, and vibrantly sexual femaleness represented by idol dancers on the other. While both images are designed to be marketable, the cute style, considered trendy in the 1970s and 1980s, is criticized today on the ground that it regulates female actors' control over their own bodies and individuality. Only when this sense of confinement is overcome by the pursuit of greater public recognition do the actors find the cute style more acceptable. On the other hand, many young female performers consider it empowering to reassert their positive identities as they desire the embodiment of vibrant sexuality. This is especially the case in an era when women are considered to have become stronger and self-assertive. It is questionable, however, how empowering this image actually is. In any case, the field of pop-idol production has become a site where the appropriate form of adolescent gender is contested.

This symbolic contestation in pop-idol performances reflects, at least in part, the ongoing struggle over gender role between the dominant and the resistant forces in modern Japanese society. While the dominant force has tried to designate the home as the proper place of activities for women, and has expected them to perform the role of "good wife, wise mother," the forces of resistance have tended to reclaim women's public statuses. The way in which this power dynamic was manifested in the domain of popular culture in the past, as in the emergence of "modern girls" *(moga)* in the 1920s and 1930s, is much the same today; that is, through the opposition between vibrantly sexual post-idols and traditional cute idols – albeit with differences in scale. In this respect, gender-role construction in the pop-idol industry is seen as an offshoot of social structures rather than a contemporary phenomenon. This recurrent pattern of symbolic competition is likely to extend into the new millennium as long as gender ideology contributes to continued marginalization of women in the public sphere.

In recent case studies, popular art forms are shown not only to exist in a contested socio-cultural terrain but also to provide points of contradiction through which individuals can gain agency, sometimes by taking multiple positions (McNay 1992; Clammer 1995; Rosenberger 1995, 1996; cf. Ochiai 1989; Boiling 1998). In concurrence with these studies, the discussion in this chapter has shown the specific ways in which female pop-idol performances epitomize the ongoing struggle between images of adolescent femaleness that nevertheless perpetuates the dominant societal view of gender and sexuality.

There is a key concept in Japan called *matori,* or "space taking," referring to an idea of self-positioning in society. If one is willing, one can open up a space (or territory) within an existing socio-cultural terrain and fill it up with images, events, or contents that are spawned out of creativity – thus, social space *(ma)* is "taken" *(tori).* Bachnik (1986, 1994) calls this "indexing one's place" in a social space, or "situating oneself" in a social relationship (also Yasuda 1984). Many pop-idol producers whom I interviewed, including Nagabayashi and Iwaki, used the word *matori* to explain their pop-idol production activities, confirming that it is a form of institutional positioning – namely, within the existing terrain of gender constructs in Japanese society. I speculate that this industrial organization of gender will continue to be practised in much the same way in Japan in the new millennium, regardless of how specific features of adolescent femaleness may change.

Notes

1 Pop-idol performances first emerged in the general category of popular music, or *kayōkyoku.* Unlike many of their predecessors, which touched on more mature subjects and were targeted mainly at adults, pop idols came to represent adolescence. Most typical examples of pop idols are young, soft-core pop singers, although they can more generally include young artists from other genres such as rock and roll and hip-hop. In some respects, they are roughly equivalent to the performances of teen idols in the West such as Frank Sinatra, Paul Anka, Tony Bennett, the Shirelles, and the Shangri-Las in the 1950s to 1970s; Debbie Gibson, Menudo, Candi, and the New Kids on the Block in the 1980s; and

the Beastie Boys, Shampoo, the Back Street Boys, the Spice Girls, Britney Spears, and "2 be 3" in the 1990s.
2 There are also articles in academic journals such as the *Journal of Popular Culture, Popular Music,* and *Popular Music and Society*.
3 This form of companionship, which signifies the position of each individual as part of a unified group, is also emphasized by star characters for younger age groups, such as Power Rangers and Sailor Moon, who tend to come in groups (of five). This contrasts with the North American television stars, such as He-Man or Batman and Robin, who stand out as solo or in pairs, emphasizing individuality and partnership. In this sense, the companionship in pop-idol performances can be seen as a style one transfers from the earlier age groups on up.
4 These practices have been imitated recently by Western artists in places such as Virgin Records and HMV to enhance their public appeal.
5 Although male pop idols adopt a more "stylish" or "cool" appearance, female fans generally agreed that to appear "stylish" is what makes male idols cute; one female university student remarked that "the earnest attempts of young and innocent-looking boys to act stylish make them somewhat pitiful, and therefore very sweet."
6 Detailed historical studies on the image of cuteness in Japan have been conducted, for instance, by Ōtsuka (1989), Akiyama (1992), and Karasawa (1995).
7 Several people whom I interviewed indicated that there were "self-expressive" and "punkish" pop idols back in the 1970s and early 1980s, when the cute style was in its heyday, but they also said that these idol styles were marginalized at the time.
8 According to Kawashima (1995, 278), women's monthly contractual salary was, on average, 60.7 percent of that of men as late as 1991, and 50.8 percent on the basis of total monthly earnings that included overtime payments and bonuses. Data from the same year show that nearly half of the 5.5 million women in the labour force were either part-time, temporary, or exempt from the benefits of full-time employment.
9 In one in-company newsletter, published in 1977, I found that female employees were compared to flowers as they were introduced. This article was titled "Blossoms of Maidens in [the name of the company]."
10 These practices were not specific to Japan. Mandatory homemaking courses and separate sports teams existed in American high schools, for example. There are many schools in Britain and elsewhere that adopt different uniforms for men and women. Since Japan copied the British and American educational systems in modern times, these practices were likely to be exported to Japan. Yet, these norms and customs apparently reinforce gender differentiation in the Japanese school context.
11 Part of the implication of this positioning was that women could actively contribute to the imperial state, whose two important sectors – the military and the bureaucracy – became preoccupied with the reproduction of the nation's labour supply.
12 This was taken from a 1982 survey conducted by the Prime Minister's Office (quoted in Kameda 1995, 108).
13 Japanese sometimes refer to this as *otoko no kao o tateru,* meaning "save boys' faces" or "pay due respect to men."

References

Akiyama, M. 1992. *Shōjo Tachi no Shōwa Shi* (The girls' history of the Shōwa Era). Tokyo: Shinchōsha.

Bachnik, J.M. 1986. "Time, Space and Person in Japanese Relationship." In J. Hendry and J. Webber, eds., *Interpreting Japanese Society: Anthropological Approaches.* Oxford, UK: JASO, 49-75.

–. 1994. "Introduction: Uchi/Soto: Challenging Our Conceptualizations of Self, Social Order, and Language." In J.M. Bachnik and C.J. Quinn Jr., eds., *Situated Meaning: Inside and Outside in Japanese Self, Society, and Language.* Princeton, NJ: Princeton University Press, 3-37.

Barnouw, E., and C. Kirkland. 1992. "Entertainment." In R. Bauman, ed., *Folklore, Cultural Performances and Popular Entertainments.* Oxford: Oxford University Press, 50-52.

Bartky, S.L. 1990. *Femininity and Domination: Studies in the Phenomenology of Oppression.* London: Routledge.
Bernstein, G.L., ed. 1991. *Recreating Japanese Women, 1600-1945.* Berkeley: University of California Press.
Boiling, P. 1998. "Family Policy in Japan." *Journal of Social Policy* 27: 173-90.
Butler, J. 1990. *Gender Trouble: Feminism and the Subversion of Identity.* New York: Routledge.
Clammer, J. 1995. "Consuming Bodies: Constructing and Representing the Female Body in Contemporary Japanese Print Media." In L. Skov and B. Moeran, eds., *Women, Media and Consumption in Japan.* Honolulu: University of Hawai'i Press, 197-219.
During, S., ed. 1993. *The Cultural Studies Reader.* London: Routledge.
Ewen, S. 1976. *Captains of Consciousness: Advertising and the Social Roots of the Consumer Culture.* New York: McGraw-Hill.
Fiske, J. 1989a. *Understanding Popular Culture.* London: Routledge.
—. 1989b. *Reading the Popular.* Boston: Unwin Hyman.
Frith, S. 1983. *Sound Effects: Youth, Leisure and the Politics of Rock'n'Roll.* London: Constable.
—. 1988. *Music for Pleasure: Essays in the Sociology of Pop.* New York: Routledge.
Fujieda, M. 1995. "Japan's First Phase of Feminism." In K. Fujimura-Fanselow and A. Kameda, eds., *Japanese Women: New Feminist Perspectives on the Past, Present, and Future.* New York: Feminist Press, 323-41.
Hara, K. 1995. "Challenges to Education for Girls and Women in Modern Japan: Past and Present." In K. Fujimura-Fanselow and A. Kameda, eds., *Japanese Women: New Feminist Perspectives on the Past, Present, and Future.* New York: The Feminist Press, 93-106.
Haug, W.H. 1986. *Critique of Commodity Aesthetics: Appearance, Sexuality and Advertising in Capitalist Society.* Minneapolis: University of Minnesota Press.
Herd, J.A. 1984. "Trends and Taste in Japanese Popular Music: A Case-Study of the 1984 Yamaha World Popular Music Festival." *Popular Music* 4: 75-96.
Ivy, M. 1993. "Formations of Mass Culture." In A. Gordon, ed., *Postwar Japan as History.* Berkeley: University of California Press, 239-58.
Kameda, A. 1995. "Sexism and Gender Stereotyping in Schools." In K. Fujimura-Fanselow and A. Kameda, eds., *Japanese Women: New Feminist Perspectives on the Past, Present, and Future.* New York: Feminist Press, 107-24.
Kaneko, S. 1995. "The Struggle for Legal Rights and Reforms: A Historical View." In K. Fujimura-Fanselow and A. Kameda, eds., *Japanese Women: New Feminist Perspectives on the Past, Present, and Future.* New York: Feminist Press, 3-14.
Karasawa, S. 1995. *Bishōjo No Gyakushū: Yomigaere!! Kokoro Kiyoi, Yogore Naki, Kedakaki Shōjo Tachi Yo* (The counterattack of girls: revive!! pure-hearted, clean, and noble girls). Tokyo: Nesuko.
Kashiwagi, K. 1973. "Gendai Seinen no Seiyakuwari no Shutoku" (Acquisition of gender roles among contemporary youth). In S. Iida, ed., *Gendai Seinen no Sei Ishiki* (Gender consciousness among contemporary youth). Tokyo: Kaneko Shobō.
Kawashima, Y. 1995. "Female Workers: An Overview of Past and Current Trends." In K. Fujimura-Fanselow and A. Kameda, eds., *Japanese Women: New Feminist Perspectives on the Past, Present, and Future.* New York: Feminist Press, 271-93.
Kinsella, S. 1995. "Cuties in Japan." In L. Skov and B. Moeran, eds., *Women, Media and Consumption in Japan.* Honolulu: University of Hawai'i Press, 220-54.
Kuninobu, J. 1984. "The Development of Feminism in Modern Japan." *Feminist Issues* 4(2): 5-10.
Mackie, V. 1988. "Feminist Politics in Japan." *New Left Review* 167: 53-59.
McNay, L. 1992. *Foucault and Feminism.* Boston: Northeastern University Press.
Matsuda, S. 1980. *Ryōte De Seiko* (Seiko in both arms). Tokyo: Shueisha.
Miyadai, S., H. Ishihara, and A. Ōtsuka. 1993. *Sabukaruchaa Shinwa Kaitai: Shōjo, Ongaku, Manga, Sei no Sanjunen to Komyunikeeshon no Genzai* (Deconstructing subcultural myths: thirty years of young women, music, cartoons, and sexuality, as well as the present state of communication). Tokyo: Parco Shuppan.

Murakami, N. 1983. *Taishoki no Shokugyo Fujin* (Working women of the Taisho Era). Tokyo: Domesu Shuppan.
Ochiai, E. 1989. *Kindai Kazoku to Feminizumu* (The modern family and feminism). Tokyo: Keizo Shobō.
—. 1997a. *Nijyu Iseiki Kazoku he: Shinkan* (Towards the family of the twentieth century: new edition). Tokyo: Yukikaku.
—. 1997b. *The Japanese Family System in Transition*. Tokyo: LTCB International Library.
Ogawa, H. 1988. *Ongaku Suru Shakai* (A musical society). Tokyo: Keizo Shobō.
Ohinata, M. 1995. "The Mystique of Motherhood: A Key to Understanding Social Change and Family Problems in Japan." In K. Fujimura-Fanselow and A. Kameda, eds., *Japanese Women: New Feminist Perspectives on the Past, Present, and Future*. New York: Feminist Press, 199-211.
Ōtsuka, E. 1989. *Shōjo Minzoku Gaku: Seikimatsu No Shinwa o Tsumugu "Miko No Matsuei"* (The folklore of girls: "descendants of maidens" that spin the wheel of legend in the end of the century). Tokyo: Kobunsha.
Ōuchi, W.G. 1981. *Theory Z: How American Business Can Meet the Japanese Challenge*. Reading, MA: Addison-Wesley.
Robertson, J. 1998. *Takarazuka: Sexual Politics and Popular Culture in Modern Japan*. Berkeley: University of California Press.
Rosenberger, N.R. 1995. "Antiphonal Performances? Japanese Women's Magazines and Women's Voices." In L. Skov and B. Moeran, eds., *Women, Media and Consumption in Japan*. Honolulu: University of Hawai'i Press, 143-69.
—. 1996. "Fragile Resistance, Signs of Status: Women between State and Media in Japan." In A.E. Imamura, ed., *Re-Imaging Japanese Women*. Berkeley: University of California Press, 12-45.
Satō, A. 1991. *Shonen* (Young boy). Tokyo: Shueisha.
Sievers, S. 1983. *Flowers in Salt: The Beginnings of Feminist Consciousness in Meiji Japan*. Stanford, CA: Stanford University Press.
Silverberg, M. 1991. "The Modern Girl as Militant." In G.L. Bernstein, ed., *Recreating Japanese Women, 1600-1945*. Berkeley: University of California Press, 239-66.
Tanaka, M. 1972. *Inochi no Onnatachi E* (To the women of life). Tokyo: Takabe Shoten.
Tanaka, Y. 1995. *Contemporary Portraits of Japanese Women*. Westport, CT: Praeger Publishers.
Ueno, C. 1994. *Kindai Kazoku No Seiritsu To Shuen* (The rise and fall of the modern family). Tokyo: Iwanami Shoten.
Uno, K.S. 1993. "Death of 'Good Wife, Wise Mother'?" In A. Gordon, ed., *Postwar Japan as History*. Berkeley: University of California Press, 293-322.
White, M. 1993. *The Material Child: Coming of Age in Japan and America*. New York: Free Press.
—. 1995. "The Marketing of Adolescence in Japan: Buying and Dreaming." In L. Skov and B. Moeran, eds., *Women, Media and Consumption in Japan*. Honolulu: University of Hawai'i Press, 225-73.
Williamson, J. 1980. *Consuming Passions: The Dynamics of Popular Culture*. London: Marion Boyars.
Yamane, K. 1986. *Hentai Shōjo Moji no Kenkyū* (An anomalous research of teenage handwriting). Tokyo: Kōdansha.
—. 1990. *Gyaru No Kozo* (The structure of gals). Tokyo: Sekai Bunkasha.
Yano, C. 1997. "Charisma's Realm: Fandom in Japan." *Ethnology* 36(4): 335-49.
Yasuda, T. 1984. *Kata No Nihonbunka* (The Japanese culture of forms). Tokyo: Asahi Shinbunsha.

8
A Century of Juvenile Law in Japan
Stephan M. Salzberg

It is now 100 years since juvenile offenders and delinquents came to be treated differently from adults in Japan. Three major laws, passed in 1900, 1922, and 1948, have framed the successive policies, institutions, procedures, and attitudes that have been brought to bear in dealing with wayward youth, many of whom have committed crimes. Each law was formulated in part with reference to foreign models, especially those in the United States. A peak of foreign influence occurred in connection with the 1948 Juvenile Law, the law currently in force, which was drafted and passed during the early years of the postwar American Occupation.

This sweep of 100 years has covered one of the most dynamic periods of all of Japanese history. This was a period of almost unimaginable social change, certainly as rapid as that of any other society on earth, and arguably more so, given the fact that Japan's nearly 250-year isolation under the feudal Tokugawa regime had ended only in 1868. Change was incessant as Japan was transformed, first into a modern industrial and urbanized society, then an imperial power, and now, at the dawn of the twenty-first century, into one of the world's most advanced post-industrial societies.

By contrast, perhaps the most striking feature of Japan's juvenile justice system over that period is a remarkable consistency. Juvenile courts have not had judicialized fact finding and imposition of punishment as their primary function. The juvenile justice system has not been guided by a philosophy that treats juveniles who have broken the law or shown a propensity to do so in isolation from their families, their schools, or their communities, or as deserving of such isolation by virtue of their offences. Instead, the juvenile courts and all of the other institutions concerned with juvenile justice have sought to involve the family, the schools, and the communities. They have engaged them as active participants in the reformation and reconciliation of individual youths, whose problems cannot be understood or dealt with except within the particular social context enfolding that individual. Indeed, only as a last resort and only in an overwhelmingly small number of cases will the juvenile justice system isolate a juvenile and remove the juvenile from his or her family and community to a correctional institution. Even then, the aim of the state, through the institution, is to replicate the family and community, substituting for them in the task of education and rehabilitation.

To the extent it is possible to speak of a Japanese model of juvenile justice, it is a social work model. It is one where the law functions to identify individuals at risk, and where procedures are aimed at inculcating compliance and personal change less through formal judicial procedures and attendant punishment than through exposure to symbols of the state's authority and through the involvement of family and community. It is a model where the juvenile courts themselves are but one small element nested within a larger community-based apparatus designed to identify and protect wayward youth, and where the juvenile court's judicial function is overshadowed by its social work functions. It is a model where rights discourse has played a very small part and where the aim of protecting society through the social protection of youths has far outweighed concerns about protecting the formal legal rights of juvenile criminal defendants. Moreover, it is a model that, by most measures, has been extraordinarily successful.

This chapter traces the development of Japan's juvenile justice system over the last century, describes and analyzes its characteristic features and forms, identifies some of the underlying, persisting tensions that have marked its formulation and practice, and examines some of the challenges it will face in the years to come.

Japan's First Juvenile Law: The *Kanka Hō* of 1900
Japan's first piece of legislation specifically concerned with wayward youth, including those who had been found guilty of criminal offences, was the Juvenile Reformatory Law of 1900.[1] In a narrow sense, the law served only to authorize the establishment of youth reformatories *(kanka'in)*. However, as will be discussed below, by setting out the categories of youths who could be confined in those reformatories, the law had substantive force in delineating those juveniles who, by virtue of their acts or status, could be made subject to this new jurisdiction and special compulsory power of the state.

In terms of Meiji legal development, by 1899 Japan had put in place a working judicial system, a constitutional order of governance, and a body of basic substantive law in the form of the first Criminal Code and Code of Criminal Procedure, the Civil Code and Code of Civil Procedure, and the Commercial Code.[2] With the turn of the twentieth century, the courts began to apply the codes, sometimes in very creative fashion, to the cases brought before them, cases that arose out of the daily life and clashes of interest that developed in the midst of rapid and accelerating social change.

Similarly, the legislature, still led largely by the aging Meiji oligarchs, began an era of new legislative initiatives, filling out and refining the positive law structure that would carry Japan through its process of modernization. The Juvenile Reformatory Law is an example of such legislation, tied by its nature to the criminal law but essentially social in its orientation and intended effect.

Until 1900, the only way in which the law formally recognized special treatment for juvenile offenders was through provisions in the 1880 Criminal Code that allowed for the reduction of punishment when the convicted offender was less than twenty years of age.[3] There were no separate procedures or separate houses of detention for juveniles. The 1900 Juvenile Reformatory Law took the initiative with respect to the need for a separate correctional regime.

The law directed that reformatories were to be established in each prefecture under the direction of the Chief Local Officials *(chihō chōkan)*, administrators appointed by the Home Ministry, roughly equivalent to postwar elected prefectural governors. With the approval of the Home Minister, private groups or individuals could also establish substitute reformatories in place of those that were publicly established and maintained.

As originally passed, the law specified three categories of youths who were to be detained in these reformatories, Japan's first custodial reform schools. These were: (1) children between the ages of eight and sixteen who lacked either proper parental supervision or proper guardians, and were deemed to be vagabonds or beggars or to be keeping bad company; (2) juveniles who had been sentenced by courts to correctional institutions *(chōjiba)* for violations of the Criminal Code; and (3) those who, with the approval of a court under the Civil Code,[4] were to be placed by their parents in a disciplinary institution *(chōkaiba)*.

The law focused primarily on the correctional aspect of the juvenile problem. Court procedures, whether under the Criminal or the Civil Code, pursuant to which juveniles might be sent to these new institutions remained unchanged. They were the procedures of the adult courts. Although lawmakers were well aware of the very recent establishment in the United States of juvenile courts – separate courts with special procedures for juveniles – there was as yet no adoption of such models. Instead, the Diet implemented only the idea of special reformatories for juveniles. This innovation had been in place in certain US states for decades, and, with the American model in mind, had also been attempted on an experimental basis in Japan in separate juvenile blocks that had been established within some of Japan's adult prisons over the preceding several years (Morita 1993, 8).[5]

Beyond the question of the institutional setting within which juveniles might best be detained and rehabilitated, however, the law also expanded considerably the range of juveniles who were deemed to require rehabilitation. Those youths who were, by the law, brought newly within the ambit of the state's legal power were those vagabond or wayward juveniles who did not have the supervision, guidance, and protection of parents or guardians. They had not been adjudicated by a court of law as deserving custodial detention because of what they had done. Instead, they were brought within the scope of the law because they were at risk. Based on the status of these youths as being at risk, the *protective* power of the state was brought to bear. The *parens patriae* power of the state, the state acting in the role of parents, or protectors, of vulnerable members of society, was embodied in the 1900 Juvenile Reformatory Law.

That power would, in the view of the government of the time, be invoked but infrequently. In the Diet debate on the bill, a government spokesman indicated that as of October 1899, there were 174 juvenile detainees in adult prisons. Moreover, there were probably very few, if any, being held under Civil Code authority (if only because there were no appropriate "disciplinary institutions" to which juveniles could be sent). The largest category that would be detained under the proposed new law, according to the government's estimates, would be wayward youths. Judging from experience in Tokyo (where there had been a reformatory since 1885, and which held 66 juveniles in 1899), Okayama, Chiba, and Mie, it was expected that there would be, on average, about 50 juveniles per prefecture requiring detention in reformatories (Morita 1993, 83-85).[6]

The exact institutional nature of the reformatories is not made clear in the law itself, nor is there much clarity added in the Diet deliberations. It appears that at one stage there was an idea to try to place even criminal offenders with families or with other volunteer groups or individuals who would provide a more supportive family-style environment, an idea heavily influenced by American theory and practice. In response to a question in the Diet, the head of the Home Ministry's Office of Prisons indicated that reformatory staff would be familiar with teaching, perhaps chosen from among volunteers and hired based on criteria normally applied for elementary school teachers. It was estimated that two teachers would be needed for every fifty juveniles. Preferably, these would be husband and wife, who could better create a family atmosphere (Morita 1993, 89-90).[7]

Three important features of Japan's juvenile law, features that would persist over the next 100 years, became apparent even as early as the 1900 Juvenile Reformatory Law. The first is the formulation of the juvenile justice system, and the initial impetus for its creation, as centred around the protection of juveniles, rather than as a criminal law process per se. Any sanctions imposed as a result of juvenile law processes were to be carried out in institutions specifically intended for juveniles and guided by principles of social rehabilitation rather than punishment and retribution.

Beyond that, however, the protective orientation of the law may be seen in the expansion of the range of juveniles who would be subject to its custodial compulsory protective measures (Morita 1993, 133).[8] All who might be deemed wayward youth, either through their own antisocial behaviour or even the company they kept, as well as those who lacked sufficient familial guidance or authority and thus became vagabonds, were within the scope of the law. The system contemplated by the law might best be characterized as one framed more by a social than by a strictly legal orientation.

Even if constructed on the basis of social protection of youth, however, the law and its operations bespoke another concern, that of social control. This is the second important feature of the regime established under the 1900 Law. One notes, for instance, that the new institutions under the law, the reformatories, were to be under the jurisdiction of the Home Ministry's Office of Prisons. In a very sharp exchange during the Diet debate on the bill, one parliamentarian raised the apparent anomaly of assigning to the Office of Prisons responsibility for what the government itself described as essentially an educational venture. In light of the negative public perception of "children's prisons," demanded the questioner, shouldn't the Ministry of Education properly take jurisdiction? The head of the Office of Prisons (again part of the Home Ministry, which was chiefly responsible for domestic security and policing) responded that although some thought had been given to precisely that idea, and although the law's general scheme related to social welfare work (*kyūhin jigyō*, literally, "relief work for the poor"), it still bore a direct relation to judicial administration and to the work of the police, and therefore properly fell within the mandate of the Home Ministry (Morita 1993, 90).

The social control aspect of the law looms even larger when one considers the contemplated intake methods under the law. Obviously, some of the juveniles would go to reformatories directly from the courts. Article 10 of the law also provided, however, that "administrative agencies" (*gyōsei chō*) should report wayward youths (those corresponding to category 1 under the law, essentially youths engaged in, or deemed liable to engage in, bad behaviour) to the Chief Local Official. Those so reported could then be detained for up to five days, during which time, it would appear, a determination would be made as to whether the youth actually fit within category 1 and should be sent to a reformatory for detention. As pointed out during Diet debate in February 1900, in practice that "administrative agency" would be the police (Morita 1993, 91-92).

In a subsequent amendment to the law, another intake path was added, under which parents or guardians could request placement of their own children or wards in a reformatory. Should the Chief Local Official deem such placement necessary, it would be so ordered.

This points to the third important feature of Japan's juvenile law regime: the way in which, since its beginning, it has been situated at the narrow end of a much broader intake funnel, in a system that relies primarily on police and parents to maintain social control conceived in a protective sense, both for youth at risk and for society at large.

The 1922 Juvenile Law

The juvenile protective and reformatory scheme envisioned under the 1900 Law never fully developed. In many prefectures, public reformatories were not established, nor were private "substitute" reformatories (Morita 1993, 7).[9] The scheme, which vested almost absolute discretion with respect to "wayward youth" in the Chief Local Official, had an ad hoc rather than systematic quality to it. As Japan advanced headlong into the twentieth century, and as social change accelerated, with urbanization and the loosening of traditional cultural mores, the lives that young people led seemed increasingly unhinged from those of earlier generations, and the number of such youths, especially in the cities continued to grow. Public discussion and debate pointed the way towards a more formal and comprehensive system that could deal effectively with youth problems in general, while removing the handling of youthful criminal offenders from adult criminal courts.

The debate gained momentum as early as 1907, immediately after adoption of the new Criminal Code (based largely on German models and replacing the French-influenced 1880 code), with the need, at the least, for conforming amendments to the Juvenile Reformatory Law. This was an opportunity seized upon by leading members of the legal community to press for complete reform of the juvenile regime. A primary inspiration and model for reform proposals came from recent developments in the United States, where, in 1899, special juvenile courts had been established in Chicago and Denver. In contrast to Japan's early approach under the Juvenile Reformatory Law, the pioneering juvenile courts in the US were judicial institutions that adopted features designed to minimize the stigmatization of juveniles. With social rehabilitation as the primary aim, the idea was to avoid the reinforcement of criminal tendencies resulting from an overly rigid punitive approach in the judicial and correctional systems (Schlossman 1977, 82).

Japan's legal world was well aware of even the most recent foreign developments. In May 1907, shortly after adoption of the new Criminal Code, the renowned legal scholar and advisor to government, Prof. Hozumi Norishige of Tokyo Imperial University's Faculty of Law, delivered a detailed lecture to the university's Legal Theory Research Society on the theory and practice of juvenile courts in the United States (Morita 1993, 1129-40).

This lecture, which was soon published (ibid., 8), became a key starting point for a wide-ranging debate over reform of the juvenile justice system, a debate that culminated in the 1922 Juvenile Law.

Criticism of the then current regime centred on its fundamental reliance on administrative discretion. One of the most vocal critics of the 1908 amendments to the Juvenile Reformatory Law, the parliamentarian and highly respected legal scholar Hanai Takuzō, stated in no uncertain terms that deprivation of liberty was quintessentially a *judicial* task. Citing the examples of juvenile courts in both Germany and the United States, he advocated a judicialized youth court as the central organ in a system of protection and education marked by empathy, warmth, and tenderness (ibid., 10).

For its part, the government, or at least the Home Ministry, while seeking the same goal, advocated continued reliance on an administrative approach, one much more conducive, it believed, to responsive, warm-hearted treatment of juveniles than a cut-and-dried judicial approach. The basic theme of this debate in many ways prefigured by a decade the concerns of government policy makers that led to the establishment of the Special Investigation Commission on Legal Institutions *(Rinji hōsei shingikai)* in 1919. The commission's establishment was prompted by the perception that Japanese were all too readily adapting to Western-style legal and judicial forms. Increasingly, they chose to litigate and rely on absolute notions of rights and obligations, rather than on the "beautiful and virtuous" traditional ways of the nation in which the warmth of human relations and mutual social obligations were seen as the key to the adjustment of competing interests. Not surprisingly, the commission's 1922 report, and the spirit that motivated it, coincided with the first of a series of conciliation statutes, as eventually many categories of civil disputes came to be routed away from the courts.[10]

Although the 1908 amendments were relatively minor (Morita 1993, 1: 10),[11] the debate that it set off continued over the next fourteen years, including a struggle between the Ministry of Justice and the Home Ministry over the shape that the juvenile justice system would finally take. In the end, the Home Ministry won out, and in 1922, after four rounds of Diet debate over the preceding two years, a new Juvenile Law was passed.[12]

The 1922 Law established a comprehensive juvenile law system that regularized the treatment of young people to whom the law applied. Jurisdiction over the system moved from the Home Ministry to the Ministry of Justice (Article 17), which controlled the courts in prewar Japan, but the system itself remained administrative, not judicial. The organizational core of the system was the Juvenile Determination Offices *(shōnen shimpansho)* that were established in each judicial district nationwide. Each office was staffed by a Juvenile Determination Official *(shōnen shimpan kan)*, who would conduct determination proceedings singly (rather than in a panel, as was the practice generally in judicial cases heard in the District Courts) and be responsible for managing the Juvenile Determination Office. Each such office would also have Juvenile Protection Officers *(shōnen hogoshi)* and clerks *(shoki)* on staff (Article 18). As will be seen, Juvenile Protection Officers played a key role in the principal work of the Juvenile Determination Offices, perhaps best characterized as administrative organs fulfilling a social-work function related in part to the institutions of the criminal law.

The range of juveniles who fell within the scope of the 1922 Law was broad, although arguably less so than the 1900 Juvenile Reformatory Law. Still, the 1922 Law applied to juveniles, those under the age of eighteen, who had "engaged in behaviour *touching upon* penal laws" *(keibatsu hōrei ni fururu kōi o nasu shōnen)* or "those *in danger of* committing" such behaviour *(keibatsu hōrei ni fururu kōi o nasu osore aru shōnen)* (Articles 1 and 4, emphasis added). The very language of the statute makes it clear that Juvenile Determination Offices were not to be concerned with judicial determination of criminal guilt. In that sense, theirs was not a judicial function.[13]

Instead, their task was to administer appropriate "*protective* dispositions" upon those who fell within their jurisdiction. The breadth of the offices' jurisdiction, evident from the definition of juveniles set out above, was reinforced all the more by the intake mode(s) contemplated in the statute. Article 29 provided that "*a person* who knows of a juvenile in need of protective disposition afforded by a Juvenile Determination Office shall so advise the office or one of its personnel," including, pursuant to Article 30, such details as were known (emphasis added). The category of "person" is as broad as one can delineate under any law, embracing not only, of course, the police but any individual. The reporting requirement is similar to those featured worldwide in child protection statutes, imposing upon all persons a duty to report, for instance, child abuse when a person comes to know of, or reasonably suspect, its occurrence.[14]

Upon such a report and the office's initial judgment that the juvenile should be subject to determination proceedings, a Juvenile Protection Officer would investigate the details of the particular incident(s), if any, together with the character and general behaviour of the juvenile, his environment, background and past experience, physical and mental condition (for which an examining physician would also be consulted to the extent possible), extent of education, and so on (Articles 31-32). The office could also order the juvenile's guardian to investigate the relevant facts, or entrust the investigation to a (private) juvenile protection organization *(hogo dantai)* (Article 33).

When the results of the investigation indicated that it would be appropriate, there would then be a "determination proceeding" *(shimpan),* after which a "disposition" would be imposed. Pending such a proceeding, the juvenile could, as appropriate, be left in the care of parents or guardian, with or without conditions attached; entrusted to a temple, church, protective association or other appropriate person or organization, or hospital; or placed under the supervision of a Juvenile Protection Officer. When there was no other alternative, the juvenile might be entrusted to a reformatory or correctional institution *(kyōsei'in)* pending the proceeding (Article 37).

The juvenile and the parents or guardian would be called to attend the proceeding, which would be closed to the public (Articles 43 and 45).[15] The Juvenile Determination Official would preside, with a clerk in attendance; a Juvenile Protection Officer need not, but might, be in attendance.

"When necessary" *(hitsuyō ga aru toki)* (a preliminary decision as to such necessity presumably would be made by the Juvenile Determination Official), another adult, selected by the juvenile, parent, or guardian, or the protective organization, with the approval of the court, might also attend. This other "attending adult" *(tsukisoinin)* could be an attorney, a person engaged in the work of juvenile protection, or someone else who had received the approval of the office (Article 42).

At the proceeding, the Juvenile Protection Officer and the parents or guardian would be allowed to state their opinions. Except where there were appropriate reasons for the juvenile to remain in the room, the juvenile would be absent from the proceedings when those opinions were stated (Article 44). The statute itself does not indicate that the opinions of the juvenile were to be heard, either permissively or mandatorily, at any time.[16]

It is in the procedures of the Juvenile Determination Offices, embracing intake, investigation, and determination proceedings, that one sees most clearly that which critics in the Diet so vehemently opposed – the almost completely administrative and discretionary nature of the juvenile law process under the 1922 Law. Any of the earmarks of true judicialized proceedings, such as a presumption of innocence, a dispassionate examination of evidence, the opportunity to know the evidence against one, and the opportunity to cross-examine, were wholly absent. When viewed as a protective process, however, implemented in the best interests of the juvenile and aimed at restoring the juvenile in better-adjusted fashion to society, those essential protective aspects of an adversarial process brought by the state *against* an individual made no sense. The system was intended to function in a protectively paternalistic fashion, and the administrative discretion it bestowed upon the offices served that end.

Nowhere can the social work/reintegrative function of the offices be seen more clearly than in the nature and flexibility of the "dispositions" it could impose. The Juvenile Determination Official had an extraordinary array of "remedies" at his disposal, to be applied as appropriate given his view of the content of the investigation and any further opinions or information made available during the determination proceeding. The Juvenile Determination Official could, where he deemed appropriate, issue a warning *(kunkai)* to the juvenile, or have the head of the juvenile's school do so. He could obtain from the juvenile a promise in writing to change his ways. He could return the juvenile to his parents or guardians with conditions attached, or could entrust the juvenile to a temple, church, protective organization, or other appropriate person or entity. The juvenile might also be placed under the protective supervision of a Juvenile Protection Officer, sent to a reformatory *(kanka'in)*, to a correctional institution *(kyōsei'in)*, or sent or entrusted to a hospital (Article 4).

In sum, the juvenile law system as implemented under the 1922 Law was a system of social protection rather than a judicial system. In that sense, it resembled models from the United States, yet, in its full-blown, stern but compassionate paternalistic approach, it had a distinctly Japanese cast. Its key features were the prominent role of the Juvenile Protection Officer, fulfilling, in effect, a social work function, and the role of the Juvenile Determination Office in coordinating community resources (parents or guardians, schools, workplaces, protective organizations, and so on) in attempting to restore and reconcile wayward juveniles to their communities.

The Juvenile Law of 1948: Reform under US Influence

Japan's defeat in the Second World War had, as is commonly known, far-ranging consequences for its legal system.[17] Guided by the Potsdam Conference Declaration, the Occupation authorities (referred to as the Supreme Commander for the Allied Powers, or SCAP[18]) sought to bring Japanese law and legal institutions more in line with the principles of democracy, equality, and individual rights. The juvenile law system did not escape the attention of SCAP as it guided legal reform in Japan, especially in the early years of the Occupation.

The chief flaw that the Occupation authorities saw in the juvenile law system was that it was an administrative rather than a judicial system. Indeed, Burdett G. Lewis, Chief of Prison Administration, SCAP, stated in November 1948, after passage of the new Juvenile Law but prior to its coming into force on 1 January 1949, that "the [former] so-called Juvenile court, which was established in the Ministry of Justice, in reality was not a court at all."[19]

One principal change in the Juvenile Law of 1948[20] thus was organizational. Part of the SCAP reform of the judiciary involved establishment of the Family Court, associated with each District Court, as part of Japan's judicial system, newly independent of government administrative control as a separate and independent branch of government under the 1946 constitution. The Family Court's jurisdiction included juvenile matters, and juvenile determination proceedings (still referred to as *shimpan*, as distinct from trials) were, and are, presided over by judges of the Family Court. These are regular members of the judiciary assigned for a term of duty to the Family Court by the Supreme Court of Japan, which administers the nation's unitary judicial system.

There was little substantive change in the 1948 Law, however. The definition of juvenile was extended, by amendment in 1951, to include youths up to twenty years of age (Article 20).[21] Juveniles who had committed offences were, of course, within the scope of the law. This was a law that also embraced those juveniles who were "prone to commit an offence" on the basis of not subjecting themselves to the reasonable control of guardians, or staying away from home without good reason, associating with people of criminal propensity or immoral character, frequenting places of evil reputation, or having the propensity to commit acts harmful to their own moral character or that of others (Article 3).[22] One sees, therefore, that the 1948 Law, like its predecessor, was not conceived exclusively as a criminal statute per se, providing for trials to determine whether offences have been committed. Its aim was protective, and thus it included within its scope juveniles *in danger* of committing offences.[23]

The 1948 Law also retained the same basic procedures set out in the 1922 Law. Thus, initial reports to the Family Court concerning a juvenile to whom the law may apply may be made by "any person" (Article 6). In practice, most (95.2 percent in 1997) are referred by public prosecutors who have received reports from police (Supreme Court of Japan 1998, 54). When the Family Court, based on a preliminary inquiry, deems that the juvenile is subject to its jurisdiction, it is to direct the Family Court Investigation Officer *(katei saibansho chōsakan)* to investigate the behaviour, background, character, and surrounding environment of the juvenile, the parents or guardians, and other relevant persons, using medical, psychological, educational, sociological, and other specialized knowledge.[24] In practice, the investigation involves gathering information from parents, schools, employers, physicians, and others with relevant information, all of whom, in most cases, cooperate fully, providing information that frequently goes well beyond that strictly related to the particular acts alleged.[25]

The Family Court can act upon cases that are investigated in any of three ways. If, based on the investigation, the Family Court deems that it is impossible or inappropriate to commence determination proceedings, the court is to render a decision to that effect (this is referred to as *fukaishi,* or non-commencement). If, as a result of determination proceedings, the court deems that it would be impossible or unnecessary to impose "protective measures," it is to render such a decision (this is commonly referred to as *fushobun,* or non-disposition). Finally, if the court deems that the previous two (in effect) non-actions are inappropriate, it can impose the following "protective measures" *(hogo shobun):* (1) protective supervision *(hogo kansatsu)* through a probation office, (2) commitment to either of two types of facilities established under the Child Welfare Law, or (3) detention in a Juvenile Training School *(shōnen'in)* (Article 24).[26]

The essential focus of the Family Court in juvenile matters remains protective and restorative rather than punitive. This may be seen in part in the statistical breakdown of the disposition of cases that have been made the subject of investigation by *chōsakan*. For instance, of a total of 164,327 such cases (exclusive of traffic offences) disposed of in 1997, fully 66.6 percent (109,455) resulted in non-commencement *(fukaishi,* or dismissal without hearing). Another 9.9 percent (16,344) were dismissed after hearing *(fushobun)*. Only 12.1 percent of all cases formally investigated led to imposition of "protective dispositions" *(hogo shobun)*.[27] In turn, only 2.8 percent of all cases (22.9 percent of all cases in which protective dispositions were imposed) resulted in commitment to a Juvenile Training School. Thus, in 1997 only 4,535 juveniles in the entire nation were committed to custody in training schools, institutions that remain considerably below their authorized capacity (Supreme Court of Japan 1999, 48).[28]

One obvious continuity in the juvenile justice system both before and after the war has been the central role of the *chōsakan,* Family Court Investigation Officers. These officers constitute the very heart of the system. They are chosen competitively from among applicants possessing professional knowledge of and academic qualifications in psychology, sociology, social work, education, and other social and medical sciences. All officers receive intensive training in a two-year program at the Supreme Court of Japan's Research and Training Institute for Family Court Probation Officers (the official English translation used by the Supreme Court), established in 1957. They are thus extremely well qualified and receive uniform training, supplemented by continuing in-service training. Their work is not only investigatory but may involve counselling, testing, psychological evaluation, and the coordination of social resources in the community (Supreme Court of Japan 1999, 13-14).

Typically, judges do not become involved in a case until deliberation proceedings (hearings) are commenced. As noted earlier, in two-thirds of the cases that are investigated, such proceedings are not begun, although in almost every case there has been delinquent or criminal behaviour. What, then, do judges do, and, as a corollary, how does the Family Court seek to achieve its goals? It may be that the bare fact of contact with the system, with a corollary indication of seriousness and the involvement of family, school, and employers, functions as a sufficient signal and corrective for the juvenile. The juvenile is not isolated in the process. If anything, the importance of the juvenile's links to the community are underscored, as are the effects that delinquent behaviour has on family and community. The Family Court becomes a focus for family and community to reassert itself.

Even in those instances where a deliberation proceeding is held (such proceedings are closed to the public), the juvenile sits facing the judge in a room marked by quasi-informality (tables and chairs with no raised dais). The accused is flanked by his or her parents or guardians, with the Family Court Investigation Officer who handled the case at a table to the left. A court clerk and bailiff will sit at a table to the juvenile's right. Only in very rare instances will the proceeding deal with disputed matters of fact, which is to say denial of guilt. Juveniles will again only rarely be represented by counsel (the latter fact is obviously related to the first: why would one need an attorney unless one were disputing the facts?).[29]

The proceeding is judicial only in the sense that it is a judge who will make a decision in the relatively small number of cases where protective dispositions are made, dismissing the matter in 45.3 percent of cases that reach this stage, referring for probation in 41.3 percent, and committing for training in custody at a Juvenile Training School in 12.5 percent.[30] Rather than a judicial proceeding, the hearing is more of a ritual occasion, at once admonitory, confessional, and restorative. The investigative officer's report is read, the juvenile and/or parents may have something to say, and then the judge speaks. Detention is imposed only when there appears to be no alternative, generally with repeat offenders who have pronounced criminal tendencies. In only 10 percent of all cases investigated is probation imposed. In other words, deterrence and future behavioural compliance are being sought, and, according to recidivism figures, achieved primarily, it would appear, through the mere exposure of the juvenile and those comprising his or her support system to the machinery of the juvenile justice system, rather than through any dispositive, coercive judicial action.[31] The judge is a symbol in a ritual performance, a symbol of authority, power, the state, and the community.[32]

How is it possible to run a juvenile justice system within a Family Court in this fashion? In part this may be because it is still possible in Japan to mobilize family and community resources that can, in many cases, serve as a social support system, a community to which a "wayward" juvenile can return. It may also be that many juveniles have a genuine concern as to their ability to function in society without that support system. Moreover, it is still possible in Japan to outline, and even catalogue, the specific behaviours that embody community norms (at least in an idealized sense), such that compliance with them would evidence, and foster, reconciliation with the community.[33]

It was precisely an institution facilitating such a process that the US Occupation authorities envisioned in their reform plans, culminating in the Family Court and the 1948 Juvenile Law. Aside from the organizational reforms introduced, the juvenile justice system carried out by the Family Courts was remarkably similar to that of the prewar Juvenile Determination

Offices, in purpose, attitude, and method. This was in fact a conscious choice made by SCAP. In his radio press conference of 30 November 1948, Burdett G. Lewis, SCAP's chief prison administrator, commented on the philosophical foundations and historical antecedents SCAP had tried to incorporate into the new Family Court-based juvenile law system:

> The law creating this court restores the sway of some of the best Oriental principles relating to children and families as a whole or as a social unit. The principles peculiar to Far Eastern society which find such vital re-emphasis in the new Family Court's Juvenile Division hark back to an ancient and honorable institution, the Council of Elders. Instead of resting upon force as basis for its power, the Council of Elders ... rests with the unanimity developed by discussion among men of equal status in the framework of a stable society ... In the old Far Eastern villages when the problems became too great for the head of family to handle, or when the members of the family, by their actions were impinging upon the rights or activities of others, it was customary for the other heads of families concerned to gather around the most respected and usually the most venerable of their numbers and discuss the situation until a consensus was arrived at concerning the matters in hand. *The men going out from such a conference needed no policeman or military leader to enforce the decision. The sanctions for enforcement were not thought of as fetters, cords, or restrictions, but rather as guides of thought and action for all concerned.*[34]

In fact, the juvenile justice system that the Americans put in place within the Family Court had, in all essential respects, a much more recent antecedent, the system of Juvenile Determination Offices implemented under the 1922 Law. In substance, very little had changed.[35]

Future Directions and Tensions in Juvenile Law

Ironically, some twenty years after Japan's Family Court was established, it was the American juvenile justice system that underwent a massive transformation. In 1967, the US Supreme Court issued its decision in *In re Gault*,[36] ruling unconstitutional juvenile justice procedures in which juveniles were not afforded the full range of due process protections that had been extended to criminal defendants generally in the Warren Court's groundbreaking decisions of the 1960s. The years – decades – of protective paternalism in US juvenile courts had ended, replaced by an adversarial due process model.

Some Japanese academics and attorneys, obviously aware of *Gault* and its aftermath, began to press for law reform in Japan from the 1970s, and draft amendments to the 1948 Juvenile Law incorporating more due process features, including greater use of legal counsel for juveniles, were proposed and discussed. This debate, however, was nothing new to Japan. The influence of *Gault* merely reawakened arguments that had first been voiced as early as the debates of 1907 and 1908.[37] Change has been slow, to say the least. A quarter of a century after due process-style amendments were first proposed, none has ever passed the Diet. Those introduced in the 145th Diet session (1999) include granting the Family Court discretion, when it deems necessary, to have a prosecutor participate in proceedings with respect to offences punishable by more than three years' imprisonment. In addition, when a prosecutor so participates, provision was made to ensure that the juvenile would be represented by an attorney, the court appointing one if necessary.[38] It must be noted that these due process reforms, even were they to be adopted, would do little to change the overall structure and practice of Japan's juvenile justice. At best, only the conduct of determination proceedings, held in a minority of cases, would be affected, and even then the reforms would apply primarily to cases where facts, and thus the question of guilt, are placed in dispute. Those cases are also exceedingly rare.

Thus, although there has been steady pressure from due process legal reformers for several decades, now reinforced by the protections afforded juveniles under the United Nations Convention on the Rights of the Child,[39] to which Japan acceded in 1994, there is little likelihood that substantial change will result.

On the other hand, there may be a growing "get tough" attitude among the public as a result of widespread and serious concern about youth crime. This concern has been prompted and fuelled by a series of extremely violent youth crimes, heavily reported by Japan's highly concentrated national media. The most prominent of these was the murder of two junior-high-school children in Kobe by a fourteen-year-old boy in March and May of 1997, in which one victim's head was left impaled upon the school's gates. These murders came as a severe shock to the entire nation and set in motion a wave of nationwide self-reflection (*Japan Times* 1997a, 1997b).

Serious incidents have not abated, seeming at times too much for the nation's consciousness to absorb. On 1 May 2000, for example, a 65-year-old housewife was brutally murdered by a 17-year-old youth who said he just wanted to experience the act of killing someone. Only two days later, a 17-year-old hijacked a highway bus in Fukuoka prefecture, slashing one passenger to death and holding ten others hostage. On 12 May, a 17-year-old tried to kill a 48-year-old male train passenger, a stranger, with hammer blows to the head (*Japan Times* 2000a, 2000b, 2000c). Public perceptions of a younger generation out of control, and perhaps dangerous, may have begun to threaten long-held beliefs in a safe and secure society (*Japan Times* 2000d).

What is the objective picture? Statistics, as always depending on their presentation and interpretation, are ambiguous. They have, however, been taken as presenting a worrisome picture. Although the overall juvenile crime rate, like the adult rate, has been declining, the proportion of violent and serious crimes is increasing. Similarly, juvenile offenders constitute a rising proportion of all criminal offenders (Keisatsuchō 1998, 110).

Can one expect major changes in Japan's juvenile justice policy? To date, that policy has not been subject to what Thomas J. Bernard (1992, 4) has referred to as the cycle of juvenile justice. It has not fluctuated between harshly punitive and lenient approaches that have been taken alternately as the cause of juvenile crime rates perceived to be unusually high. As Bernard (1992, 34) explains, such a cycle depends upon the belief that the system of processing juvenile offenders increases, or even affects, juvenile crime.

Unless perceptions of a violent and uncontrollable younger generation come to dominate in Japan, it is likely that Japan will not experience this cycle. This has to do in part with the Family Court's nature and function. It is nested at the narrow end of a funnelling set of social institutions, including the volunteer patrol members and counsellors, the police, schools, and government at all levels, that aim to control youth crime by trying to ensure that youth remain part of the communities that surround them. There appears to still be a realistic awareness that the juvenile justice system, and specifically the Family Court's juvenile division, is but one agency in an overall social response to juvenile crime and the effort to reintegrate and restore youth to society.

Thus, the vision and spirit of Japan's juvenile justice system, first articulated in 1900 and embodied in the 1922 Law, have continued until today under the 1948 Law. Should violent youth crime, however, continue to affect the nation's consciousness as profoundly as it has in recent years, that system may not be able to withstand compelling pressures for change. Such change in all likelihood would entail the adoption of more punitive approaches to juvenile offenders, reversing the philosophy that has guided Japan's juvenile justice policy since its formal inception a century ago.

Notes
1 *Kanka Hō*, Law No. 37 of 1900.
2 There was, of course, a large volume of subsidiary legislation, such as would be necessary in the establishment and administration of any modernizing or modern nation-state. For a detailed description of Meiji period legislation, see Ishii 1958 and Takayangi's excellent essay (1963).
3 Punishment could be reduced by two degrees when the offender was at least twelve years of age but less than sixteen, and by one degree if at least sixteen but less than twenty (*Chizai Hō* [Code of Criminal Instruction], Great Council of State Decree No. 37 of 1880, arts. 80[2] and 81).
4 *Minpō* ([Old] Civil Code), Laws No. 89 of 1896 and No. 9 of 1898, art. 882, gave parents this right under the rubric of parental powers. The provision remained moribund, however, for lack of an appropriate "disciplinary institution" to which juveniles could be sent.

5 Professor Morita's work, a collection of painstakingly selected and edited Diet debates and other materials, together with a very useful introductory essay, is essential to an understanding of developments in Japanese juvenile law during the first quarter of the twentieth century.
6 Stenographic Record of the House of Representatives' Special Committee to Deliberate on the Proposed Juvenile Reformatory Law, 19 February 1900.
7 Stenographic Record of the Special Committee, 20 February 1900.
8 In the course of Diet debate on amendments to the law in 1908, Hanai Takuzō, the well-known legal thinker, noted, in an extremely critical vein, that the idea of compulsory "protective education" made Japan's system unique in the world. Stenographic Record of the House of Representatives Committee on Revision of the Juvenile Reformatory Law, 26 February 1908.
9 By 1907 only five public reformatories had been established, housing 117 juveniles. Private reformatories held 176 juveniles.
10 On the development of conciliation from the early Meiji through the late prewar period, see Henderson 1965, 208-17.
11 The age of juveniles subject to the law was raised to eighteen years, subsidies from the national government for the building of reformatories were authorized, and, in ancillary legislation, provision was made for the establishment of national, rather than prefectural, reformatories. In addition, the catch-all category 1 in Article 5(1), defining juveniles within the scope of the law, was changed to a more general designation of youths with respect to whom appropriate parental authority was not being exercised, and who either engaged in, or were liable to engage in, "wayward behaviour" *(furyō kōi)*, an even broader category than in the original law.
12 Juvenile Law, Law No. 42 of 1922 (hereafter referred to as the 1922 Law).
13 That the phrase "touching upon penal laws" is to be taken in the broadest sense is abundantly clear when comparison is made to Article 7, dealing with reduction of sentences for juveniles under the age of sixteen who *commit* [the most serious of] *crimes (tsumi o okasu ... mono)* (emphasis added). The phrase "touching upon penal laws" could be taken in quite sweeping terms.
14 One would not expect such an intake mode in a criminal procedure law. Juveniles could also enter the juvenile justice system by virtue of arrest for actual commission of crimes or, in certain cases, through referrals by prosecutors from District Courts, where they would otherwise be tried as adults.
15 With permission of the office, the juvenile's relatives, juvenile protection workers, or others deemed appropriate might also attend (Article 45). However, when the parents or guardian were deemed not to have an interest in the matter, they would not be called to the proceeding (Article 43).
16 The statute does not, however, set out detailed rules for the conduct of such proceedings, so one would assume that the Juvenile Determination Official had considerable leeway in conducting them. Formal constraints such as those that would bind judges and prosecutors in judicial proceedings were absent in accordance with the design and spirit of the law itself. Under the circumstances, one would assume that the voice of the juvenile would be heard in most cases, if only to express contrition.
17 For a comprehensive and very readable treatment of law and government reform during the Occupation, see Oppler 1976.
18 A name both revealing and obfuscating; revealing insofar as it makes singular reference to General Douglas MacArthur, the larger-than-life Supreme Commander, and obfuscating insofar as it makes reference to "Allied Powers," who had little or no say in Occupation policies. The Occupation was essentially an American operation.
19 Remarks of Burdett G. Lewis, Radio Tokyo Press Conference, 30 November 1948 (SCAP Document). Indeed, under the Meiji Constitution of 1889, the entire court system was not structurally independent but was organized as part of the Ministry of Justice.
20 *Shōnen Hō* (Juvenile Law), Law No. 168 of 1948 (hereafter referred to as the 1948 Law).
21 The new law also provided that only juveniles sixteen years or older could be referred to public prosecutors for trial as adults.

22 This language paraphrases the unofficial English-language version of the law set out in UNAFEI (United Nations Asia and Far East Institute for the Prevention of Crime and the Treatment of Offenders), *Criminal Justice Legislation of Japan* (n.d., n.p.), which reprints the Eibun Hōreisha (EHS) translation.
23 So-called *guhan shōnen*, youths in danger of offending, under Article 3(3). The purpose of the law is expressly stated in Article 1 as "with a view to the wholesome rearing of juveniles, to carry out protective measures relating to the character correction and environmental adjustment of delinquent juveniles."
24 *Chōsakan*, whom I have referred to as Family Court Investigation Officers, are called Family Court Probation Officers in official publications of the Supreme Court of Japan. This is unfortunate because it gives a mistaken impression of the officers' role and duties. Similarly, the equivalent used in the EHS translation of the law, "Pre-Sentence Investigator," conveys that role too narrowly and would give readers the mistaken impression that what goes on in juvenile determination proceedings culminates in "sentencing," an impression that would equate such proceedings with criminal trials, which they clearly are not. Fukuda (1990) refers to *chōsakan* as Family Court Social Caseworkers.
25 Interviews with Family Court personnel, 1995.
26 The Family Court may also refer a juvenile sixteen years of age or older alleged to have committed an offence punishable by death or imprisonment with or without forced labour to the Public Prosecutor for trial as an adult when the court finds it appropriate in light of the nature and circumstances of the offence (Article 20). Juvenile Training Schools, established under the *Shōnen'in Hō* (Juvenile Training School Law), Law No. 169 of 1948, provide a nationally uniform and comprehensive approach to reform education under custody, with an emphasis on social, educational, and occupational rehabilitation.
27 About 11 percent of all cases were joined to other cases or transferred to other Family Courts.
28 This source-translated material contained in Supreme Court of Japan 1998, 28-29. Of the 12.1 percent of all cases reaching final disposition, 9.1 percent of all cases resulted in probationary supervision (14,912 total), while 1.5 percent of such cases (0.2 percent of all cases, 288 total) resulted in commitment to child education and training homes or other juvenile facilities. Only 0.2 percent of all cases (292 total) were referred to Public Prosecutors for trial as adults in light of the nature and circumstances of the offence.
29 Figures as to the number of cases where juveniles dispute the facts (and thus claim innocence) do not appear to be readily available. Out of the 204,824 cases (this figure, in contrast to the statistics given in Supreme Court of Japan 1999, includes negligent vehicular homicide cases, but not other traffic cases) that the Family Courts decided nationwide in 1997, attorneys participated on the juvenile's behalf (as an attending adult, *tsukisoinin*) in 2,968 cases (out of 3,139 total attending adults) (Supreme Court of Japan 1998, 91). Juveniles were thus accompanied by attorneys in only about 1.4 percent of all cases. It is probably a safe assumption that most, if not all, juveniles professing innocence would be accompanied by an attorney and that some of those with attorneys were not professing innocence. Thus, it is most likely that disputed juvenile cases did not exceed 1.4 percent of all juvenile cases decided by the Family Court in 1997.
30 Percentages are based on Supreme Court of Japan 1999, 48.
31 This model of behavioural compliance may be likened to the process at work in electrical transformers, where a response of a specified type is induced through the mere placement of the coil acted upon within the range of the active master coil. There is none of the direct physical contact that one would metaphorically associate with a punitive approach.
32 A number of judges with Family Court experience have concurred with this characterization in my discussions with them.
33 The educational programs in the Juvenile Training Schools aim to inculcate those sorts of behaviours and social and occupational skills. See *Shōnen'in Hō* (Juvenile Training School Law), Law No. 169 of 1948, Article 4.
34 Remarks of Burdett G. Lewis, Radio Tokyo Press Conference, 30 November 1948 (SCAP Document), pp. 3-4 (emphasis added). Lewis also notes, on p. 3, that "in a sense this system seems simpler, and to some, more democratic than many current patterns of action in the Western World."

35 One substantive change related to the formal judicialization of the juvenile law system, however, was the reduction in the number and flexibility of dispositions, or remedies, available to the presiding officer at determination hearings (under the 1948 Law, the judge). As Abe (1963, 355) suggested as early as 1963, this reduced the ability of the chief organ responsible for juvenile justice to serve a social function through stern but less stigmatizing actions such as discipline or warnings either from the court or through school principals or others, or return of the juvenile to the home with conditions. To a certain extent, these less formal and less intrusive forms of social control have devolved upon the police and volunteers who, in their patrol activities aimed at wayward and misbehaving youth, come into contact with numbers far in excess of those whose cases reach the Family Courts. In this sense, the Japanese police may be a much more visible, powerful, and effective organ of social control with respect to juveniles than the Family Courts. Indeed, in 1997 police gave "guidance" (warnings, advice, escorts home, and even continuing checks) to 814,202 young people, amounting to about 8 percent of all youths between the ages of fourteen and nineteen nationwide, for such wayward behaviour *(furyō kōi)* as smoking, drinking, and playing around late at night (Keisatsuchō 1998, 119). With regard to the nature and scope of Japanese police activity concerned with juveniles, see Yokoyama 1981, Murai 1988, and Fukuda 1990.
36 387 U.S. 1, 87 S.Ct. 1428, 18 L.Ed.2d 527 (1967).
37 See the section above, on the 1922 Juvenile Law.
38 Ministry of Justice, *Shōnen hō tō no ichibu o kaisei suru hōritsuan yōkō* (An outline of the bill to amend the Juvenile Law), 1999.
39 The text of the convention may be found in UN General Assembly Resolution 44/25 (20 November 1989). The government of Japan takes the view that no revision of domestic law is needed to comply with the convention (Iwasawa 1998, 3). Some have argued that Article 40 of the convention requires much greater procedural protections than the Juvenile Law provides to alleged juvenile offenders.

References

Abe, H. 1963. "The Accused and Society: Therapeutic and Preventive Aspects of Criminal Justice in Japan." In A.T. von Mehren, ed., *Law in Japan: The Legal Order in a Changing Society*. Cambridge, MA: Harvard University Press, 324-63.

Bernard, T.J. 1992. *The Cycle of Juvenile Justice*. New York: Oxford University Press.

Fukuda, M. 1990. "A Critical Analysis of [the] Juvenile Justice System in Japan: Debasement of the Juvenile Law to Attain Unarticulated Social and Economic Purposes." *Hitotsubashi Journal of Law and Politics* 18: 1-13.

Henderson, D.F. 1965. *Conciliation and Japanese Law – Tokugawa and Modern*. Seattle: University of Washington Press.

Ishii, R. 1958. *Legislation in the Meiji Period*. Translated by W.J. Chambliss. Tokyo: Pan-Pacific Press.

Iwasawa, Y. 1998. *International Law, Human Rights and Japanese Law*. Oxford: Oxford University Press.

Japan Times. 1997a. "Two Girls Found Stabbed in Kobe," 17 March, 2.

–. 1997b. "Boy's Severed Head Found near School," 28 May, 1-2.

–. 2000a. "Woman Stabbed to Death, Boy Wanted to Experience Killing," 3 May, 2.

–. 2000b. "15 Hour Ordeal: Cops Storm Hijacked Bus, Detain Knife-Wielding Boy," 5 May, 1.

–. 2000c. "Teen Attacks Sleeping Train Passenger with Hammer," 13 May, 2.

–. 2000d. "Proposal to Revise Law: Juveniles Face Longer Prison Terms," 19 May, 2.

Keisatsuchō (National Police Agency). 1998. *Keisatsu hakusho* (Police white paper). Tokyo: Okurasho Insatsukyoku.

Morita, A., ed. 1993. *Taishō shōnen hō* (The Taishō Juvenile Law of 1922). Vols. 18 and 19 in the series *Nihon rippō shiryō zenshū* (A complete collection of Japanese legislative materials). Tokyo: Shinzansha.

Murai, T. 1988. "Current Problems of Juvenile Delinquency in Japan." *Hitotsubashi Journal of Law and Politics* 16: 1-10.

Oppler, A. 1976. *Legal Reform in Occupied Japan: A Participant Looks Back*. Princeton, NJ: Princeton University Press.

Schlossman, S.L. 1977. *Love and the American Delinquent*. Chicago: University of Chicago Press.

Supreme Court of Japan. 1998. *Shihō Tōkei Nenpō, Shōnen Hen (Heisei 9 nen)* (Annual report of judicial statistics for 1997 – juvenile cases). Tokyo: General Secretariat, Supreme Court of Japan.

–. 1999. *Guide to the Family Court of Japan*. Tokyo: General Secretariat, Supreme Court of Japan.

Takayangi, K. 1963. "A Century of Innovation: The Development of Japanese Law, 1868-1961." In A.T. von Mehren, ed., *Law in Japan: The Legal Order in a Changing Society*. Cambridge, MA: Harvard University Press, 5-40.

Yokoyama, M. 1981. "Delinquency Control Programs in the Community in Japan." *International Journal of Comparative and Applied Criminal Justice* 5(2): 169-78.

Part 3
Urban Living and Beauty

One of the most dramatic social changes in the postwar period has been the rural-to-urban shift in the Japanese population. By way of illustration, between 1920 and 1980, the urban population in officially designated cities increased from 10 million to 89 million, and from 18 percent of the population to 76 of the population (Harris 1982). By the end of the twentieth century, however, a tension had developed between the interests of urban and rural dwellers. Many of the former began to resent the high cost of subsidizing what were perceived as "wildly inefficient farmers and agriculture in Japan" (Ohmae 1995, 48). It was often argued that cheaper and more available farmland for development would reduce the cost of housing and essential public works in the city suburbs where most of the population now lives. At the same time, rejection of the suburban lifestyle, and rapidly changing economic and political environments, have evoked memories of an idyllic rural *furusato,* or native village (Robertson 1998).

The contributors to Part 3 address different aspects of urban culture in Japan. In Chapter 9, David W. Edgington explores why the quality of urban life has failed to match the strong growth in economic activity. It is astonishing to many observers that Japan's riches are to be seen not in the places where people live but in the luxurious postmodern buildings in the hubs of major cities and alongside vast waterside projects. The "bubble economy," for example, spawned high-tech factories and "intelligent" offices, elegant hotels and spanking new auditoriums, and glittering rows of fashionable shops. By contrast, amenities in the suburbs for long-time residents, such as sewer connections, paved roads, and open spaces were either forgotten or postponed. Indeed, the image of a "rich country but poor people" has recurred in Japan over much of its modern history (Inoguchi 1987).

Edgington argues that economic goals have nearly always outweighed quality of life goals, and examines the progress made in upgrading the amenities of Japan's cities over the last 100 or so years. By analyzing the city planning movement in Japan, he shows how the state has modified what was originally a Western concept to suit its own tastes and needs. He traces the evolution of city planning in Japan – from its original importation from the West at the turn of the century to support economic growth and modernization, to attempts to copy British "new towns" in the interwar years. His chapter considers the rapid population increases associated with postwar urbanization, through to the 1992 Economic Plan to make Japan a "quality of life superpower." Despite the rhetoric in this plan, which claims to put quality of life first and to support decentralization, he argues that there are very real constraints in upgrading Japanese cities in the years to come.

Other essays in this section touch on the capacity of the Japanese to create an idealized past. Nowhere has this been more prevalent than in the evocation of *furusato,* the old town or community. The call for the re-creation of the old community as a touchstone of unchanging values and culture has also been used in relatively recently created suburbs (Robertson 1991). Moreover, in recent years Japan has seen a spate of museum construction in local towns and major cities. Scheiner (1998, 67) notes that "this sort of past has also been invoked by the Tokyo metropolitan government in its efforts to create museums and exhibitions to remind Japanese of the greatness of the culture of old Edo, at the very point when Japan and Tokyo have seemingly been internationalized." In part also, this phenomenon heralds the growth of a leisure-conscious society and a new cultural business (Foreign Press Center 1993). Certainly, the "museum construction rush" is indicative of a remarkable rise in public interest over Japan's previous cultural wealth and a growing need for "place based social meaning" (Steffensen 1996, 164). Still, the question arises of just how Japan's rich and varied past has been brought to consumers in the closing years of the last century.

Joshua S. Mostow analyzes this phenomenon by looking at a series of major museum and art shows held in Japanese cities during the 1990s with the theme of *Nihon no Bi* (Japanese beauty). While 1995 was the 50th anniversary of the end of the Second World War, 1994 was celebrated as the 1,200th anniversary of the establishment of Kyoto as the Japanese capital, a status it enjoyed from the year 794 to the late nineteenth century. In Chapter 10, Mostow asks what objects and time period were taken at this historical moment as representative of "Japanese beauty," and how was such a concept constructed? By examining the objects chosen for a representative selection of exhibitions, and the texts provided to explain them, Mostow maps the present-day narratives deployed in the nationalistic reification of a "Japanese aesthetic consciousness" *(nihon-teki bi'ish-iki)*. Following the work of anthropologists such as Marilyn Ivy (1993), he explores Japan's "self-exotification" and the alliance between postmodernism and consumer commodification.

At century's end, it appeared that Japan was indeed in the middle of a "history boom," one that had occurred spontaneously without anybody having conducted a concerted campaign to start or spread it. Nakanishi (2000) notes that a renewed sensitivity to history and tradition, especially in the form of a heightened appreciation of rural and open landscapes, could be an important trigger in raising people's consciousness of the need to protect the Japanese environment and improve overall living conditions.

In the past, individual Japanese would never have complained about a system that appears so unbalanced between corporate wealth and impoverished urban landscapes and social amenities in general. They were taught and trained not to object to what the government said or did, but to accept it without a murmur *(shigata ga nai)*. Today, however, a marked disparity in economic burden, coupled with an equally marked disparity in urban and rural lifestyles, has begun to tear at the old social fabric. The current debate boils down to which should be given priority – the individual or the group? It is a ponderous question, one that runs through many of the essays in this volume and relates to a fundamental difference between Western and Japanese ways of thinking. Addressing this will almost certainly be an ambitious undertaking involving change in the roots of Japanese society. The delicate interplay between change and continuity in the new millennium is the material left for discussion in the concluding chapter of this book.

References

Foreign Press Center. 1993. *Leisure and Recreational Activities*. About Japan Series 4. Tokyo: Foreign Press Center, Japan.
Harris, C.D. 1982. "The Urban and Industrial Transformation of Japan." *Geographical Review* 72: 50-89.
Inoguchi, K. 1987. "Prosperity without the Amenities." *Journal of Japanese Studies* 13: 125-34.
Ivy, M. 1993. "Formations of Mass Culture." In A. Gordon, ed., *Postwar Japan as History*. Berkeley: University of California Press, 239-58.
Nakanishi, T. 2000. "Goals for Japan in its 'Second Postwar Period.'" *Japan Echo* 27(2): 8-13.
Ohmae, K. 1995. *The End of the Nation State: The Rise of Regional Economics*. New York: Free State.
Robertson, J. 1991. *Native and Newcomer: Making and Remaking a Japanese City*. Berkeley: University of California Press.
–. 1998. "It Takes a Village: Internationalization and Nostalgia in Postwar Japan." In S. Vlastos, ed., *Mirror of Modernity: Invented Traditions of Modern Japan*. Berkeley: University of California Press, 110-29.

Scheiner, I. 1998. "The Japanese Village: Imagined, Real, Contested." In S. Vlastos, ed., *Mirror of Modernity: Invented Traditions of Modern Japan*. Berkeley: University of California Press, 67-78.

Steffensen, S.K. 1996. "Evolutionary Socio-Economic Aspects of the Japanese 'Era of Localities' Discourse." In S. Metzger-Court and W. Pascha, eds., *Japan's Socio-Economic Evolution*. Folkestone, Kent: Japan Library, 142-72.

9
Japan Ponders the Good Life: Improving the Quality of Japanese Cities
David W. Edgington

> The notorious Japanese rabbit-hutch is too small to allow a family to relax. We tire as we ride packed like sardines on crowded trains for long periods. The roads leading to the nearby leisure facilities are jammed with cars on holidays, wasting our precious free time as we wait in traffic jams ... these problems are familiar to virtually all Japanese.
>
> – Ministry of Construction, *White Paper on Construction 1991*

> "Rich Japan, poor Japanese *(tomeru Nihon, mazushii Nihonjin)*."
>
> – popular phrase

The 1995 *White Paper on the National Lifestyle* (Economic Planning Agency 1995a) provided an apparently robust and remarkably positive review of Japan's economic and social achievements over the previous fifty years. The country's standard of living, it noted, measured in average nominal per capita income was now the highest among major advanced countries. Nonetheless, following this good news there came a caution. As a result of the bursting of the "economic bubble" in the early 1990s, a tangible unease had grown over Japan's economic future and social development. Indeed, the white paper went on to record that even in the period of the "bubble economy" only a few benefited, and that after fifty years of intense effort, Japanese lifestyles still did not live up to the country's economic success. The principal causes of dissatisfaction were reported to be long working hours, lengthy commuting times, high living costs, low housing standards, a poor living environment, and delays in providing social infrastructure (Economic Planning Agency 1995a). In this official document, as in many popular books and articles, there was the feeling that Japan at the turn of the century was less affluent than other industrialized countries, in terms of space, time, and purchasing power. In other words, Japan was still "the poor little rich country" (Woronoff 1996).

Currently, there are many debates about how to arrange things differently and change Japan from a producer-oriented to a consumer-oriented nation. Thus, one government poll found that while 90 percent of Japanese considered themselves middle class, some 60 percent also wanted to

194   David W. Edgington

improve the quality of their lives. But to improve the quality of life in Japan really means improving the urban quality of life, as there are now about 110 million urbanites and about 85 percent of the population lives in urban areas (Statistics Bureau 1996). While most people have achieved a measure of consumer satisfaction through the purchase of cars and consumer goods (Figure 9.1), they now seek more qualitative affluence – more living space, bigger houses, more vacation time.[1] Still, for those aspects of the quality of life that are quantifiable – such as sewerage, parks, housing

Figure 9.1

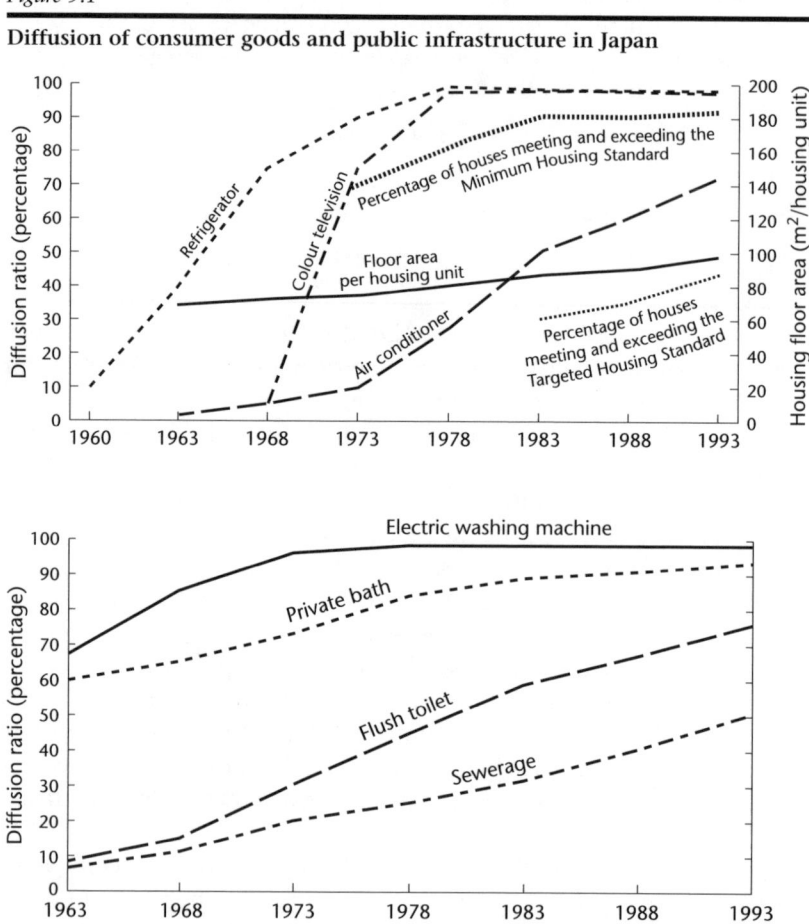

Diffusion of consumer goods and public infrastructure in Japan

Note: In the upper graph, the percentages of houses meeting and exceeding the Minimum Housing Standard for 1960, and percentages of houses meeting and exceeding the Targeted Housing Standard for 1983 and 1998, are estimates by the Ministry of Construction.
Source: Data from the Ministry of Construction based on data from the Management and Coordination Agency and the Economic Planning Agency (Ministry of Construction 1995).

Table 9.1

Japan's infrastructure and housing standards compared with other countries

Sector	Japan At present	Japan Early 21st century[a]	Other countries UK	Other countries Germany	Other countries France	Other countries US
Sewerage diffusion rate[b]	55% (FY 96)	90%	97% (1994)	92% (1995)	81% (1994)	71% (1992)
City park area per resident	7.3 m² (nation) 2.9 m² (Tokyo ward area) (FY 96)	20 m²	25.3 m² London (1994)	27.4 m² Berlin (1995)	11.8 m² Paris (1994)	29.1 m² New York (1997)
Average floor area per resident	31 m² (FY 93)	—	38 m² (1991)	38 m² (1993)	37 m² (1992)	60 m² (1993)
Length of expressways	7,265 km (FY 97)	14,000 km	3,141 km (1994)	11,143 km (1994)	9,000 km (1994)	73,271 km (1994)
Flood control rates[c]	52% (1996)		Probability of damage by tidal waves: once in 1,000 years	Probability of damage through flooding: once in 500 years	Probability of damage through flooding: once in 100 years	Probability of damage through flooding: once in 500 years
	Major rivers 65% (1996)	**Major rivers** Projects to prevent flood damage completed: once in 30-40 years	Thames River completed (1983)	Rhine River completed (1993)	La Seine completed (1988)	Mississippi River 79% (embankment for mainstream 1993)
	Smaller rivers 44% (1996)	**Smaller rivers** —				

[a] Figures for the early twenty-first century are long-term goals set by the Ministry of Construction.
[b] Sewerage diffusion rate data for other countries are from OECD Environmental Data Compendium 1997.
[c] Floods in the table refer to those caused by rainfall of 50 mm per hour and over.
FY = fiscal year.
Source: Based on Ministry of Construction 1998.

standards, and road transport – Japan clearly lags and scores badly against other affluent Western countries (Figure 9.1 and Table 9.1). Moreover, the way Japan has lagged in its levels of social infrastructure cannot be blamed entirely on its status as an island nation with a limited land area. Many European countries with similarly limited land have more spacious housing, many large parks, and less crowded rail systems. In Japanese cities, there are only a small number of parks where people can relax. A little away from big cities, open space is more plentiful and housing more affordable, but flush toilets and gas pipes are often unavailable. Traffic congestion and exhaust pollution in Japan's *dai toshi* (major metropolitan areas) continue to break records. Most power lines and utility poles remain above ground in the middle of narrow sidewalks, constituting a pedestrian hazard as well as an eyesore. There appears no end to the list testifying to the country's inferior infrastructure.[2]

In this chapter, I seek to understand how Japan arrived at this point and, more importantly, what is possible to change in the years ahead. To explore this issue required an assessment of urban planning practice in Japan, both currently and back through the postwar years and even to earlier periods. I examined official attitudes towards urban policy and planning and their role in Japan's modernization, patterns of postwar urbanization, and the "Tokyo problem," as well as more recent policy debates over Japan's quality of urban life in the 1990s. I did this by asking a range of officials working at central and local government levels to explain the history of Japan's urban planning system, together with the more contemporary changes in social infrastructure, planning regulations, and administrative procedures.

History of Japanese Approaches to Urban Planning

Many cities in Japan had their origins in Tokugawa period (1605-1867) castle towns (called *jōkamachi*), which Smith (1979, 64) has referred to as "one of the world's greatest efforts in the planned construction of new cities." Yet for nearly a century after the year 1605, the shogun's castle towns were concerned primarily with defence and the spread of fires through the densely built wooden houses of the commoners' areas surrounding the central castle district. Originally, their narrow streets radiated from the central manor in a zigzag pattern (Fujioka 1980). Modern city building originated with the Meiji Restoration in 1868, around the same time that urban planning as a concept emerged in the West, growing out of the socio-historical conditions of late nineteenth-century Europe and America. In Western countries, the pollution, crowding, and rapid growth of national capitals and other industrial cities were seen as a threat to the physical, social, and even political welfare of the people living there

(Ashworth 1954; Cullingworth and Nadin 1997). Planning was therefore institutionalized as a government function at the turn of the twentieth century, with a strong public health element as well as features allied to social reform and urban beautification. Together these attitudes had a built-in "anti-metropolitan bias" that led to a system of stringent controls over land use, urban sprawl, and disorderly expansion and development (see Chapin 1965). These initiatives were in general firmly supported by the emerging middle classes, who with increasing political power wanted to move out into suburban areas previously open only to the more affluent classes (Mumford 1961).

A sharp contrast to these beginnings is presented by Shunichi Watanabe (1984) in his account of the history of the Japanese urban planning system, one in which an anti-urban or anti-metropolitan bias has been virtually alien. Pioneering Japanese planners in the Meiji period (1868-1912) were imbued with the thinking of their day: *fukoku kyōhei,* or "strong army: strong nation." Edo (the former Tokyo) in the mid-nineteenth century was second only to London as the world's largest city. And as city building was a strong urban tradition in Japan, the centralized planning powers attained under Meiji Japan allowed the new generation of bureaucrats to foster the metropolis as a component that would aid Japan's catch-up modernization. Tokyo, the nation's new capital, in particular became a symbol of the country's progress in the late nineteenth century (Seidensticker 1983).[3]

The first recorded urban planning legislation in Japan, the Tokyo Municipal Improvement Act (1888), was instigated directly by the central government and was much more concerned with the capital's economic and political functions rather than its appearance or the social and housing conditions of its citizens (International Affairs Division 1994). From the very beginning, therefore, urban planning philosophy in Japan emphasized the provision of "hard" infrastructure over the introduction of planning regulations, and thus was very public works-oriented *(toshi keikaku).* The plan approved by the government under the legislation included, for example, the building or improvement of 315 streets, 34 rivers and moats, 1 elevated railway, many bridges, 8 markets, 5 crematoria, 6 cemeteries, and 49 parks (Watanabe 1984, 411). Notably, this emphasis on public works totally ignored housing and local residential environments.

The act also established a pattern under which the national government held responsibility for planning while municipal governments (with some national subsidies) held responsibility for the expenses and implementation of various projects. Watanabe (1984, 411) notes that "this planning system was appropriate to the highly centralized power which produced it, and it had an immense impact on all subsequent planning concepts." Nonetheless, shortages of urban infrastructure had plagued Tokyo even from early times. Almost all streets untouched by the Municipal Improvement Program were unpaved and unfit for vehicular traffic. Water and electricity were available only in the commercial centres around Tokyo station. Trams were the main means of transport for the masses, and their services were congested and inadequate. Sewerage systems were the least developed service of all.[4]

Sawamoto (1981) and Mizuuchi (1991, 1999) provide an interesting snapshot of the infrastructure priorities of the new Meiji government. Their analyses show that government investment led private investment throughout the first twenty years of the new regime. Apart from a vast military expenditure, the main emphasis of government investment was on infrastructure for economic development, such as national railways, rivers, and highways, as well as agriculture, forestry, and fisheries, and erosion control alongside rivers to control flooding (Figure 9.2). Thereafter, the weight of non-infrastructure investment increased, for example, on public school construction and public offices. Priority was invariably given to the Tōkaidō north-south axis linking the international port cities of Tokyo/Yokohama and Osaka/Kyoto/Kobe, and their neighbouring urban areas along the Pacific coast (Mizuuchi 1999). Road improvement gained importance as the number of automobiles increased by the early

Figure 9.2

Japan's infrastructure priorities, 1870-1993

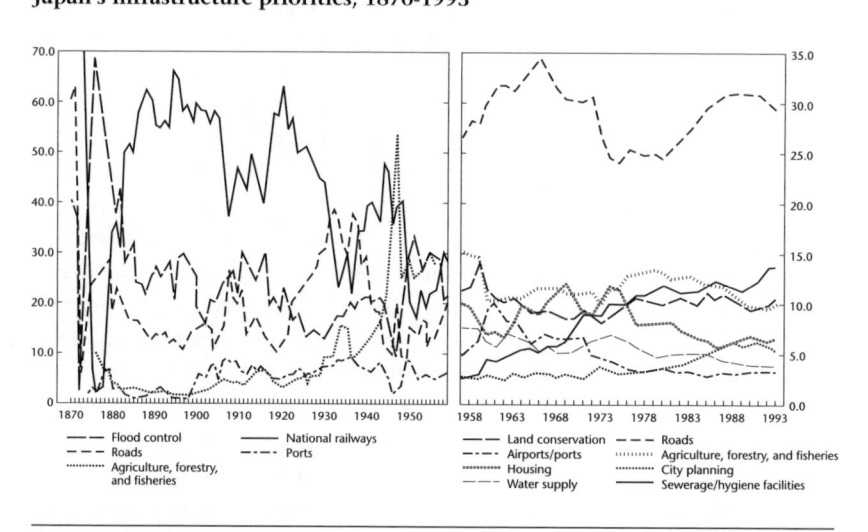

Notes: The left graph is based on data from the Economic Planning Agency (the ratio of six project fields to the total amount of investment [=100]). The right graph is based on data from the Ministry of Home Affairs (adjustments made due to privatization of National Telephone and Telegraph and Japan National Railways).
Source: Ministry of Construction 1997.

1930s (see Figure 9.2). In the interwar years, the pace of industrialization quickened even further when the nation fell under the control of militarist factions. Their priorities promoted economic infrastructure, such as ports and transportation, and were commonly expressed in the saying "roads are most important, housing the least" (Sawamoto 1981).

Tokyo's initial public works plan was virtually complete by 1918 but included no land use controls or building regulations on private sector construction. Eventually a City Planning Act (1918) was instigated by the central government and provided a rudimentary legal zoning control separating large-scale factories from residential areas. It was first applied only to the six largest cities in Japan, and eventually to the smaller ones also. Together with the Urban Building Act of the same year, it generated a Japanese-style planning system that crystallized into public works projects on the one hand and site-specific building regulations on the other. Land use controls were weak and practically nullified by the need to accommodate the traditional mixed uses of Japanese cities (International Affairs Division 1994). This history is in sharp contrast to the Western experience, where urban planning centred traditionally on the separation of land uses and strict controls over local neighbourhood amenities, especially regarding road widths, construction setbacks from lot boundaries, and provision of sufficient open space between buildings (Chapin 1965). A further consequence of Japan's approaches in the Meiji and Taishō (1912-26) periods was the separation of public health controls from those of urban planning. Public health, which had been a major factor in the origins of Western-style urban planning, was in Japan placed under the control of the police administration and its activities were limited to the prevention of epidemics such as tuberculosis (Watanabe 1984).

In the interwar years, the Den-en Toshi (Garden City) Company of Shibusawa Eiichi popularized suburban living and provided a "garden suburb" in the southwest of Tokyo, with an environmental quality that the statutory planning system of the day could not attain or provide for (Watanabe 1980). Following the Great Kantō Earthquake of 1923, a special City Planning Act was enacted to apply site consolidation techniques to the ruined areas of Tokyo and Yokohama (called *kukaku seiri*, or "land readjustment" in Japan; see Minerbi et al. 1986).

To sum up, Japanese urban planning, at least until 1945, took a form significantly different from that practised in Europe and North America. While British planners emphasized public housing and redevelopment, and American planners strict land use controls in suburban areas, Japan followed a system of weak regulations and strong public works programs geared heavily towards economic infrastructure (Watanabe 1993). This pattern was set early in the twentieth century and thus narrowed the field of urban planning in Japan, which, until the Second World War at least, concentrated on the promotion of civil engineering projects dealing with the construction of roads and bridges and the improvement of river systems. The weak regulatory powers, together with insufficient financial provisions for urban infrastructure, were a constant frustration to Japanese planners into the postwar period. The early preoccupation of planning with facilitating economic growth was encouraged by the need to catch up with the West, and strengthened by the rise of a military regime in the 1930s. The extensive Allied bombing during the last years of the Second World War destroyed Japan's industrial capacity and much of its urban infrastructure. Once again, rapid industrialization became the goal of economic and urban policies. Other fundamental issues, such as housing and adequate services for a burgeoning urban population, either were not considered or were given lower priority. This contributed to the significant problems faced in planning major city developments after 1945.

Postwar Patterns of Urbanization

A prominent challenge addressed by urban planners in the postwar years was how to cope with rapid urbanization, which increased dramatically in keeping with the government's policy of high economic growth. Private investments were concentrated along the Pacific coastal region as heavy and chemical industries mushroomed, using domestic coal at first and cheap imported oil later on. Population followed industry from rural areas, and as a result the percentage of Japanese living in cities with a population greater than 100,000 rose from around 28 percent in 1945 to 70 percent in 1970 (Harris 1982). Approximately one-third of this new urban population was clustered within a fifty-kilometre radius of the three huge metropolises of Tokyo, Osaka, and Nagoya, in a combined land area about 1 percent of the entire archipelago. The Greater Tokyo Metropolitan Area[5] alone had about 22 million people in 1970 - almost 21 percent of the total national population - and registered a population density of nearly 5,000 people per square kilometre. In only two and a half decades, therefore, Japan transformed itself from a rural nation into a predominantly urban society. Although urbanization in Japan lagged behind that of the United States and England, it took Japan only 25 years to reach a level that had taken the US about 100 years to attain, and European countries about 300 years (Kawabe 1980; Harris 1982).

During this time, money was indeed spent on basic health care and education programs, together with the mass production of public housing. However, little effort and resources were directed towards improving the quality of housing and other urban amenities in this high-growth period; these were still deemed a low priority. For instance, more than 40 percent of the total public works budget in the 1960s was allocated for industry-related infrastructure such as industrial roads, harbours, and airports.[6]

Moreover, the regional distribution of these funds was biased in favour of rural areas as part of Japan's regional equity drive (see Calder 1988; Fukai 1990; Edgington 2000a).

The problems created for urban dwellers through such a gross budgetary mismatch soon became obvious. For instance, one indicator of the insufficiency of investments in urban roads was the shockingly high number of highway traffic accidents. In 1960 there were 112 deaths per million vehicle kilometres in Japan, compared with only 3.2 in the United States. While highway safety is the result of many factors, the highways' poor quality – with a lack of paving, open ditches, and a lack of sidewalks for pedestrians in suburban areas – was a major contributing factor. As late as 1960, only 3.1 percent of all roads in Japan were paved. The situation improved somewhat thereafter, as more kilometres of road were paved each year in the 1970s than had been paved throughout the nation up to 1960.

Other indicators demonstrate a similar lack of urban social infrastructure. As late as 1963, less than 10 percent of all Japanese dwellings were equipped with flush toilets (i.e., connected to sewerage treatment systems). In the same year, only 2.2 percent of all households had access to a telephone service. Besides these deficiencies, perhaps the most pressing problem was how to overcome a critical housing shortage. By 1973 it was estimated that 790,000 Tokyo households continued to live under inadequate conditions of accommodation (e.g., in only one-room family apartments) (Bennet and Levine 1976; Lincoln 1986). An exodus to the suburbs in search for affordable family housing led to a multitude of new developments in the 1970s, but this brought fresh problems. Particularly in Tokyo and Osaka, morning and evening trains connecting the new communities to downtown centres became crammed with commuters, many of whom travelled up to two hours each way in rail coaches filled to two or three times their intended capacity (Okamoto 1997).

The urban planning system could not prevent increasing air and water pollution (soon to be discussed), and neither could it provide for the efficient development of suburban areas. Despite the extensive postwar urbanization and inherent shortage of land, Japanese cities allowed the spread of small one-storey, one-family houses in the suburbs. By contrast, the genuine need was for large-scale comprehensive developments at higher densities that made better use of well-serviced urban land – along lines developed in the new towns of Singapore, Hong Kong, and South Korea (Philips 1987). Besides the overall lower densities of development, factories, retail stores, and other commercial uses sprang up in an ad hoc fashion amid new residential neighbourhoods, many of which continued to be interspersed with patches of farmland on the urban fringe to create widespread urban sprawl (Hebbert and Nakai 1988). The only exceptions were the planned *danchi* (mass-produced public high-rise housing complexes) and "bed towns" developed by government agencies in certain areas, such as Tama New Town in western Tokyo and Senri New Town to the north of Osaka (Public Enterprise Bureau 1972; Tokyo Metropolitan Government et al. 1976).

In 1968 the existing City Planning Act was finally revised to force developers to make contributions towards new construction of local public roads, open space, and sewers (Japan International Cooperation Agency 1981). In both the older inner areas and the new suburbs, land readjustment *(kukaku seiri)* was attempted over large areas to regularize irregular and chaotic land subdivisions. In suburban areas, this was done on land that until recently had often been rural rice fields *(tambo)*. In existing built-up districts, the severity of this task was complicated by the fact that many cities were developed with their original *jōkamachi* street patterns intact. Except for Nagoya (where extensive replotting of the urban street pattern occurred in the late 1940s; see Edgington 1996, 2000b), this feudal ground plan persisted throughout the postwar period, to the consternation of most city planners (Itoh 1976).

In an administrative sense, the planning system that emerged in the postwar period was still based on very centralized controls exercised by nonprofessional bureaucrats located in the central Ministry of Construction (MOC). Zoning for all of Japan's cities followed the narrow set of restrictions prescribed for every plan throughout Japan as laid down in the 1968 legislation. Even though the "new" Urban Planning Act attempted to decentralize planning down to the Japanese prefectural level, in practice the MOC continued to retain the important privilege of checking local decisions and had the ultimate power to make ad hoc adjustments to every city plan. Local government, on the other hand, while confronted with the very tangible and direct challenge of coping with urban growth pressures, was usually unable to find the necessary skilled personnel to implement its plans in a sensitive way. Indeed, Masser and Yorisaki (1994) have shown that the exercise of planning discretion in city bureaucracies has been undertaken mainly by "generalists" (career administrators) who relied on the strict interpretation of the nationally prescribed laws, rather than professional planners. This overly heavy-handed approach to urban planning was already in place by the time the 1968 City Planning Act was drafted, and reflects the continuing centralization of government in postwar Japan (Edgington 2000a).

Pollution and Urban Amenity

Despite the rapid expansion of cities, many commentators argue that the Japanese people, at least initially, shared a rather broad consensus on the desirability of rapid economic growth after 1945. Besides the paucity of urban amenities in this period, they note that people were willing to work long hours and endure a lack of investment in social infrastructure on the assumption that this represented the best route to future prosperity (Lincoln 1986). Whether or not these observations reflect elitist thinking by just a few privileged intellectuals, this broad public consensus regarding the desirability of economic growth eventually broke down in the late 1960s, most visibly and dramatically over issues relating to pollution.

Rapid industrialization was accompanied by a severe degradation of the environment, one that ultimately resulted in a series of incidents of pollution-induced illnesses. In Minamata (southern Kyushu), mercury from an industrial process that was routinely dumped in a fishing bay poisoned hundreds of people and deformed their offspring. In Yokkaichi (west of Nagoya), smoke and fumes from a new complex of petrochemical plants caused an upsurge in asthma and other serious respiratory conditions. *Itai-itai* disease (episodes of severe cadmium poisoning) was caused in various parts of the country by the dumping of wastes from lead and zinc smelting operations into rivers. In addition to these acute incidents, some of which led to protracted and highly publicized court struggles, a broad segment of the urban public suffered more generally from increased air and water pollution.

One characteristic of postwar urbanization and industrialization had been the concentration of large-scale manufacturing plants on reclaimed land along Tokyo Bay, Osaka Bay, and Ise Bay (Nagoya). Conditions worsened as the number of these factories increased and as the economy shifted from coal to heavy oil for its fuel requirements. During the early 1960s, the consumption of heavy oil in Japan surpassed that of coal, and the amount of soot in the air decreased, but sulphur dioxide concentrations from smokestack industries (mainly steel and metal fabrication) increased rapidly. Further, by 1964 the number of motor vehicles in Tokyo and other cities exceeded the million mark, and automobile exhaust fumes led to harmful levels of carbon monoxide that compounded the pollution problem in Japan's industrial cities (Huddle and Reich 1987; Hoshino 1992).

As public pressure mounted, the government reacted with new legislation and administrative regulations. In 1970 the Diet passed fourteen pollution control laws and created an Environmental Agency (Barrett and Therivel 1991). From 1970 to 1973, the central government's pollution control budget more than tripled, and if investments in related organizations for pollution control are added, anti-pollution expenditures almost quadrupled to ¥430 trillion ($1.6 billion at 1973 exchange rates). Increased government spending for pollution control was matched by rapid increases in expenditures by private industry. In the iron and steel industry, spending for pollution control in relation to total sales rose from 0.9

percent in 1970 to 1.8 percent in 1974. These increased expenditures eventually brought about a significant and visible improvement in environmental quality (OECD 1977).

While less dramatic than pollution, gaps in social amenities also received increased government attention in the 1970s. The severe pollution problems spawned by rapid growth saw a diversification of official goals, away from "economic growth at all costs" to "improving the quality of life" (Lincoln 1986). These changes coincided with both the end of Japan's miracle high-growth period and a dramatic fall in the size of the Liberal Democratic Party (LDP) majority in the Diet. The latter result in particular led to a rapid rise of government spending on social welfare as well as public investments in social infrastructure. For instance, the length of roads paved in 1980 exceeded that of all roads paved in Japan throughout the 1960s. The distance of roads paralleled by sidewalks doubled between 1970 and 1975, and almost doubled again by 1981. As might be imagined, investments in paved roads and sidewalks alone represented a general improvement in quality and safety, contributing to a dramatic reduction in traffic fatalities.

The quality of urban life improved in other ways. Thus, 58 percent of Japanese dwellings had flush toilets in 1983, up from 9.3 percent in 1963, with much of the expansion taking place after the late 1960s. The total area of local parks doubled from the 1970s to 1981. The percentage of households with telephone service tripled from 1970 and 1980, from 25 percent to 77 percent (Lincoln 1986). Housing, too, showed some improvement as the share of government expenditures directed towards this sector increased. The greater availability of public funds, rising income levels, and changing demographics (fewer people per household) gradually produced an improvement in housing quality (as opposed to mere quantity), measured by increasing amounts of space per person and increases in the average size of dwelling units (Kirwin 1987; Donnison and Hoshino 1988).

In the early 1980s, fears over ballooning government debts limited any further growth of public investments, and in some years thereafter the levels of public works were actually cut. Yet another constraint on urban infrastructure was an increasing shortage of suitable building sites due to the higher cost of real estate following land price inflation and widespread land purchases by speculators in the early 1970s. This soon led to problems for city governments providing public services in the big cities; it was not unusual for the expansion of main roads and the purchase of sites for public use to exceed as much as 70 percent of the total project's cost. Consequently, many social overhead investments tended to be postponed just when city officials began to consider more seriously the factors necessary to attain a higher quality of life. Their belated efforts were frustrated by reductions in central government subsidies and a shortage of available space for large-scale housing projects, play areas for children, and sewerage and refuse treatment plants, together with the prevalence of extremely high land prices (Lincoln 1986). During the following years, major official government reports – such as the Maekawa Report in 1985 and the Fourth Comprehensive National Development Plan *(yonzensō)* in 1987 – continued to recommend improvements to the national stock of housing and social infrastructure, together with the decentralization of central government activities away from Tokyo. Nonetheless, reduced funds and increased land prices meant that the implementation of these goals often proceeded at a snail's pace (Lincoln 1988).

The "Tokyo Problem" and the Land Price Crisis

Indeed, the most pressing planning issue in the 1980s concerned the amplification of Tokyo's role as the nation's primary urban centre. This occurred against the backdrop of another round of spectacular increases in land prices and stock market levels, known as the economic bubble (1987-91). The 1980s saw a shift in Japan's economic structure from industry to the service sector. In turn, this led to an increase in commercial, political, and cultural functions in the nation's capital, bringing with it a higher concentration of government offices, company headquarters, financial institutions, high-tech industries, research agencies, and universities. The end result was a dramatic imbalance in economic development between Tokyo and all other Japanese cities. By the end of the 1980s, therefore, the problem of poor urban amenities and infrastructure was more and more a "Tokyo problem" caused by overconcentration *(ikkyoku shūchū)* in the capital (Kantō) region (Douglass 1993; Hill and Fujita 1995).[7]

Land prices in central Tokyo first started to show a dramatic rise from around 1983 (Mera 1993). For instance, the price in the three central wards of Tokyo rose by around 20 percent in 1983, 30 percent in 1984, 54 percent in 1985, 50 percent in 1986, and 13 percent in 1987. This price hike was transmitted to the surrounding suburban areas of Tokyo with a time lag of about one to two years in the initial phase. By the end of 1989, the average price of commercial land in the entire Tokyo metropolitan region was 3.28 times higher than at the beginning of 1983, and 2.35 times higher in the case of residential land. The Osaka region started to witness a noticeable rise in land prices during 1986, and subsequently the price moved steeply to reach a level 3.60 and 2.78 times, respectively, for commercial and residential land within two years. Similar price rises were observed during the late 1980s in other large and intermediate-sized cities throughout the Japanese archipelago.[8]

Hasegawa (1992) notes that this massive land price inflation, while benefiting financial institutions, affected consumers hardest. It forced many urban dwellers to buy small, expensive houses far from work or to give up entirely any aspiration to own their own home. The average price of a new 75-square-meter condominium in the Tokyo metropolitan area in 1990 was around ¥69.5 million, or almost ten times the average annual income of salaried workers (Fukai 1990). High prices also gave rise to further subdivision of regular lots into substandard "mini-developments." Consequently, by the end of the bubble period, a great paradox had occurred: Tokyo residents had average income levels increasingly higher than in other parts of the country, but lived in housing that was considerably worse. Prices were so high in the 1980s that according to the government, more than 80 percent of housing lots sold in fiscal 1990 in the Tokyo metropolitan area were 30 kilometres or more away from the centre of the city, over an hour's commute. Land price inflation also disrupted the smooth development of social infrastructure. Perhaps the most celebrated case was when the Tokyo Metropolitan Government widened a half-kilometre of road in Mita, Minato Ward, during 1989. Acquiring the land cost the city ¥200 million per metre, or 99.5 percent of the total cost (Fukai 1990).

This land price crisis in Tokyo may in fact have been precipitated by increasing demand for, and perceived shortage of, office space in the central district.[9] Nonetheless, great blame must also be ascribed to the government's failure both to control quickly the spate of loans by banks that fuelled speculative real estate deals and to bring more land onto the market in a rational and regulated manner. By the end of the 1980s, however, it was apparent that three sets of structural factors had prevented government action, and this led to a crisis in urban policy (Hanley and Yamamura 1992).

First, zoning regulations were much too loose to effectively control urban development patterns and to prevent land hoarding. In particular, there were estimated to be 36,000 hectares of potentially developable farmland lying within the so-called Urbanization Promotion Areas (UPA) in the three major metropolitan regions, and 8,300 hectares in Tokyo alone. Land within a UPA is supposed to be developed for urban uses within ten years from the date of zoning, but many local mayors in urban fringe municipalities had little political will to enforce these plans and antagonize the farming sector in their communities (Fukai 1990).

Second, fragmented administrative authority over land in the national government, together with a lack of local policy-making autonomy, greatly hindered effective and flexible responses to the rapidly changing circumstances and needs of urban residents. In 1974 a National Land Agency was established to oversee urban and regional polices. However, interministerial friction over land policy continued between the Ministry of Construction (MOC), the Ministry of Agriculture, Forestry and Fisheries (MAFF), the Ministry of International Trade and Industry (MITI), the

Ministry of Transport (MOT), and the Ministry of Home Affairs (MHA), which held mutually conflicting views (Anchordoguy 1992).

Third, the tax system in Japan tended to suppress the supply of land coming onto the market. Thus, up to the 1990s, both agricultural land and corporate-held land enjoyed preferential tax treatment that was not afforded to residential land owned by urban households. Consequently, corporations bought large amounts of excess land as a hedge against inflation or to speculate with, and only 2-3 percent of farmland held with the UPAs was converted each year to residential and other uses. While tax on the income from land sales was high in Japan, to penalize speculative investments, this actually limited the supply of lots put on the market, and so further worsened the demand-to-supply relationship.

As a result of this policy impasse, the government produced only one significant piece of new legislation at the end of the 1980s to deal with the urban land crisis – the Basic Law on Land, passed in December 1989. While this act boldly declared that the welfare of the general public should be given top priority in land policy, by itself it did nothing at all to change the myriad of specific land regulations and taxation policies that obstructed that particular goal. Moreover, it did not contain any badly needed detailed interpretation or procedures by which the legislation could be enforced (Kurokawa 1990).

Policy Changes in the 1990s

During the 1990s, there was a feeling in some government and bureaucratic quarters that the last decade of the twentieth century would be a critical time in which to improve living space and prepare for urban conditions in the new millennium (Shishido 1991). In terms of policies aimed at improving the urban quality of life, the new decade started off well enough, especially with a concerted effort to increase expenditures on infrastructure and to reduce land prices.

Ironically, improvements in both public works expenditures and land policy were triggered in part by *gaiatsu* (external pressure) exerted during the Structural Impediments Initiative (SII). This was a series of high-level talks held during 1989 and 1990 between Japanese and American bureaucrats over opening up Japan's rather closed domestic markets to foreign imports. First, the US called for a substantial expansion of public works expenditure in Japan to reduce the nation's domestic budget surplus and to offset the country's high savings rate. Second, with an eye to the balance of trade issue, it called for broad changes in land policy aimed at bringing down skyrocketing land prices, an issue that the Americans argued kept up savings and depressed both personal consumption and public investment. High land prices in the 1980s had also made the cost of doing business and setting up distribution networks for overseas importers prohibitively expensive (Bacow 1990). Importantly, the US also wanted results-oriented quantitative targets for these and other proposed reforms to be included in the SII agreement. This was necessary, so it was argued, in order to show Japan's willingness to make changes that could be measured later on (Schoppa 1997).

Following these negotiations, the Japanese government in 1990 crafted an ambitious plan to invest a substantial ¥430 trillion in public works during the decade up to fiscal year (FY) 2000, representing about 6-7 percent per annum growth in this budget item. Social infrastructure, such as sewerage and public housing projects, was set to account for 60 percent of total public works budgets rather than the 50 percent or so estimated in the previous decade. Quantitative goals to keep the Japanese promises were written into a special ten-year Public Works Plan.[10] The Ministry of Construction was responsible for implementing these broad goals through its own five-year plans and programs for such items as sewerage, city parks, traffic safety facilities, and housing (see Table 9.2) (Ministry of Construction 1998).

Besides encouraging infrastructure spending, US pressure also helped to produce a new package of tax measures taken in 1991 to address land prices and speculative transactions. These included a new Land Holding Tax that was based on capital values and levied on idle commercial waterfront land owned by major companies (Mera 1993).[11] Even more effective, however, were the administrative restrictions imposed by the Ministry of Finance between 1989 and 1991 on real estate loans issued by banks and other financial institutions, together with a dramatic change in monetary policy. The latter saw a rise in the bank discount rate from 2.5 percent in 1989 to 6.0 percent in mid-1990. Following an abrupt fall in the Tokyo stock market during 1990, Japan's bubble economy burst the very next year, and land prices began to tumble thereafter (Hasegawa 1992; Japan Real Estate Institute 2000).

Quality of life issues again came to the fore in 1992, when Prime Minister Miyazawa Kiichi released his "Lifestyle Superpower Plan" *(seikatsu taikoku)*, one of the many consecutive five-year economic plans prepared in the postwar period (Tanimura and Edgington 2001). Going beyond merely indicating the desired direction of medium-range economic management, for the first time it spelled out clearly the government's policy, with specific concrete goals echoing those included in the SII agreement and Public Works Plan of 1990. A notable feature was a housing and land policy aimed at providing affordable quality housing in urban areas (for roughly five times the average worker's annual income), and social infrastructure improvements in twenty-seven specific fields (Economic Planning Agency 1992).[12] By the middle of the 1990s, various studies showed that housing prices had indeed stabilized and returned to around five times the average annual income level. More importantly, private sector sentiments towards holding land for speculative purposes has changed. There is now every indication that the downward trend in land prices that commenced in 1992 will remain unchanged for the foreseeable future. Consequently, prices are expected to drop to a level that reflects the practical value of land rather than include speculative values that assume future price rises (Japan Real Estate Institute 2000).

While it might be thought that lower land prices would assist public works efforts in Japanese cities, it is interesting to note that actual public works budgets alternately accelerated and decelerated throughout the decade according to the national political environment. Thus, while the ¥430 trillion Public Works Plan projected an annual growth of around 3 percent in projects commencing in FY 1991, real growth rates were pushed up to an average of 10 percent annually over the next two years. This was done in order to stabilize the collapsing real estate market and national economy. Indeed, during 1994 the government of Prime Minister Hosokawa Morihiro revised the Public Works Plan, increased the budget, and called for a total of ¥630 trillion to be disbursed by 2004. A new five-year economic plan in 1995 also committed the government of Prime Minister Murayama Tomiichi to accelerate social infrastructure improvements. This included new programs related to the needs of Japan's rapidly aging population as well as economic infrastructure in cities, such as fibre optic networks and increased expenditure on research and development facilities (Economic Planning Agency 1995b). The more positive environment surrounding public works eventually evaporated, however, when in FY 1997 it became clear that Japan was facing huge budget deficits caused by continuing slow growth and even recession. Under the government of Hashimoto Ryutaro, a fiscal reform package was announced and public works were cut by 7 percent in FY 1998. However, in order to address a further deterioration in economic conditions in 1998, these reforms were suddenly frozen in favour of economic stimulus measures. Consequently, Obuchi Keizo, who replaced Hashimoto in July 1998, switched back to a big-spending policy, and the budget for FY 1999 contained a record growth in public works spending (*Nikkei Weekly* 1999).

Apart from increased infrastructure budgets and tax reform, changes in land use planning and affiliated regulations emerged as important initiatives to promote urban amenity. For instance, revisions of the Urban Planning Act and the Building Standards Act occurred in 1992, resulting in a more detailed zoning system. This allowed planners to, in certain cases, restrict the inefficient mingling of housing and commercial property and so protect the amenity of entire residential areas (Ministry of Construction 1992). Further changes in 1997 established districts where the construction of high-rise apartment buildings could be encouraged by easing floor area-to-site area restrictions and other building controls. The intent here was to

Table 9.2

Five-year (and seven-year) infrastructure plans of Japan's Ministry of Construction

Name of plan	(Period: FY)	Total projected investment (¥100 million)	Achievement rate[1] (% end of FY 1998) (outlook)	Goals
The Ninth Seven-Year Flood Control Program	1997-2003	240,000	33.0	Flood controlled ratio: 52% → 59%
The New Five-Year Road Improvement and Management Program	1998-2002	780,000	17.1	Total length of national expressways: 5,929 km → 7,806 km
The Eighth Seven-Year Sewerage Improvement Program	1996-2002	237,000	48.9	Sewerage diffusion ratio: 54% → 66%
The Sixth Seven-Year Program for Developing City Parks	1996-2002	72,000	48.1	Per capita urban park area: 7.1 m^2 → 9.5 m^2

The Sixth Seven-Year Traffic Safety Facilities Improvement Program	1996-2002	24,800	48.5	Length of roads with sidewalks: 128,000 km → 153,000 km
The Seventh Housing Construction Five-Year Plan	1996-2000	7.3 million houses (3.6 million public houses)	70.9	Floor area per house: 91.9 m^2 (1996) → 100 m^2 (2000)
The Sixth Seven-Year Seacoast Project Program[2]	1996-2002	17,700	48.2	Ratio of protected/unprotected seacoast: Approx. 40% → 50%
The Fourth Five-Year Prevention Program for Collapse of Steep Slopes	1998-2002	11,900	17.8	Proportion of landslide protection measures undertaken: 25% → 33%

Notes:
1. Achievement rate is the amount of total investment of the current plan divided by that of the previous plan.
2. Investment in the Seacoast Project Program is the total investment in this project by all government ministries.

Source: Based on Ministry of Construction 1998.

encourage a higher ratio of condominium apartments and to facilitate a higher population in inner city districts (Ministry of Construction 1997). On top of this, the government reformed the Land Lease and Building Lease Act in 1992 to allow fixed-term land lease contracts. In this way, consumers could find a way around high prices by building houses on leased land, potentially halving the price they would pay if they bought the property outright (Ishizawa 1994).

In a rare occurrence of interministerial cooperation, decentralization of population and jobs from congested Tokyo was promoted through the Core Cities Law, passed in 1992 and supported by MOC, MITI, MAFF, MHA, and the National Land Agency (NLA). This program was aimed at taking much of the increase in public works spending outside of Tokyo, and focusing it on just one or two core cities in each prefecture, targeting each as a centre for local development. Furthermore, low-interest loans from the Japan Development Bank and tax exemptions were made available for the private construction of office buildings, as well as private educational and health care facilities, in the centres designated under this program. Fourteen areas were picked initially, especially in prefectures experiencing decreasing populations (see Figure 9.3), but eventually the program covered 50 to 80 regional centres with populations of 100,000 to 200,000 spread throughout Japan, with one or two designated for special treatment in each prefecture (*Nikkei Weekly* 1992a, 1992b). An example where funds were allocated under the program is Kitakyūshū in Fukuoka prefecture. To arrest its population decline to a level of around 1 million, the city received special funds from the national government to improve its downtown area and enhance the Murasakigawa River, which flows through the city centre (Ministry of Construction 1993).

A more strident move to shift the balance away from Tokyo to the regions came from a bipartisan commitment to investigate the removal of national capital functions. The debate over this issue *(sentoron)*, and where a new location for the Diet and central ministries might be found, dominated urban policy in the 1990s. A number of sites were suggested – including western Japan at Lake Biwa in Kansai, along the base of Mt. Fuji, as well as further north in the central Tōhoku region. An interim report recommending removal of the national government from Tokyo was delivered by the Diet's own committee in 1992. Not surprisingly, it received severe criticism from the Tokyo Metropolitan Government, but it was widely supported by the business community (Eckert 1992a, 1992b).

Eventually, the ruling LDP and the opposition parties combined to pass a basic law governing the future transfer of the central government's legislative, administrative, and judicial functions. This also provided a blueprint for a new capital to be located on a 9,000-hectare location lying at least sixty kilometres from Tokyo, and suitable to accommodate a population of 600,000. The legislation then led to a multiparty study of the feasibility of relocating the Diet and national government ministries in an effort to ease Tokyo's congestion. The 1995 Hanshin-Awaji earthquake, which killed over 6,000 people in Kobe and surrounding areas, brought home the need to reinforce the disaster prevention capacity of cities, as well as the urgency of moving government functions away from the earthquake-vulnerable Kantō (Tokyo) region (United Nations Centre for Regional

Figure 9.3

Regional core cities targeted as centres for local development under the Core Cities Law of 1992

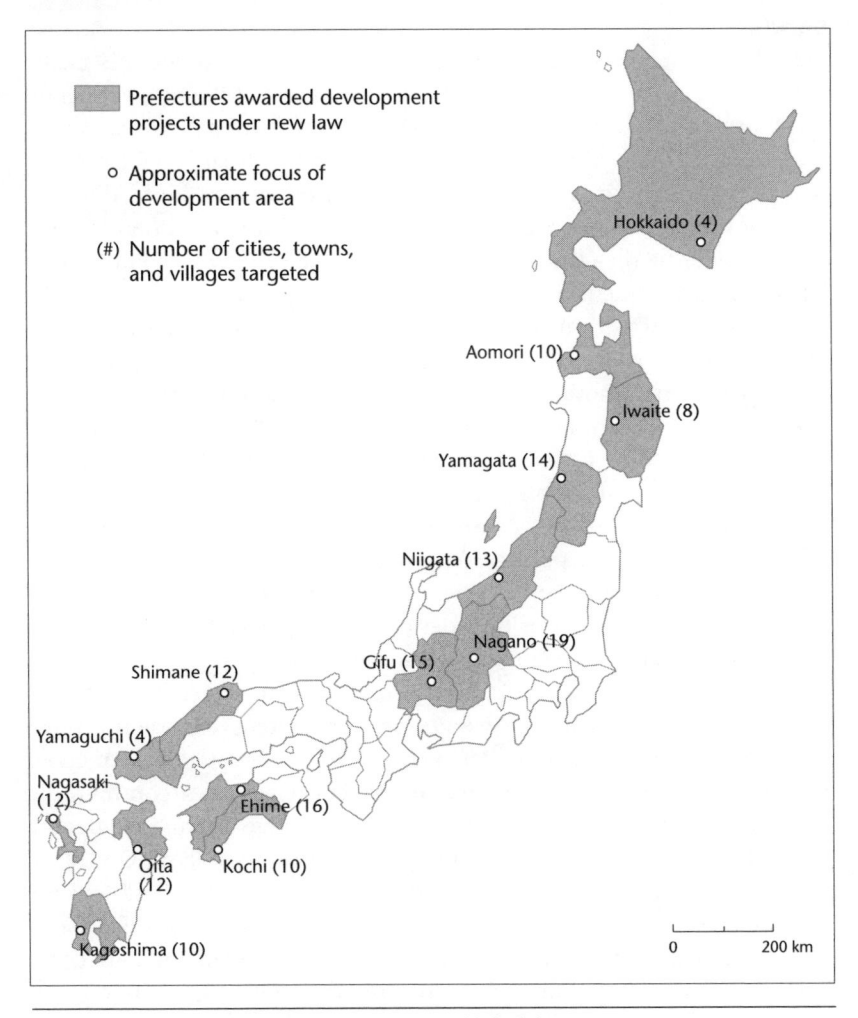

Source: Based upon Ministry of Construction, unpublished data.

Development 1996). By the end of the decade, however, the final location for a new capital had not been designated.

Yet another reform worthy of note was the bipartisan support for local government reform and administrative decentralization, as embodied in the Law for the Promotion of Decentralization *(Chihō Bunken Suishinho)* and the Committee for the Promotion of Decentralization *(Chihō Bunken Suishin Iinkai)*, both established in 1995. The latter made a series of important recommendations, including increasing the autonomy of local governments and their ability to make a greater number of decisions without national interference in the field of city planning, based purely on local circumstances (Kamo 1997).

Conclusions

This chapter suggests that while there have indeed been changes in the value placed on urban quality of life in Japan, most of the postwar period can be seen to have been a continuation of trends and patterns set in the Meiji and Taishō periods. Only in the 1990s has there been anything resembling a concerted effort to bring urban quality of life to the forefront, and even this has been encumbered by the current economic crisis. Still, considering the rather severe geographical and climatic conditions in Japan, the government has worked hard to improve its housing and social overhead capital within a relatively short period, with many achievements. While certain indicators, such as housing, sewerage, parks, and roads, lag behind those of other industrialized nations, others, such as health and education, are in some cases well ahead. Moreover, Japanese cities can cite some astonishingly impressive social statistics on crime, longevity of the population, urban culture, or pollution abatement, and these can easily rebut any Western quip about "workaholics living in rabbit hutches."[13] It is perhaps only natural that Japan typically shows "poorer" features of amenity when compared with Europe and North America, which have longer histories of capital accumulation and whose rates of urbanization have long since slowed down.

Improving housing standards, expanding the urban expressway network, local sewerage system improvements, and urban redevelopment – these will continue to present formidable tasks for Japanese urban planners in the twenty-first century. However, land prices have fallen continuously for a decade, and sudden dramatic increases through speculative buying and selling are now unlikely to cause further social problems. On top of this, the 1995 population census tended to show that the trend towards massive population inflow to Tokyo during the bubble period had virtually ceased, which should allow some catch-up of urban amenities to occur in the current century (Ministry of Construction 1998). Thus, while Tokyo and the other big cities in Japan are unlikely to ever have uncluttered landscapes, they can look forward to higher levels of neighbourhood amenity and incremental improvements in infrastructure.[14]

Several factors remain as substantial challenges for the years to come. First, the aging of the population will require a new set of facilities, including easier physical access to public transportation, safer sidewalks, and special access to buildings. In fact, because of Japan's aging society, it is feared that the capacity to invest in housing and social capital may well be eroded by the shrinking of the productive workforce, lower savings rates, and the growing limitations of fiscal policy. Second, in light of recent construction scandals, increasing the infrastructure budget has lost credibility in the eyes of the public.[15] Third, projects in Japan are often about 30 percent more expensive than in the United States, mainly because of the closed bidding *(dangō)* system and lack of true open competitiveness. Also, the cost of repair and replacement of an earlier generation of infrastructure, including public housing and urban expressways, is likely to rise substantially over time (Woodall 1996).

Above all else, there are serious political limitations on what can be accomplished in quality of life without substantial pressure from grassroots citizen movements. To put it bluntly, the Japanese style of social engineering has placed an emphasis upon the fulfillment of institutional requirements at the expense of the encouragement of individual rights and choices. This study has shown that when it comes to shaping the physical structure of cities, Japanese government authorities and private developers have almost always been in control (see also Sorensen 2002). Whether it is the paving of a road, the creation of a park, or the simple planting of a tree, local residents' voices are generally unheard. Japanese society solicits an abysmally low level of accountability from its elected officials or bureaucrats, and local groups have traditionally been unwilling to challenge authority.[16]

Despite low amenity and inefficient public works, the common expression *shikata ga nai* (it cannot be helped) reflects a fatalism that may yet bolster the status quo. For real improvements in the urban quality of life, a change is required in the thinking of the average Japanese. The concept of *machizukuri* or "bottom-up" town building involves a willingness to be involved in community affairs (Sorensen 2002). Voluntary movements of this sort by residents, while not unheard of, are comparatively rare in Japan, despite the *jichikai* (residents council) movement of local neighbourhood groups that goes back to the 1950s (Bestor 1989).[17] In 1995 the Great Hanshin-Awaji Earthquake galvanized the forces already at work attempting to build a stronger civil society in Japan. Sudden attention was focused on this issue, thanks in large part to the outpouring of support by over 1.3 million volunteers in Kobe and elsewhere. The media attention given to volunteerism in Kobe paved the way for legislative proposals to facilitate the formal acknowledgment of the work of nongovernmental organizations (NGOs) and provided incentives for tax-deductible contributions. Still, even more voluntary activities are required, and in certain cases these should be combined with the power and vitality of the private sector to improve urban design and neighbourhoods in conjunction with local government authorities. Otherwise, the status quo will continue to favour narrow producer interests, such as the construction industry, banking groups, big manufacturers, and small urban farmers (Yamamoto 1999).[18]

Acknowledgments
The author wishes to thank the large number of government officials and academics interviewed as part of this project during 1996 and 1998. Special thanks go to Prof. Watanabe Shunichi of the Tokyo University of Science, Taketoshi Makoto of the Ministry of Land, Infrastructure and Transport, and Ikeda Junichi of Osaka City Government.

Notes
1 Living conditions in Japan began to improve rapidly during the high-growth period (1953-73). This was marked by the diffusion of durable goods, at first symbolized by the "three sacred treasures" (the electric washing machine, the refrigerator, and the vacuum cleaner) and later, in the 1970s, by the "new three sacred treasures" (automobiles, air conditioning, and colour television). This was a time of rapid urbanization with a greater movement of people from rural areas into the cities (Ministry of Construction 1997).
2 "Quality of life" conveys, of course, different meanings to various groups within society (Frick 1986; Proshansky and Fabian 1986; Rogerson 1999). In Japan, urban planners have defined this concept in a rather limited way, referring mainly to the promotion of civil engineering projects, such as highway construction, river improvements, and large-scale housing projects. This type of "top down" big-project planning is known in Japan as *toshi keikaku* and associated with the public works budgets of the central government's ministries (construction, transport, agriculture, and so on). With few exceptions, a more local "bottom up" approach to planning, one that focuses on community and neighbourhoods (called *machizukuri*, or local "town building"), has been less pronounced (I am indebted to Prof. Watanabe Shunichi for this insight). Further, the closely linked concept of "amenity," one that is widely used in the field of urban planning in North America and Europe, is rarely found in Japan. Amenity in this sense implies not just the provision of higher levels of social infrastructure or individual building landscape but also wider issues of local neighbourhood planning, enhancement of local urban design, traffic and noise abatement, social welfare, and security.
3 Watanabe (1980) notes that this stands in contrast to British planner Ebeneezer Howard's turn-of-the-century notion of the "Garden City." This was to be laid out with both elements of the countryside (wide streets, open space, low densities) and land set aside for more traditional urban uses (industrial estates for factories as well as residential areas for workers and social elites).
4 Tarr (1984) shows that at the same time in North American cities, the development of more local and democratic government structures led to a wider array of infrastructure provision. Thus, while much infrastructure in the US was also related to commerce and development, an equally important driving change stemmed from considerations related to public health and public order. Consequently, expenditures on street improvements, planned water supply, and sewerage systems were consistently higher from the middle of the nineteenth century. Later on, into the first decade or so of the twentieth century, new public infrastructure developments in US cities included the rapid diffusion of street lighting and the beautification of city centres. These were joined by the planned rebuilding and improvement of streets, roads, parkways, and bridges in order to improve traffic circulation.

5 The Tokyo Metropolitan Region includes Metropolitan Tokyo and the surrounding prefectures of Chiba, Kanagawa, Saitama, Yamanashi, Gunma, Tochigi, and Ibaraki. This area has a radius approximately 150 kilometres from Tokyo's central business district, Marunouchi.
6 Construction of industry-related infrastructure was promoted systematically in the high-growth period by a series of legislative enactments, such as the Land Reclamation Law (1946), the Law for the Construction of Roads (1952), Law for the Harbours (1951), and Law for the Construction of Airports (1956). The official mentality was reflected in the Enterprises Rationalization Promotion Law of 1952, which committed the central and local governments to build ports, highways, electrical power grids, gas mains, and industrial parks "at the public expense" (Johnson 1982).
7 There have been several scholarly articles describing Japan's shift towards a service economy and the restructuring of Tokyo into a "world city" (Fujita 1991; Sassen 1991; Machimura 1992; Hatta and Tabuchi 1995; Nakamura 1996). Census results showed that the population of the Tokyo Metropolitan Region increased from 17.9 million in 1960 to 31.8 million in 1990, while the national population increased from 94.3 million to 123.6 million during the same period. This meant that natural growth and net in-migration to this single region together accounted for about 50 percent of Japan's total population increase during these thirty years. About 25 percent of Japan's population was concentrated in the Tokyo metropolitan area during the 1980s, compared with about 18 percent for the comparable London and Paris metropolitan regions. Population density recorded in Tokyo was around 14,000 persons per square kilometre, while the average for Japan stands at about 322 per square kilometre (Fukai 1990).
8 For commentary on the land problem in Japanese cities during the 1980s, see Hanley and Yamamura 1992. I am persuaded by the perceptive analysis provided by Woodall (1992), which suggests that Japan's leaders have long treated economic growth as a "public good" while treating social infrastructure and land as a "private good."
9 While real estate agents and developers often mentioned this factor, it took place along with other trends occurring in the background. These included excess liquidity caused by Japan's escalating trade surplus, slow domestic growth and poor opportunities for investment in manufacturing, deregulation of financial markets, the Bank of Japan's easy credit policy (which caused asset prices to skyrocket), reckless bank lending for speculative real estate deals, the Nakasone government's policy of encouraging private sector infrastructure activities (*minkatsu* development), and the government's own sale of public lands in Tokyo (Bank of Tokyo 1990).
10 For instance, the plan aimed to increase the average house floor space from 89 square metres to 100 square metres by the year 2000. Other goals included doubling the area of city parkland per urban resident from 5.4 square metres at the end of FY 1988 to 10 square metres by the year 2000, and increasing the national average sewerage diffusion ratio from 44 percent in FY 1989 to 70 percent over the same period (Ministry of Construction 1992).
11 For commentary and criticism regarding the overall effectiveness of the new taxes, see Anchordoguy 1992.
12 A concrete example of how extra infrastructure funds were used concerns the new Jōban railway line northeast of Tokyo in Ibaraki prefecture. This will connect towns along the way to Akihabara Station in central Tokyo in less than forty minutes, allowing the development of residential areas close to the new stations by the government's Housing and Urban Development Corporation *(Kōdan)* (Kobayashi and Takashima 1993).
13 The average length of life in Japan reached a record high in the 1990s – 76.3 years for males and 82.5 for females. Increasing concerns are now being raised about how to cope with the rapid aging of the population. In 2002, one in four Japanese is expected to be 65 or older, and it is estimated that the number of elderly people in need of care will rise from 2 million in 1993 to 5.2 million in 2050 (Economic Planning Agency 1995a).
14 Some regional core cities (Sapporo, Sendai, Hiroshima, and Fukuoka) have grown continuously in the postwar period. Thus, if current population trends continue, the regional core cities (especially those with populations of 1 million and above) and their immediate hinterland will increase in size and take a larger proportion of the Japanese population. However, those with less than about 1 million are expected to see their populations level

off or decrease over the next twenty years as the national population itself falls (Ministry of Construction 1992, 1999).
15 Newspaper stories involving major construction companies spread nationwide following the massive tax-evasion scandals of former Liberal Democratic Party vice-president Shin Kanemaru in 1992. The Miyagi prefecture governor and Sendai city mayor were also arrested, and in Ibaraki prefecture, the governor and a local town mayor were taken into custody. Following these and many other breaches, certain local governments have since introduced stringent ethics ordinances (Komatsuzaki 1995).
16 A recent exception was the outcry over inappropriate high-rise commercial buildings and the destruction of traditional houses in Kyoto (see *Kyoto Journal* 1994).
17 An example of the *machizukuri* approach concerns Tokyo's Setagaya's Ward council, which established a Setagaya Community Design Centre to help associations of local residents express their views on what their community should look like. One proposal being considered calls for electricity lines and poles to be laid underground in areas near parks so as not to mar the scenery (Nishimura 1992).
18 Ebisu Garden Place is an example of successful urban redevelopment in Tokyo, where a redundant factory site was made into a new complex with hotel, housing, office, and commercial facilities. Opened in 1994, it attracted 40 million visitors in the first two and a half years. Canal City Hakata in Fukuoka, opened in 1996, is an example of successful redevelopment in a regional core city. This complex, with commercial and amusement facilities, has attracted visitors not only from Kyūshū but also from neighbouring Asian countries, and so has had a positive impact on the local economy (Ministry of Construction 1997).

References
Anchordoguy, M. 1992. "Land Policy: A Public Policy Failure." In J.O. Hanley and K. Yamamura, eds., *Land Issues in Japan: A Policy Failure?* Seattle: Society for Japanese Studies, 77-112.
Ashworth, W. 1954. *The Genesis of Modern British Town Planning*. London: Routledge and Kegan Paul.
Bacow, L.S. 1990. *The Tokyo Land Market*, Working Paper No. 26, Center for Real Estate Development. Cambridge, MA: Massachusetts Institute of Technology.
Bank of Japan. 1990. *The Recent Rise in Japan's Land Prices: Its Background and Implications*, Special Paper No. 193. Tokyo: Research and Statistics Department, Bank of Japan.
Barrett, B.F.D., and R. Therivel. 1991. *Environmental Policy and Impact Assessment in Japan*. London: Routledge.
Bennet, J.W., and S.B. Levine. 1976. "Industrialization and Social Deprivation: Welfare, Environment, and Postindustrial Society in Japan." In H. Patrick, ed., *Japanese Industrialization and Its Social Consequences*. Berkeley: University of California Press, 439-92.
Bestor, T.C. 1989. *Neighborhood Tokyo*. Stanford, CA: Stanford University Press.
Calder, K.E. 1988. *Crisis and Compensation: Public Policy and Political Stability in Japan*. Princeton, NJ: Princeton University Press.
Chapin, F.S. 1965. *Urban Land Use Planning*. Urbana: University of Illinois Press.
Cullingworth, J.B., and V. Nadin. 1997. *Town and Country Planning in the UK*. 12th ed. London: Routledge.
Donnison, D., and S. Hoshino. 1988. "Formulating the Japanese Housing Problem." *Housing Studies* 3: 190-95.
Douglass, M. 1993. "The 'New' Tokyo Story: Restructuring Space and the Struggle for Place in a World City." In K. Fujita and R.C. Hill, eds., *Japanese Cities in the World Economy*. Philadelphia: Temple University Press, 83-119.
Eckert, P. 1992a. "Momentum Builds for Relocation of Capital outside Tokyo." *Nikkei Weekly*, 1 August, 10.
–. 1992b. "Measure Would Move Diet Out of Tokyo: City to Remain Japan's Cultural Economic Hub." *Nikkei Weekly*, 23 November, 10.
Economic Planning Agency. 1992. *The Five-Year Economic Plan: Sharing a Better Quality of Life around the Globe*. Tokyo: Economic Planning Agency.

–. 1995a. *White Paper on the National Lifestyle, Fiscal Year 1995*. Tokyo: Printing Bureau, Ministry of Finance.
–. 1995b. "Social and Economic Plan for Structural Reforms towards a Vital Economy and Secure Life." Mimeograph. Tokyo: Economic Planning Agency.
Edgington, D.W. 1996. *Planning for Industrial Restructuring in Japan: The Case of the Chukyo Region*. AURN (Asian Urban Research Network) Working Paper No. 11. Vancouver: Centre for Human Settlements, University of British Columbia.
–. 2000a. "Central-Local Government Fiscal Relations and Regional Equalization." Paper presented at the Understanding Japan in the 21st Century conference, University of British Columbia, Vancouver.
–. 2000b. "New Directions in Japanese Urban Planning: A Case Study of Nagoya." In P. Bowles and L.T. Woods, eds., *Japan after the Economic Miracle*. Dordrecht, Netherlands: Kluwer Academic Publishers, 145-68.
Frick, D. 1986. "Introduction." In D. Frick, ed., *The Quality of Urban Life: Social, Psychological, and Physical Conditions*. Berlin: de Gruyter, 1-12.
Fujioka, K. 1980. "The Changing Face of Japanese *Jōkamachi* (Castle Towns) since the Meiji Period." In Association of Japanese Geographers, ed., *Geography of Japan*. Tokyo: Teikoku-Shoin, 146-60.
Fujita, K. 1991. "A World City and Flexible Specialization: Restructuring the Tokyo Metropolis." *International Journal of Urban and Regional Research* 15: 269-84.
Fukai, S. 1990. *Japan's Land Policy and Its Global Impact*. USJP Occasional Paper 90-01, Program on US-Japan Relations. Cambridge, MA: Harvard University.
Hanley, J.O., and K. Yamamura, eds. 1992. *Land Issues in Japan: A Policy Failure?* Seattle: Society for Japanese Studies.
Harris, C.D. 1982. "The Urban and Industrial Transformation of Japan." *Geographical Review* 72: 50-89.
Hasegawa, T. 1992. "Land Prices and Economic Growth in Japan: The Bursting of the Bubble Economy, and the Direction of Land Prices." *JCR Financial Digest* (22): 1-6.
Hatta, T., and T. Tabuchi. 1995. "Unipolar Concentration in Tokyo: Causes and Measures." *Japanese Economic Studies* 23(3): 74-104.
Hebbert, M., and N. Nakai. 1988. *How Tokyo Grows: Land Development and Planning on the Metropolitan Fringe*. London: Suntory-Toyota International Centre for Economics and Related Disciplines, London School of Economics.
Hill, R., and K. Fujita. 1995. "Osaka's Tokyo Problem." *International Journal of Urban and Regional Research* 19: 181-93.
Hoshino, Y. 1992. "Japan's Post-Second World War Environmental Problems." In J. Ui, ed., *Industrial Pollution in Japan*. Tokyo: United Nations University Press, 64-76.
Huddle, N., and M. Reich. 1987. *Island of Dreams: Environmental Crisis in Japan*. Cambridge, MA: Schenkman Books.
International Affairs Division. 1994. *A Hundred Years of Tokyo City Planning*. TMG Municipal Library No. 28. Tokyo: Tokyo Metropolitan Government.
Ishizawa, M. 1994. "Tokyo Home Buyers Opt to Build on Leased Land." *Nikkei Weekly*, 28 February, 5.
Itoh, S. 1976. "Land Problems in the Tokyo Region: The Existing Situation and Land Policy." In J. Wong, ed., *The Cities of Asia: A Study of Urban Solutions and Urban Finance*. Singapore: Singapore University Press, 48-70.
Japan International Cooperation Agency. 1981. *City Planning in Japan*. Tokyo: Japan International Cooperation Agency.
Japan Real Estate Institute. 2000. *Urban Land Price Index and National Wooden House Market Value Index as of the End of March 2000*. Tokyo: Japan Real Estate Institute.
Johnson, C. 1982. *MITI and the Japanese Miracle: The Growth of Industrial Policy 1925-1975*. Stanford, CA: Stanford University Press.
Kamo, T. 1997. "Time for Reform? Fifty Years of the Postwar Japanese Local Self-Government System." In Foreign Press Center, Japan, ed., *Japan. Eyes on the Country: Views of the 47 Prefectures*. Tokyo: Foreign Press Center, Japan, 8-17.
–. 1999. "Urban-Regional Governance in the Age of Globalization: The Case of Metropolitan

Osaka." In J. Friedmann, ed., *Urban and Regional Governance in the Asia Pacific*. Vancouver: Institute of Asian Research, University of British Columbia, 67-80.

Kawabe, H. 1980. "Internal Migration and the Population Distribution in Japan." In Association of Japanese Geographers, ed., *Geography of Japan*. Tokyo: Teikoku-Shoin, 379-89.

Kirwin, R.M. 1987. "Fiscal Policy and the Price of Land and Housing in Japan." *Urban Studies* 24: 345-60.

Kobayashi, A., and Y. Takashima. 1993. "The Jōban Plan: Japan's New Deal?" *Nikkei Weekly*, 1 March, 11.

Komatsuzaki, K. 1995. "Corruption in Local Government Stifles Desire for Decentralization." *Yomiuri Shimbun*, 17 January, 7.

Kurokawa, N. 1990. "Getting Serious about Land Prices." *Japan Quarterly* 37: 392-401.

Kyoto Journal. 1994. "Special Edition: The Death and Resurrection of Kyoto," 27: 1-100.

Lincoln, E.J. 1986. "Infrastructural Deficiencies, Budget Policy and Capital Flows." In M. Schmiegelow, ed., *Japan's Response to Crisis and Change in the World Economy*. Armonk, New York: M.E. Sharpe, 153-80.

–. 1988. *Japan: Facing Economic Maturity*. Washington, DC: Brookings Institution.

Machimura, T. 1992. "The Urban Restructuring Process in Tokyo in the 1980s: Transforming Tokyo into a World City." *International Journal of Urban and Regional Research* 16: 114-28.

Masser, I., and T. Yorisaki. 1994. "The Institutional Context of Japanese Planning: Professional Associations and Planning Education." In P. Shapira, I. Masser, and D.W. Edgington, eds., *Planning for Cities and Regions in Japan*. Liverpool: Liverpool University Press, 113-23.

Mera, K. 1993. "Risks of Accelerating Land Taxation: Lessons from the Japanese Experience." Mimeograph. Salem, OR: Tokyo International University of America.

Minerbi, L., P. Nakamura, K. Nitz, and J. Yanai. 1986. *Land Readjustment: The Japanese System*. Boston: Oelgeschlager, Gunn and Hain.

Ministry of Construction, Japan. 1992. *White Paper on Construction 1991*. Tokyo: Research Institute of Construction and Economy.

–. 1993. *White Paper on Construction 1992*. Tokyo: Research Institute of Construction and Economy.

–. 1997. *White Paper on Construction in Japan 1997*. Tokyo: Research Institute of Construction and Economy.

–. 1998. *White Paper on Construction in Japan 1998*. Tokyo: Research Institute of Construction and Economy.

–. 1999. *White Paper on Construction in Japan 1999*. Tokyo: Research Institute of Construction and Economy.

Mizuuchi, T. 1991. "Patterns in Public Service Provision and Urban Development in Prewar Japan before 1945." *Geographical Review of Japan* 64 (Series B): 1-24.

–. 1999. "Development Policies and Spatial Integration in Japan from 1868 to 1941." In T. Mizuuchi, ed., *Nation, Region and the Politics of Geography in East Asia*. Osaka: Osaka City University, 30-42.

Mumford, L. 1961. *The City in History: Its Origins, Its Transformations and Its Prospects*. New York: Harcourt, Brace and World.

Nakamura, N. 1996. "The 'Tokyo Problem' and the Development of Urban Issues in Japan." In J.S. Jun and D.S. Wright, eds., *Globalization and Decentralization: Institutional Contexts, Policy Issues and Intergovernmental Relations in Japan and the United States*. Washington, DC: Georgetown University Press, 157-75.

Nikkei Weekly. 1992a. "Bill to Push Regional Development," 18 January, 7.

–. 1992b. "Fourteen Outlying Areas Picked for Development Boost," 14 December, 13.

–. 1999. "Fiscal Policy: Reform Plans Take Back Seat to Recharging the Economy." In *Japan Economic Almanac 1999*. Tokyo: Nihon Keizai Shimbun, 58-59.

Nishimura, H. 1992. "Citizen's Groups Seek Say in Planning: Quality of Life Decisions Are No Longer Being Left to Corporations." *Nikkei Weekly*, 3 October, 11.

OECD (Organization for Economic Co-operation and Development). 1977. *Environmental Policies in Japan*. Paris: OECD.

Okamoto, K. 1997. "Suburbanization of Tokyo and the Daily Lives of Suburban People." In P.P. Karan and K. Stapleton, eds., *The Japanese City*. Lexington: University of Kentucky Press, 79-105.

Philips, D.R., ed. 1987. *New Towns in East and South East Asia: Planning and Development*. Hong Kong: Oxford University Press.

Proshansky, H.M., and A.K. Fabian. 1986. "Psychological Aspects of the Quality of Urban Life." In D. Frick, ed., *The Quality of Urban Life: Social, Psychological, and Physical Conditions*. Berlin: de Gruyter, 19-30.

Public Enterprise Bureau. 1972. *Senri New Town*. Osaka: Osaka Prefecture.

Rogerson, R.J. 1999. "Quality of Life and City Competitiveness." *Urban Studies* 36: 969-85.

Sassen, S. 1991. *The Global City: New York, London, Tokyo*. Princeton, NJ: Princeton University Press.

Sawamoto, M. 1981. "One Hundred Years of Public Works in Japan: Lessons of Experience." In H. Nagamine, ed., *Nation Building and Regional Development: The Japanese Experience*. Singapore: Maruzen Asia, 99-135.

Schoppa, L.J. 1997. *Bargaining with Japan: What American Pressures Can and Cannot Do*. New York: Columbia University Press.

Seidensticker, E. 1983. *Low City, High City: Tokyo from Edo to the Earthquake*. Tokyo: Charles E. Tuttle.

Shishido, T. 1991. "President's Message." In Research Institute of Construction and Economy (RICE) and Ministry of Construction, Japan, *White Paper on Construction 1990*. Tokyo: Ministry of Construction and RICE.

Smith, H. 1979. "Tokyo and London: Comparative Conceptions of the City." In A. Craig, ed., *Japan: A Comparative View*. Princeton, NJ: Princeton University Press, 49-99.

Sorensen, A. 2002. *The Making of Urban Japan*. London, Routledge.

Statistics Bureau. 1996. *1995 Population Census of Japan*. Tokyo: Management and Coordination Agency, Government of Japan.

Tanimura, P., and D.W. Edgington. 2001. "National-Level Economic and Spatial Planning in Japan." In R. Alterman, ed., *National-Level Planning in Democratic Countries: An International Comparison of City and Regional Policy-Making*. Town Planning Review Special Study No. 4. Liverpool: Liverpool University Press, 197-218.

Tarr, J.A. 1984. "The Evolution of the Urban Infrastructure in the Nineteenth and Twentieth Centuries." In R. Hanson, ed., *Perspectives on Urban Infrastructure*. Washington, DC: National Academy Press, 4-66.

Tokyo Metropolitan Government, Japan Housing Corporation, and Tokyo Metropolitan Housing Supply Corporation. 1976. *Tama New Town*. Tokyo: Tokyo Metropolitan Government.

United Nations Centre for Regional Development (UNCRD). 1996. *Relocation of Capital Function as a New Urban Strategy for Decongestion of Major Metropolises*. UNCRD Proceedings Series No.12. Nagoya: UNCRD.

Watanabe, S.J. 1980. "Garden City Japanese Style: The Case of Den-en Toshi Company Ltd., 1918-28." In G.E. Cherry, ed., *Shaping an Urban World*. London: Mansell, 129-44.

–. 1984. "Metropolitanism as a Way of Life: The Case of Tokyo, 1868-1930." In A. Sutcliffe, ed., *Metropolis 1890-1940*. London: Mansell, 403-30.

–. 1993. *The Birth of "Urban Planning": Japan's Modern Urban Planning in International Comparison* (in Japanese). Tokyo: Kashiwa-shobō.

Woodall, B. 1992. "The Politics of Land in Japan's Dual Political Economy." In J.O. Hanley and K. Yamamura, eds., *Land Issues in Japan: A Policy Failure?* Seattle: Society for Japanese Studies, 113-48.

–. 1996. *Japan under Construction: Corruption, Politics and Public Works*. Berkeley: University of California Press.

Woronoff, J. 1996. *Japan as Anything but Number One*. 2nd ed. Houndmills, Basingstoke, Hampshire, UK: Macmillan Press.

Yamamoto, T., ed. 1999. *Deciding the Public Good: Governance and Civil Society in Japan*. Tokyo: Japan Center for International Exchange.

10
Museum as Hometown: What Is "Japanese Beauty"?
Joshua S. Mostow

Introduction

A number of scholars have recently written on what is called the *furusato būmu*, or "hometown boom." This involves a renewed interest in village Japan, inaugurated to no small extent by the phenomenally successful Japanese National Railways (JNR) tourist campaign of the 1970s, "Discover Japan." Indeed, the whole nostalgia industry has come under repeated scholarly investigation. However, these studies focus on travel out from an urban centre into a rural periphery, and they firmly identify this movement with that of folklore and its search for authenticity in the premodern, pre-industrial landscape. The role of art, rather than folkcraft, and the role of early modern urban culture in this search for Japanese identity have been largely ignored.

In this chapter I analyze four museum exhibitions that took place in Japan in the fall/winter season of 1994-95.[1] Each of these exhibitions claimed to be presenting, and thus defining, *Nihon no Bi*, that is, "Japanese beauty" or "the beauty of Japan." Each used markedly different strategies, and focused to a certain extent on significantly different time periods and genres. Yet in all cases we can observe the kinds of discourse that are constructed in Japan for Japanese audiences to instill a sense of cultural uniqueness, that is, cultural nationalism.[2]

Marilyn Ivy's "Discover Japan" and "Exotic Japan"

Marilyn Ivy describes how the JNR Discover Japan campaign, inaugurated in 1970, was conceived of as a kind of "de-advertising" *(datsu kōkoku)*, setting itself in contrast to more typical tourist advertising. Rather than showing a famous tourist spot, such as Mount Fuji, "in Discover Japan ... the appeal was non-specific, to a Japan in general – unnamed, yet somehow recognizable. The encounter of young women – marginal to the workaday world – with natural beauty and rusticated 'tradition' (also marginal to the urban centers of Japan) created a repertoire of standard images of a Japan timelessly held in reserve for the traveler, ready to be discovered" (Ivy 1995, 47).

Such journeys were set in direct contrast to the everyday work world and urban society. Again, in Ivy's words: "*Tabi* [travel] is everything that society is not: it is the natural, the free, the rural, the humane, the nonordinary. In travel there is the promise of a retrieval of everything lost in the current age ... Self-discovery had to be rearticulated with the national-cultural object of Japan, the discovery of 'myself' mapped onto the terrain of the Japanese archipelago, now colonized by this expansive ego" (40). Ivy argues that the trope for this process is synecdoche (47):

> In previous domestic travel advertisements, a poster or a television commercial depicting a resort, a famous landscape, or an historical site had a specific, direct appeal. There was no necessary linkage between their specificity and a traditional Japan writ large, although undoubtedly those associations were made in the case of especially potent natural symbols of Japaneseness, like Mount Fuji. In the new campaign's strategy, however, the trope of synecdoche dominated, with parts of Japan, almost always vaguely identified, standing for Japan itself in all its native purity. Similarly, the (re)discovered "myself" also operated as a synecdoche of an essentially coterminous Japan.

In other words, the Discover Japan campaign was part and parcel of the renewed interest in Japanese folklore of the 1960s and 1970s. Japan was defined in contrast to its postwar self; it was, again in Ivy's words, "rural, remote, non-American, and non-rational."

By contrast, the JNR 1984 Exotic Japan campaign "reversed the terms ... [I]nstead of urging the (re)discovery of native Japan, it enticed travelers with images of non-native Japan" (Ivy 1995, 48). Ivy's description of the typical Exotic Japan poster sounds like the description of a museum exhibition (49):

> In none of these is the model set within a unified landscape, identified or otherwise. Rather, she is located – or dislocated – within an array of parts that indicate the exotic within Japan. The dominant rhetorical trope is metonymy – a contiguous linking of related objects – but the linkages do not constitute a narrative; the parts are not unified to form a totality, to tell a story. Exotic Japan is described by the elements it contains, its fragments, as the exotic is reduced to the level of objects. No longer is there the lure of tabi as self-discovery and holistic encounter with the scenic native, but rather the seductiveness of rare objects within a fragmented yet sumptuous space.

Ivy sums up the new relationship between Self and Other as: "Exotic Japan presents Japanese difference from and identity with both the Occident and the Orient as a matter of style" (51-53):

> Exotic Japan implies a counternarrative strategy: Japan is represented as a montage of exotic objects – brocades, statuary, paintings – around a New Wave teenager who looks enigmatically out from the montage, appearing herself as an object among objects. We are led to believe that what is really exotic is a Japan that can montage such disparities with such exciting aplomb. The seemingly indiscriminate cultural mixing and matching that some have taken as the hallmark of modern Japan becomes, in the global matrix of advanced capitalism, the stylish prerogative of an affluent nation.

My original hypothesis in this study was that, especially in the post-bubble economy of the 1990s, the museum or art exhibition has to some extent replaced the rural destination as "hometown" for the Japanese cultural consumer. Marilyn Ivy's work would suggest that if my hypothesis is true, then the museum-as-*furusato* trend would have two distinctive characteristics. The first would be an emphasis on visual style – evacuating content, and emphasizing what has been called the "visual distinction" of the object over its historical context (see Karp and Lavine 1991) – and the second, consequently, would be an erasure of history. In other words, one would expect both an absence of narrative or expository text, and at the same time an obfuscation of chronological specificity.

Japanesque – Rediscovery

The first art exhibition reviewed here is the *Nihon Bi Saihakken: Furi-Mukeba Japanesuku* (Japanesque – Rediscovery of Japanese Aesthetic Designs) at the Mitsukoshi Department Store in Tokyo (see Figure 10.1). At first glance this show would seem to be paradigmatic. Held in a major department store, produced by NHK Promotions (a quasi-governmental corporation), with a large number of tickets given away free, on show during the height of the New Year holiday season, this exhibition had a massive attendance. The original Japanese subtitle could be translated more literally: "When you look back, it's Japanesque!"[3]

This show, I would argue, is the 1990s version of the Exotic Japan campaign Marilyn Ivy has described. In fact, as the catalogue's introductory essay makes clear, the exoticizing of the Japanese past is the basis of the show. The apparent organizer, Yasumura Toshinobu, starts with the Meiji Restoration and repeats a completely standard (and largely discredited) narrative of modern Japanese history. In other words, the entire Meiji period is blanketly characterized by "indiscriminate" and "uncritical" westernization. This is followed by a total elision of the Taishō and early Shōwa periods, the replacement of Europe by America after 1945, with its "pragmatic thought and civilization," leading to the phenomenal economic growth of the 1970s and the culmination in a new reign, the Heisei Era. The new era has brought about attention to a new generation, in fact a "new Japanese," "who have been raised in an environment where the fact that Euro-American culture has been brought into everyday life is an extremely normal *(futsū)* thing." For these new Japanese, artifacts from Japan's past are seen as the same kind of object as artifacts from other Asian countries; in other words, they have become "ethnic."

This, of course, is the same premise found in the Exotic Japan campaign. Yet this discourse has a turn that saves it from complete self-alienation, in Yasumura's words: "It goes without saying that this spiritual pattern of incorporating alien cultures into daily life and taking pleasure in experiencing alien nations is a traditional expression of Japan." This Japan-as-exotic montage is what is defined as the "Japanesque." The idea here of Japanesque objects fitting into "our westernized ways of life" is not metaphorical, as the exhibition included several displays of Japanese *objets d'art* in use in a modern Japanese household setting (for example, a Western-style dinner table set with traditional Japanese plates; interestingly, the table was set for only two, indicating a relatively young couple without children).

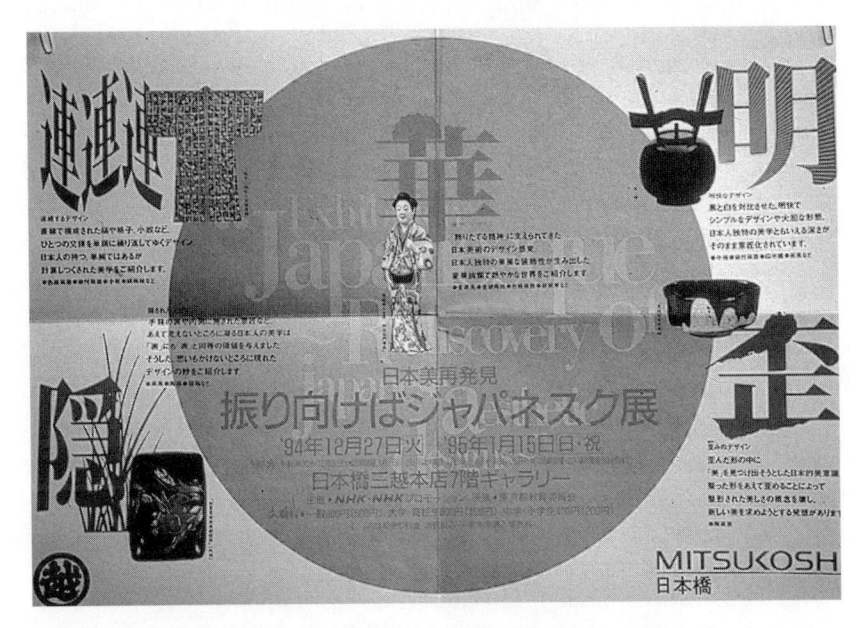

Figure 10.1 Catalogue cover from *Nihon Bi Saihakken: Furi-Mukeba Japanesuku* (Japanesque – Rediscovery of Japanese Aesthetic Designs), Mitsukoshi Department Store, Nihonbashi, Tokyo (27 December 1994 to 15 January 1995).

Whereas, according to Ivy, the *name* of the geographical location was virtually hidden in Discover Japan ads, in the "Japanesque" show it is the *dates* of the pieces that are hidden. While they in fact range from the Momoyama period up to Meiji, or the mid-sixteenth to the early twentieth century, one has to turn to the very end of the catalogue to ascertain the age of any specific piece, and the dates were not made part of the exhibition labels. Yet, given the emphasis on style that Ivy sees as central to the Exotic Japan mode, it is perhaps surprising that the images in the Japanesque show are heavily mediated by text. While the catalogue essays are relatively short (just one page), well over half of all the objects have their own commentary. In addition, all the objects are classified under one of five rubrics related to their design *(dezain)*:

- "Straightforward design" *(meikai na dezain)*
- "Hidden design" *(kakusareta dezain)*
- "Gorgeousness design" *(hanayagu dezain)*
- "Design that continues" *(renzoku suru dezain)*
- "Design of distortion" *(hizumi no dezain)*.

"Straightforward" (*meikai na dezain*)

Certainly the cover of the catalogue suggests an essay in cultural nationalism, with the *Hinomaru* Rising Sun appearing out from under the silhouette of a saké cask. If we were to enter the show's catalogue through this image, we would be led to the section on the *meikai*, or "straightforward." In fact, this was the largest section of the show, with the most objects, and also the longest section of the catalogue, with the most pages devoted to it. More importantly, its introductory essay was written by the same man who wrote the introduction to the whole show, Yasumura.

Kenkyūsha's New Japanese-English Dictionary defines *meikai* as "clear (thinking); articulate (pronunciation); lucid (explanation); explicit (statement); perspicuous (expression); clear-cut (answer); clear-cut (argument); unequivocal (statement)." Yasumura quotes the definition from the *Shōgakkan Nihon Kokugo Daijiten*: "*sappari to shite kimochi no yoi koto.*" *Kimochi no yoi koto* is something that "feels good" or "has or gives a good feeling." *Sappari to shite* is much more complicated; again, *Kenkyūsha* defines *sappari shita* as "clean; neat and tidy; frank; openhearted; plain and simple; refreshed." Clearly, in terms of design we are talking about "plain and simple," but, as we shall see, the moral dimension – "frank; openhearted" – cannot be ignored.

Yasumura defines "straightforward *dezain*" as simplified and magnified: "When an object is seized impressionistically, a simplification of the object takes place; and when there is bold decoration, an enlargement of the pattern occurs." His paradigm is found on the *hanten,* or jackets, with trademarks *(shirushi-banten)* of the Edo period, one of which just happens to be from the show's sponsor, Mitsukoshi. Yasumura also quotes approvingly from Yashiro Yukio's *The Character of Japanese Art (Nihon no Bijutsu no Tokushitsu),* which identifies four distinctive features in Japanese art (Yashiro 1942):

- its impressionistic nature *(inshō-sei)*
- its decorative nature *(sōshoku-sei)*
- its symbolic nature *(shōchō-sei)*
- its sentimental nature *(kanshō-sei).*

According to Yashiro, the Japanese appreciate nature "impressionistically." This term and concept, of course, are completely anachronistic when applied to Japan before the late nineteenth century, in other words, Japan before the introduction of Impressionism, which was used by poets such as Masaoka Shiki to justify the continued existence of such poetic genres as *tanka* and haiku. Nonetheless, according to Yashiro's explanation, the Japanese of all periods perceived and appreciated nature impressionistically, and the decorative characteristic of their art is what results when "nature that is felt impressionistically is expressed in art."[4] Such decoration, of course, is not *mere* decoration, but "symbolizes some kind of spiritual content." The Japanese seize on objects that would appeal "to a child's heart," and that look attractive when enlarged. Such childlike impressions are transferred to the picture-plane, uncorrected by "scientific [read 'Western'] knowledge" but rather as a "pure and naive dream."

Yasumura gives as an example a scene from the late Heian period, *Nezame Monogatari Emaki* (which he incorrectly identifies as a frontispiece, or *mi-gaeshi).* This painting – with its "large blossoms on the branches of the young cherry-trees, violating natural perspective, that all turn towards us, and are in simultaneous bloom, as if fireworks had been set off" – appeals "to the Japanese, who love cherry-blossoms" (remember, this is written in Japanese, for a Japanese audience).

Jumping to the Edo period, which is the touchstone of the show, Yasumura insists that the "aesthetic consciousness of feeling good with the plain and simple" *(sappari to shite kimochi ga yoi to iu bi-ishiki)* has something in common with the Edo natives' *(Edokko no)* concept of *iki,* or chic.[5] Such a consciousness is born from an *"isagiyoi* disposition." *Isagiyoi* is also a term with a variety of translations in English; Nelson's *Japanese-English Character Dictionary* gives: "pure, clean, righteous, manly, gallant, sportsmanlike." In Yasumura's words, it is the temperament of a man who would feel shamed if he had not spent all his money by the time a night of carousing was through (a well-worn Edo chestnut), who "rejects quarrelsome, confused and mixed-up countrified things *(gotagota shita yabottai mono)*, and likes open forms that keep nothing to themselves. The simplicity that we see in the trade-mark *hanten* that our chic older brothers *(iki na o-niisan-tachi)* liked to wear, with its straightforward contrasting colors and bold patterns resist-dyed in white on dark blue grounds, can indeed be called the acme of straightforward *dezain*."

"Hidden" *(kakusareta dezain)*

One might expect that the "hidden" *(kakusareta)* would be the opposite of the straightforward, but in fact it turns out to be much the same. The author of this essay starts by invoking the image of Tōyama Kinsan (Kinshirō), famous from a long-running television show. Tōyama is one of the two magistrates of Edo in its final days, and keeps an eye on the citizens by means of his persona of Kinsan, a playboy of the entertainment district. The *sutōrīno kuraimakkusu* is when the episode's miscreants are brought before Magistrate Tōyama and deny all charges, only to be confronted with the evidence of Kinsan, who is recognizable from his famous *sakura-fubuki*, or "cherry-blossom storm," tattoo, which he reveals in the midst of the court, stripping off his formal robe from one shoulder while his speech falls from the measured tones of the magistrate to the slangy rhythms of the street. Having evoked and rehearsed this icon from popular culture, the author of the essay notes: "Though the historical facts differ some from the story, and although it is known that the historical Tōyama Kinshirō never exposed to public view the tattoo he had applied in an excess of youthfulness, and never wore thin robes even in the hottest times of summer, still ... from the fact that even now he has become a popular television show, we can feel the tradition of the aesthetic consciousness towards concealing."

As can be guessed from this introduction, this section in particular is largely ahistorical. Although a variety of *haori*, or over-jackets, with interior designs are shown (including one with a gruesome execution, related, no doubt, to the fact that the recreations of torture chambers are a popular exhibition at such "living museums" as Edo Mura), not once does the author discuss or even mention the strict sumptuary laws of the period, which forbade all but the simplest decoration to the lower classes, including the merchants. In fact, some scholars have argued that it was the sumptuary restrictions imposed by the Tempō Reforms of the 1740s that led to the creation of a new kind of urban understated elegance, called *iki*. On the other hand, often "hiding" or "concealing" seems hardly the point: as in the showcased image of a rabbit that forms the decoration on the inside of the lid of a writing box, the outside of which can hardly be called plain.

The "Edo boom" is also apparent in the inclusion in this section of the only erotic image in the show, a set of Ōshima weave robes. The label entry reads:

In the zest for life seen in the chic *(iki)* way of wearing clothes, there is a difference in the designs of the plain outside and bold inside. While disguised in the plainness of Ōshima and Yūki weaves on the outside, in the under-robes and under-wear that can usually not be seen, they liked to display pictures that would surprise people. A "pillow-picture" ("spring picture," *shunga*) that paints a private joke of a man and woman in the bedroom is also one such example. Unfortunately, we are not allowed to show you this in the catalogue, but there is nothing offensive in the expression, and it is finished up in a frank *(sappari to shita)* design that reflects magnanimous *(oorakana)* Edo sexual consciousness.

As one can see, we are back to *sappari to shita* ("frank; openhearted"). In short, from all that we have seen so far, we would conclude that *Nihon no Bi,* or "Japanese beauty," was chiefly characterized by the Edo period and had a strong relationship to Edo chic, or *iki*. It is the bold, straightforward patterns of the urban merchants, who spent, expressed, and made love freely.

"Gorgeousness" *(hanayagu dezain)*

The most fascinating aspect of the Japanesque show was the contestation it manifested, that is, the evidence of art historians attempting to tell a story other than that already inscribed in the popular consciousness. For instance, "gorgeousness" is literally central, modelled by the female figurine who serves to mark the predominantly female viewers' point of entry and identification (see Figure 10.1). Yet, the catalogue entries tell a very complex story of identity construction. The showcased figurine appears together with another *bijin,* or "beauty," on a vase with the design of dancing women. The catalogue entry for the vase reads:

> Three scenes of kabuki dancing are painted in the three colors of gold, silver, and vermilion. This is the first work in which a "Japanese" *(nihonjin)* makes her appearance as a pattern in ceramics. Before this, only aliens, such as Southern Barbarians [Europeans] and Chinese, had been painted. The present piece was probably manufactured in the 1650s to 1670s.
>
> During this period, in painting as well, the "Kambun [Era] Beauty" was isolated from the genre paintings of the early Edo period and independent pictures of beautiful women *(bijinga),* which became the beginning of *ukiyo-e,* were popular. The wave of that vogue caused a large-scale revolution even as far as designs in porcelain.

This is followed by the entry for the figurine:

> This is a standing figurine, as if a Kambun [Era] Beauty had become three-dimensional. It was made with a mold, and that earthen mold has become

a topic in the news, having been rediscovered a few years ago in the ruins of Arita-machi's Akae-chō. Based on the luminous polychroming that is the distinctive feature of the Kakiemon style, a design of gorgeous water-drops has been painted on the woman's over-robe *(uchi-kake)*. No kimono with this kind of design is extant today, and it is an imaginary design of the painter's.

From the 1660s, the kilns of Bizen were facing a period of large-scale exporting to Europe. There are many examples of this figurine that have been handed down, chiefly in Europe, and no doubt it was something that was manufactured with an eye to export.

Together, then, these two works tell a curious tale. It was the alien (European, Chinese) that was first represented on porcelain, and next the indigenous Other, that is, Woman. In other words, the first depictions of "Japanese" in porcelain were as Other. And around the same time, such representations, such "beautiful women *(bijin),*" were being manufactured specifically to be sent to Europe – a kind of ceramic *kara-yuki,* or "export prostitution." The combination of object – "wares," in the sense of both "earthen-wares" and "wares to sell" – gender, national representation, and identity come together here in a fascinatingly overdetermined way. Whether most viewers of this exhibition saw this issue is, of course, another matter.

"Continuity" *(renzoku suru dezain)* and "Distorted" *(hizumi no dezain)*

Likewise, "continuity" refers not to unbroken tradition but to *renzoku suru dezain,* that is, repetitive patterns. The strongest contrast is provided by the smallest section, the "distorted" *(hizumi).* Here we are *not* regaled with quotations from the *Tsurezure-gusa* (a classical piece of Japanese literature) on the Japanese love of the incomplete, asymmetrical, warped, or bent. Rather, the historian situates the popularity of a certain kind of pottery in connection with the famous tea-master Furuta Oribe, and traces its rise and fall in popularity over a clearly defined historical period.

In other words, it would seem that we can see differing visions of Japanese beauty presented in this show. While the exhibition presented a trite image of Japanese tradition largely consonant with constructions supported by the *nihonjinron* industry and other forms of cultural nationalism, packaged in a exoticizing, postmodern format, a minority view suggests other perspectives, carefully historicized, that work against the very thesis of the show.

Japonisme in Vienna

Japanese exceptionalism can be seen as a form of "reverse orientalism," that is, as a defensive response to the orientalism of the West. The abiding orientalism of certain segments of the European community, and its coordination with the project of certain Japanese, was evident in *Uīn no Japonizumu* (*Japonisme* in Vienna), which ran from 20 December 1994 to 12 February 1995 at the Tōbu Museum of Art of the Tōbu Department Store (Figure 10.2). This show was co-organized with the MAK-Austrian Museum of Applied Arts, and received the support of the Austrian embassy in Japan (it also received assistance from Japan Airlines, the Japanese national carrier). The preface by the organizers contains echoes of things heard in the Japanesque show, but these expressions of understandable Japanese pride pale in comparison with the mystification of the introductory remarks of Peter Noever, Executive and Creative Director of the MAK (Austrian Museum of Applied Arts):

> A Japan that opens up to the West, admits reciprocal influences, yet at the same time preserves its own mystery, is something Europe has known since the first opening of Japan more than 120 years ago. That was a time when enigmatic objects, arcane in their simplicity, began to flood European markets. It was also the time when Europe began to imitate the Japanese vocabulary of forms in order to saturate them with Western content, because their real content, no matter how open and apparently accessible, remained hidden. The endurance of this mystery, which is obvious to Western eyes without the loss of any of its aura, has by no means been affected by a seeming reversal of *Japonisme* – the Americanization of the Far East, which makes out of Japan a more perfect America – since it is within this very perfection that the enigma is safeguarded yet again. The prejudice of the West distorts our vision. With amazement we can only speak about "Japan's lack of prejudice," its ability to absorb things from the outside, develop and in the end surpass them, without losing itself in the process.

This is such an amazing document, and so rich, that I would like to comment on it in sections. The basic scheme that Noever is using is that of the "Hollow Centre Model," or "Unchanging Core," most developed, with regard to both literature and visual art, by Katō Shūichi, who argues that Japan's unique character lies in the seemingly wholesale adoption of foreign influence, which yet never touches its unchanging and essential cultural core (see Miller 1980; Chino 2003). Note that in Noever's essay it is Europe that recognizes this always-mysterious Japan, not America, although it was obviously the Americans who caused "the first opening of Japan more than 120 years ago." Although Europe was "flooded" by Japanese objects, these objects remained and still remain unknowable, not because of any obfuscation on the part of the Japanese but because of their very simplicity. Such absolute alien-ness means that it is the Westerners

Figure 10.2 Catalogue cover from *Uīn no Japonizumu* (*Japonisme* in Vienna), Tōbu Museum of Art of the Tōbu Department Store, Tokyo (20 December 1994 to 12 February 1995).

(notice Noever's easy alternation between defining himself as a "Westerner" and a "European," depending on whether he wishes to include America in his condemnation or exclude Europe from it) who are the real "imitators" – indeed, the Japanese, who are completely without "prejudice," are able to absorb the foreign and surpass the West, while the West can only uncomprehendingly imitate Japan.

So we are experiencing today another twisting of the spiral of influence. High-tech and cars from Japan are flooding Western markets, at the very moment when Americanization seemed to have taken over where *Japonisme* left off. In the shortest time imaginable the tables have been turned. The West is again staring spellbound at Japan, again surrounded by Japanese utilitarian objects, and again uncomprehending.

But why is there an artificiality clinging to every example of *Japonisme*, one that never achieves a satisfying integration of the "alien" element and remains, so to speak, flashy, half-baked exoticism? To put it another way, why is it that not one work of "Japanized" graphic art created at the turn of the century will ever have the unforced naturalness of a Honda or a Sony Walkman? Or that a "Haikuized" sketch by Altenberg will never have the ease displayed by Japanese interpreters of Bach?

This is an amazing display of cultural self-flagellation. It also questions the very raison d'être of the show itself: if Viennese Japonesque design is so unsatisfying, why is the exhibition visitor about to look at 270 examples of it?

How, then, does the Japanese perfecting of Western technology differ from the Japanisms of our century, as they developed from the introduction of Far Eastern motifs and ornaments, the acquisition of compositional techniques, the supposed adoption of an "attitude to life," which had been promoted by Hermann Bahr? It would be comforting to believe that cool and calculating technique is opposed to philosophical engagement. But the truth is that the Western strategies of appropriation are based just as much on expediency and self-interest as the Eastern ones, all the way from the improvement of indigenous handicrafts to Zen seminars for the managers of the 1990s. The fact is that every form of *Japonisme* expresses an attempt to find oneself in the alien element, exposing a sense of cultural deficiency that stands in sharp contrast to Japanese self-assurance.

I do not know Mr. Noever's field of expertise, but one senses that he has no love of *Japonisme* or, for that matter, Asia. For by his logic it is clear that every attempt to borrow, adopt, or indeed learn something foreign must not only fail but be driven by the need for mere self-recognition, and an admission of cultural deficiency. Presumably an Austrian replete with a secure sense of cultural self-identity would have no need to look for or at anything beyond his own borders. "Yet the enigma still remains, at least in our eyes. The emphasis has merely shifted from the mysteries of an inimitable command of line and an inexplicable gift for 'extracting the essence out of every object' (Gustav Gugitz, *Ver Sacrum* 1, 1898) to an equally inexplicate technical and commercial competence."

It seems to me that this appears to be exactly what we do not want art and other cultural forms to do, that is, to serve as mystifications of and substitutes for real economic and political explanations. It will come as no surprise that Noever's essay ends with admiring quotations from Roland Barthes's *Empire of Signs*.[6]

The academic essays and labels of this show surprisingly have none of this mystifying orientalism. In fact, one of the very premises of the show is the distinctive nature of Vienna's *Japonisme,* that it is significantly different from the Japanese-inspired art found in Paris or London, based both on the different nature of artistic patronage and marketing in Vienna at the turn of the century and on the distinctive selection of Japanese artifacts that found their way to Vienna. Surely such difference in effect undermines the belief in some invariable essence inherent in Japanese art. The essays are fine, historically specific examinations of the introduction to and use of certain kinds of Japanese objects in Vienna at a certain period of time, and the influence they can be seen to have, along with other influences such as Byzantine and Egyptian, on the art of Gustav Klimt and others. The show was in fact based on an earlier one mounted in Vienna in 1990. Yet again, one wonders how much of their message got through to the viewers in Japan. Reading only the organizer's statement, not reading the catalogue or its fine essays, isn't it likely that what the average Japanese viewer saw was simply the evidence of Japan's undeniable, and unjustly neglected, influence on (a) Western culture?

Two *Nihon no Bi*

In the six-month period between October 1994 and March 1995, there were two shows entitled *Nihon no Bi,* or "The Beauty of Japan," and they form an instructive contrast. The more straightforward (if I may be allowed the term) of the two was *(Heisei 6-nendo Kokuritsu Hakubutsukan/Bijutsukan Chihō Junkai-ten) Nihon no Bi* (Annual Exhibition of National Museums and National Art Galleries Held in Provincial Regions for the Year 1995: Japanese Beauty). As the title suggests, this is a travelling show that took works belonging to the national museums out to the provinces, this year to Gunma prefecture. In other words, this is a state-supported enterprise, presenting a national history of art to a peripheral community. This involved some unacknowledged repatriation, as 6 of the 155 objects originally came from the area that is now Gunma. One of the introductory sections (p. 3) gives the kind of thumbnail sketch of Japanese beauty that we are looking for:

> While our country did receive the influence of Chinese continental culture, we came to support a unique aesthetic consciousness [or "awareness of beauty"]. From this was born the fine and elegant *yamato-e* ["Japanese painting" of the Heian period], and again the tea-masters of the Muromachi and Momoyama periods discovered a sublime beauty in coarse objects which had not been recognized on the continent, and they brought the art of tea-ceremony to perfection. Japanese art, in general, values abstraction rather than naturalistic accuracy, and it is pointed out that it is plain and simple, as well as decorative. In the present exhibition, where many beautiful works from various fields compete with each other under one roof, we expect that the aesthetic consciousness that runs through Japanese art will arise in you.

Clearly the counter-narrative strategy of Exotic Japan has not yet reached the staid halls of the Tokyo National Museum or Agency for Cultural Affairs *(Bunkachō)*. The exhibition was organized in a roughly chronological/generic order, as the following list will make clear:

Antiquities *(kōko)*	27 objects
Sculpture *(chōkoku)*	5
Metalwork *(kinkō)*	14
Swords *(tōken)*	6
Lacquerwork *(shikkō)*	8
Pottery *(tōji)*	15
Tea ceremony *(chanoyu)*	9
Noh theatre *(nō)*	12
Textiles *(senshoku)*	2
Painting *(kaiga)*	18
Ancient calligraphy *(shoseki)*	11
Modern painting *(kindai kaiga)*	22
Modern sculpture *(kindai chōkoku)*	6

It is apparent that, after "Antiquities," it is modern painting that gets the largest representation. Likewise, in the premodern category, painting is best represented. Sculpture, modern and premodern, is clearly marginal, as are antiquities, to the narrative we heard above, despite their large numbers. "Antiquities" starts with *dogū* clay figurines, and features three striking *haniwa* from Gunma. "Sculpture" consists of Buddhist art from the seventh century to the thirteenth, reflecting the common wisdom that the Kamakura period represents the acme of Japanese sculpture, with nothing of significance being produced subsequently. "Metalwork" consists of Buddhist implements and more mirrors, but not "swords," which also encompasses their mountings. The distinctive Japanese sword dates, of course, from the Kamakura period, and the lacquer mountings on display, although actually dating from the nineteenth century, lead naturally into the next category of "lacquerwork." Here again we follow a chronological progression, from a late Heian-period saddle (the catalogue tells us that the shape of Japanese saddles is unique in the world) to an eighteenth-century mirror stand. "Pottery" goes from Heian jars to eighteenth-century plates, and in this section in particular the entries constantly insist on the distinctively Japanese character of the objects.

The major departure from this taxonomy is the sudden introduction of the categories of tea ceremony *(chanoyu)* and Noh drama. What the category of *chanoyu* first allows is the inclusion of Chinese works in a show on Japanese beauty. We have ink paintings and calligraphy from the Southern Sung period. The introductory essay to this section also speaks of the transformation of Chinese tea drinking into Japanese *chanoyu,* and the creation of such aesthetic concepts as *hie, sabi,* and *karabi.* In the Noh section, we move from masks to costumes (all Momoyama and Edo period), the latter segueing to regular *kosode* of the Edo period. In contrast to the Japanesque show, with its emphasis on textiles, there are only two kimonos in the Gunma show.

Painting brings us back to the Heian period. Interestingly, there is only one example of *yamato-e,* a piece from the *Satake-bon Imaginary Portraits of the Thirty-Six Poetic Immortals.* Three Muromachi *suiboku-ga,* then in quick succession Kano, Rimpa, Tosa, and Ōkyo (Figure 10.3). Back to Kano screens, then Ike no Taiga, *ukiyo-e* by Miyagawa Chōshun, and ending with fan paintings by Watanabe Kazan, that is, a thoroughly standard rehearsal of canonical artists and the genre therefore most closely identified with.

Next comes calligraphy, with Buddhist sutras; the *Nihon Shoki* (appropriately enough); the *Man'yōshū;* and examples up to GoYōzei's neoclassical forms. Finally "modern painting" with *nihonga* from 1908 to 1974, then "Western painting" from 1890 to 1934, and then "modern sculpture," with five pieces ending with a Rodinesque bronze from 1910. The isolation of "modern" painting and sculpture serves to protect the supposed purity of "premodern" Japanese art.[7]

In contrast to this rather standard historical survey of Japanese art, we have an exhibition mounted in conjunction with the celebration of the 1,200th anniversary of the founding of Kyoto: *Dentō to Kindai - Nihon no Bi* (translated in the catalogue as "Traditional Beauty in Japanese Art," but more literally "Tradition and Modernity: The Beauty of Japan"). This show was held at the National Museum of Modern Art, Kyoto (12 October to

Museum as Hometown: What Is "Japanese Beauty"? 237

13 November 1994) and the National Museum of Modern Art, Tokyo (22 November to 18 December 1994) (Figure 10.4). Clearly, the purpose of this show was to demonstrate the continuity between premodern and modern Japanese art. Interestingly, the objects were limited entirely to paintings (remember the relative emphasis on painting in the Gunma show as well). This decision is explained by the Director of the National Museum of Modern Art, Kyoto, Tomiyama Hideo, thus: he claims that *Nihon no Bi* is too multifarious and complex to present in its entirety, so the organizers of the show have concentrated on just one part, that is, painting from the Heian period onwards, and within this genre they thought to focus on "line" *(sen)* and "colour" *(iro)*. Even that is too broad, and so they have concentrated on "the beauty of the drawn line" *(senbyō no utsukushisa)*, its transformations and transitions.

Tomiyama goes on to explain that the painting tradition that Japan inherited from China, with its emphasis on line, stands in contrast to the Western tradition, in which such artists as Delacroix and Cezanne deny the existence of the line in nature. Tomiyama's next task is to distinguish Japanese art from Chinese. He does this by using the hackneyed theory of

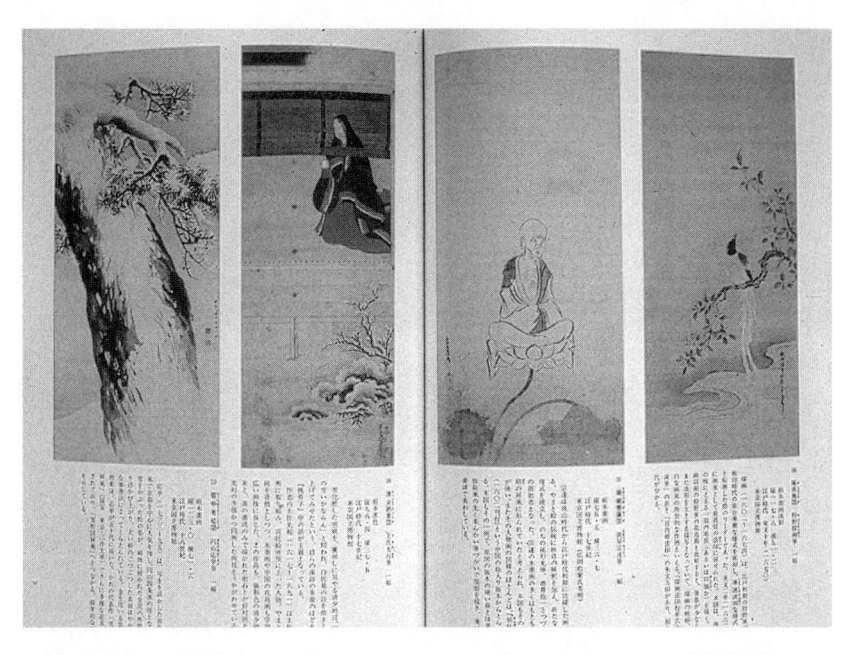

Figure 10.3 Double-page spread from the catalogue for the exhibition *(Heisei 6-nendo Kokuritsu Hakubutsukan/Bijutsukan Chihō Junkai-ten) Nihon no Bi* (Annual Exhibition of National Museums and National Art Galleries Held in Provincial Regions for the Year 1995: Japanese Beauty), Gunma Prefectural Museum of Modern Art (25 February to 26 March 1995).

Figure 10.4 Catalogue cover from *Dentō to Kindai – Nihon no Bi* (Traditional Beauty in Japanese Art), National Museum of Modern Art, Kyoto (12 October to 13 November 1994) and National Museum of Modern Art, Tokyo (22 November to 18 December 1994).

ebbs and flows of foreign influence. That is, the Japanese alternate times of massive importation of Chinese (or foreign) influence with other periods of introspection in which they develop "beauty peculiar to Japan" *(nihon koyū no bi)*.

Such "beauty peculiar to Japan" was, according to Tomiyama, undoubtedly concentrated in the Heian period, which gave rise to *yamato-e*. The term *yamato-e* appears for the first time in the Heian period as a term paired with *kara-e* ("China pictures"). Akiyama Terukazu demonstrated long ago, however, that throughout the Heian period these two terms did not refer to differences in style but simply content – *yamato-e* were "pictures of Yamato," that is, Japan, while *kara-e* were pictures of China (Akiyama 1964). "The first firmly documented use of 'Yamato-e' in a stylistic sense, in fact, is not found before the 15th century. During the Muromachi period (1473-1568) the influx of Chinese ink painting of the Sung and Yūan tradition apparently stimulated a consciousness of 'style' that prompted a particular distinction between *kara-e* as Chinese ink painting *(sumi-e)*, and Yamato-e as the brilliant colored court style and traditional subject matter of the Tosa school" (McDonald 1976, 3-4).

In light of this definition, one would expect the organizers to concentrate more on colour than on line, but in fact the first work in the show that Tomiyama refers to is the *Scroll of Frolicking Animals (Chōjū jinbutsu giga)*. However, this scroll has no relation to any known *monogatari* (court literary romance), which Tomiyama previously identified as a characteristic of *yamato-e*. Nor is it a product of the court, but of the monastery atelier. If it is true that *yamato-e* had no stylistic significance in this period, then there is nothing about this scroll's use of line that makes it distinctly Japanese. Tomiyama's discussion completely ignores the heavily pigmented paintings, such as the *Tale of Genji Illustrated Scrolls,* that are typically thought of as representative of courtly *yamato-e* of the Heian period. Instead, when he considers pigmented works, he goes to the more lightly pigmented works of the Kamakura period, such as *Hell Scrolls* or the various depictions of battle.

In light of Tomiyama's specialty, that is, modern art, it is perhaps not surprising that the individual artist and his genius are given far more stress in this show than in the Gunma show (we might note that no female artists are included in the show). In fact, the catalogue entries focus, whenever possible, on the *artists,* not the objects, and several works by individual artists are included, again in contrast to the Gunma show or the craft orientation of the Japanesque show. Here we start to find the concessive grammatical constructions of cultural nationalism: "despite the fact that he continued to learn Chinese painting, this is a work in which it is possible to indicate the decorative, Japanese, elements." Talented individuals become the means of uniting Japanese and Chinese, or Japanizing the foreign. The catalogue repeats the party line about Kano Motonobu from the

Honchō Gashi, that he "combined the Japanese with the Chinese" *(kan nishite wa o kaneru),* what Gene Phillips has called "the Kano myth," which elides the very existence of Buddhist painters and reduces everything to a thesis/antithesis/synthesis between China and Japan (Phillips 1994).

The nationalistic emphasis on the scroll format, and scrolls of the Kamakura period, is also seen in a show presented in the new gallery of the Imperial Palace from 8 October to 1 December 1994. Here, too, we are told: "Even from among all our country's cultural heritage, whether seen from the aspect of their form, their pictorial expression, the calligraphy of their textual passages, or their literary content, illustrated handscrolls are certainly one thing in which Japanese uniqueness is especially rich." This chauvinism of the imperial gallery is not just limited to ancient works – as the emperor is the "symbol of the people," so, apparently, must his art collection be the symbol of the nation. The next exhibition was in celebration of the New Year, and was in fact on works of celebration, starting with the familiar words: "From of old in our country" *(furuku kare waga kuni dewa)* (Figure 10.5).

In Lieu of a Conclusion

A number of observations can be made from these reviews of "museum as *furusato*" art displays, which inform our understanding of the "museum" or "exhibition" boom in contemporary Japan, and the commodification of Japan for modern urban consumers.

First, the display of Japanese art in Japan today is an intensely nationalistic activity. Rarely is Japanese art shown in a larger Asian context;[8] rather, its focus is always on the retrieval of some putative identity. While trendier shows, such as the Mitsukoshi Japanesque, may employ a new postmodern counter-narrative strategy, most of the shows are firmly based on teleological narratives created shortly after the end of the Greater East Asian and Pacific war. Just as during that war, Japan is situated within Asia, primarily in contrast to a monolithic West that is largely conceived of in post-Renaissance terms. In other words, the West is the modern West, and Japan is a premodern, pre-West Japan. Western influence is not recognized until after the Meiji Restoration, and similarities between Japan's, for example, twelfth century and the twelfth century of any culture in Europe are never broached.

Second, just two time periods are typically chosen as the touchstone for Japanese beauty. The first is the Heian period, when the term *yamato-e* first arose, and the second is the Edo period. Yet, the reference to the Heian period does not necessarily entail a valorization of court culture, and a deceptively quick slide is made from the Heian period to the Kamakura period, the latter being the period from which most illustrated scrolls survive. In other words, the Heian period is seen as important because of

Figure 10.5 Handbill for an exhibition, *Keiga ni yosete* (Gathering Felicitations), the Museum of Imperial Collections, Sannomaru Shozokan Imperial Palace, Tokyo (4 January to 20 February 1995).

the term *yamato-e*, but the extant works that are shown are from the Kamakura period and derive from a culture that is not necessarily strictly aristocratic or courtly.[9] On one hand, then, we have the "Japanese beauty" of what is identified as the Heian period but is actually represented by Kamakura-period illustrated handscrolls. On the other hand, there is the tendency to situate Japanese beauty in the Edo period, as derived from eighteenth- and nineteenth-century urban culture (no doubt under the influence of Kuki Shūzō) (Pincus 1996). This was a period of rapid commodification in Japan, and it is not surprising that its recommodification is of interest to Japanese publishers and other purveyors of cultural products.

The majority of scholars and curators in either period are careful, conscientious, historically specific researchers. What we have been examining here, however, are shows sponsored either by large commercial enterprises – department stores and national newspapers – or governmental and quasi-governmental agencies – NHK Productions, the Imperial Household Agency, and the national museums. It is here that the *Nihon no Bi* discourse appears and is ritualistically enacted. Or rather, it is here that it is purveyed. In the end, Japanese beauty is a commodity that interpolates its consumers, a commodity that, like any good commodity, creates the need for itself in the consumer. Japanese beauty, and Japaneseness, are both something that the state and big business need to sell to the inhabitants of the Japanese archipelago, whose national identity is defined by their consumption.

Such a trend, of course, is only strengthened through globalization, where each country attempts to "brand" itself, that is, create an image of itself and its products with a "brand-name" identity to be purveyed abroad. In a way, then, the manufacture of such brand-name cultural products for the domestic market serves partly as a run-up to the greater competition in the international market, much as happened in the field of electronic goods. What will be intriguing to watch as we move into the twenty-first century is how a discourse of cultural nationalism and aesthetic uniqueness will interact with the equally important emerging discourse of "the Asia-Pacific" and Japanese efforts at closer regional integration in Asia under its own political lead.

Notes

1 The art museum exhibitions and catalogues examined in this chapter are:

- *Nihon Bi Saihakken: Furi-Mukeba Japanesuku* (Japanesque – Rediscovery of Japanese Aesthetic Designs), Mitsukoshi Department Store, Nihonbashi, Tokyo (27 December 1994 to 15 January 1995)
- *Uīn no Japonizumu* (*Japonisme* in Vienna), Tōbu Museum of Art of the Tōbu Department Store, Tokyo (20 December 1994 to 12 February 1995)
- (*Heisei 6-nendo Kokuritsu Hakubutsukan/Bijutsukan Chihō Junkai-ten*) *Nihon no Bi* (Annual Exhibition of National Museums and National Art Galleries Held in Provincial Regions

for the Year 1995: Japanese Beauty), Gunma Prefectural Museum of Modern Art (25 February to 26 March 1995)
- *Dentō to Kindai – Nihon no Bi* (Traditional Beauty in Japanese Art), National Museum of Modern Art, Kyoto (12 October to 13 November 1994) and National Museum of Modern Art, Tokyo (22 November to 18 December 1994).

2 On cultural nationalism in Japan, see Yoshino 1992 and Befu 1993.
3 Ivy (1995, 57), speaking of the "neo-Japonesque," writes: "The Japonesque, of course, already references the French appropriation of things Japanese in the realm of the aesthetic. In the realm of styled surfaces and commodity bodies, the neo-Japonesque counterpoints the distinctions that Exotic Japan rhetorically enfolds: the repetitively ever-new domestic (re)appropriation of what the French did to Japanese style, now retrofitted for hip Japanese delectation." The current Japanese spelling of the word, however, is *japan-esuku*, rather than *japonesuku*, as would be expected if the term derived from French.
4 On the "decorative in Japanese art," especially the Rimpa school, see Tamamushi 1999. In English, see Clark 1998. In fact, as both Tamamushi and Clark's research show, the "decorative" Rimpa school has been held as axiomatic of Japanese art since the beginning of the twentieth century. Space will not permit, however, consideration of the one "Japanese Beauty" show devoted to Rimpa in the 1994-95 season (see Asahi Shinbun-sha 1994).
5 The identification of *iki* with Japanese aesthetic consciousness comes from Kuki (1930), who started the modern tradition of what has been called "key-word essentialism." On Kuki, see Pincus 1996.
6 Noever's quote is the following: "I do not look at 'the essence of the East' with infatuated eyes: the Orient is a matter of complete indifference to me ... What we can strive for in our contemplation of the East are not different symbols, are not different metaphysics, is not a different wisdom ... but the possibility of a difference, of a mutation, of a revolution in the character of the symbol system ... A dream: to descend into the untranslatable and feel the shock, without it ever weakening, until the entire Occident within us begins to totter."
7 On the ideological alignment between genre and theme in modern Japanese painting, see Ikeda 1998, 194-200.
8 An important exception to this was the "Japanese, Korean and Chinese Art of the 16th Century" show held from 26 April to 29 May 1988 at the Osaka Municipal Museum of Art.
9 However, the association between Japanese art and the Imperial Household is one that is made repeatedly in the last quarter of the twentieth century. See Mostow 1999. The related issues of the feminization of cultural consumerism and its link to nationalism and, in particular, the emperor system, are beyond the scope of this chapter. See, however, Kamakura and Chino 1999.

References

Akiyama, T. 1964. *Heian jidai sezokuga no kenkyū* (Research on the secular painting of the Heian Period). Mimeograph. Tokyo: Yoshikawa Kōbankane.
Asahi Shinbun-sha. 1994. *Nihon-bi no Seika: Rimpa* (The flower of Japanese beauty: Rimpa). Tokyo: Asahi Shinbun-sha.
Befu, H., ed. 1993. *Cultural Nationalism in East Asia: Representation and Identity.* Research Papers and Policy Studies 39. Berkeley: Institute of East Asian Studies, University of California.
Chino, K. 2003. "Gender in Japanese Art." In J.S. Mostow, N. Bryson, and M. Greyhill, eds., *Gender and Power in the Japanese Visual Field.* Honolulu: University of Hawaii Press (in press).
Clark, T. 1998. "'The Intuition and the Genius of Decoration': Critical Reactions to Rimpa Art in Europe and the USA during the Late Nineteenth and Early Twentieth Centuries." In Y. Yamane, M. Naitō, and T. Clark, eds., *Rimpa Art from the Idemitsu Collection, Tokyo.* London: British Museum Press, 68-82.
Ikeda, S. 1998. *Nihon Kaiga no Josei-zō* (The image of women in Japanese painting). Tokyo: Chikuma Shobō.

Ivy, M. 1995. *Discourses of the Vanishing: Modernity, Phantasm, Japan.* Chicago: University of Chicago Press.
Kamakura, T., and K. Chino, eds. 1999. *Onna? Nihon? Bi? Aratana Jendaa Hihyo ni Mukete* (Woman? Beauty? Japan? Towards a new gender criticism). Tokyo: Keio Gijuku Daigaku Shuppan-kai.
Karp, I., and S.D. Lavine, eds. 1991. *Exhibiting Cultures: The Poetics and Politics of Museum Displays.* Washington, DC: Smithsonian Institution Press.
Kuki, S. 1930. *"Iki" no Kōzō* (The anatomy of "chic"). Tokyo: Iwanami.
McDonald, L. 1976. "The Masculine and Feminine Modes of Heian Secular Painting and Their Relationship to Chinese Painting – A Redefinition of Yamato-e." Unpublished PhD dissertation, University of Michigan.
Miller, R.A. 1980. "Plus ça change, ..." *Journal of Asian Studies* 49(4): 771-82.
Mostow, J. 1999. "Nihon no Bijutsushi Gensetsu to 'Miyabi'" (Art historical discourse in Japan and "courtliness"). In Tokyo Kokuritsu Bunkazai Kenkyūjo, eds., *Kataru Genzai Katarareru Kako: Nihon no Bijutsushi 100-nen* (The present that tells, the past that is told of: 100 years of art history in Japan). Tokyo: Heibonsha, 232-39. Also published in English as: "'Miyabi' and Japanese Art Historical Discourse." In International Symposium on the Preservation of Cultural Property, *The Present, and the Discipline of Art History in Japan.* Tokyo National Research Institute of Cultural Properties (1999), 70-76.
Phillips, Q.E. 1994. "*Honchō gashi* and the Kano myth." *Archives of Asian Art* 47: 46-57.
Pincus, L. 1996. *Authenticating Culture in Imperial Japan: Kuki Shūzō and the Rise of National Aesthetics.* Berkeley: University of California Press.
Tamamushi, S. 1999. "Kōrin-kan no Henken – 1815-1915" (Transitions in the image of Kōrin – 1815-1915). *Bijutsu Kenkyū* (Journal of Art Studies), no. 371 (March): 1-70.
Yashiro, Y. 1942. *Nihon no Bijutsu no Tokushitsu.* Tokyo: Iwanami Shoten.
Yoshino, K. 1992. *Cultural Nationalism in Contemporary Japan: A Sociological Enquiry.* London: Routledge.

11
Continuity and Change in Japan
David W. Edgington

> Japan – Land of Contrast, is everybody's cliché: the country seems so modern and Western, but so traditional and Japanese, changing rapidly yet staying the same.
>
> – J.C. Campbell, *Politics and Culture in Japan*

Introduction

Our discussion thus far has concentrated on Japan's underlying continuities, linking the past with the present. But what of the future? What changes should or could occur? The results of these studies suggest that, for better or worse, history, continuity, and certainty have assuredly made a difference. Indeed, stability and predictability in economic, political, and social life have undoubtedly been good for postwar, "catch-up" Japan (Kingston 2001). But now, in the new century, the past is widely seen as an unhelpful model. The traditions of the 1950s and the 1960s were designed to gain rapid and unimpeded national economic growth under difficult circumstances. Nevertheless, this older system, should it continue, is almost certainly going to lead to widespread economic, political, and social failure. There now appears to be such a crack in the existing paradigm that Japan's postwar system cannot continue indefinitely. Many are calling for a "regime shift" (Pempel 1998). But if the postwar arrangements for governing the country have really played themselves out, and if the Japanese are actually ready for something new, then to what degree do Japan's history and traditions really provide a barrier to change?

Just after the essays in this book were prepared, the events of 2001 brought a new set of issues into play. First, in the early summer, Japan had a new prime minister, Koizumi Junichiro, who was intensely committed to reform and change. Then, the 11 September terrorist attacks on the United States caused the Japanese economy to descend into yet another recession. By the end of the year, Japan was close to slipping into a crisis, with the economy entering negative growth and unemployment and company bankruptcies at record levels, along with declining trade surpluses and the declining value of the yen (Katz 2001).

In light of this continuing turbulence and volatility, I propose in this concluding chapter to address a number of questions, including: What needs to be done? What reforms are in the wind? And can Japan really change? Let us first consider what is at stake.

Economic and Political Issues

The first broad area of concern comprises economic and political issues. Many other books explore the causes and cures of the country's present economic crisis (e.g., Katz 1998; Freedman 1999; Porter et al. 2000; Lincoln 2001). The underlying challenge here is structural; namely, how to transform a system that so effectively built a manufacturing base in the postwar period into one that can instead support a mature economy, while also having to support an aging population.

To begin with, one area that has to be addressed is the balance of support given to Japan's internationally competitive industries and those that are inefficient but still overly protected. As noted by Keizo Nagatani in Chapter 2 of this book, the government has explicitly assisted a number of ineffective industries to facilitate their "soft landing" in a time of structural change, such as agriculture, heavy manufacturing, and certain service industries. However, this has surely harmed the more successful sectors of the economy that are competitive but that depend on Japanese-made inputs. Moreover, the high cost structure of many domestic services (especially finance, retailing, transportation, and construction) has burdened other economic activity and given Japan the highest consumer prices among member countries of the Organization for Economic Co-operation and Development (OECD) (Katz 1998). Besides, Japan in the new millennium cannot rely only on basic manufacturing to create its economic strength, since many of its Asian neighbours can offer lower production costs. Unless Japan revives its overall productivity and overcomes its high-cost and dual economy at home, it will continue to lose the most efficient manufacturing firms to offshore investment. While Japanese firms have certainly moved on to higher-technology areas, they currently lag behind the US and other Western countries in developing both new service sector business as well as "new economy" technologies, such as the Internet.

Another important pressure on the economy in Japan concerns changes playing out in the country's labour force.[1] The dearth of children and a rapidly aging society will lead to a labour shortage in the first two decades of the millennium. By one estimate, the working population is predicted to decline by an annual rate of at least 1.5 percent by the year 2014 (Kingston 2001, 94). By another, from the year 2010, the government estimates that two workers will retire for every new worker entering the workforce (Kingston 2001, 87). This will have an enormous impact on the employment practices of Japanese firms. As mentioned by Lonny E. Carlile in Chapter 3, labour unions such as Rengō have failed to address this new challenge. Accordingly, they must expect to see a decline in the role of enterprise unions, together with the other "sacred treasures" of lifetime employment and seniority-based wages (Sako and Sako 1997).

What changes are necessary in the Japanese labour market? First, there must be more effective utilization of older people. This will mean revision of pension schemes from fifty-five to sixty, and even sixty-five years or more. There must also be an age discrimination employment act to allow people to find new jobs after their official retirement. Second, current attitudes must change to integrate women more fully into the labour force. This can be done only by firms shifting towards paid maternity leave and less gender discrimination. Third, a larger influx of foreign workers to Japan has to be accommodated, especially in the information technology (IT) sector.[2] Finally, for individuals there must be public support for lifetime retraining programs in response to firms moving towards merit-based promotion and pay. All these changes are certainly possible in the coming years, but are nonetheless daunting. How the union movement responds will be an important factor in its viability.

When considering the future of the Japanese economy, Katz (2000, 10) has made a rather startling finding. He argues that sluggish productivity growth and a falling working population probably mean that Japan's "high-water mark" may have already passed: "After a spectacular rise from the 1950s onwards, Japan's share of the world economy probably peaked at 9 percent some time between 1986 and 1991." Moreover, he asserts that Japan cannot expect economic growth much higher than just 1-2 percent annually for the foreseeable future, even with a move towards Western-style deregulation. Yet a further encumbrance to growth, as pointed out by Roger Smith in Chapter 4, is Japan's particular vulnerability to disruption of large-scale imports of resources from overseas. Food security in particular is an ongoing concern, and this has been further heightened by the impact of the 11 September terrorist attacks. The Ministry of Agriculture, Forestry and Fisheries has drawn attention to the country's special vulnerability to imported foods, and to the fact that priority should be placed on ensuring that Japan is a safe nation in which people can live in security in the new millennium (*Japan Today* 2001a).

Reforms in the economy, in the workplace, and in corporate life must be mirrored by changes in political life. A discussion of the problems of Japanese politics at century's end has been presented by Schlesinger (1997) and Curtis (1999). Pertinent issues include Japan's pork-barrel style of politics, a secretive and powerful bureaucracy, and a general inability of the political system to effectively articulate and deal with a range of domestic and international policy problems. Apart from a new breed of politicians, political reform in Japan also needs stronger consumer movements and stronger nongovernmental organizations (NGOs). The discretionary power of government makes people overly submissive because they do not know what their rights are. Japan has never developed a forceful consumer movement and civil society with NGOs that could expose unfairness and heavy-handed government, and inform citizens of the precise ways in which they are disadvantaged. Nowhere in Japan today are to be found strong general-purpose watchdog groups that can blow the whistle on corruption and bid-rigging or harmful chemicals. The usual cast of civil society individuals that might have mounted some challenge to the powerful bureaucracies, business groups, and politicians – the present-day press, the union movement, and the universities – seem incapable of doing so.

Japan's Identity Abroad and at Home

Japan's objectives for the twenty-first century must go beyond that of economic growth at all costs, a goal that appeared to dominate most of the twentieth century. As noted by Bill Sewell in Chapter 5, Japan has for a long time denied its own history and focused only on a policy of catching up with the US and other Western countries. But now Japan must think about the sort of nation it wishes to become and its relationship with the rest of the world.

Better relations with its neighbours in Asia are called for, especially with China, as Japan's corporate diaspora continues. For the foreseeable future, Japan's international identity will revolve more around its relations with the rest of Asia than with the United States, which has been its mainstay for most of the past fifty years.

Japan's relations with China remain a paradox, however. On the one hand, and despite the many problems involved in their bilateral trade relations, it is likely that trade between China and Japan will grow significantly over the next two decades and possibly surpass that between Japan and the US. Thus, one study suggests that China and Japan could generate up to 28 percent of world trade in 2075, compared with just 13 percent in the mid-1990s (East Asia Analytical Unit 1996). One rather optimistic scenario arising from this trend is that an economic partnership between China and Japan will occur, creating a "double yolk" economy in East Asia, similar to the relationship between France and Germany, partners in the European Union. On the other hand, mutual trust on the political level is still not very high between these two countries. There are also likely to be continuing problems and controversies, for instance, over territorial issues, the status of Taiwan, China's military power, its human rights record, and "Japanese militarism." The central question concerning Sino-Japanese relations, therefore, is whether relations between the two Asian powers will remain amicable or whether their historical rivalry will reignite.

Whatever happens, considering their cultural and geographical proximity, one may expect that bilateral interaction will move beyond trade relations to an unprecedented level in the twenty-first century. One is struck by the staggering human interaction between China and Japan in recent years. For instance, not only have student numbers increased but the two-way flow of visitors is now over 1 million persons per year (East Asia Analytical Unit 1996). Consequently, the future of Sino-Japanese relations probably lies somewhere between the "friendly neighbour" and "potential rivals" schools of analysis. It will be a challenge to steer diplomatic policy so that China and Japan emerge not as military rivals but as both economic partners and competitors for influence in East Asia.

At home, Japan must accept more diversity in its population, especially in the area of minority rights, as expressed by Millie Creighton in Chapter 6. Presently, Korean residents, Burakumin, Ainu, and Okinawans are rarely welcome into corporate or other Japanese formal situations. Multiculturalism is also likely to become a bigger issue in the twenty-first century. Even by the mid-1990s, Japan had 1 million officially registered foreign residents, not including an estimated 300,000 illegal foreign workers – mainly from South Korea, China, Bangladesh, Southeast Asia, and Pakistan – employed without permits or residents' rights (Douglass and Roberts 2000). This growing presence of foreigners, and particularly the "visible foreign," in Japanese society is often referred to as Japan's so-called third stage of globalization, following the Meiji and postwar periods (see Eades et al. 2000). However, there continues to be a marked reluctance in Japan to accept greater numbers of foreigners in a society that thinks of itself as homogeneous and prizes an imagined ethnic purity. The current situation allows the government to keep immigrant labour in legal limbo, thus preventing the emergence of a permanent community of immigrants (Shimada 1994).

Besides immigration, new values are also coming into Japan through new companies setting up there, both from East Asia and from North America and Europe. Inward foreign direct investment (FDI) to Japan has increased sharply since the mid-1980s and is playing a greater role in Japan's economy. Foreigners now own about 20 percent of the shares on Japan's stock market, compared with only 3 percent in 1990 (Shinozaki 1999). On the one hand, this has brought enormous benefits in terms of economic resources, capital, technology, and know-how.[3] But it also brings changing values in other ways. As Morris-Suzuki (1998, 175) explains, "in this age of information technology, the flows of influence are complex and intersecting. While Japan exports cartoon films, computer games and broadcasting technology, it is also on the receiving end of new information systems devised and developed abroad." Moreover, while roughly 80 percent of foreign capital-affiliated firms in Japan have Western partners, the proportion from Asia is gradually rising (e.g., from South Korean companies and overseas Chinese business groups). Even more inward investment by East Asian companies is likely in the twenty-first century, as the prospect of more rapid growth and increased competitiveness in mainland Asia underscores their potential to set up operations in Japan. Conversely, locating in Japan has tremendous advantages for Asian companies, especially given the size of the market, its leading economic position, and favourable geographic location (Helweg 2000).

All this discussion of Japan's changing identity leads to the question of whether Japan needs a new constitution. Many commentators believe that a discussion of a new constitution, including the elimination of the no-war Article 9, is long overdue. It may be the only cure for Japan's "neurosis of history" (Smith 1998, 305). While the Diet has often thought about revision, especially of the controversial Article 9, this is not likely to happen soon. Still, a new document is probably the only way by which Japan will be able to assume the responsibilities that must accompany its economic pre-eminence in Asia, and the debate involved in such a bold step would surely have more to do with the future than the past.

Social Change

Yoshihara (1994, 187) argues that despite its past reputation for high economic growth, Japan's particular style of development over the last fifty years or so led to an "unfinished revolution." This is because while the Japanese economy has been hugely productive, the lives of the people who run the productive machine are often "relatively narrow and impoverished" (Preston 2000, 210). Problems that are routinely cited in this stream of critical commentary include: long hours of work, inequality between genders, schooling that is excessively examination-centred, lack of leisure time for families, habits of conformity that are overstressed, the problems of an aging population, and so on (Preston 2000, 214).

As pointed out earlier, and emphasized by Hiroshi Aoyagi in Chapter 7, Japan clearly needs to integrate women more fully into the economy and tap this largely squandered pool of human capital. Working mothers, caring for children and nursing aged parents, need a more flexible employment system, one that is sensitive to their life cycles and enables them to reconcile the competing demands of home and work more effectively. There is a need for more nurseries for children in Japan.

Conversely, many experts agree that Japanese society is not yet ready to cope with the burdens and needs of a large elderly population. Indeed, it is generally agreed that the aging crisis is one of the most serious challenges facing Japan in the twenty-first century as it struggles to balance the needs and interests of the young and the old. The question of improving the future welfare system and raising the necessary funds to support the retirement system is an urgent matter. Local governments have provided facilities for seniors in the form of nursing care since April 2000, but there will continue to be tremendous implications for health and pension costs.

Another important area, one not considered expressly in this book, is education reform. Previously admired around the world for their rigour, Japan's highly disciplined schools are coming under scrutiny at home. A wave of juvenile crime was considered by Stephan M. Salzberg in Chapter 8 in the context of the legal system. This has also raised questions about whether the educational pressure-cooker, with its emphasis on rote learning and examination, is turning out well-rounded citizens. Educational experts also say that schools are failing to produce creative thinkers, which is a problem for a modern economy that depends upon innovation (Porter et al. 2000, 144).

Another area of social reform concerns the quality of urban life. As shown by David W. Edgington in Chapter 9, one dark side of the Japanese economic system has been the systematic underprovision of neighbourhood facilities, such as quality housing and public open space. The study of "Japanese beauty" by Joshua S. Mostow in Chapter 10 suggests that there has been a search for quintessential Japanese culture idealized as the source of basic values and national character – values that are remote from the frequently shoddy lives of the urban-based majority.

The types of reforms and improvements that are required include better housing, living closer to work, and more time for family life. In considering solutions to these and other social problems, Sheridan (1998) argues that an opportunity was lost in the "miracle years" of the long boom to extend the productive capacity of the economy from consumer goods to the provision of better family and neighbourhood life. By contrast, Itakura (2000) maintains that with proper budgetary allocations, the quality of life and work in Japanese cities, and expanding the amount of space available to the public, could be achieved in the twenty-first century. This is because, unlike other countries, Japan has wealth stored up in $13 trillion of private savings, and so all this is possible without borrowing money from abroad.

One bright spot among the economic bad news in Japan is that falling land prices have allowed a new generation of public works and affordable condominium apartments in Japanese cities. Ten years or more of falling land prices have brought the cost of residential land in Tokyo to around half its 1991 peak (*Japan Today* 2001b). However, a new urban problem of Japan's largest cities is the number of homeless on city streets and in city parks. The numbers have leapt as a grinding economic downturn and corporate restructuring have thrown people out of work. While homelessness in the past was confined to day labourers on building sites, a rash of bankruptcies and layoffs has forced former office workers to join them on the streets, broadening the problem to all age groups and all localities (*Japan Today* 2001c). At the same time, smaller cities in more peripheral and rural areas (for example, Kyushu and Hokkaido) need stronger leaders and more attention. At present, Japan's administration is too centralized. An important step in greater decentralization would be to remove capital city functions, such as the Diet and government administration, out of congested Tokyo. A number of sites for a new capital have already been identified; including the Tochigi-Fukushima region in the northeast, the Gifu-Aichi region in the central Tokai area, and Mie-Kio in Kansai (Cybriwsky 1998; Hasegawa 2001).

Reformers in the 1990s

How can Japan set about charting a new course? In the 1990s, the Japanese state remained as the central site where debates over social, political, and economic change were conducted. However, it had nothing on its "old map" about the end of the Cold War, the globalization of markets, the rise of China, or the invention of the Internet. Japanese officials knew that they had to implement some form of deregulation over the economy,[4] but the reforms canvassed in this chapter will likely require improvements in a much wider number of areas. Are there any bases for optimism that such changes will occur? Let us look first at several initiatives since the beginning of the 1990s, when a number of deregulators and interventionists advocating change appeared on the political scene.

The overthrow of the Liberal Democratic Party (LDP) in 1993 by then Prime Minister Hosokawa Morihiro presented an opportunity to dismantle the old conservative system. While only a few members of his Japan New Party strongly advocated sweeping reforms, the coalition government began to put forward proposals that could have led to significantly new institutions. However, Hosokawa and his reform movement proved exceptionally short-lived (Schlesinger 1997; Curtis 1999). Diet member Ozawa Ichiro, currently leader of the minority Liberal Party, also advocated reform in his book *Blueprint for a New Japan,* with a very un-Japanese emphasis on individualism and political reform (Ozawa 1994). He and his followers comprised former LDP dissidents who left the party in the early 1990s, paving the way for Hosokawa's anti-LDP coalition. When the LDP returned to power with a majority government in 1996, Prime Minister Hashimoto Ryutaro and the Administrative Reform Council called for deregulation in six broad areas: bureaucratic restructuring, budgeting and economic reform, finance, education, and welfare (Harano 1997). In the life of his government, perhaps his most notable success was the "Big Bang" initiative to liberalize the Japanese financial system.[5] The reconfigured financial regulatory bodies created by Big Bang made possible some changes in the economic sphere and allowed new entrants into the financial marketplace to challenge the former banking and insurance giants (Takenaka 1997).

Further ideas for reform came in a controversial report by a private study group set up by Prime Minister Obuchi Keizo in 1999 to draw up a national vision for the coming century. The Prime Minister's Commission on "Japan's Goals in the 21st Century" consisted of the country's top thinkers, including an astronaut and a playwright, and pointedly excluded the bureaucrats who have usually dominated policy making in Japan. In its final report of January 2000, entitled *The Frontier Within: Individual Empowerment and Better Governance in the New Millennium,* the commission wrote: "We share a sense of urgency. We fear that as things stand Japan is headed for decline" (quoted in Mulgan 2000, 52). The report addressed many of the concerns raised in this book, and concluded that certain qualities that used to be considered Japan's greatest strengths – homogeneity, conformity, egalitarianism, consensus – were in fact holding it back. According to the report, Japan should consider adopting English as a second language, permit more immigration, decentralize government and slash the bureaucracy, and lower the voting age from twenty to eighteen years. It also advocated lifelong learning, educational reform, and greater options for parents and students, as well as a more active policy to build neighbourly relationships *(rinko)* of long-standing stability and trust with Korea and China. While this report was considered just too ambitious to ever implement, it generated an unprecedented debate over Japan's identity in the new century. Specifically, two conflicting visions of the future crystallized: one where Japan became a more open and multilingual and multicultural nation, versus Japan as a homogeneous, monolingual, and largely closed nation (*Japan Echo* 2000; Yoshide 2000).

Another positive move was made by Japan's next prime minister, Mori Yoshiro, who advocated a more knowledge-based society in Japan and an extension of IT networks at the annual G7 summit that Japan hosted in Okinawa in July 2000. The Mori government took the initiative in arguing for "a Japanese IT society," one aimed at enabling every Japanese to enjoy the benefits of IT (*Nikkei Weekly* 2001a). But following the ruling LDP's weakened support in the elections of that year, the vigour behind any political reform or policy initiatives waned (*Oriental Economist* 2000).

What emerges from this narrative is that there has been no shortage of reform-minded politicians in the last decade of the twentieth century. Many, including former Prime Ministers Hosokawa, Hashimoto, and Obuchi understood the need for change and offered solutions. However, determining the right pace and depth of liberalization policies has always been a major challenge. Most politicians eventually stressed implementing a reform agenda at medium speed, appealing to a broad middle ground between no change and the views of the most progressive conservatives.

The bureaucrats in particular have been associated with a conservatism that has often impeded reform measures. Their mind-set is often said to linger from the bygone period of Meiji Japan, when former samurai became officials in the first national government and thus gained much prestige (Kim et al. 1995). While this group has contributed much to the country's postwar development, it is no longer regarded as an omniscient elite. Indeed, many Japanese regard them, along with politicians, as being at the core of Japan's problems, and believe that the substantive reform that Japan needs will not occur if certain ministries retain their strong authority vis-à-vis the prime minister and other key cabinet politicians.

Accordingly, one of Prime Minister Hashimoto's legacies was to streamline the administrative structure and to establish a system in which the government was steered by elected politicians, with the prime minister in the lead. Introduced in January 2001, it has streamlined the number of Japanese ministries from twenty-two to just twelve, and set up a new Cabinet Office to strengthen the prime minister's ability to organize budget and policy (see Figure 11.1). The enabling legislation and government implementation provided for a reduction of 10-25 percent in the number of central government employees over a ten-year period. The prime minister's power to generate the government's budget, a task formerly undertaken by the Ministry of Finance, was greatly enhanced by the new arrangements. In essence, the Ministry of Finance has been downgraded to a treasury ministry, and even its authority to supervise banks and other financial institutions has been transferred to a new agency (*Japan Echo* 2001a; *Look Japan* 2001).

Despite this bold initiative, Japan began the new millennium in 2001 with the same sluggish economy and political confusion that characterized almost a decade of economic decline and political turbulence. Some positive developments, such as corporate reforms and banking mergers, initiatives to advance information technology, and a modicum of economic recovery, did not improve Japan's overall outlook for the future. This continued to be clouded by a massive public debt, high levels of unemployment, and a rapid aging of the population. With deeply entrenched bureaucrats and political interests, as well as a dearth of creative lawmakers, Japan's political landscape remained ineffectual, leading to growing apathy, frustration, and a distrust of politicians among the public. Externally, despite some activism on foreign and security policy, Japan's influence in the international arena was perceived by many observers to be declining (Segal 1999).

The Koizumi Phenomenon

Until 2001 real reform was hard to come by. In April of that year, however, there was a sudden turn of events in Japan that previously would have been unthinkable. The LDP embarked on a bold gambit by selecting as its leader Koizumi Junichiro, a quirky nonconformist who favoured economic austerity and pain as policy options. Koizumi was inaugurated as prime minister after a landslide victory in the LDP presidential race (Kawachi 2001). He promised to carry out sweeping reforms of the nation's economic, fiscal, administrative, social, and political systems, including putting a priority on improving the nation's fiscal balance and deepening cooperation with China and South Korea. He also pledged to privatize the state-run postal business and have prime ministers directly elected by the voters rather than party bosses, the latter requiring an amendment to a

Figure 11.1

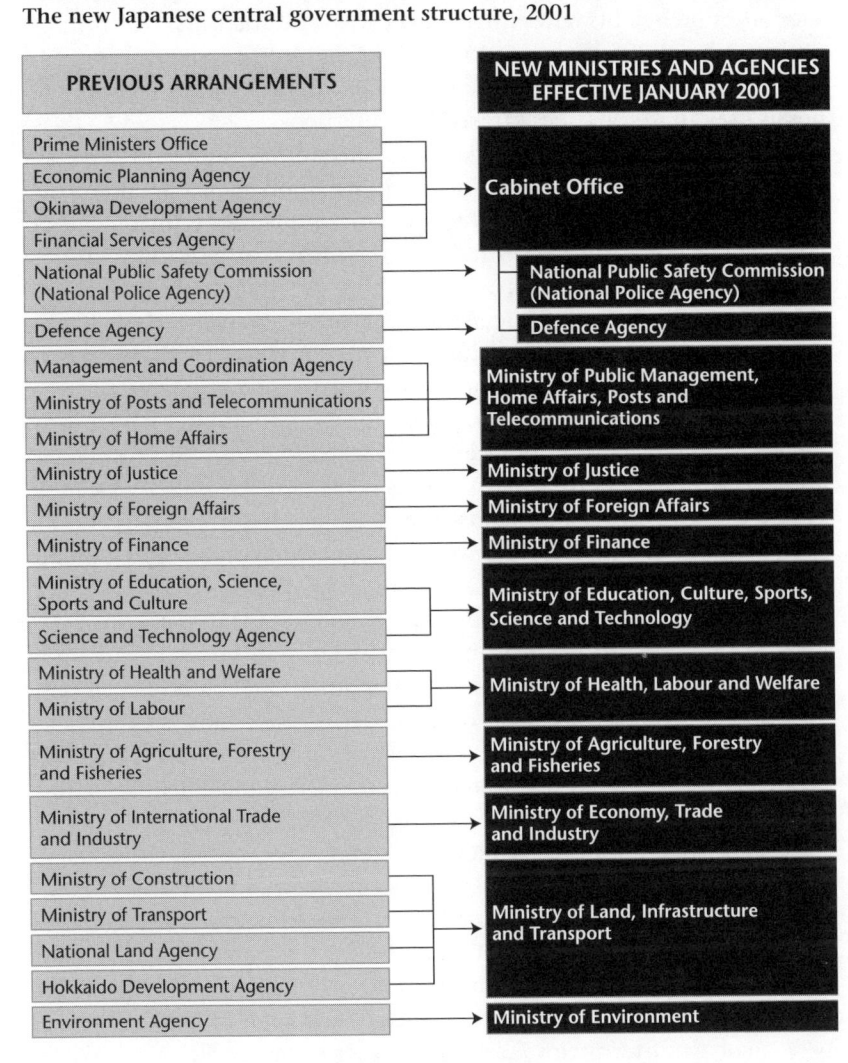

The new Japanese central government structure, 2001

PREVIOUS ARRANGEMENTS	NEW MINISTRIES AND AGENCIES EFFECTIVE JANUARY 2001
Prime Ministers Office	Cabinet Office
Economic Planning Agency	
Okinawa Development Agency	
Financial Services Agency	
National Public Safety Commission (National Police Agency)	National Public Safety Commission (National Police Agency)
Defence Agency	Defence Agency
Management and Coordination Agency	Ministry of Public Management, Home Affairs, Posts and Telecommunications
Ministry of Posts and Telecommunications	
Ministry of Home Affairs	
Ministry of Justice	Ministry of Justice
Ministry of Foreign Affairs	Ministry of Foreign Affairs
Ministry of Finance	Ministry of Finance
Ministry of Education, Science, Sports and Culture	Ministry of Education, Culture, Sports, Science and Technology
Science and Technology Agency	
Ministry of Health and Welfare	Ministry of Health, Labour and Welfare
Ministry of Labour	
Ministry of Agriculture, Forestry and Fisheries	Ministry of Agriculture, Forestry and Fisheries
Ministry of International Trade and Industry	Ministry of Economy, Trade and Industry
Ministry of Construction	Ministry of Land, Infrastructure and Transport
Ministry of Transport	
National Land Agency	
Hokkaido Development Agency	
Environment Agency	Ministry of Environment

Source: Adapted from *Japan Echo* 2001a, 324.

hitherto untouched constitution (*Oriental Economist* 2001a). Then, in July 2001, Koizumi won the upper house elections for the LDP-led coalition with slogans of structural reform and a display of determination to make it happen. Throughout the election campaign, he stressed themes such as "structural reform without sanctuary," "reform with no sacred cows," and "no pain, no gain" (Kabashima 2001).

Prime Minister Koizumi is certainly part of a new generation of political leaders. He is also a maverick, not a consensus builder. His two stunning political victories not only reversed the plunging political fortunes of the LDP but also signalled that a great many Japanese wanted change. His supporters praised his refreshingly direct style and charisma, which shone out amid the dull features of other politicians. Still, popularity and charisma are no substitute for good policy. Let us look at Koizumi's reform proposals in light of the issues canvassed in this book.

The policy manifesto that Koizumi unveiled in the summer of 2001 had several striking features. First, his administration aimed to drastically reduce wasteful expenditures. Thus, he quickly pledged to place caps on government bond issues, starting from the fiscal year beginning in April 2002, and to review the government's notorious public works budget. The latter had been a source of largesse for rural areas of Japan and small business ever since Prime Minister Tanaka Kakuei first launched his drive to "remodel the Japanese archipelago" in 1974 by covering large tracts of the country in concrete (*The Economist* 2001). Enthusiastic government spending on public works in recent years failed to return the economy to faster growth. Both of these new policies made sense to ordinary Japanese as well as to the LDP's anti-mainstream members. Japan's long economic slump left voters with serious questions about the party's ability to manage the economy. Ten years after the price of property and shares collapsed, the economy, households, banks, and companies still struggled under a mountain of debts. Consequently, Koizumi focused on gaining control of the budgetary process by attempting to cut subsidies to public corporations, such as the Housing Loan Corporation, and agencies in charge of providing public infrastructure, such as the Japan Highway Public Corporation and the Water Resources Development Corporation, involved in dam construction (*Japan Today* 2001d).

Second, while drastically reducing wasteful expenditures, the Koizumi administration aimed to boost the allocation of funds towards strategically important areas. The overall aim is based upon shifting public resources from low-productivity to high-productivity areas. Seven strategic areas were targeted: information technology, urban redevelopment, the environment, the aging population, the revitalization of local communities, science and technology, and human resources development (*Nikkei Weekly* 2001b).

A third major policy initiative was the use, for the first time, of the Self-Defense Forces (SDF) in a supporting role alongside the US forces in the war in Afghanistan at the end of the year (*Oriental Economist* 2001b). The Koizumi government introduced legislative changes soon after the 11 September terrorist attacks to allow the dispatch of naval vessels and troops to gather intelligence, provide medical services, and provide humanitarian aid for refugees. This enabled the SDF to provide medical support and transportation of supplies to American and other allied forces. Japan, of course, has been no stranger to attacks by extremist groups – the Japanese doomsday cult Aum Shinrikyō launched sarin gas attacks in a crowded Tokyo subway train in 1995, killing twelve people and injuring hundreds more (Brackett 1996). Thus, even though the expressed priority was to reconfirm links with Asia, Koizumi was desperate to show support for the United States. He feared another debacle like that of 1991, when Japan dithered about its contribution to the allies in the Gulf War, sent a huge cheque instead of troops, and got no thanks in return (see Reading 1992, 276).

A number of mini-budgets at the end of the year allowed the Koizumi administration to further state its policy directions, at least on the important economic front. These were modest in size but focused on employment measures that would produce structural reforms, such as promoting information technology in government offices and in schools.[6] The prime minister's free market philosophy also turned from rhetoric to reality when he trimmed at least US$24 billion from the 2002 budget plan. This led almost immediately to conflict within the LDP ranks. Most economists believed that Japan's existing public sector was extremely wasteful and needed to be reformed. As Japan's fragile economy worsened during late 2001, however, many economists feared that severe fiscal cuts were inappropriate given the weak state of the global economy following the 11 September terrorist attacks. Moreover, Koizumi's plans left one of the major economic problems, the disposal of the nonperforming loans of the country's banks, virtually untouched (*Japan Times Online* 2001a).

During 2001 the Koizumi government had to put most of its effort into fighting both the reactionary section of its own party and the equally reactionary bureaucrats. Other reforms promised by Koizumi slipped to the backburner as helping the US fight against terrorism and addressing the sick economy topped the policy agenda. Domestic policy initiatives here were aimed at improving Japan's labour market. By the end of the year, however, the economy took a turn for the worse as unemployment and bankruptcies rose to historic levels, the yen sank lower against the US dollar, and the economy went into negative growth (Katz 2001). Many of Koizumi's promised social reforms, such as those that would promote women's rights, were few and far between, but he did select five women as cabinet ministers, reflecting his election promise to make Japanese society truly gender-equal. The Koizumi government planned to include in its reform program a plan to increase by 150,000 the number of children's spaces in nursery schools by fiscal year 2002, and to increase the number of spaces in after-school child care centres to 150,000 (*Japan Today* 2001e).

How Will Japan Change?

By the time this chapter was finished, the jury was still out as to whether the government could implement its bold reform program. By the end of 2001, it appeared that Prime Minister Koizumi was locked in stalemate. His administration was still popular and continued to obtain 80 percent support among the voters, but in reality he had accomplished little. Some commentators branded the prime minister "Mr. Nato" – No Action, Talk Only – indicating that his enormous degree of personal popularity was no substitute for effective implementation of reform (*Japan Today* 2001f; *Oriental Economist* 2001c).

There were three reasons for this stalemate. The first obstacle to change was a rapidly declining economic situation. In the summer of 2001, many large corporations, such as Hitachi and Toshiba, announced unprecedented job layoffs as their profits in the IT sectors tumbled (*Japan Today* 2001g). The tentative recovery that had begun in the spring of 1999 depended heavily upon growth in Japan's high-technology manufacturing base. When world demand for silicon chips, fibre optics, and other IT equipment collapsed at the end of 2000, Japan was hit especially hard. High-tech goods piled up in warehouses and production collapsed. While the longer-term effects of 11 September terrorist attacks remained unclear, their immediate impact was to further dampen the economy and increase unemployment. By the end of 2001, the economy had contracted by almost 1 percent on an annual basis and, for the first time, the unemployment rate of 5.5 percent was higher than in the US (*Japan Today* 2001h). Japan's largest labour organization, Rengō, called on the prime minister to tackle rising unemployment immediately through supplementary budget measures (*Japan Today* 2001i). Accordingly, Koizumi was forced to restore traditional pump-priming expenditures in a late-autumn mini-budget, albeit dressed up as reform (*Japan Today* 2001j). Other programs to privatize public corporations such as the country's postal services, while not abandoned, were put on hold.

A second obstacle involved resistance within the LDP itself. Despite his overwhelming popularity, there were many critics of the Koizumi reform movement, especially the "policy tribes" (*zoku*) who supported rural electorates, farmers, small shopkeepers, and the construction industry. To meet this backlash within his own party, and from equally reactionary bureaucrats, the prime minister focused most energy in his first six months on gaining control of the government's budgetary process. Traditionally, the process had been orchestrated by powerful officials and the major *zoku*. In attempting to cut public works spending and subsidies given to public corporations, Koizumi upset his parliamentary colleagues within the LDP. He made it clear that he wanted to redirect these funds to address the problems that would come from bank restructuring, through programs such as social support and retraining. However, he faced stiff opposition to these reforms on all fronts (Maeda 2001).

A third dimension was trouble on the international scene. Much goodwill was lost here when the prime minister made an official visit to the Yasunuki Shrine in Tokyo in August 2001, to pray for the souls of Japan's war dead, including the Class A war criminals enshrined there (*Japan Echo* 2001b). China and South Korea were incensed by this as well as by the revisionist history textbooks approved by the government for use in schools (Matsumoto 2001). In addition, Japan's foreign diplomacy was dealt a further blow when China and the ASEAN (Association of Southeast Asian Nations) trade bloc announced plans to bypass Japan and negotiate their own free-trade agreement (FTA). This involved a potential trade bloc that could compete with the US, Europe, and Japan in the World Trade Organization (*Nikkei Weekly* 2001c). By contrast, Japan could only point to its proposed FTA with Singapore (Masaki 2001).

All of these forces will undoubtedly further slow down the reform movement. Beyond that, there is the conservative Japanese electorate. As intimated earlier, Japan's recent political history is littered with the corpses of reformers. From Prime Minister Nakasone's Maekawa Commission in the mid-1980s to the report on Japan's goals in the twenty-first century of Prime Minister Obuchi, these initiatives were swept in on a wave of hope, only to be swept out again when these hopes were crushed. At the end of the day, voters are likely to prefer slow change. Thus, despite a basic sympathy with the reform agenda, an underlying conservatism in the electorate has fostered concern that the reform might come too fast. Opinion polls suggest that over 60 percent of Japanese are satisfied with their lives, a figure that has not changed in twenty years, despite the boom of the 1980s and the bust of the 1990s (*The Economist* 2001). Indeed, a number of factors might make the Japanese electorate and political climate arguably even more conservative in the future, since the proportion of older voters, who are less likely to support radical change, is increasing all the time.

Despite the urgency of Japan's problems, it is likely that this and future governments will adopt a step-by-step, incremental approach to planning and formulating policies, and that the fight over reform will continue to dominate Japan's economic and political life for some time to come. The many dramatic changes now unfolding in Japan are indeed path-dependent, meaning that many links and similarities with the past remain.

In many ways, Japan is like the former communist regimes in the former Soviet Union and Eastern Europe. It is clear that the old regime has been displaced and transition is under way, but precisely how that transition will play out is less clear-cut. This underscores the value of interdisciplinary research in revealing the exact links between continuity and change in Japan. The "regime shift" that Pempel (1998) talks about will most likely take some years yet.

Still, catalysts for change emanate from several sources. First, as already noted, foreign companies and foreign workers are entering Japan in growing numbers, bringing with them new ideas regarding both labour markets and sources of capital. Second, within Japan a new generation of CEOs and politicians are assuming leadership in many Japanese companies and in political life. Third, deregulation and policy change are in fact proceeding, although the speed of change and the extent of the government's resolution to achieve change remain to be seen. In the absence of any single and well-defined goal, the future course of Japan must now be found by a trial-and-error process. At the beginning of the new millennium the question is whether Japan can surprise its critics by carrying out a "third revolution," one comparable to the Meiji Restoration and American-imposed Occupation reforms, in order to revive the country's flagging fortunes and improve its social and political systems.

Notes

1 Japan's population stood at 126.92 million in 2000. The most important trend is that the economically active population, aged between 15 and 64 years old, fell by 1.1 percent from the previous five-year census results in 1995, to 86.22 million. The population of people aged over 65 rose 20.5 percent to 22.01 million, or 17.3 percent of the total population, whereas the population of children under 15 totalled 18.47 million (*Japan Today* 2001k).
2 One trend that appears to be continuing is the immigration of foreign workers to Japan. There is a growing trend among industrial nations to actively accept immigrant workers in the fields of information technology and nursing. Japan also needs to accept such workers. Because of the falling birthrate, Japan's population will be approximately 127 million around the year 2005. It is likely to then fall to around 92.3 million by 2050 and down to about 51 million by 2100 without any immigration program. Just to replenish the labour force, it is forecast that Japan should accept around 70,000 workers every year, which would bring the total to 180,000 immigrants when families are included. The goals of such a policy would be to replenish the labour force, the population, and purchasing power while further developing the nation's culture. In order to accomplish this, it is argued that Japan should adopt as a national goal for the twenty-first century the integration of the three stages of residency, permanent residency, and naturalization, and the creation of a system in which the indigenous and immigrant populations can coexist harmoniously (*Japan Today* 2001l).
3 For example, Renault Motor Company of France, after acquiring 37 percent of Nissan Motor Corporation in 1999, became its largest shareholder and appointed Carlos Ghosen as Nissan's new chief executive officer (Ghosen 2000). Similarly, DaimlerChrysler AG purchased a controlling (34 percent) stake in debt-ridden Mitsubishi Motors during 2001. This deal means that all but two of the major Japanese automakers will have a capital affiliation with a US or European company (Landers and Dvorak 2000).

4 According to Japan's Fair Trade Commission, when comparing the extent to which different countries' economies are subject to regulation, Japan ranks thirty-fifth (below even Russia). About 30 percent of its economy is still controlled by national bureaucrats, compared with America's 7 percent (*The Economist* 1998).
5 Hashimoto's "Big Bang" initiative got its name from the Big Bang launched in the United Kingdom by Prime Minister Margaret Thatcher to reform the economy during the 1980s. Japan's Big Bang was intended to make the financial system more transparent and accessible by loosening the insurance and securities sectors, providing tax cuts for corporations, and restricting the regulatory power of the Ministry of Finance. The government established a Financial Reconstruction Commission, a Financial Supervisory Agency, and improved market access (*Nikkei Weekly* 1998).
6 The main feature was the hiring of fifty thousand unemployed people as assistant school teachers, forestry workers, and other public sector employees for up to a year. It is hoped that the assistant teachers would share knowledge gained from their previous jobs with students and help improve corporate education. The government's spending on IT projects involved upgrading high-speed school computer networks and so-called "e-government" programs (*Japan Times Online* 2001b).

References
Brackett, D.W. 1996. *Holy Terror: Armageddon in Tokyo*. New York: Weatherhill.
Campbell, J.C. 1988. *Politics and Culture in Japan*. Ann Arbor: Center for Political Studies, Institute for Social Research, University of Michigan.
Curtis, G.L. 1999. *The Logic of Japanese Politics: Leaders, Institutions, and the Limits of Change*. New York: Columbia University Press.
Cybriwsky, R. 1998. "Moving the Capital?" In *Tokyo: The Shogun's City at the Twenty-First Century*. Chichester, UK: John Wiley and Sons, 225-28.
Douglass, M., and G.S. Roberts, eds. 2000. *Japan and Global Migration: Foreign Workers and the Advent of a Multicultural Society*. London: Routledge.
Eades, J.S., T. Gill, and H. Befu, eds. 2000. *Globalization and Social Change in Contemporary Japan*. London: Routledge.
East Asia Analytical Unit. 1996. *Asia's Global Powers: China-Japan Relations in the 21st Century*. Canberra: Department of Foreign Affairs and Trade, Australia.
The Economist. 1998. "Three Futures for Japan: Views from 2020," 21 March, 25-28.
–. 2001. "The Voters Give Koizumi a Chance: Will the LDP?" Special Report: Japan's Election, 4 August, 21-23.
Freedman, C., ed. 1999. *Why Did Japan Stumble? Causes and Cures*. Cheltenham: Edward Elgar.
Ghosen, C. 2000. "Putting Nissan Back on Track." *Japan Echo* 27(2): 38-40.
Harano, J. 1997. "The Hashimoto Reform Program." *Japan Echo* 24(3): 30-33.
Hasegawa, M. 2001. "Movin' on Out." *Nikkei Weekly*, 8 October, 3.
Helweg, M.D. 2000. "Japan: A Rising Sun?" *Foreign Affairs* 79(4): 26-39.
Itakura, H. 2000. "What's the Capital of Japan?" *Look Japan* 46(530): 5.
Japan Echo. 2000. "Reinventing Japan: Report of the Commission on Japan's Goals in the Twenty-First Century (Outline)," 27(2): 17-20.
–. 2001a. "Reorganization of Japan's Ministries and Agencies," 28(1): 57-58.
–. 2001b. "Yasunuki Revisited," 28(6): 48-50.
Japan Times Online. 2001a. "Japan Faces a Balancing Act," 4 October. <http://www.japantime.co.jp>, accessed October 2001.
–. 2001b. "Cabinet Approves 3 Trillion Yen Extra Budget for Fiscal 2001," 8 November. <http://www.japantime.co.jp>, accessed November 2001.
Japan Today. 2001a. "Food Supplies Secured in the Wake of US Chaos," 11 September. <http://www.japantoday.com>, accessed September 2001.
–. 2001b. "Land Prices Down for 10th Straight Year," 24 September. <http://www.japantoday.com>, accessed November 2001.
–. 2001c. "Japan's Homeless Population Increases to 24,000," 16 December. <http://www.japantoday.com>, accessed November 2001.

–. 2001d. "Koizumi Says He's Going to Ax Public Corporations," 5 September. <http://www.japantoday.com>, accessed November 2001.
–. 2001e. "More Child Care Needed, Says Koizumi," 14 September. <http://www.japantoday.com>, accessed November 2001.
–. 2001f. "Koizumi Branded 'Mr. NATO' – No Action, Talk Only," 6 December. <http://www.japantoday.com>, accessed December 2001.
–. 2001g. "Hitachi, Toshiba Planning to Cut 20,000 Jobs Each," 26 August. <http://www.japantoday.com>, accessed November 2001.
–. 2001h. "Jobless Rate Hits Record High 5.5% in Nov," 27 December. <http://www.japantoday.com>, accessed December 2001.
–. 2001i. "Rengō Urges Koizumi to Save Jobs," 28 August. <http://www.japantoday.com>, accessed August 2001.
–. 2001j. "Koizumi Instructs Cabinet to Draft Second Annual Budget," 27 November. <http://www.japantoday.com>, accessed November 2001.
–. 2001k. "Japan's Population at 126.92 Million in 2000," 10 November. <http://www.japantoday.com>, accessed December 2001.
–. 2001l. "Japan Needs 8.37 Million Immigrants," 12 October. <http://www.japantoday.com>, accessed November 2001.
Kabashima, I. 2001. "The Birth of the Koizumi Administration and the July 2001 Election." *Japan Echo* 28(6): 19-25.
Katz, R. 1998. *Japan, the System that Soured: The Rise and Fall of the Japanese Economic Miracle*. Armonk, NY: M.E. Sharpe.
–. 2000. "Shrinking Japan." *Oriental Economist* 68(9): 10-11.
–. 2001. "Economy Heading Backwards." *Oriental Economist* 68(12): 3-4.
Kawachi, T. 2001. "New Prime Minister: How Will Koizumi Fare." *Japan Echo* 28(4): 6-11.
Kim, H., M. Muramatsu, T.J. Pempel, and K. Yamamura, eds. 1995. *The Japanese Civil Service and Economic Development: Catalysts of Change*. Oxford: Clarendon Press.
Kingston, J. 2001. *Japan in Transformation, 1952-2000*. Harlow, UK: Pearson Education.
Landers, P., and P. Dvorak. 2000. "Wave of Foreign Capital Washes over Japan." *Globe and Mail* (Toronto), 28 March, A7.
Lincoln, E.J. 2001. *Arthritic Japan: The Slow Pace of Economic Reform*. Washington, DC: Brookings Institution Press.
Look Japan. 2001. "Kasumigaseki Shake-up," 46(538): 6-10.
Maeda, T. 2001. "Koizumi Struggles against Resistance Forces." *Japan Times*, 3 December, 3.
Masaki, H. 2001. "Singapore FTA Coming." *Japan Times*, 24 November, 10.
Matsumoto, K. 2001. "East Asian Countries Begin to Rewrite History." *Japan Echo* 28(6): 56-60.
Morris-Suzuki, T. 1998. *Re-inventing Japan: Time, Space, Nation*. Armonk, NY: M.E. Sharpe.
Mulgan, A.G. 2000. "Japan: A Setting Sun?" *Foreign Affairs* 79(4): 40-52.
Nikkei Weekly. 1998. "Big Bang Special." In *Japan Economic Almanac 1998*. Tokyo: Nihon Keizai Shimbun.
–. 2001a. "IT Policy: Government Joins Revolution with IT Strategy." In *Japan Economic Almanac 2001*. Tokyo: Nihon Keizai Shimbun, 8-9.
–. 2001b. "Koizumi Unveils Blueprint of Battle for Reform," 4 June, 19.
–. 2001c. "China, ASEAN to Negotiate Final Touches to Free Trade Pact," 5 November, 18.
Oriental Economist. 2000. "Days Are Numbered for Miscast Mori," 68(9): 1-2.
–. 2001a. "One Giant Step for Reform in Japan: The Koizumi Factor," 69(5): 1-2.
–. 2001b. "Japan Embarks on a New Security Policy: Normal Country?" 69(11): 1-2.
–. 2001c. "Koizumi Stalemate: Premier Still Popular, but Little Reform Progress," 69(12): 1-2.
Ozawa, I. 1994. *Blueprint for a New Japan*. Tokyo: Kodansha.
Pempel, T.J. 1998. *Regime Shift: Comparative Dynamics of the Japanese Political Economy*. Ithaca, NY: Cornell University Press.
Porter, M.E., H. Takeuchi, and M. Sakakibara. 2000. *Can Japan Compete?* Houndmills, Basingstoke, Hampshire, UK: Macmillan Press.

Preston, P.W. 2000. *Understanding Modern Japan*. London: Sage Publications.
Reading, B. 1992. *Japan: The Coming Collapse*. London: Orion Books.
Sako, M., and H. Sako. 1997. *Japanese Labour and Management in Transition: Diversity, Flexibility and Participation*. London: Routledge.
Schlesinger, J. 1997. *Shadow Shoguns: The Rise and Fall of Japan's Postwar Political Machine*. New York: Simon and Schuster.
Segal, G. 1999. "Japan's Other Crisis." *Newsweek*, 25 January. <http://www.segal.org/gerald/nw26ja99>, accessed November 2001.
Sheridan, K. 1998. "Japan's Economic System." In K. Sheridan, ed., *Emerging Economic Systems in Asia: A Political and Economic Survey*. St. Leonards, NSW: Allen and Unwin, 9-44.
Shimada, H. 1994. *Japan's "Guest Workers": Issues and Public Polices*. Translated by R. Northridge. Tokyo: University of Tokyo.
Shinozaki, A. 1999. "Investing in Japan: What's the Attraction?" *Look Japan* 45(518): 4-12.
Smith, P. 1998. *Japan: A Reinterpretation*. New York: Vintage Books.
Takenaka, H. 1997. "Prospects for the 'Big Bang.'" *Japan Echo* 24(3): 22-29.
Yoshide, S. 2000. "The Frontier Within." *Look Japan* 46(529): 23.
Yoshihara, K. 1994. *Japanese Economic Development*. Oxford: Oxford University Press.

Contributors

Hiroshi Aoyagi is a cultural anthropologist who is currently Director of the Laboratory for Iconographic Studies in Tokyo. He was previously a visiting lecturer and Mitsubishi Scholar at the Department of Asian Studies, University of Texas at Austin, and a postdoctoral fellow at the Edwin O. Reischauer Institute of Japanese Studies, Harvard University. His research interests include symbolism, cultural industries, socialization and enculturation, and socio-linguistics. He is author of the essay "Pop Idols and the Asian Identity" in *Japan Pop! Inside the World of Japanese Popular Culture*, edited by Timothy Craig (M.E. Sharpe, 2000).

Lonny E. Carlile is an Associate Professor at the Center for Japanese Studies and Asian Studies Program at the School of Hawaiian, Asian and Pacific Studies, University of Hawaii at Manoa. His research interests span a broad range of topics in the area of Japanese political economy. Recent publications include *Is Japan Really Changing its Ways? Regulatory Reform and the Japanese Economy*, co-edited with Mark Tilton (Brookings Institution Press, 1998).

Millie Creighton is Associate Professor in the Department of Anthropology and Sociology at the University of British Columbia. Her research and publications include work on Japanese mass consumer industries (department stores, advertising, tourism), work and gender issues, education, traditional crafts, and minorities in Japan. Recent publications include "Weaving the Future from the Heart of Tradition: Learning in Leisure Activities," in *Learning in Likely Places: Varieties of Apprenticeship in Japan*, edited by John Singleton (Cambridge University Press, 1998). She was winner of the Canon Foundation Prize in 1998 for an article on Japanese department stores that appeared in the journal *Japan Forum*.

David W. Edgington is Associate Professor in the Department of Geography at the University of British Columbia, where he teaches courses on the geography of Japan and the Pacific Rim. His research interests focus on spatial development and planning in Japan, as well as Japan's overseas trade and investment. His publications include *Planning for Cities and*

Regions in Japan (co-edited with P. Shapira and I. Masser) (University of Liverpool Press, 1994) and *Japan and the West: The Perception Gap,* co-edited with Keizo Nagatani (Ashgate, 1998).

Joshua S. Mostow is Associate Professor and Acting Head of the Department of Asian Studies at the University of British Columbia. His research interests include Japanese culture and Tokugawa art and poetry. He is the author of *Pictures of the Heart: The Hyakunin Isshu in Word and Image* (University of Hawaii Press, 1996), which was selected by *Choice* magazine as one of its Outstanding Academic Books of 1997.

Keizo Nagatani is Professor Emeritus, Department of Economics, University of British Columbia. He is currently Professor at Ryūtsū Kagaku University (University of Marketing and Distribution Sciences) in Japan. His research includes monetary theory, macroeconomics, and Japanese economics. Recent works include *Japan and the West: The Perception Gap,* co-edited with David W. Edgington (Ashgate, 1998), *Nakanaka Kuni Nippon* (Japan Is Not a Bad Country) (Chūō Keizaisha, 1998), and *Nippon Keizaigaku* (Japanese Economics) (Chūō Keizaisha, 1999).

Stephan M. Salzberg is Associate Professor at the Faculty of Law, University of British Columbia, and Director of its Centre for Asian Legal Studies. His teaching and research interests include comparative medical law and Japanese law. Recent publications include "Taiwan's Mental Health Law" (*Chinese Law Reporter,* 1993) and a number of studies in Japanese on mental health law.

Bill Sewell is Assistant Professor in the Department of Asian Studies at Saint Mary's University, Halifax. His research focuses on imperialism, urbanism, and definitions of modernity in northeast Asia. His PhD dissertation at the Department of History, University of British Columbia, focused on the evolution of the city of Changchun, Jilin Province, People's Republic of China, between 1905 and 1945.

Roger Smith is currently a doctoral student in international relations at St. Anthony's College, Oxford University. He completed his MA at the Department of History, University of British Columbia, on Japanese international fisheries relations. He has held positions at the Asia Pacific Foundation in Vancouver and the Asian Development Bank Institute in Tokyo, and served as a freelance writer for the *Japan-Canada Business Journal.*

Index

Abstention Line, 75, 77, 80, 81
Ainu
   and discrimination, 9, 13, 92, 93, 124, 125, 126, 127, 130, 135, 136, 141n9, 249
   gods, 129
   hunter-gatherers, 123, 126
   language, 126, 127, 128, 134, 136, 139
   networking, 121, 133, 134, 135, 137, 138
   revival, 93, 121, 125, 127-28, 129, 133
   self-identity, 121, 124, 129, 131, 133, 134
Ainu Cultural Promotion Act, 136
ambiguity tolerance, 35-36, 40, 46n12
American economics. *See* economics, American art
   Chinese influence, 235, 237, 239-40
   commodification of, 191, 240, 242, 243n3
   Edo period, 227-29, 236, 240, 242
   Heian period, 227, 235, 236, 237, 239, 240-41
   Meiji period, 224-25, 226
   and national identity, 222, 240
   ukiyo-e, 229, 236
   and the West, 224, 225, 227, 230, 231, 233-34, 237, 240, 243n3
   yamato-e, 235, 236, 239, 240, 242
art exhibits
   emphasis on style, 224, 226
   erasure of history, 224, 225, 226, 227, 228, 242
   and Exotic Japan, 224, 225
   as *furusato*, 224, 240
"Asian flu," 9
assimilation, 122, 123, 125, 126-27, 136, 137, 139, 140n3
Association of Southeast Asian Nations (ASEAN), 259

Axelrod experiment, 45n11
Ayukawa, Yoshisuke, 108, 110

Basic Law on Land, 207
Big Bang, 7, 252, 261n5
Bristol Bay (Alaska), 70
bubble economy, 4, 25, 40, 46n13, 61, 62, 92, 109, 189, 193, 205, 208
Burakumin, 92, 127, 249

capitalism, 19, 30, 43, 45n3, 53, 106, 137, 159, 224
catch rates (fish), 69, 70, 71, 76-77, 78, 81, 88n4
Central Intelligence Agency (CIA), 74-75
Chief Local Officials, 170, 172, 173
China
   cultural influence, 235, 236, 237
   and fisheries, 72, 73, 74, 75, 79, 80, 83, 85, 87
   and Manchuria, 91, 100, 105-6, 109, 110, 113, 114n3
   nationalism, 102
   rivalry with Japan, 9, 91, 248-49, 252, 259
   ties with Japan, 8, 12-13, 91, 248-49, 253, 255
   and USA, 103, 106-7
Chinese
   in art, 229, 230
   discrimination against, 13, 92
   perceptions of Manchuria, 97-98, 101, 110
   work camps, 99
City Planning Act, 202
civil minimum policies, 14-15
coexistence principle, 19, 37-38, 43, 47n16
Cold War, 8, 52, 80, 84, 92, 100, 252

Columbus, Christopher, 133
comfort women, 112
comics, 111
communism, 50, 51, 71, 74, 100, 110
competition
  attitudes regarding, 36, 37, 38, 41, 46n13, 60, 61
  drawbacks, 29, 45
  foreign, 20, 22, 23, 250, 259
  global, 15, 40, 242, 246
  and labour relations, 55
  lack of, 23, 215
  and Newtonian physics, 28, 30
  in USA, 31, 32, 33-34, 35, 37, 45n7
Conference on Hunting and Gathering Societies (CHAGS), 136-37, 138
Confucianism, 38, 45n3
constitution, 6, 46n12, 58, 60, 135, 159, 169, 177, 184n19, 250, 256
Core Cities Law, 212
cute pop idols
  alternative to post-idols, 163, 164
  characteristics, 148, 153-55, 156, 158, 163
  creation, 152-56
  decline, 151-52, 156, 161
  handwriting, 148
  historical roots, 14, 93, 148, 151, 161, 165n6
  rebellion against adult culture, 151-52
  See also pop idols
Cutie Smile, Ltd., 152-56, 157, 163

Dairen. *See* Dalian (city)
Dalian (city), 98, 110
Dance-Jet Agency, 156-58, 163
dangō (rigged building contracts), 46n14, 215
Decade of Indigenous Peoples (1995-2004), 120, 137, 139
decentralization, 3, 50, 190, 202, 205, 212, 214, 252, 253
Democratic Party, 63
Democratic Socialist Party (DSP), 55, 59, 63
Dentō to Kindai – Nihon no Bi (art exhibit)
  and Chinese influence, 237, 239-40
  and continuity, 237
  emphasis on genius, 239
  emphasis on line, 237, 239
  and Kyoto, 236
Discover Japan, 222-23, 226
Dōmei (labour organization), 55-56, 57, 58, 60
DSP. *See* Democratic Socialist Party (DSP)
Dulles, John Foster, 72

earthquakes, ix, 4, 199, 213-14, 215
e-commerce, 20, 44
Economic Research Bureau, 100, 104, 106, 108, 111, 114n5, 115n7
economics
  American, 31-35
  Japanese, 35-42
economy
  attempts to stimulate, 25, 41, 42, 47n16, 256, 258
  crisis, 245, 246
  decline, 4, 5, 6, 7, 8, 11, 12, 21, 25, 40, 42, 46n13, 47n16, 62, 209
  Meiji, 36-37
  peak, 247
  postwar recovery, 6-7, 26, 51, 52, 53, 54-55, 56, 62, 200, 204, 216n1
  and quality of life, 250
  reform, 252-54, 261n4
  and service sector, 205, 217n7
  stock market crash (1990), 4, 208
  and terrorism, 245
  and Western models, 11, 19, 26, 43, 46n13, 207-8, 247, 248, 261n5
Edo, 197, 227, 229
Edo period. *See* art, Edo period
EEZs. *See* exclusive economic zones
efficiency
  dynamic, 28-29, 31, 32, 36
  and equity, 19, 35, 37, 38, 45
  small-business, 41
  static, 28-29, 30, 32
electorate, 6, 64, 130, 255, 256, 258, 259
emperor, 113, 114n3, 120, 121, 124, 138, 140n3, 159, 240, 243n9
enclosure movement, 70, 78-81, 82, 84, 87
enterprise unions, 49, 50-51, 53-54, 55, 57, 59, 60, 61, 64, 247
environmentalism, 12, 84, 87, 88n8, 132
Equal Employment Opportunity Law (EEOL), 160
equity
  and efficiency, 19, 31, 35
  ex ante, 29, 32, 37, 45n7
  ex post, 29, 30, 32, 33, 37, 38, 40, 45, 46n14
era of high-speed growth. *See* economy, postwar recovery
exclusive economic zones (EEZs), 79, 80, 81, 82, 85, 87
Exotic Japan, 223, 224, 226, 235, 243n3

Family Court Investigation Officers, 178, 179, 180, 185n24
Family Courts, 177-81, 182, 183, 185n26, 185n27, 185n28, 185n29, 186n35

fascism, 102, 104
feminism, 161-62
fish
  conservation, 23, 72, 74, 77, 78, 79, 80, 81, 83, 88n4, 88n5
  declining stocks, 86-87
  and diet, 67-68, 69, 71, 72, 88n3, 88n7
  exports, 71, 75
  farming, 81, 86-87, 88n7
  imports, 23, 81, 85, 86
  salmon, 22, 68, 69, 70, 74, 75, 76-77, 80, 82, 83, 88n5, 131, 132, 136
  species taken, 68, 69, 76
fisheries
  attempts to limit, 12, 22, 74, 75, 76, 80
  coastal, 67, 68, 70, 72, 80, 81, 85, 86, 87
  and environment, 22-23, 69, 72, 83, 85
  offshore, 68, 69, 70, 81
  overseas, 22, 68, 69
  prewar, 67, 68, 69, 70, 75
  resentment of, 70, 72
  treaties, 73-74, 75-77
fishing
  areas, 68, 69, 72, 73, 75, 76
  driftnet, 22, 76, 77, 81-83, 84
  techniques, 68, 69, 71, 76
flag, 124, 138, 140n5, 226
"flying geese model" of development, 91
food security. *See* food self-sufficiency
food self-sufficiency, 19, 22, 67, 71, 84, 85, 86, 247
Fordism, 53-55, 58, 62
foreign direct investment (FDI), 249, 260n3
forgiveness, 38-39, 45n11
Formosa. *See* Taiwan
free trade, 19, 30, 44, 259
freedom of the seas, 70-71, 74, 75, 77, 78, 79, 80, 81, 84, 85, 88n4
Fukuzawa, Yukichi, 37
Fundamental Welfare Theorem, 30, 32
furusato ("home place"), 129, 141n13, 189, 190, 222, 224, 240

gals, 156, 161
General Agreement on Tariffs and Trade (GATT), 45
Gini coefficient, 32, 38, 43
globalization, 6, 11, 12, 13, 21, 40, 41, 43, 95, 137, 242, 249, 252
Gotō, Shimpei, 100-1, 104
Greater East Asia Co-Prosperity Sphere, 91
Greenpeace, 12, 23, 82

Heisei period, 120, 225
high technology, 12, 20, 246, 258

Hinomaru. *See* flag
Hokkaido Former Aborigines Protection Act, 126, 131, 136
Hokkaido Utari Kyōkai (Ainu association), 127, 128, 141n9
Home Ministry, 170, 171, 172, 174
homelessness, 251
homogeneous society, 9, 13, 92, 93, 120-22, 125, 131, 134, 135, 136, 140n2, 140n3, 249
Hoshino, Naoki, 103-4, 105, 108
housing
  improvements, 204, 207, 214, 217n10, 251
  shortage, 201, 206-7, 208
  and tax system, 207, 208, 209
  Tokyo, 201, 205-6, 251
  zoning regulations, 206, 209, 212

IDE. *See* Institute of Developing Economies (IDE)
idol dancers. *See* post-idols
Ienaga, Saburō, 101-2, 105, 109
Iizawa, Shigekazu, 108
iki ("chic"), 227-28, 229, 243n5
Imperial Army, 99
imperial rule assistance associations, 49
imperialism, 92, 101-2, 106-7, 108, 109, 111, 113, 114n2, 114n6, 140n5
Indigenous Peoples, 120, 121, 126, 132, 134, 135, 137, 138, 139, 140n2
individualism, 31, 33, 35, 37, 41, 45, 252
inflation, 56, 57, 58, 59, 61, 205, 207
information technology (IT), 20, 44, 247, 249, 253, 254, 256, 257, 258, 260n2, 261n6
infrastructure
  Allied bombing of, 200
  improvements, 15, 204, 205, 206, 207, 208, 209, 214, 215, 217n10, 217n11, 251
  inferiority of, 14-15, 194, 196, 197-98, 201, 205, 251
Institute of Developing Economies (IDE), 100
International Confederation of Trade Unions, 51
International Metalworkers Federation – Japan Charter (IMF-JC), 55-56, 57, 58
International North Pacific Fisheries Commission (INPFC), 75, 78, 79, 80, 81, 83, 88n5
International North Pacific Fisheries Convention, 75-77, 80
International Whaling Commission (IWC), 84, 88n5

International Whaling Convention, 70, 88n4
internationalization, 93, 121, 137, 138, 190
Internet, 20, 44, 246, 252
Itō, Takeo, 104-5, 111
Ivy, Marilyn, 191, 222-24, 226, 243n3

Japan
  economic miracle, 6
  lost decade, 4
  as quality of life superpower, 15, 190
Japan Federation of Employers Associations. *See* Nikkeiren (Japan Federation of Employers Associations)
Japan Inc., 6
Japan National Railways (JNR), 46n14, 58, 60, 222, 223
Japan New Party, 252
Japan Railways, 47n14
Japan Socialist Party (JSP), 52, 53, 56, 59, 63
Japan Times, 3
Japanese economics. *See* economics, Japanese
Japanese economy, hollowing out of, 7
Japanesque – Rediscovery (art exhibit)
  continuity design, 226, 230
  distortion design, 226, 230
  and Edo period, 227-29
  erasure of history, 225, 226, 227, 228
  and Exotic Japan, 224, 225
  gorgeousness design, 226, 229-30
  hidden design, 226, 228-29
  straightforward design, 226-28
  and the West, 224-25, 227
Japonisme in Vienna (art exhibit)
  and hollow centre model, 231, 233
  orientalism, 230-34, 243n6
  and the West, 233-34, 243n6
JSP. *See* Japan Socialist Party (JSP)
Juvenile Determination Offices
  role, 174-77, 180-81, 184n15
  staff, 174-77, 184n16
juvenile justice system
  continuity, 14, 94, 168, 174, 178, 179, 180-81, 182, 183
  and foreign models, 94, 168, 170, 171, 173-74, 177, 181, 185n34
  philosophy, 168-69, 171-72, 181, 183
  role of parents, 172-73, 176, 177, 178, 179, 180, 183n4, 184n15
  role of police, 172-73, 175, 178, 183, 186n35
  and social change, 94, 168, 170, 173, 182-83

as social work model, 94, 169, 172, 173, 175, 176, 177, 178, 179
Juvenile Law (1922)
  compared to Juvenile Reformatory Law, 174, 175
  comprehensiveness, 174
  discretionary nature, 176
  youth protection, 175, 176, 177
Juvenile Law (1948)
  revisions, 95
  and US model, 94, 177
  youth protection, 178, 179, 180, 185n23
juvenile offenders
  categorization, 95, 169, 170, 171, 172, 175, 178, 184n11, 184n13, 185n23
  differentiated from adult offenders, 168, 170, 172, 173, 184n14, 184n21, 185n26
  violent crimes, 5, 94, 182, 183
Juvenile Protection Officers, 175, 176, 177
juvenile reformatories, 169, 170-71, 172, 173, 177, 184n9, 184n11
Juvenile Reformatory Law (1900)
  and modernization, 169-70
  reform of, 173-74
  social control, 172, 173
  youth protection, 171-72, 173, 174

Kantōgun. *See* Kwantung Army
Kayano, Shigeru, 125, 126, 128, 129, 131, 133, 134-35, 136, 137, 139, 140n7
Keidanren (Federation of Economic Organizations), 39, 47n15
Keynes, John Maynard, 29
Kishi, Nobusuke, 99-100, 103, 104, 108
Koizumi, Junichiro
  maverick, 5, 256
  popularity, 6, 256, 258
  reforms, 5-6, 16, 245, 254-55, 256-59, 261n6
  resistance within LDP, 258-59
  stalemate, 258-59
  and Yasunuki Shrine, 259
Komai, Tokuzō, 103, 104, 105, 108
Korea
  competition with Japan, 20
  and fisheries, 12, 22, 23, 68, 69, 72, 73, 74, 76, 79, 80, 83, 87
  nationalism, 102
  ties with Japan, 249, 253, 255
  urban development in, 201
  and USA, 103
  war in, 51, 74
Koreans, 13, 92, 249

Koshizawa, Akira, 111
Kwantung Army, 103, 104, 110

labour force
  aging, 246, 247
  female, 58-59, 94, 160-61, 165n8, 165n9, 247, 250
  foreign, 9, 13, 247, 249, 260, 260n2
  full-time, 22, 54, 58-59, 165n8
  part-time, 11, 22, 58-59, 165n8
  relations with management, 11, 20, 54, 55, 58, 63, 64n4
  shortage, 246
  temporary workers, 22
labour movement
  decline, 11, 20, 49, 61, 64
  ideology, 50, 51, 56, 64n4
  militancy, 51, 52, 53, 56, 57, 59, 64n4
  prewar, 49-50, 51
labour unions
  decline, 11, 61
  democratization, 50
  membership, 21, 49, 50, 61
  private sector, 21, 55-56, 58, 59, 60
  public sector, 52, 56, 57-58, 59, 60
land
  prices, 204-5, 206, 207-8, 209, 212, 214, 251
  use, 209
Law of Capture, 71
LDP. *See* Liberal Democratic Party (LDP)
Liberal Democratic Party (LDP), 4, 5, 10, 21, 59, 62, 63, 99, 204, 212, 252, 253, 254-55
Liberal Party, 252
lifetime employment, 11, 19, 21, 47n14, 49, 54, 62, 247

MacArthur Line, 72, 76, 88n4
macroeconomics, 29-30, 31, 34, 39, 58
Manchukuo
  bureaucrats, 102, 103-4, 109
  chimera, 113-14
  in comics, 111
  demise, 110, 114n4
  economy, 111, 112
  establishment of, 99, 114n3, 115n7
  and imperialism, 104
  migration, 99, 114n4
  progressiveness, 107
Manchuria
  atrocities, 109, 112, 115n9
  interest in, 92, 97-98
  and Japanese identity, 13, 97-98, 111-12, 113
  Marxist analysis, 92, 106-7
  military, 102, 104-5, 107, 112
  progressiveness, 92, 101, 105, 107, 108, 111, 112, 113
  public figures, 98-99
  settlers, 98, 99, 110, 114n4, 115n9
Manchuria Heavy Industries, 100, 102, 108
Manchurian Incident, 99, 102, 104-5, 107, 112, 114n3, 115n7
Mantetsu. *See* South Manchuria Railway (Mantetsu)
mare liberum. See freedom of the seas
Maruyama, Masao, 102, 104, 105
matori ("space taking"), 164
Meiji period
  art, 224-25, 226
  assimilationism, 93, 126
  bureaucrats, 253-54
  city planning, 196, 197-98, 199, 214
  coexistence principle, 19, 46n12
  dissociation from the past, 113
  internationalization, x, 249
  legal system, 102, 169-73, 183n2, 184n10, 184n19
  progressiveness, 108
Meiji Restoration, 8, 46n12, 102, 196, 224, 240, 260
microeconomics, 29, 31, 39
militarism, 102, 105, 140n3, 140n5, 248
Minimata, 203
Ministry of Agriculture, Forestry and Fisheries (MAFF), 75, 79, 206-7, 212, 247
Ministry of Construction (MOC), 202, 206, 208, 212
Ministry of Health and Welfare, 5
Morimura, Sei'ichi, 109
mother ship operations, 68, 76
Mukden (city), 98, 99, 100, 114n3

Nakamura, Shigeo, 110
National Diet
  and Ainu, 125, 129, 133, 134-35, 136, 140n7
  and constitution, 250
  and fisheries, 80
  and flag, 140n5
  and juvenile law, 94, 95, 170, 171, 172, 174, 176, 182, 183n5, 184n8
  and labour movement, 52, 53, 64
  and pollution control, 203
  relocation, 212-14, 252
national identity
  and art, 190-91, 222, 240, 242
  denial of diversity, 13, 121, 122, 123, 124, 134, 135, 137, 138, 249

and Manchuria, 13, 97-98, 111-12, 113
and minority groups, 120, 122, 124, 125
rice and, 122-23, 124, 126, 137-38, 140n6
sun and, 122, 123-24, 137-38
National Land Agency (NLA), 206, 212
National Railways. *See* Japan National Railways (JNR)
nationalism
 anti-feminist, 161
 attitudes to, 40
 cultural, 222, 226, 230, 239, 240, 243n2, 253n9
 and economics, 31
 and Manchuria, 102, 106, 107, 112
neoclassical economic theory, 26-31
 critiques of, 45n6
 and Newtonian physics, 27-28, 30
 and USA, 31-35, 39, 43
neo-corporatism, 59-60
new millennium, 3, 120
Nibutani
 as home place, 129, 130
 language school, 128
 and Nibutani Forum, 133, 134
 sacred, 121, 129, 138
 and Saru River, 129, 131
Nibutani Dam
 construction, 132, 136
 court decisions, 132, 135-36, 138
 effect on fish, 132
 government compensation, 131
 impact on Ainu, 129, 130-32, 136
 opposition to, 93, 121, 130-33, 135-36
Nibutani Forum, 133, 134, 137, 138
Nihon no Bi (art exhibit), 234-35, 236, 237
Nikkeiren (Japan Federation of Employers Associations), 57, 62-63
1940 system, 19
Nippon Suisan (fishing company), 68, 81
Nippon Telegraph and Telephone Corporation (NTT), 21, 60
Nishizawa, Yasuhiko, 111-12
Nissan, 21, 102, 108, 109, 110, 260n3
nongovernmental organizations (NGOs), 247-48
North American Free Trade Agreement (NAFTA), 9
North Pacific Anadromous Fisheries Commission. *See* International North Pacific Fisheries Commission (INPFC)
NTT. *See* Nippon Telegraph and Telephone Corporation (NTT)

Occupation (US)
 comfort women, 112
 and fisheries, 71
 and juvenile law, 94, 168, 177, 180-81, 184n17
 and labour movement, 50, 51, 52
 and Manchuria, 100
 reforms, 260
oil crisis, 21, 22, 56, 60
Okabe, Michio, 110
Okinawans, 9, 13, 92, 123, 124, 133, 249
Organization for Economic Co-operation and Development (OECD), 9, 32, 38, 246
overfishing, 70, 72, 78, 80, 88n4

Pareto efficiency. *See* efficiency, static
Pelagic Fisheries Encouragement Act (1905), 69
Policy Promotion Labour Council, 59, 60
policy tribes, 6, 258, 259
pop idols
 commodities, 14, 93, 144, 145, 146, 152
 gender ideals, 93, 145, 152, 156, 163, 164
 manufactured images, 93, 146, 152, 154, 162-63
 objectification, 158
 relations with fans, 144, 146-48, 165n3
 role models, 144-45, 163
 and role of women, 14, 145, 152, 162-63
 trend creation, 144, 145, 146, 159
 youth culture, 146-48, 151, 163, 164n1
 See also cute pop idols; gals; post-idols
population
 aging, 209, 215, 217n13, 246, 250, 254, 256, 259, 260n1
 statistics, 189, 194, 200, 260n1, 260n2
 of Tokyo, 200, 214, 217n7
 urbanization of, 14, 189, 200, 212, 216n1, 217n14
post-idols
 alternative to cute idols, 163, 164
 characteristics, 156-58, 163
 creation of, 156-58
 female empowerment, 152, 158, 163
 manufactured images, 162-63
 sexuality, 158, 162
 stereotypes, 158, 162-63
price busting, 41
Pu Yi (last emperor), 113, 114n3
Public Works Plan, 208, 209

Recruit Scandal, 63, 64n7
reform
 of bureaucracy, 254, 256
 economic, 252-54, 255, 256, 257, 258, 259
 of justice system, 95, 173-74
 political, 252-54, 255-56
 regime shift, 245, 260
Rengō (labour organization), 21, 59, 63, 64n3, 246, 258
retirement age, 47n14, 247
rice, as symbol, 122-23, 124, 126, 137-38
right to strike, 52, 57-58, 59
Russia, 12, 22, 68, 106
Russo-Japanese War, 99
ryōsai kenbo ("good wife, wise mother"), 144, 159, 161, 162, 164

saké, 39, 226
San Francisco Peace Treaty, 51-52, 72, 74
Sanbetsu (labour organization), 50
Saru River, 129, 130, 131, 132, 135
scandals, ix, 5, 8, 26, 63, 64n7, 215, 218n15
SCAP. *See* Supreme Commander for the Allied Powers (SCAP)
Second World War, 6, 10, 92, 93, 97, 139n1, 140n3, 140n5, 177, 190, 199, 200
Self-Defense Forces (SDF), 257
Shenyang. *See* Mukden (city)
shinjinrui ("younger generation"), 13
shōjo ("unmarried girl"), 148, 161
Shuntō. *See* wages, bargaining
small-business sector, 21, 41, 46n13, 62
Sōdōmei (labour organization), 50
Sogō, Shinji, 104, 108
Sōhyō (labour organization), 51, 52, 53, 55-56, 57, 58, 64n3
South Manchuria Railway (Mantetsu), 100, 104, 105-6, 107, 108, 109, 111, 114n2, 114n3, 115n7
Soviet Union. *See* USSR
Structural Impediments Initiative (SII), 207-8
sumptuary laws, 228
sun, as symbol, 122, 123-24, 137-38
Supreme Commander for the Allied Powers (SCAP), 71, 72, 73-74, 88n2, 88n4, 177, 181
Suzuki, Takeshi, 108-9
synecdoche, 223

Taiwan, 20, 23, 68, 83, 100, 248
Taiyō Gyogyō (fishing company), 68, 81
Takasaki, Tatsunosuke, 102-3, 105

terrorism
 Aum Shinrikyō, ix, 4, 14, 257
 11 September 2001 (attack on World Trade Towers), 245, 247, 257, 258
Tokugawa period, x, 46n12, 168, 196
Tokyo Municipal Improvement Act, 197-98

Udagawa, Masaru, 110
Uilta, 133
ukiyo-e, 229, 236
unemployment
 among Ainu, 125
 and economic decline, 4, 5, 245, 254, 257, 258
 and layoffs, 7, 21, 47n14, 251
 rates, 42, 62
 and reform, 6
 and terrorism, 245
United Nations, 120, 121, 122, 133, 134, 137, 138, 140n2
United Nations Conference on the Law of the Sea (UNCLOS), 78, 79, 80, 84, 87
United Nations General Assembly, 78, 83
urban planning
 and centralization, 197, 202, 205
 and citizens' movements, 215, 218n16, 218n17
 and industrialization, 200, 217n6
 and modernization, 196, 197, 200
 and pollution, 201, 202-4, 214
 prewar, 196, 197-99, 202, 214
 and public health, 199
 public works orientation, 197, 198-99, 200, 204
 and quality of life, 15, 189-90, 193-94, 196, 197, 204, 207, 208, 214, 215, 216n2, 251
 suburbs, 189, 199, 201-2
 Tokyo, 196, 197-98, 199, 201, 202, 205, 212, 215, 218n18
 and western models, 190, 196-97, 199, 214, 216n2, 216n3, 216n4
Urbanization Promotion Areas (UPA), 206, 207
USA
 economy, 31-35, 38, 42
 relations with Japan, 8-9, 13, 37, 40, 46n12, 51, 52, 103, 207-8, 248
USSR, 72, 74, 76, 79, 80, 81, 82, 99, 108, 110, 260

wages
 bargaining, 22, 54, 55, 56, 57, 58, 62, 64
 and labour movement, 60, 63

merit-based, 22, 247
post-oil shock, 21
seniority-based, 247
of women, 94, 165n8
Wajin ("Japanese"), 93, 124, 125-26, 127, 129, 130, 131, 133, 134
wakon yōsai, 46n12
war crimes trials, 99, 100, 101, 103, 105
welfare state, 60
westernization, 12, 19, 23, 46n12, 174, 225
whales and whaling, 22, 68, 69, 72, 82, 83-84, 89n8
women
 in art, 229-30
 discrimination against, 159-60, 162
 in labour force, 58-59, 94, 160-61, 165n8, 165n9, 247, 250
 marginalization, 144, 159, 160, 162, 164
 rights, 159, 160-62, 163-64, 257
 role, 93, 144, 145, 159-60, 161, 162
World Trade Organization (WTO), 45, 259

xenophobia, 9, 35

Year of Indigenous Peoples (1993), 120, 121, 133, 134, 137
yen, 7, 61, 64n6, 245, 257
Yoshida, Shigeru, 100
Yoshino, Shinji, 100
youth culture, 13-14, 93, 144-65

Set in Stone by Brenda and Neil West, BN Typographics West

Printed and bound in Canada by Friesens

Copy editor: Frank Chow

Proofreader and Indexer: Deborah Kerr